S0-AZP-938

Battleships of the World

1905-1970

Battleships of the World
1905-1970
SIEGFRIED BREYER
MAYFLOWER BOOKS
NEW YORK

Published in the United States by
Mayflower Books Inc, 575 Lexington
Avenue, New York City 10022.
First edition published 1977–79
as three volumes under the title
Grosskampfschiffe 1905–1970

First English language edition,
with revisions, published 1980 by

Library of Congress Catalog Card No: 80–13715

ISBN 0–8317–0705–4

MANUFACTURED IN GREAT BRITAIN

FIRST AMERICAN EDITION

Foreword

This pictorial book is a result of numerous requests which have been made over several years by owners of the standard work *Battleships and Battle Cruisers 1905–1970*. These people have repeatedly voiced the feeling that they would greatly appreciate a series of selected photographs of these ships to complement the hundreds of drawings in the aforementioned volume. This wish can now be fulfilled, after sifting through the very extensive library of photographs in the Bibliothek für Zeitgeschichte (Library of Contemporary History) at Stuttgart. As far as possible, only pictures which either have never been published before or have been known only to a small circle of warship enthusiasts have been selected. The aim has not been to present an endless series of ship portraits, but rather to provide a lively cross-section through all the battle fleets of the world.

The choice of photographs was difficult, especially with respect to US and Japanese ships. There is a superabundance of good photos of US warships, but most of the available photos of Japanese vessels have already appeared in other, mainly Japanese publications. This situation was bound to create problems, particularly with the *Yamato* class; there are relatively few photographs of these vessels, and it is hoped that the reader will make allowances if he does not find any new pictures in this book.

As a special 'extra' a section on the preparations which were made in Germany in 1939 for the building of battleships under the 'Z-Plan' has been included; this is intended to show how all the necessary forces were mobilised and organised with the aim of achieving the target within the time limit. Further appendices cover the events of 7 December 1941 at Pearl Harbor and the atomic bomb tests at Bikini in the summer of 1946, and these include some photographic material. There is also an appendix giving a detailed account of the building of capital ships in the Soviet Union, before and after 1945, and this includes much information only gathered over the last few years. Of necessity, some of the material has already appeared elsewhere, but there are also a large number of facts that have not hitherto been published. The resumption of capital shipbuilding in the Soviet Union after the end of the Second World War is also dealt with, and for the first time the reader will find details of the ships begun in that period.

A tabular summary is included, in order to provide brief information on the capital ship types discussed and depicted in the photos: this will enable the reader to extract the essential facts about the ships for the purpose of comparing their performance in battle. Where the information does not agree with that given in *Battleships and Battle Cruisers 1905–1970*, the data provided here should be considered correct as most of it has been drawn from recent research. In some instances only average values could be given, for example the figures for displacements.

I am deeply indebted to Dr Jürgen Rohwer, Director of the Bibliothek für Zeitgeschichte, who allowed me a free hand in selecting photographic material and also gave frequent help with his valued suggestions. I am equally indebted to Frau Ilse Kasper for the translation of many Russian texts, and to Messrs Barilli, Bertermann, Huan, Stockinger and Todorov, and Dr Kowark, who provided photographs. I am grateful to Messrs Franke and Lohberger, who built the model of the Austrian 'Ersatz Monarch' class battleship and photographed it for this book. I also wish to thank my many friends and correspondents who have time and again provided valued assistance; even if their help may seem to them to have been minimal I can assure them that I could not have managed without it.

If this volume provides a few small items of new information to warship enthusiasts it will have fulfilled its purpose.

Siegfried Breyer

Editor's note

This book originally appeared as three volumes under the title *Grosskampfschiffe 1905–1970*, published by Bernard & Graefe Verlag, Munich. In order to meet the requirements of a single publication, a number of revisions, affecting particularly the introductory notes and end matter, have had to be incorporated, and the text has also been amended to take account of, for example, British nautical terminology, a switch (where necessary) from Central European to Greenwich Mean Time, and Imperial measures. Metric equivalents are, however, also quoted, for comparative purposes. In addition, a number of minor corrections to the original German text have been made and many of the maps and diagrams have had to be redrawn to accommodate English labelling. The latter task has been ably undertaken by John Roberts.

Roger Chesneau

Contents

Introduction

DAWN OF THE DREADNOUGHT ERA

At the turn of the century, the Royal Navy possessed the largest fleet of battleships in the world: 37 units were in service, none more than 25 years old, and by 1905 this number had risen to 56. Germany possessed only one-third of this number – in 1900 there were 10 comparable units, in 1905 just 17. The disparity appeared to guarantee British superiority for the foreseeable future, as the Imperial German Navy would have to make an enormous effort to close the gap. Development work was already being strongly directed towards the 'all-big-gun' battleship, and sooner or later this was bound to bear fruit; the Russo-Japanese War of 1905, and the lessons relating to naval warfare learned from it, also had an accelerating effect on events. One of the most prominent advocates of the 'all-big-gun' battleship was Admiral Sir John Fisher. As Commander of the British Mediterranean Fleet he had already spent a good deal of time considering the question of capital ship development; when he became First Sea Lord in 1904, he was in a position to put his ideas into effect. It was thanks to his initiative that designs for the 'all-big-gun' battleship were worked out, and soon afterwards these designs became a reality – spurred on by reports from the United States, where similar projects were being drawn up. The *Dreadnought* was built – and thus began the 'dreadnought era'. With this move the British believed that they had produced a trump card and secured a lead which no other country was capable of making up; they were thinking primarily of the German Navy, which had been growing at an ever-increasing rate since the passing of the Naval Laws of 1898–1900.

At the same time, Great Britain also laid down *Invincible* and her two sister-ships – the first battlecruisers. Compared with *Dreadnought*, the building of which represented merely a logical next step in the development of capital ships, *Invincible* was a genuine leap forward, since the armoured cruiser, the predecessor of the battlecruiser, was a much more recent concept: her ancestor, the armoured corvette, only had its origins in the 1880s.

It was indeed the German Navy upon which these British moves had their greatest effect. In Great Britain it was hoped that the building of these first dreadnoughts would take Germany so much by surprise that she would be unable to begin the construction of comparable ships immediately. However, extensive preparatory work had in fact already been carried out on the other side of the North Sea, and this served as a basis for the Germans' own designs when the pattern of further development was finally settled.

On the German side, it was considered important to keep the new capital ships down to a size which would allow them to use existing port facilities and also the Kaiser Wilhelm Canal. The limit this imposed was around 15,000 tons. However, it was already realised that the limit was too low, unless design weaknesses were to be accepted from the outset, and for this reason the decision was taken to raise the limit to 19,000 tons, involving very costly extension work to ports and docks, but above all to the Canal. Early in 1906, three months after *Dreadnought* was launched, the *Reichstag* authorised the necessary funds, and five days later the construction of the first German dreadnought, the *Nassau*, was sanctioned. Germany also kept pace in the building of battlecruisers: in 1908 the first ship of this type, *Von der Tann*, was laid down.

Great Britain's expectations were somewhat thwarted by these moves, and it must also be understood that by her own actions she rendered almost all her powerful fleet of pre-dreadnoughts obsolete. The British were therefore obliged to order increasingly large and powerful battleships and battlecruisers, which imposed a considerable financial burden.

THE RISE OF JAPAN

As the nineteenth century drew to a close, the USA was reflecting upon the war against Spain which they had just brought to a successful conclusion. In this war most of the decisive actions had taken place at sea, for example the Battle of Manila

Bay on 1 May 1898 and the naval engagement near Santiago da Cuba on 3 July of the same year. In both cases the Americans destroyed the Spanish units opposing them. The balance of power had been far from even: at Manila four fairly modern American cruisers faced two old Spanish cruisers, and at Santiago four poorly armed Spanish armoured cruisers, four battleships and two armoured cruisers opposed the Americans, who were able to exploit their superior gunnery to the full. The war brought substantial territorial gains for the USA in the Caribbean and Pacific, and formed the basis for America's emergence as a world power. This in turn demanded a greater role for the US Navy, which had been allowed to decline by American politicians since the end of the Civil War, and whose renaissance had only started in the 1880s. The tasks which befell it lent a significant new impetus: when the new century began, the USA only had five capital ships, but seven more were under construction, and by 1905 orders for a further thirteen had been placed.

Japan, the island empire on the other side of the Pacific Ocean, had been victorious in a war with China in 1894–95, which had also been to a large extent fought at sea. The conflict had been started by Japan when she realised that her position vis-à-vis China and Russia was becoming dangerous – with China because of her aspirations as a naval power, and with Russia because of her penetration into the Far East in the search for ice-free ports. The war ended with the military occupation of Korea and with the cession to Japan of Formosa, the Pescador group of islands and Port Arthur; Japan's naval superiority in the East China Sea was firmly established.

The outcome of the Sino-Japanese War was bound to lead to conflict with Russia, who was setting about securing new zones of influence in East Asia. However, Japan was quite soon forced by diplomatic pressure to withdraw her troops from Korea and to evacuate Port Arthur. From that time on, Japan began to build up her military strength (and her Navy in particular) at a rapid pace, to prepare herself for a war with Russia, whose expansionist intentions threatened to relieve Japan of the fruits of her victory over China. The Russo-Japanese War broke out in February 1904 with the Japanese attack on Port Arthur, which the Russians had occupied shortly before the turn of the century. The numerically superior Russian Far East Fleet suffered serious defeats, culminating on 28 May 1905 in the naval battle off Tsushima, which ended with the destruction and defeat of the Russians, forcing them to negotiate peace. Thus Japan had achieved her aim: Russia's position in East Asia was enormously weakened, her military strength was almost entirely destroyed, and the Japanese were unassailable. When the war ended, Japan possessed four battleships with two more under construction, and also had the use of five Russian capital ships, which had been taken as prizes; these vessels more than compensated for the two battleships lost by the Japanese.

The conflicts that took place around the turn of the century provided the lessons and experience that accelerated the further development of the capital ship towards an 'all-big-gun' battleship, but they were not its initial cause: the evolution was almost entirely predictable, and continued inexorably. Even in 1903–04 – before the outbreak of war with Russia – the Japanese were working on designs for battleships armed with eight 12in (30.5cm) guns, which placed them well ahead of their time.

These designs were in fact the preliminary stage of the *Satsuma* class: these vessels had been ordered before Tsushima, and thus would have been the first real 'all-big-gun' battleships in the world if they had been built to the original plans. They were then intended to be fitted with a main armament consisting of twelve 12in guns, which would easily have eclipsed all other ships of the period, but the enormous strains imposed by the war made it impossible for Japan to keep to her plans: she still had to buy her heavy guns abroad, but as her coffers were almost entirely exhausted extreme frugality was called for. The result was that these ships were only fitted with four 12in guns instead of the planned twelve, and the others were replaced by twelve 10in (25.4cm) units, a decision which effectively pushed the two vessels back into the ranks of the pre-dreadnoughts.

In March 1905 the US Congress authorised the construction of two more capital ships, whose designs had been in preparation since 1904. Their mere authorisation would not have been grounds for particular attention, had it not been made known at the time that their main armament was to be double that of previous vessels. They were thus the first 'all-big-gun' battleships to be authorised – and as such pre-dated the British *Dreadnought*. However, construction work on these American ships – *South Carolina* and *Michigan* – was protracted, as everything was carried out very carefully and with no hint of urgency. For Great Britain, this news was the signal to accelerate the design work on *Dreadnought* and proceed with her building with all despatch. It is likely that national pride was the guiding force behind this urgency, and by the time the Americans laid down their first 'all-big-gun' battleships *Dreadnought* had been completed. When the US vessels were commissioned early in 1910, Great Britain was already involved in the 'second dreadnought phase' – the transition to the 'super-dreadnought', whose main feature was an increase in main calibre.

THE ARMS RACE INTENSIFIES

From 1907 onwards, all the great naval powers began building dreadnoughts, which gave each of them the opportunity to make a fresh start, where there had been no such prospect before. General re-armament now took place. To safeguard her lead, Great Britain authorised the building of seven battleships and two battlecruisers in the 1906–08 Estimates; Germany responded with eight dreadnoughts (*Nassau* and *Helgoland* classes) and one battlecruiser (designated a 'heavy cruiser'). On 31 December 1910, the Royal Navy had seven battleships and three battlecruisers in service, while Germany's Imperial Navy had four and one respectively.

In the 1909 financial year, the hectic race in the building of capital ships intensified once more. Great Britain ordered six battleships, and four more in each of the following two years, as well as five battlecruisers. That year also marked the first increase in calibre for the British vessels. With the exception of two battleships and one battlecruiser, all the new vessels were to be fitted with 13.5in (34.3cm) guns.

For various reasons the German Navy had adhered to a 28cm (11in) calibre, and it was only in 1908 that an increase to 30.5cm (12in) was introduced. The Navy was apparently not particularly impressed by the increase in the British calibre, and stayed with the 30.5cm gun initially, as trials had shown that its shells had considerably more penetrative power than British shells of the same calibre. In the meantime, the United States and Japan had progressed to an even heavier calibre – 14in (35.6cm) – and reports reaching Great Britain suggested that the German Navy was soon to take a similar step. For these reasons Britain decided to adopt the 15in (38.1cm) gun. The four *Queen Elizabeth* class battleships authorised in 1912 (a fifth was contributed by the Malayan States as a gift) were the first to be equipped with these new weapons. In the same year Germany began building her first two ships with 38cm guns (*Bayern* and *Baden*); the British countered this with five more battleships with 15in guns in 1913 (*Revenge* class).

MEDITERRANEAN RIVALRY

Although there existed a treaty of alliance between Italy and Austria-Hungary, the deep-seated rivalry between these two powers never completely disappeared; in fact, it intensified. For the Danube monarchy, Italy was considered to be the most likely political opponent, not least because of her naval superiority, regardless of all the other potential crisis points in the Mediterranean area. This line of thinking could not be concealed from Italy, who therefore adopted a policy of re-armament in response. Thus Italy became the first Mediterranean state to take up the building of modern capital ships, with the object of underlining her superiority – and by the end of 1908 she possessed eleven capital units as opposed to six on the Austro-Hungarian side. An amendment to the 1905 Fleet Act was made in 1909, which authorised the construction of four more capital ships, the first of which, *Dante Alighieri*, was ordered that same year. A year later the three *Conte di Cavour* class units followed, with two *Caio Dulio* class soon afterwards, the latter being authorised in 1912. All six were armed with a large number of 30.5cm (12in) guns – *Dante Alighieri* had twelve, all the others thirteen – in line with current thinking on capital ship design.

Austria-Hungary responded almost immediately, and in the summer of 1910 the keel of the first unit of the *Tegetthoff* class was laid. The Austro-Hungarian monarchy had Admiral Rudolf Montecuccoli to thank for the fact that she was able to react so swiftly to Italy's moves. He was the commander-in-chief of the navy, and despite the fact that the naval budget of 1910 did not include any such provision, he agreed to the proposal put forward by Stabilimento Tecnico Triestino to start the construction of two new dreadnoughts, in order to maintain full employment at the yard. He later succeeded in obtaining authorisation for these two ships, and then a further two. Their fighting value was not essentially different from that of the Italian capital ships: they also were equipped with 30.5cm guns, twelve barrels per ship. When the First World War broke out in 1914, only one of Italy's dreadnoughts had been commissioned, while Austria already had three. By 23 May 1915 – when Italy declared war on Austria-Hungary – the relative position was very different: Austria's four dreadnoughts were opposed by Italy's five.

The westernmost Mediterranean state, the kingdom of Spain, decided to acquire dreadnoughts in 1908, although they had to be ordered from British yards. Spain embarked on this course to add impetus to the reconstruction of her navy after the war with the United States in 1898, which had so depleted her fleet. These Spanish vessels turned out to be very modest: they were the smallest and weakest dreadnoughts in the world, despite their eight 12in guns, and they were never repeated.

RUSSIA AND FRANCE JOIN IN

Russia was in a similar position to Spain when she resolved to build dreadnoughts, also in 1908. The war with Japan had rendered her fleet practically unserviceable, and had greatly dented her standing, especially in the Baltic and Black Sea. In addition she had grave internal problems – the 'tip of the iceberg' was seen in the *Potemkin* mutiny. In these circumstances the transition to the 'all-big-gun' battleship must have been welcome in Russia in spite of the heavy and increasing financial burden which this would bring, as it gave the chance of a new start in an international situation where conditions were approximately the same for all nations. Thus the *Duma* – the legislative body during the Tsarist period – ordered the four capital ships of the *Gangut* class in 1908, all of which were laid down in 1909. They too were equipped with 30.5cm guns, but they had one great advantage over most dreadnoughts in that their top speed was 23kts – a clear step ahead of the rest. Whilst this class was intended for the Baltic Sea, the *Imperatrica Mariya* class, begun in 1911, was intended for the Black Sea, to provide a counter to Turkey's naval re-armament efforts. These ships were fitted with the same number of 30.5cm guns as the *Gangut* class, although they were slightly slower owing to their somewhat heavier armour.

At this time France was too heavily under the influence of her *Jeune Ecole* to be able to join the race immediately. Her first capital ships were not ordered until 1910, and these were the four units of the *Courbet* class. They, too, were fitted with a large number of 30.5cm guns, and all were completed by the end of 1914.

Great Britain had progressed to the 'super-dreadnought' as early as 1909 by adopting a heavier gun calibre (13.5in) and she was followed by Italy, Austria-Hungary, Russia and France; these developments did not take place immediately, some countries only acting after the outbreak of the First World War. It was Russia that first adopted a still larger calibre – 35.6cm (14in) – with the four battlecruisers of the *Borodino* class, begun late in 1912. They were authorised by a new long-term Fleet Act passed on 6 July 1912, which could hardly have been directed at any power other than Germany. This Act laid down the strength of the Russian Baltic Fleet alone at 36 capital ships – 24 battleships and 12 battlecruisers – a target which was to be met by 1930. A programme of this size (it also included 24 cruisers, 108 destroyers and 36 submarines) was only possible with extensive foreign assistance, as Russia's industrial capacity was in no way adequate for the task. Russia sought this help in Germany, as well as in other countries, and she was not refused – despite the threat which this expansion in fleet building involved.

France was the next naval power to take up building 'super-dreadnoughts'. The three *Provence* class battleships were built there from 1912 on, and 34cm (13.4in) guns had been developed for them, ten in number and all of them in twin turrets. Just one year later work began on the four units of the *Normandie* class, and in 1914 a fifth was approved. For these ships the 34cm calibre was retained, but a new layout was chosen – three quadruple turrets. The first designs for the *Lyon* class were drawn up before the start of the war; these featured the same calibre, but the number of barrels had risen by 33 per cent, an arrangement which enabled the highest number of heavy guns to be fitted that had ever been planned for a single capital ship: sixteen barrels in four quadruple turrets, which constituted a unique concentration of firepower for a capital ship. Great Britain had led the way with fast battleships by ordering the *Queen Elizabeth* class in 1912; Italy kept pace when she produced plans for the battleships of the *Francesco Caracciolo* class in 1912. These ships, displacing 30,000 tons, were to have a top speed of 25–28kts and be fitted with an armament identical to that of the British *Queen Elizabeths*: eight 15in and twelve 6in guns. Two of these ships were laid down. At the same time the Austro-Hungarian monarchy was also preparing for the construction of 'super-battleships'. Four such vessels were authorised, their main armament consisting of 35.5cm (14in) guns.

THE 'DREADNOUGHT FEVER' SPREADS

In the last years before the outbreak of the First World War, smaller states were drawn into the whirlpool of naval re-armament, including Greece and Turkey. Increasing tension between Italy and Turkey was the latter's reason for building these ships; these tensions resulted in open war in the autumn of 1912. Even before this conflict was over, the Balkan War involving Greece, Bulgaria, Serbia and Montenegro began. Turkey blamed her defeats on her maritime weakness, and she was substantially correct; it was therefore understandable that she would seek ways and means of acquiring the power which would guarantee her superiority at sea – and this power resided in the capital ship. For this reason, Turkey ordered two battleships from Great Britain in 1911, and made preparations for building a third in her own yard, although this yard had yet to be constructed. Moreover, in 1914 Turkey was able to acquire a battleship which was being built in England for Brazil, and the ship was continued on the Turkish account. Greece also found herself forced to seek an opportunity of acquiring her own battleships, and to this end a ship was ordered in Germany in 1913, followed by a second in France in 1914.

An arms race also developed among the 'ABC states' of South America. Brazil began it by ordering two units in Great Britain, which were delivered by 1910. The contract for a third, even larger and more powerful vessel was imminent when Argentina ordered her two *Rivadavia* class capital ships in the USA in response.

The capital ships ordered by Brazil and Argentina were all fitted with 12in guns, and thus were comparable to other ships which characterised the first 'dreadnought phase'. Guns of the same calibre were also planned for the battleship *Rio de Janiero*, which was ordered by Brazil from Great Britain in 1911, but in Autumn 1913 the Brazilian Naval Command no longer considered this size adequate, and ordered a completely new battleship, this time to be equipped with 15in guns. She sold *Rio de Janiero* to the Turks for whom the ship was completed. Chile did not join in the race immediately, and only placed contracts for her first two ships (from Great Britain) in 1911 and 1912. These were fitted with 14in guns and can be considered as belonging to the category of super-dreadnoughts.

WORLD WAR I

In August 1914, when the great struggle between the nations began, the Royal Navy possessed 28 capital ships – 19 battleships and 9 battlecruisers – opposed on the German side by 18 units – 14 battleships and 4 battlecruisers. During the war the British Fleet was supplemented by the units begun in peacetime – 13 battleships and 1 battlecruiser – and also three battleships, built for foreign customers, which were taken over at the outbreak of war and placed in service with the Royal Navy. An additional two battlecruisers and three light cruisers with a battleship-type main armament were completed during the war.

The Royal Navy suffered heavier losses in the war than the German Navy – five units (two battleships and three battlecruisers) as against only one capital ship, *Lützow*. When the war ended, Great Britain had 45 heavy units in service – 33 battleships, 9 battlecruisers and the three 'large light cruisers'. A few weeks earlier *Hood* had been launched, the *ne plus ultra* of British battlecruisers. The Imperial German Navy comprised 24 heavy units – 19 battleships and 5 'heavy cruisers' (excluding *Goeben*, which had been transferred to Turkey). In various stages of construction were a further two battleships and seven 'heavy cruisers', the first four of which were to be fitted with 35in (13.75in) guns, the last three with 38.0cm (15in).

The First World War affected the building of capital ships for the smaller navies in several ways:

1 None of the capital ships being built at the time in Great Britain for Turkey and Chile was delivered to the customers, as they were requisitioned and added to the Grand Fleet on completion.
2 The contracts placed in Great Britain by Brazil, and in France by Greece, shortly before the start of the war, were not fulfilled.
3 Work on the ships being built in Germany for Greece was halted.
4 The building of 'super-dreadnoughts', which had been begun or planned in France, Italy, Russia and Austria-Hungary was either stopped and the contracts annulled, or completion was postponed for the duration of the war. Only those ships which were at an advanced stage of construction were completed, although in some cases building was not halted until a fairly late stage of the war.
5 In none of these states were new capital ships begun for the duration of the war.

Russia and Italy each lost one capital ship during the war, while Austria-Hungary lost two of hers. A further Russian capital ship was sunk by her own naval forces to avoid it falling into German hands.

TENSION ACROSS THE PACIFIC

Japan, for good or evil, was forced to keep pace with developments taking place far from her shores, in order to maintain and secure her new-found superiority in the Far East. In 1909 her first two dreadnoughts were laid down and they were fitted with the main armament which had been intended for the *Satsuma* class. Admittedly, the Japanese still had to buy their guns and machinery abroad, but they succeeded extraordinarily quickly in acquiring the technological skills of the great industrial nations, thus making themselves independent of foreign countries. In 1912 their first dreadnoughts – *Settsu* and *Kawachi* – were commissioned.

A 'battleship race' was soon in full swing outside the confines of Europe. The development of the two Pacific navies took place along virtually parallel lines. By 1910 the USA had ordered six more capital ships, and in 1911 adopted the 'super-dreadnought' type, following the British example; these ships featured 14in (35.6cm) guns. Japan followed immediately: in 1911 the battlecruiser *Kongo* was laid down in Great Britain (this was the last warship which Japan ordered abroad), and only a short time after this three more units were built to the same design in Japanese yards – also fitted with 14in guns. This calibre was retained for the four capital ships which were ordered in the years 1912 to 1915. In Europe the war had brought a virtual halt to the building of capital ships, but the two Pacific powers, whose relationship with each other was tending ever more towards that of enemies, continued their work unhindered. In February 1916, Japan approved the so-called '8–8' plan, which provided for the building of eight battleships and eight battlecruisers. This scheme had been drawn up and proposed in 1910, but financial stringencies prevented it from being carried out. In the short term, the Japanese parliament authorised two vessels, *Nagato* and *Mutsu*, but they were not actually ordered immediately, as their designs had to be altered as a result of the experiences of the Battle of Jutland. They were the first capital ships to be equipped with 16in (40.6cm) calibre guns, which had been developed and built in Japan in total secrecy, isolated from the war.

The American answer was not long in coming: in the summer of 1916 Congress authorised a wide-ranging fleet construction programme, which included the building of ten battleships and six battlecruisers, for which the Americans also adopted 16in guns. At first, however, only one of these new battleships, *Maryland*, could be started. The reason lay in the involvement of the American shipbuilding industry in the construction of a large number of destroyers which were needed to counter the German U-boats in the Atlantic. The building of nine battleships therefore had to be postponed initially, and the same happened with the six battlecruisers, the design of which also had to be revised after the experiences at Jutland.

It was only after the end of the war that the Americans could tackle their programme. Understandably, Great Britain had little enthusiasm for the American naval construction plans, as the US Navy was threatening to overtake the Royal Navy, and this would start a new naval arms race. Some ill-feeling arose between the two Anglo-Saxon sea powers, which intensified when the USA realised that their previous allies were by no means inclined to co-operate in the creation of the absolute freedom of the seas proposed by the American President. The US reaction to this was unequivocal – not only were three more battleships ordered, but preparations were made to lay down the remaining six battleships and six battlecruisers by 1920. This move caused disappointment and resentment in Great Britain, but also provoked thoughts on how the American intentions could be countered by her own building programme.

Japan, however, felt far more threatened than Great Britain. Her reaction was a new '8–8' programme, which was authorised in the summer of 1920, and established that the future active battle fleet would comprise eight battleships and eight battlecruisers, of which no ship would be older than eight years (calculated from the date of its completion). Hence the two *Tosa* class battleships and two *Akagi* class battlecruisers were laid down that same year, followed the next year by two more *Akagi* class battlecruisers. From 1922 it was expected that eight more battleships would be ordered, the last of which was to have 18in (45.7cm) guns.

THE WASHINGTON TREATY

The Armistice dictated that the German High Seas Fleet was to be interned at Scapa Flow. In the following year, the ships were scuttled by their crews: the German Navy now possessed no capital ships at all, since any ship not sunk at Scapa Flow had to be handed over to the victorious powers. The Royal Navy now had no opposition – but this apparent state of affairs was deceptive. The new US-Japanese rivalry was casting its shadow, leading to the threat of another arms race.

Great Britain could by no means view this situation with equanimity. On the one hand any Japanese predominance in East Asia was just as uncomfortable for Great Britain as for the United States, and on the other hand the US Navy threatened to become so powerful in the near future that it might take over the Royal Navy's role as the foremost naval power in the world, and thereby deal a heavy blow to British prestige. For these reasons, the British Parliament authorised the preparation of materials for four heavy battlecruisers with 16in guns in the summer of 1922, to be followed by two groups of four further battleships with 18in guns. However, Great Britain was financially exhausted after 1918 and urgently needed time to reorganise her resources; so she tried using peaceful means to slacken the tensions which had built up. The United States had also recognised that her original aim could not be achieved without creating rivalry between the British and US fleets; it was also observed that Japanese predominance in East Asia could hardly be prevented by naval re-armament, as Japan appeared to be prepared for any sacrifice to carry out her fleet construction plans. The idea of halting Japan's naval build-up by means of suitable treaties therefore seemed more and more attractive. Japan had enjoyed an enormous boom period during the war, and the end of the war brought serious consequences for her – high unemployment, an economic crisis which proved impossible to overcome, and the build-up of enormous internal tensions; these were unmistakable, even to outsiders.

As usually happens after a lengthy conflict, treaty considerations were fostered by general pacifist tendencies. For this reason all the naval powers concerned welcomed – at least privately – the United States' tentative overtures, in which she made known her readiness to start disarmament negotiations. Thus the Washington Naval Conference came about in 1921, followed in 1922 by the Treaty named after it. The signatory powers had to accept heavy cuts in quality and quantity as a result of this treaty. For one thing, the highest permissible standard unit displacement of all ships to be built in the future was limited to 35,000 tons, and the gun calibre was not to exceed 16in. For another, the relative strengths of the sea powers were laid down in unit numbers. This meant that all the nations had to abandon their current construction programmes, and that all units which exceeded the limits had to be disposed of. At the same time a ten-year 'holiday' on the building of battleships was agreed.

As a result of these measures, Great Britain had to take fifteen capital ships out of service. Britain admittedly had been allowed the right to build two battleships within the new limits before the expiration of the 'holiday', but this was a special exemption; she took advantage of this in 1922, by beginning the construction of the new *Nelson* class vessels. By the late 1920s the Royal Navy possessed sixteen battleships (amongst them the newly-built *Nelson* and *Rodney*) and four battlecruisers. As applied to the USA and Japan, the treaty included the following provisions:

1 The relinquishment of their current building programmes, and the scrapping of all capital ships under construction (although each of the nations was permitted to complete two battlecruisers as aircraft carriers).

2 A limitation on the capital ships in service to 18 and 10 units respectively.

3 The withdrawal from service of all other capital ships, including the pre-dreadnoughts already in existence.

4 A ten-year moratorium on the building of capital ships.

5 Qualitative limits on new capital ships.

Both powers respected these treaty conditions absolutely, and for several years had to make do with the capital ships they already possessed. This gave them the opportunity gradually to carry out a thorough modernisation programme.

France and Italy were granted parity in battleship tonnage, with 175,000 tons allowed to each. In addition, both were given the right to replace one of their oldest battleships with a new vessel. They had to scrap the new ships which had already been laid down, and any more units planned had to be abandoned. In Russia – now the Soviet Union – the building of new capital ships was inconceivable during these years, and also for the foreseeable future. The 'ABC states' of South America were not subject to the treaty, nor were the European states which had only small numbers of capital ships, or which had had ambitions towards capital ship ownership before the war. In any case, none of them would have been in a position to build their own capital ships, and assistance from the great naval powers was outlawed by the Treaty.

GERMANY REAWAKENS

The London Naval Treaty, which was signed in 1930, was concerned mainly with the building of cruisers, but it also affected capital ships in that the moratorium on building was extended to 1936. The stock numbers were aligned with the relative strengths laid down in the Washington Treaty, *viz* 5:5:3 for Great Britain, USA and Japan respectively, which meant a reduction to 15, 15 and 9 units, and the removal from service of other capital ships.

This naval treaty was the last to which Japan was a signatory. Her efforts from then on were aimed at reclaiming her position of pre-eminence in the Far East, which had been greatly weakened by the two agreements.

The Treaty of Versailles had placed strict limitations on the reconstruction of the German Navy, for example there was a complete ban on building ships of over 10,000 tons. After the *Reichsmarine* had struggled by for a decade with the entirely obsolete pre-dreadnoughts that remained in front-line service, their replacement became so urgent that something had to happen. Preliminary discussions were concentrated on what could be made out of the prescribed size. Two types of ships were considered: a strongly armed, well-protected, but necessarily slow type – a sort of armoured coast defence ship; and a faster, less well-armed and armoured type, which would have greater versatility than the former. Initially the first idea was preferred, but eventually the decision was taken to go ahead with the cruiser-like, 'high seas' type. The result was the famous *Panzerschiff* (armoured ship), the first of which was *Deutschland* (later renamed *Lützow*). This type was more powerful than any faster ship, and faster than any more powerful ship, with the exception of three vessels – the surviving British battlecruisers. By 1932 three of these armoured ships were authorised, and by 1936 they had been completed.

When Adolf Hitler came to power in 1933, there was little change at first as far as the German Navy was concerned. In 1934 two more armoured ships – slightly bigger than their predecessors – were laid down, but then the decision was taken to build two larger, faster and better-armoured battleships in their place, although they were not to have guns of a larger calibre. These were *Scharnhorst* and *Gneisenau*, begun in 1935. In the same year the Anglo-German Naval Agreement, which Hitler had striven for, was signed, and this decreed that the strength of the German fleet should be limited to 35 per cent of the Royal Navy's, thus enabling Germany to authorise the building of two much larger and more powerful battleships (*Bismarck* class) soon afterwards.

COUNTER-MOVES IN EUROPE

France ordered her first new battleship in 1932 – *Dunkerque* – which was followed two years later by *Strasbourg*. Both were declared to be a reply to the German 10,000-ton *Panzerschiffe*. In their case the French were satisfied with smaller size and a lighter calibre than those permitted by the treaty regulations; this sacrifice was chiefly for financial reasons, but the French may also have hoped to find agreement amongst other naval powers, and spur them into following a similar course.

Italy could not, however, remain indifferent to the French move. Her initial reaction was to completely modernise the two old *Conte di Cavour* class battleships, work on which was begun late in 1933; at the same time, preparations were made for building new ships, the first two, *Vittorio Veneto* and *Littorio*, being laid down the following year. In their case, the qualitative limits were only partially exploited: they were declared as 35,000-ton ships – although in fact they displaced more – but instead of the 16in (40.6cm) guns permitted, they were fitted with 15in (38.1cm) weapons. This course of action caused the French to build battleships which exploited the permitted limits. *Richelieu*, the first of them, was laid down in 1935, and the second, *Jean Bart*, one year later. This action confirmed that a naval arms race between the two powers was now in full swing.

Immediately after the end of the battleship building 'holiday', Great Britain began the construction of five units of the *King George V* class. They were not intended as an addition to current strength, but as replacements for the five least battleworthy capital ships. If World War II had not intervened, dissolving all treaty-dictated regulations on fleet construction, five old ships would have had to be taken out of service at the time when the new vessels of the *King George V* class were completed. In 1938, steadily growing opposition to Germany gave rise to the authorisation to build four further battleships. In this case the 35,000 tons and 14in (35.6cm) guns of the *King George V*s were raised to 40,000 tons and 16in (40.6cm) guns; this was permitted by a supplement to the London Naval Conference agreement, signed in 1938, which had raised the limit for battleships to 45,000 tons.

The political situation in Europe at that time led to a massive fleet construction programme in Germany – the so called 'Z-Plan'. The core of this plan was six battleships each with a displacement of around 56,000 tons, a top speed of 30kts, and a main armament of eight 40.6cm (16in) guns. Their armour was designed to be so strong that they would be able to withstand the effects of any weapon. An especially important feature was their great range of 19,000nm.

For Italy the situation was reasonably satisfactory: in June 1940 – the time of Italy's entry into the war – she had four completely modernised and two brand-new battleships at her disposal, and by 1942 a third new battleship was finished.

The Soviet Union resumed the building of new battleships and battlecruisers in 1938, but none of them was ever finished*. Thus she had to carry on through the war with the three old and only partially modernised ships of the *Gangut* class. Of these, one was so badly damaged that for all practical purposes it did not exist. The Soviet Union received support from Britain in 1944 when the latter loaned her a *Revenge* class battleship.

Shortly before the start of the war in 1939, the Netherlands again made preparations for acquiring capital ships – for the second time in the history of her navy. Three battlecruisers were to be built with German assistance, but the war thwarted this intention once again.

In Italy, when the modernisation of the *Conte di Cavour* class was complete, the two *Caio Duilio* class units followed immediately, and they were converted along similar lines. In 1938 the Italians laid down two more 35,000-ton battleships – *Impero* and *Roma* – which were answered by France with *Clemenceau*, the third ship in the *Richelieu* class, in 1939; a fourth vessel of an improved class, *Gascogne*, was also announced.

* The history of Soviet capital shipbuilding is described in detail in the appendices.

WORLD WAR II

The French Navy had seven battleships in service by 1939, but two of these were very antiquated and could only be used as training ships. Three others were not much younger, and their usefulness was limited. Only the two *Dunkerque*s were really modern. By the time of the Armistice in the summer of 1940, only *Richelieu* had been completed to supplement the fleet. During the war the French Navy lost one old battleship in action, whilst another old ship and the two *Dunkerque* class vessels were scuttled. The Italian Navy lost one of its modernised battleships in action, and one new unit. When the war ended, France still possessed one old and one new battleship; another, *Jean Bart*, which had been begun before the war, was completed in the years following 1945. At the time of her capitulation Italy still had three modernised and two new battleships, but of these one of the old ships had to be handed over to the Russians, and the two new ones had to be scrapped, under the terms of the peace treaty.

The *North Carolina* class battleships ordered by the USA in 1937, and the *South Dakota* class vessels which followed in 1939, can be considered as replacements for their six oldest battleships. They were followed by six 45,000-ton battleships of the *Iowa* class, which were laid down from 1940 onwards, after the treaty provisions had been altered in mid-1938 to permit an increase in displacement to 45,000 tons.

At this time two classes of superlative battleships evolved on each side of the Pacific: the Japanese *Yamato* class, which became the world's most powerful battleships; and the American *Iowa* class, which were the fastest battleships that had ever existed. The aim of the Japanese 'super battleship' programme was to place the USA under massive pressure:

1 The Japanese hoped that they had raised the fighting strength of these 'super battleships' to such a level that even the USA, which economically and industrially was one of the strongest nations, would find it very difficult to keep pace.

2 In addition, it was intended to force the US Navy into building such large vessels in response, that they would be unable to utilise the strategically important Panama Canal.

By passing the Two-Ocean Navy Bill in the summer of 1940, the USA foiled the Japanese plans: this Bill allowed the USA to expand her navy to such an extent that the problem of the Panama Canal was of very little consequence. If the USA had until then considered this point as being of fundamental importance in the building of heavy warships, she now for the first time ignored it altogether in the construction of the 60,000-ton 'super battleships' of the *Montana* class, the building of which ships was authorised by the Bill.

THE DEATH OF THE BATTLESHIP

When Japan began the war with the USA by attacking Pearl Harbor on 7 December 1941, the relative strengths in battleship terms was 10:7 in favour of the United States. After the outbreak of war the Japanese were only able to commission two new battleships, while the USA added eight, plus two battlecruisers. At the end of the war the Japanese had lost all their battleships but one, but the Americans had lost only two. However, the battleships had not played a decisive role in this war on either side: the era of the battleship had already come to an end.

Great Britain had fifteen capital ships in service in 1939; Germany had only two, plus the three *Panzerschiffe*. During the war Britian completed a further five units, the Germans only two. None of the battleships which were begun last – the 40,000 ton *Lion* class units on the British side and the first two of the 'Z-Plan' on the German side – was completed, although in 1941 Great Britain laid down *Vanguard*, a sort of substitute *Lion*. During the war the Royal Navy lost five capital ships, Germany all four, and also her *Panzerschiffe*. When hostilities ended in 1945, the Royal Navy still had sixteen capital ships in service, of which the majority were obsolete. These were the first to go to the breakers, but the others followed soon afterwards. *Vanguard* was sold for scrapping in 1960 – just over half a century after the building of *Dreadnought* – at a time when the role of the battleship had long since been assumed by the aircraft carrier.

For France, Italy, the Soviet Union and the few smaller powers, the battleships which remained in service past the end of the war disappeared silently from the stage, most of them in the 1950s, the last in the late 1960s. From then on only *Yavuz Sultan Selim* – the former German *Goeben* – remained, the only capital ship that the Turkish Navy had ever been able to commission. She too has now been scrapped. Not one capital ship has been kept in Europe as a floating memorial for subsequent generations, in contrast to the position in the USA. The desire for profit, and a lack of insight, have evidently been stronger than the concern of those groups of people who wanted to preserve the ships.

Great Britain

The Royal Navy possessed more than fifty capital ships when the construction of the world's first 'all-big-gun' battleship began in the autumn of 1905. The last pre-dreadnoughts were *Lord Nelson* and *Agamemnon*, which had been laid down only a few months earlier; these two ships were completed in 1908, at a time when they were already to a large extent obsolete since foreign powers had reacted so strongly to the British move. During the First World War the *Lord Nelsons*, together with several other pre-dreadnoughts, were used against the Dardanelles fortifications: *Agamemnon*, shown here in 1915 during these operations, was hit more than fifty times by Turkish coastal batteries and was severely damaged. *BfZ*

Dreadnought

Dreadnought heralded a new era in warship design as the first 'all-big-gun' battleship. She came into being as a result of initiatives by Admiral Lord Fisher, who had made a series of studies relating to a vessel of this type since the beginning of the century. He was not at first over-enthusiastic about a 12in (30.5cm) calibre, preferring the 10in (25.4cm) gun because its rate of fire was so much higher, but the experience gleaned from the Russo-Japanese war of 1905 prompted him to settle for the larger weapon. When he became First Sea Lord in the autumn of 1904, he set up a commission to study and draw up the technical design aspects of the capital ship of the future; the sixth of the suggested designs was approved, and this formed the basis on which *Dreadnought* was built. The ship was commissioned in December 1906. *BfZ*

Another view of *Dreadnought*. *BfZ*

DREADNOUGHT

In contrast with *Dreadnought*, the battlecruiser represented a real innovation, for whilst the former was arguably a logical, inevitable step involving only a moderate increase in size, the battlecruiser represented an enormous increase in capability over its progenitor, the armoured cruiser. The first battlecruisers were *Invincible*, *Inflexible* and *Indomitable*. Firepower and speed were accorded absolute top priority, but this was achieved only at the expense of no less an important factor – strength. The gravity of the error of judgement made by the battlecruiser's champion Admiral Lord Fisher – whose basic dictum was 'Speed is the best protection' – was made plain at the Battle of Jutland: under the salvoes of the German battlecruisers, *Invincible* broke up in a massive explosion after a shell had penetrated one of her midships turrets and ignited the magazine below. Only five men survived. *Indomitable*, pictured here, was the third ship of the class and was commissioned in the summer of 1908. The forefunnel was raised by 6ft in 1910. *BfZ*

After the tragic loss of *Invincible*, her sister-ships were given improved protection – principally a strengthening of the turret roofs and magazine crowns; improvements to the flooding systems inside the shell rooms were also worked in. Nevertheless, they remained poorly protected vessels. This photograph shows *Invincible* in 1918. *BfZ*

The Second Battlecruiser Squadron on 21 November 1918 off the Firth of Forth, waiting for the German High Seas Fleet on its way to internment. The *Indefatigable* class battlecruisers *Australia* and *New Zealand* lead *Indomitable*. *BfZ*

Bellerophon class

Bellerophon, Superb, Temeraire

In the winter of 1906–07 a class of three 'all-big-gun' battleships was begun for the Royal Navy. They carried the same main armament as *Dreadnought*, arranged in identical fashion, but these ships showed two improvements: first, the strengthened anti-torpedo-boat battery, consisting of 4in (10.2cm) guns – *Dreadnought* had to rely exclusively on 3in (7.6cm) guns for this purpose – and second, the anti-torpedo bulkhead. The latter was an important advance, since *Dreadnought* had only armoured longitudinal bulkheads where the main shell rooms were situated. The *Bellerophon* class differed externally from their predecessor principally in the arrangement of the masts and funnels. This is a prewar photograph of *Temeraire*, identifiable by the two white rings around each funnel. *BfZ*

Temeraire looked somewhat different in 1918, as shown here. She had been fitted with two 4in (10.2cm) AA guns, but one of them was located on the after turret instead of on the quarterdeck as with the other ships of her class. A characteristic feature of early British dreadnoughts were the derricks to either side of the after superstructure, which were usually stowed vertically. *BfZ*

During the course of World War I the appearance of all capital ships changed as a wide variety of equipment was added, mainly in the form of extra searchlights, AA guns and fire control systems. Most ships also had their topmasts struck. This 1918 photo shows *Bellerophon*'s final appearance: she was the only ship of her class to have a clinker screen to the forefunnel. An awning is rigged over 'X' turret, and the two 4in (10.2cm) AA guns are clearly visible. To the left, above the ship, is a barrage balloon. *BfZ*

A second series of three battleships was built as the *St Vincent* class, which was largely similar to the *Bellerophon* class and therefore also belonged to the family of designs based on *Dreadnought*. The ships had few really new features, but were generally more efficient. Of the three, *Vanguard* was lost during the war – not as a result of enemy action but from an internal explosion, presumably arising from the ignition of cordite in a magazine. This photo shows *Vanguard* in peacetime. *BfZ*

From 1917 *Collingwood* featured clinker screens on both her funnels, the only ship of the *St Vincent* class – indeed, the only early British dreadnought – to have these fittings. This photograph, dating from 1918, also shows the other modifications which were made after she was commissioned, notably the aircraft flying-off platform on the after turret and the enlarged superstructure forward of it, on which a range clock and further searchlights can be made out. *BfZ*

Neptune, Colossus, Hercules

A special feature of early British dreadnoughts from *Bellerophon* to *Hercules* was the flying bridge, also known unofficially as the 'Marble Arch'. These were bridge-like structures, between the main midships turrets, on which the ships' boats were stowed. *Neptune*, *Colossus* and *Hercules* each had one of their flying bridges subsequently removed. The drawing shows a flying bridge on *Neptune*. *Author*

Neptune, laid down early in 1909, represented a new departure for the Royal Navy as far as the arrangement of her main armament was concerned. The wing turrets were disposed *en échelon*, enabling them to fire on either beam. A second change was to shift the second aftermost turret further aft, superimposed over 'Y' turret. The forward flying bridge was removed from *Neptune* in 1915, and by 1916 she had a clinker screen on her forefunnel. This photo was taken in 1918, probably in Scapa Flow, and also shows an *Orion* class battleship in the background. *BfZ*

The battleships *Hercules* and *Colossus* can be conveniently grouped together with *Neptune* but in fact they were a new design, which however showed no real progress. They had the same main armament as *Neptune*, and the disposition of the guns was similar, but their protection was not comparable to that of their predecessors: thicker armour was used, but the anti-torpedo bulkhead was abandoned in favour of a return to the *Dreadnought* arrangement, which meant that only the shell rooms for the main armament were protected by armoured longitudinal bulkheads. Thus there was no really effective underwater protection. Another unfortunate decision was the retention of the forefunnel in front of the foremast, the same layout as that originally featured by *Dreadnought*. The photograph shows *Colossus* during the second half of World War I, in company with other battleships and a few light cruisers. *BfZ*

A photograph of *Hercules*, taken before 1917 (the searchlight towers are not yet in place around the after funnel) and probably, like the previous illustration, at Scapa Flow. *BfZ*

The *Invincibles* were quickly complemented by a further three vessels, but these units showed no fundamental improvements over their predecessors, sharing their handicap of wholly inadequate protection. For this reason, *Indefatigable* suffered the same fate as *Invincible* at Jutland – a fatal hit from a 28.0cm (11in) salvo fired by the battlecruiser *Von der Tann*, followed by an explosion. There were only two survivors, even fewer than from *Invincible*. This is one of the last photographs of *Indefatigable*. *BfZ*

The battlecruisers *Australia* and *New Zealand* were financed by the dominions whose names they bore, as part of the Commonwealth defence programme. Australia also paid the running and maintenance costs of her ship and therefore laid claim to her command, but New Zealand decided against this and immediately placed the ship at the disposal of the Royal Navy. Australia later did the same, since Britain had been granted the right to make use of her ship in an emergency, provided Australia was not endangered by the ship's withdrawal. This was the case in 1914, after Tsingtau, the only German outpost in south-east Asia which could threaten Australia, was annexed by the Japanese in November that year. This act cut off the East Asia Squadron, commanded by Admiral Graf von Spee, and the light cruisers operating individually. This photo shows *New Zealand* in 1918. *BfZ*

Australia, which had to be disposed of under the terms of the Washington Treaty, was scuttled off the south-west Australian coast on 12 April 1924. The photograph shows her final moments. *BfZ*

Orion class

Conqueror, Monarch, Orion, Thunderer

During the war the external appearance of the *Orion* class battleships changed, a fact apparent from this photo of *Conqueror* taken in 1918 at Rosyth. Modifications around the bridge have made the forefunnel hardly recognisable as such, and *Conqueror* looks more like a single-funnel vessel. The searchlight towers grouped around the after funnel were also added as part of the modification programme. *BfZ*

When the Imperial German Navy abandoned its 28.0cm (11in) guns in favour of 30.5cm (12in) weapons, Great Britain reacted by adopting 13.5in (34.3cm), a move which heralded the 'super-dreadnought' era. A new generation of battleships evolved, the first of which were the *Orion* class. From this time on, classes of four were laid down instead of the previous classes of three. The main turrets were henceforth disposed along the ship's centreline; wing turrets were finally relinquished, although they reappeared later for secondary armament. This is a peacetime photograph of *Orion*: she shared the same problematic forefunnel position as *Colossus* and *Hercules*. *Author's Collection*

The three battlecruisers of the *Lion* class – *Princess Royal*, *Queen Mary* and *Lion* herself – were quickly dubbed 'the splendid cats' by the British Press. With their eight 13.5in guns they were the battlecruiser equivalents of the 'super-dreadnoughts'. The original designs called for the foremast to be sited aft of the forefunnel, and *Lion* was completed to this configuration (see photograph); however, during trials this arrangement proved to be unsatisfactory and troublesome, because flying sparks and the high temperatures of the escaping gases made the bridge virtually uninhabitable at high speed. Modifications were carried out to eliminate these problems before the ship was commissioned. *Author's Collection*

The *Lions* suffered from the same deficiencies as their predecessors: they were insufficiently robust, and the reason for this was that, despite a considerable increase in displacement (about 8000 tons), once again only a small proportion of the total was allocated to protection. In action, these weaknesses became very apparent: *Lion*, involved in the Dogger Bank action and the Battle of Jutland, was severely damaged by shellfire, and barely escaped disaster; *Queen Mary* was hit as many times at Jutland, but she exploded and sank, sharing the fate of *Invincible* and *Indefatigable*, and only nine men survived. Jutland, the greatest sea battle in history, forced the British to reconsider their capital ships designs – they had lost three of their most powerful ships, not to speak of 3321 men, on which so many hopes had been placed. Here *Queen Mary* is shown at anchor at Scapa Flow. She already carries the late war paint scheme, the midships section of the hull being finished in dark grey. *BfZ*

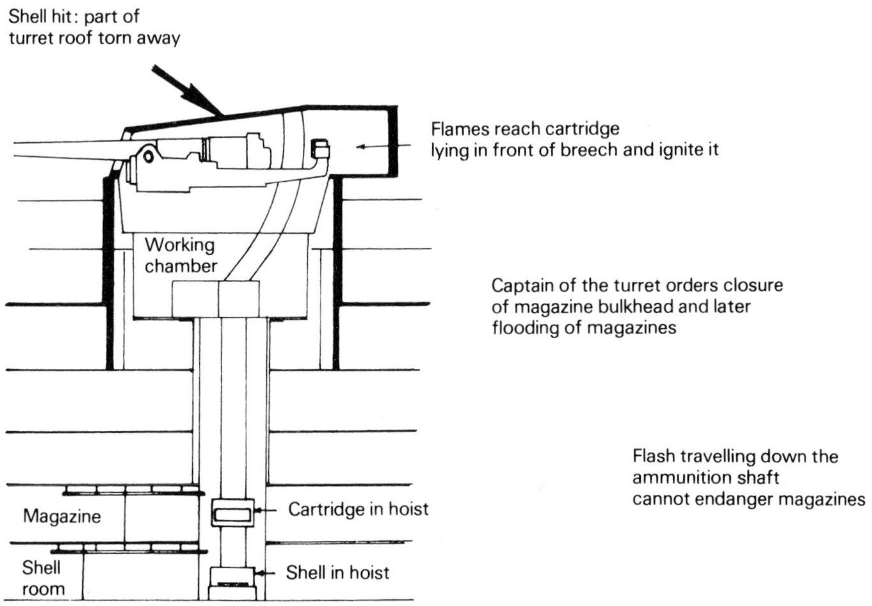

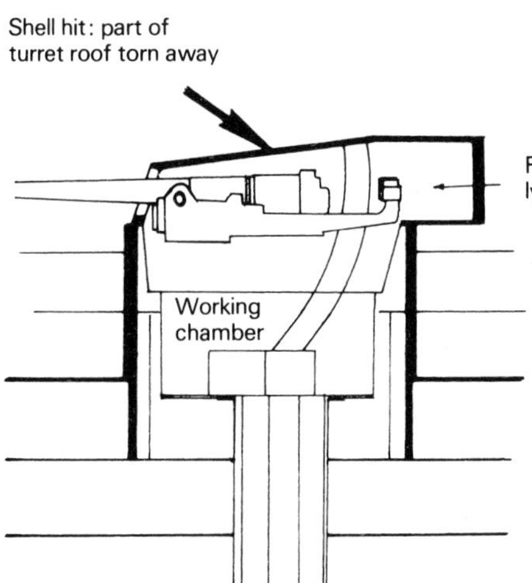
Shell hit: part of turret roof torn away
Flames reach cartridge lying in front of breech and ignite it
Working chamber
Captain of the turret orders closure of magazine bulkhead and later flooding of magazines
Flash travelling down the ammunition shaft cannot endanger magazines
Magazine
Cartridge in hoist
Shell room
Shell in hoist

During the Battle of Jutland *Lion* was hit by a 30.5cm (12in) shell from the German battlecruiser *Lützow*, which struck the roof of 'Q' turret, tore it away, and exploded inside: the entire turret crew – about 100 men – were either killed or severely injured. Nevertheless, there was good luck in this misfortune, for the captain of the turret, with his dying breath, had given the order to flood the magazines, which saved the ship. Had the shell rooms beneath the turret exploded, the ship would undoubtedly have sunk. The drawing shows the effect of this devastating blow. *Author*

Lion shortly after the Battle of Jutland – the ruptured turret has been removed, and repairs are underway. The ship was ready for action again by the second half of July 1916. *BfZ*

Lion and *Princess Royal* remained in service only for a few years after the end of the war, and were then broken up. Although the British were obliged to scrap these vessels under the terms of the Washington Treaty, the decision could not have been a particularly painful blow to them, as it had long been apparent that these battlecruisers – and their predecessors – suffered from inherent, incurable deficiencies. This 1918 photo of *Princess Royal* shows how the ship appeared in her last years of service. She has a rangefinder on the foretop, the typical searchlight towers in the region of the after funnel, and an aircraft platform on 'Y' turret. *BfZ*

Lion in 1918 was showing the same modifications as her sister-ships but in addition had a clinker screen on her forefunnel. Both this and the previous photo show a makeshift canvas shelter on the 'Y' turret aircraft platform, probably to house the aircraft and to protect it from the weather – a forerunner of the aircraft hangar. It was obviously an experiment, and was not continued. *BfZ*

The second series of four in the new generations of 'super-dreadnoughts' consisted of the ships of the *King George V* class. They were basically repeats of the *Orions*: armament, protection and machinery were virtually identical. After the ships had been laid down, there was some debate as to whether a comprehensive secondary armament should be fitted instead of the 4in (10.2cm) guns, but the idea was shelved on grounds of cost, although the necessity of a heavier secondary battery had been tacitly admitted. These ships were much more handsome vessels than their predecessors. This 1918 photo shows *King George V* at her anchorage with other battleships, and a barrage balloon overhead. *BfZ*

Audacious was the first British capital ship to be lost in World War I. She suffered severe damage on 27 October 1914 after striking a mine (laid by the German auxiliary cruiser *Berlin*) while steaming off Northern Ireland near Lough Swilly. An internal explosion followed, causing further injury. After unsuccessful attempts to take the ship in tow, she had to be abandoned, and sank. This photo shows *Audacious* in the early stages of her death throes: destroyers try to render assistance, but she is already listing noticeably to port. *BfZ*

Centurion had by no means completed her active career when placed in reserve in 1924: in 1926–27 she was modified to a remote-controlled target ship, and was used for target practice until the end of 1940. In early 1941 she was then converted again, this time into a 'dummy ship': using a great deal of wood and canvas she masqueraded as *Anson* of the new *King George V* class, and operated in the Mediterranean, the South Atlantic and the Indian Ocean. In mid-1942, while transporting 2000 tons of supplies to Malta, she was damaged by a bomb and returned to Alexandria. From the end of 1942 to the beginning of 1944 she was used as a floating AA battery on the Great Bitter Lake, and in June 1944 her career ended on the Normandy invasion beaches, where she was scuttled as a breakwater. There the wreck deteriorated, and was later gradually broken up. The upper photo shows *Centurion* as an operational battleship, taken around 1918 (note the aircraft launching platforms on 'B' and 'X' turrets); the lower picture dates from 1935, when she was already being used as a target ship. *BfZ*

Iron Duke class

Benbow, Emperor of India, Iron Duke, Marlborough

The third series of four 'super-dreadnoughts' was known as the *Iron Duke* class, laid down in 1912. They were essentially similar to the *King George V*s, having practically identical armament and armour; however, they were the first 'all-big-gun' battleships to return to a full-strength secondary armament, a design feature necessitated by the increasing size, power and strength of destroyers. The photo shows *Marlborough* in 1914. This ship was damaged at the Battle of Jutland and had to be towed home, having been torpedoed by the German cruiser *Wiesbaden*. *BfZ*

This aerial photo shows *Emperor of India*, the only member of the *Iron Duke* class not to take part in the Battle of Jutland. As the searchlight towers are already present around the after funnel, the year must be 1918. The 3in (7.6cm) AA guns on the after superstructure are also clearly visible. *BfZ*

Between 1915 and 1918 the *Iron Duke* class units carried 'baffles', which were intended to deceive enemy rangefinders. They are clearly visible here on *Benbow*, on the after edge of the forefunnel and on the derrick post behind it. *BfZ*

Emperor of India was the only ship in her class to have a clinker screen on the forefunnel from 1918 on. Here she lies at anchor, with her turrets trained to port. Gunnery practice is evidently taking place at a supply base. *BfZ*

After the end of the First World War the battleships of the *Iron Duke* class served with the Mediterranean Fleet. During this time, they were temporarily transferred to the Black Sea where they provided support for the White Russian troops fighting against the Bolsheviks. The photograph shows the *Iron Duke* firing against an advancing Bolshevik unit at Novorossijsk.

The *Iron Duke* class battleships remained in service until the end of the 1920s, after which all except *Iron Duke* herself were scrapped. This photo was taken in July 1928, and shows *Benbow*, serving with the Atlantic Fleet at the time; in the background is the battlecruiser *Renown*. *BfZ*

From August 1914 to November 1916, *Iron Duke* was the flagship of the Grand Fleet; Admiral Sir John Jellicoe directed operations from her during the Battle of Jutland. In the early 1930s *Iron Duke* was converted to a gunnery training ship, since she had to be partially demilitarised to comply with the First London Naval Conference agreement in 1930. From then on she lacked 'B' and 'Y' turrets, her armour belt, her conning tower, her torpedo tubes and some of her boilers. This photo dates from the mid-1930s, when *Iron Duke* was already operating as a gunnery training ship. *BfZ*

Tiger

Tiger was originally intended as the fourth ship of the *Lion* class, and following her a second ship – *Leopard* – was also planned, but nothing came of either of these schemes; *Tiger* was built as the sole representative of a new design, and symbolised the last phase of British prewar battlecruiser development. The design was strongly influenced by the battlecruiser *Kongo*, built by Vickers at Barrow for Japan, and produced a much more battleworthy ship, particularly as regards horizontal protection. Underwater protection was still, however, inadequate. *Tiger* was the first British battlecruiser with a full-strength secondary armament, ie 6in (15.2cm) guns, and was also the first British warship to develop more than 100,000hp; she was, moreover, the last British battlecruiser to be fitted with coal-fired boilers. The photograph shows *Tiger* after the end of the First World War, with her main topmast fitted, modifications in the bridge and foremast area, and a flying-off platform on 'B' turret. An important improvement in *Tiger* was her great freeboard forward – 23ft (7m), in contrast to the 18ft 8in (5.7m) of the *Lion* class. *BfZ*

The battlecruiser *Tiger* at Rosyth in 1917. At this time the aircraft launching platform was still in place on 'X' turret, and the canvas shelter which presumably housed the ship's aircraft is also visible. The topmast stepped on the derrick post forward of the after funnel is not fitted. The paint scheme shown was typical of British warships during the second half of World War I. *BfZ*

Agincourt

Agincourt was said to be the most powerful battleship afloat, not on account of her gun calibre, but because of the number of heavy guns she carried – no fewer than fourteen barrels, grouped in seven twin turrets, the turrets divided into three groups forward, amidships and aft. The early history of this ship is also of interest: she was begun as *Rio de Janeiro* for the Brazilian Navy, but in 1914 was sold to Turkey when half completed, and her construction was continued as *Sultan Osman I*. War broke out shortly before her delivery, and Great Britain immediately requisitioned this valuable ship; from that time on she served as *Agincourt* in the Grand Fleet. This photo shows her in 1915 at her home base. There are already changes compared with her original appearance: the 'flying bridges' have been removed, and the main topmast has been struck. *BfZ*

By 1918 *Agincourt*'s appearance had altered compared to when she commissioned in 1914: in 1916 the support struts of the mainmast were removed, and in 1918 the mast was taken out completely. The ship is seen here in this state. The searchlight towers around the after funnel are still missing, as are the 3in (7.6cm) AA guns on the quarterdeck. *Agincourt* fought at Jutland and came through undamaged. In 1921 Brazil refused an offer from the British to buy back the ship, and in 1922 she was sold for scrapping; two years later the buyers docked her, cut her in two, and broke her up. *BfZ*

Erin

The battleship *Reshadieh*, ordered by Turkey from Vickers (Barrow) in 1911, was almost complete when war broke out. She was requisitioned for the Royal Navy and shortly afterwards placed in service with the Grand Fleet under the name *Erin*. The ship took part in the Battle of Jutland and sustained no damage. In 1919 she was placed in reserve, and three years later authorised for scrap, in accordance with the conditions of the Washington Treaty. *Erin* is shown here at anchor in Scapa Flow in July 1915. *BfZ*

Erin in the Moray Firth, also in 1915. In both this and the previous photo the ship is unchanged from her appearance as completed; alterations were, however, made in 1917 to the bridge, the mast and the searchlights, and AA guns were also added. *BfZ*

Canada

In 1911 Chile had ordered two capital ships in England, which were begun in 1911 and 1913. When war broke out the first ship, *Almirante Latorre*, which had already been launched, was immediately requisitioned for the Royal Navy. In Autumn 1915 she was commissioned with the new name of *Canada*. This photo shows her at Rosyth in 1916. *BfZ*

Canada took part in the Battle of Jutland but was undamaged, and accomplished little worthy of note. She is shown here accompanied by the destroyer *Oak*, which is being used as a despatch vessel for the Fleet Commander. *BfZ*

The building of *Almirante Latorre*'s sister ship, *Almirante Cochrane*, was suspended, and she remained on the slipway. For a time the idea of completing the ship with the name of *India* was contemplated, but eventually it was decided not to do so. Finally, the Royal Navy acquired the half-finished hull and completed the vessel, not as a battleship, but as the aircraft carrier *Eagle*, as shown here. *BfZ*

The *Queen Elizabeth* class battleships, laid down in 1912–13, represented a new departure in two respects. The Americans and the Japanese had opted for 14in (35.6cm) guns, and there were signs that Germany would also shortly adopt a heavier calibre, so Winston Churchill, who had been First Lord of the Admiralty since 1911, used all his influence to ensure that new British battleships should not be caught out. The decision was quickly made: a calibre of 15in (38.1cm) was agreed upon, which had never before been used for a battleship. This was compensated for by accepting a reduction in the number of barrels: only eight guns instead of the previous ten. This meant four twin turrets, and the logical arrangement was clearly an equal grouping forward and aft; the absence of a turret amidships, moreover, made it possible to install larger and more powerful machinery, in order to attain a higher speed. The adoption of this new design resulted in the world's first fast battleships, and marked the narrowing of the gap that had separated battleships from battlecruisers. With their 15in guns the *Queen Elizabeth* class units were clearly superior to all other battleships then built, but they would also provoke other navies – principally Germany's – into opting for still larger calibres. The photo shows *Queen Elizabeth*'s 15in twin turrets and was taken shortly after the ship was commissioned. *BfZ*

In January 1915 the first *Queen Elizabeth* class ship was completed, bearing the class name. She first went into action in February 1915 in the Dardanelles operations. Although the use of this battleship – the largest and most powerful at the time – had a marked strengthening effect on the morale of the troops, she was ordered to return home in May 1915 becuase of the dangers presented by U-boats and mines. This aerial photo of *Queen Elizabeth* shows that her after 6in (15.2cm) guns have already been removed; the other ships of her class were not fitted with them at all. *BfZ*

Warspite, *Malaya*, *Barham* and *Valiant* were all temporarily fitted with 'rangefinding baffles' in 1916–18. These somewhat bizarre fittings were made out of canvas stretched over a frame, attached to the funnels and masts, and served to alter the ships' silhouettes, making recognition more difficult for the enemy. This photo shows *Warspite* in 1916. *BfZ*

The relatively high speed (25kts) of the *Queen Elizabeth* class battleships, which operated together as the 5th Battle Squadron, resulted in their being temporarily assigned to the Battle Cruiser Fleet, as part of which they were employed at Jutland; *Queen Elizabeth* was absent, however, since she was at Rosyth for refit from 24 May 1916. Together they fired 1099 rounds from their 15in guns (*Barham* 337, *Valiant* 288, *Warspite* 259 and *Malaya* 215), although they were themselves hit – *Barham* four times, *Malaya* eight times and *Warspite* thirteen times, only *Valiant* remaining undamaged. In the course of July 1916, all of them were operational again. This photo shows *Warspite* in 1917, together with other battleships, evidently in Scapa Flow. *Warspite* still carries her 'range baffles'. *BfZ*

Towards the end of the war *Queen Elizabeth* (pictured here) differed from her four sister-ships in that she alone carried tall topmasts fore and aft. Flying-off platforms are fitted on the superfiring turrets, and one of the ship's aircraft can be seen on the forward platform. Note the range clocks on the foremast. *BfZ*

The first refits for the *Queen Elizabeth* class were concerned above all with increasing protection. *Warspite* was the first ship to go into dock in 1924, *Valiant* the last in 1929. All five vessels were fitted with torpedo bulges, increasing their beam by more than 13ft (4m), which resulted in a slight decrease in speed. At the same time the funnels were trunked and a new fire control system and additional AA guns were fitted. *Valiant* differed from her sister-ships in having a catapult installed on the quarterdeck, which is clearly visible here together with the aircraft crane fitted at the same time. Fragments of the old launching platforms are still visible on the 'B' and 'X' turrets. *BfZ*

Starting in 1937, *Queen Elizabeth* and *Valiant* underwent extensive modernisation, and could hardly be recognised when the work was finished, so fundamentally had their external appearance altered. The reconstruction was carried out on the pattern of *Warspite* (which had been modernised from 1934 to 1937) and included the fitting of new engines and boilers, a strengthening of the horizontal armour, the installation of new heavy and light AA weapons (dispensing entirely with the 6in guns), increasing the elevation of the main armament, the fitting of new fire control systems and the provision of aircraft. *Queen Elizabeth*'s reconstruction was carried out in Portsmouth, but she was moved to Rosyth in December 1940, where the work was completed. This photo was taken there in February 1941. The space behind the funnel clearly shows where the new aircraft catapult is located. *BfZ*

During the night of 20 March 1941, *Malaya* was torpedoed by *U106* about 250 miles WNW of Cape Verde, while escorting convoy SL-68. She then steamed to Trinidad for temporary repairs. This illustration was published by the Germans during the war and shows *Malaya* five years earlier, after a collision with a freighter, and not after the torpedo strike as claimed in the photo caption at the time. *BfZ*

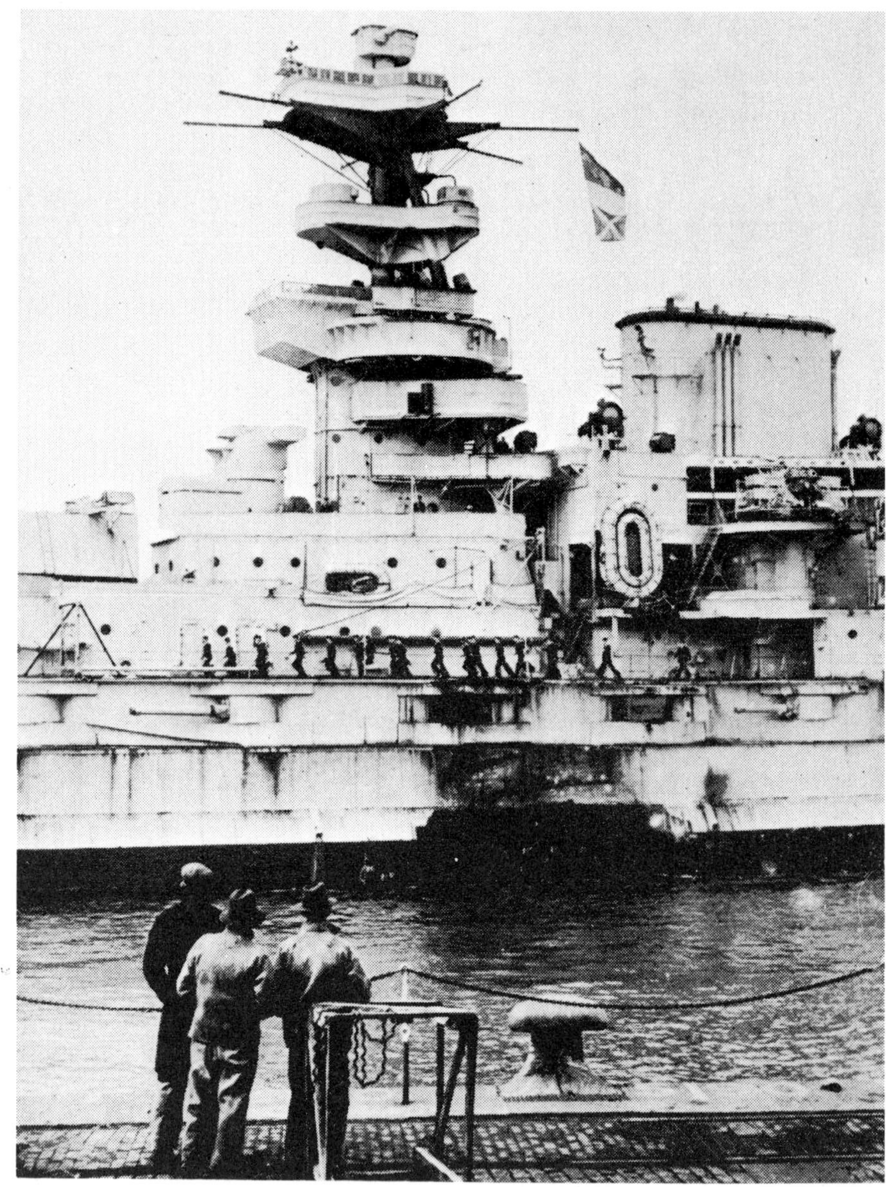

During the Second World War, damaged British battleships were occasionally repaired in the USA, even before that country declared war. This was the case with *Malaya*, following her March 1941 torpedo hit. *Warspite* – shown here – was also refitted and overhauled at Seattle, Washington, in October 1942. *BfZ*

Twice in the Second World War *Barham* crossed the path of U-boat torpedoes and was hit. The first time was on 28 December 1939 off the Clyde Estuary – a torpedo from *U30* hit the ship, but she sustained only minor damage, and was operational again in April 1940. On 25 November 1941, however, she was again hit, this time by three torpedoes from *U331* off the Egyptian Coast near Sollum, and these were fatal: the ship exploded as she capsized (see photo) and took 862 men to the bottom of the sea. *BfZ*

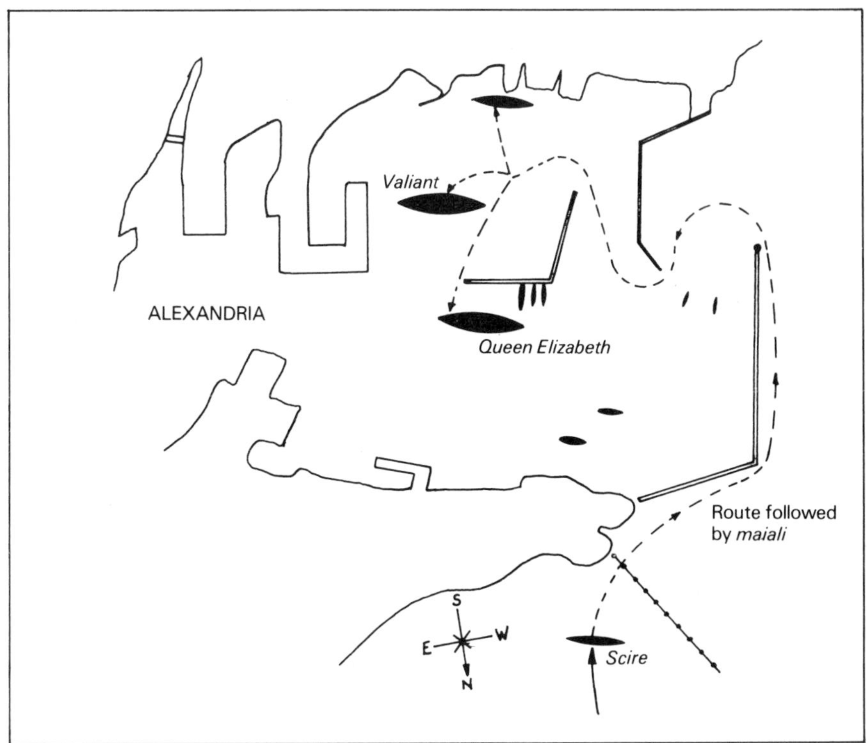

Late in 1941 the Royal Navy lost three capital ships in the space of three weeks, and two more were so badly damaged that they were out of action for several months. The first to be sunk was *Barham*, on 25 November, followed by *Repulse* and *Prince of Wales* on 10 November. On 19 December 1941 three human torpedoes carried by the Italian submarine *Scire* got through the defences at Alexandria with their *maiali*. The battleships *Valiant* and *Queen Elizabeth* were at anchor there with other vessels which had just returned from a mission. The Italians laid their charges and following detonation both battleships sank to the bottom with severe damage. It was some months before they were fully operational again. This map shows where the two British battleships lay at anchor, and the route followed by Italian human torpedoes. *Author's Collection*

The severe damage suffered by *Queen Elizabeth* on 19 December 1941 was finally repaired in Norfolk (USA). In June 1943 she returned to Britain and in December she joined the Eastern Fleet. After taking part in a number of operations, she returned once more to Britain in July 1945 and was broken up three years later. This photograph of *Queen Elizabeth* probably dates from 1943; her aircraft equipment has already been removed. *Author's Collection*

Valiant, which had also been completely modernised from 1937 onwards, joined the Home Fleet early in 1940, and shortly afterwards took part in operations around Norway. From the summer of 1940 she was assigned to the Mediterranean Fleet. The damage she sustained in Alexandria in December 1941 was repaired in the USA; thereafter she was transferred to the Eastern Fleet. One year later she was assigned to Force 'H' and took part in the conquest of Sicily and the landings in Southern Italy from September 1943, but from early 1944 she again served in the Eastern Fleet. This photograph dates from early 1944 during the operations against Soerabaja; *Valiant* is in the foreground and behind her is the French battleship *Richelieu*, detached to the Eastern Fleet at that time. *Author's Collection*

On 1 September 1944 *Malaya* undertook her final operational mission, when she bombarded the Ile de Cézèmbre, off St Malo. The war had scarcely ended when she was taken out of service; however, she spent some time as a torpedo training ship, in which role she was serving when this 12 May 1947 photo was taken off Spithead. One year later her breaking-up had begun. Since 1943 *Malaya* had had no secondary armament, as is evident here; the superstructure beneath the mainmast was also added around this time. *Author's Collection*

Warspite could claim that she had the longest battle record of any battleship. She also received more hits than any other British battleship, but she was a 'lucky' ship and always survived. For this reason she should really have earned a different fate: on 12 March 1947 she began her final voyage, which was meant to take her to the scrapyard at Faslane, but on 23 March the tow cable broke en route and she ran aground at Prussia Cove, near Land's End. There she was gradually broken up, the last remnants being removed in 1956. This photo shows *Warspite* shortly after the accident. *BfZ*

Revenge class

Ramillies, Resolution, Revenge, Royal Oak, Royal Sovereign

The *Queen Elizabeth* class were the first battleships in the world to have exclusively oil-fired boilers, but in Britain doubts were soon expressed as to whether it would be possible to maintain a sufficient reserve supply of oil in wartime. It was not possible to allay these doubts completely, so the decision was taken to return to mixed firing for the *Revenges*, the next class to be built: the majority of their boilers were to be coal-fired, and only a few oil-fired. This limited the top speed, but the 21kts attainable would allow the ships to fit in well with the concept of the battle fleet, according to the views of the Admiralty. However, one of the first of Lord Fisher's actions after he returned to office was to revise the boiler systems: the majority of them would now be oil-fired, in order to provide a slightly higher speed (23kts). *Revenge* herself is shown here. *BfZ*

In many respects the *Revenge* class were similar to the *Queen Elizabeths*, principally in the matter of armament, although armour and protection generally were somewhat better. The ships were ready half way through the war. Almost until the end of the war they carried a camouflage scheme in light grey, dark grey, black and white, as shown both in the previous photograph and in this one of *Ramillies*. *BfZ*

Revenge and *Royal Oak* were completed so far ahead of schedule that they had already joined the Grand Fleet when the Battle of Jutland took place. *Revenge* was assigned to the 1st Battle Squadron, *Royal Oak* to the 4th. *Ramillies* was the first battleship to be fitted with torpedo bulges; although installed after her completion, they were fitted before the ship was commissioned. The other ships were fitted with them shortly after being completed. Towards the end of the war and immediately afterwards, the *Revenge* class were modified to bring them into line with accepted standards: the obligatory searchlight towers either side of the funnel and on the mainmast (those in the latter position were soon removed) and also the flying-off platforms on 'B' and 'X' turrets. This photograph was taken around 1920, and shows *Revenge* with additional accommodation above and abaft the bridge; right to the end she was the only ship of her class to have this feature. The torpedo bulge is also clearly visible here. *BfZ*

In 1922 *Resolution* was the first ship in her class to be fitted with a clinker screen; for years this feature served to differentiate her from her sister-ships. However, the rest of the class – with the exception of *Royal Oak* – were also fitted with screens around 1938–39. From the beginning of the 1930s *Resolution* also carried a spotter aircraft, and a catapult was fitted aft. This photo of *Resolution* probably dates from the early 1930s. *BfZ*

By 1926, *Royal Sovereign* no longer featured flying-off platforms on her main turrets, only remnants of them still being visible. In the early 1930s she was fitted with the same quarterdeck catapult equipment as *Resolution*. *BfZ*

Royal Oak was sunk six weeks after the start of the Second World War, and was the first British capital ship to be lost in this conflict. On 14 October 1939 she was hit by at least two torpedoes from the German U-boat *U47* under the command of *Kapitänleutnant* Günter Prien. *U47* had penetrated into Scapa Flow, the British Home Fleet's anchorage at the time, and was able to escape unmolested after the attack. Within twelve minutes of the first torpedo hit, the ship sank, drowning 786 crew members. *BfZ*

Royal Oak differed from her sister-ships in her torpedo-bulges, which were carried upwards virtually to the battery deck, a modification which had been made in 1927. The previous photo shows the shape of the bulge particularly well, although it can also be seen clearly in this illustration, where the port torpedo tube doors can also be made out. These doors had been installed as an experiment in 1935 – two on each side angled at roughly 35° forward from the ship's longitudinal axis. *BfZ*

On 25 September 1940, during operations against Dakar, *Resolution* was hit by a torpedo from the French submarine *Bévéziers*. Repairs were begun at Portsmouth, but the increasingly heavy German air attacks made it necessary to carry out the rest of the work at a safe dockyard – Philadelphia. Eventually, *Resolution* joined the Eastern Fleet. This picture was taken on 28 November 1941, and shows *Resolution* in her 'warpaint'. *BfZ*

Revenge again, shown here in September 1949 whilst being broken up at Inverkeithing – a view into the bridge deck, which has already been partially dismantled. *BfZ*

During the Second World War *Ramillies* saw action in all the major theatres: initially she covered troop transport operations to France; in late 1939 she went to Aden to join Force 'J'; from mid-1940 she was assigned to the Mediterranean Fleet, escorting convoys; after that she operated in the Atlantic, also mostly on convoy protection duty; and at the end of 1941 she was transferred to the Eastern Fleet. Here she took part in the operations against Madagascar, and was hit by a torpedo from a Japanese midget submarine. She steamed to Durban for emergency repairs, but it proved necessary to send her back home. The repairs were eventually carried out at Devonport in the late summer of 1943, after which she rejoined the Eastern Fleet. In 1944 she returned to Europe and supported the D-Day landings with her shelling, first on the Normandy coast, then off the South of France. At the end of 1944 she was ordered home and served from that time as an accommodation ship until being scrapped shortly after the war. This photo dates from Summer 1944, immediately before, or possibly during, the Allied landings. *Author's Collection*

Renown class

Renown, Repulse

Shortly before the outbreak of World War I, Great Britain had developed the fast battleship, and it seemed at first that the British would continue with this design and abandon the battlecruiser. This prognosis proved incorrect: slow battleships (*Revenge* class) were built next after the fast *Queen Elizabeth* class; moreover, early experiences in the sea war had shown the battlecruiser in a new light, and it proved much more effective than might have been expected. In particular, *Invincible* and *Inflexible* were successful against the German cruisers *Scharnhorst* and *Gneisenau* at the Falkland Islands, and this success caused Lord Fisher to insist on more battlecruisers. It was therefore decided to redesign two ships, which had already been authorised, as battlecruisers, and for which the dockyards had already stockpiled a considerable amount of material. The resulting vessels were *Renown* and *Repulse*, the building of which took about 20 months each, a record time for units of this size. They were the largest, fastest and most powerful battlecruisers in the Royal Navy, but in respect of their protection the same mistakes were made as with all their predecessors: the ships were far too weak – and subsequent modifications brought little improvement. This photograph shows *Renown* before 1917, ie in her original configuration. *Author's Collection*

Renown and *Repulse* proved to be extremely unreliable during their early careers, and often had to go into dock for repairs; they were promptly dubbed 'HMS Refit' and 'HMS Repair'. Another nickname, 'Tin Cans', was a reference to their inadequate protection. In spite of their heavy main armament, they never wholly endeared themselves to the Royal Navy. This photograph shows *Repulse* in 1918, with a flying-off platform already fitted on 'B' turret and searchlight towers around the after funnel. Note that the main topmast is missing. *BfZ*

Although the battlecruiser *Repulse* was modernised from 1934 to 1936, her protection was not improved; hence she entered World War II as the weakest British capital ship – and she did not survive. Together with *Prince of Wales*, she was sunk on 10 December 1941, fatally damaged by five torpedoes and a bomb, off the Malayan Peninsula. This is a peacetime photo of *Repulse* after her refit, which was completed in 1936. *BfZ*

Following on from *Repulse*, *Renown* also underwent modernisation, but this time the modifications were much more fundamental. The most important improvement was the strengthening of the horizontal armour; in addition the ship was fitted with new machinery, and she was also re-armed, except for the six 15in (38.1cm) guns. Externally, *Renown* was scarcely recognisable when she emerged from the dockyard in mid-1939, so radically had her appearance been altered. *Author's Collection*

During the Second World War *Renown* was involved to a remarkable degree in operations against German heavy units: in late 1939 she was sent to look for *Admiral Graf Spee*, operating in the South Atlantic; on 9 April 1940 she had a skirmish with *Scharnhorst* and *Gneisenau* off Vestfjord (north Norway); and a few weeks later she unsuccessfully chased a severely damaged *Gneisenau* on her return home. In the following year she took part in the hunt for *Bismarck*, and towards the end of the war she was the only available Home Fleet capital ship which could have been pitted against *Tirpitz*. This photo dates from late 1943 and was taken at Rosyth; the following January *Renown* was transferred to the Eastern Fleet. The elderly American battleship in the background is probably *Texas* or *Arkansas*. *Author's Collection*

These vessels were not battlecruisers as such, although they have often erroneously been so called; they were officially referred to simply as 'cruisers', and 'large light cruisers' was just a term used by Lord Fisher as he steered their authorisation through Parliament. Later, when the ships were being built, this term was no longer used, although occasionally they were unofficially described as 'first class cruisers'. These unique vessels were produced in response to a project of Lord Fisher's: as early as 1909 he had suggested that, if war should break out, powerful forces should enter the Baltic and land troops on the Pomeranian coast, from where they could push on to Berlin. Late in 1914 this project was revived: the Baltic adventure was planned as part of a wide-ranging offensive, the other thrusts of which were in the Dardanelles in south-east Europe and Flanders in the north-west. The task of the Royal Navy was to penetrate the Baltic with a large number of ships, making it possible for Russian troops to land on the Pomeranian coast, while at the same time a diversionary operation against the Friesian Islands was taking place. The units in the Baltic were to be supported by the three large cruisers *Courageous*, *Glorious* and *Furious*; high speed, the most powerful armament possible and relatively shallow draught were their distinguishing features, but their protection was no better than that of light cruisers. This photograph shows *Glorious* around 1917, shortly after her completion. A striking feature is the unusually high barbette for the forward 15in (38.1cm) turret. *BfZ*

The failure of the Dardanelles campaign and the resultant downfall of Lord Fisher were two of the chief reasons for calling off the planned Baltic operation. By this time the three large cruisers had been laid down, but their construction was continued as they were seen as a welcome reinforcement to the Fleet, despite their inadequate protection. When the first two units, *Courageous* and *Glorious*, were completed, they were assigned to the 3rd Light Cruiser Squadron. *Courageous*, illustrated here, was employed temporarily as a minelayer, and two sets of rails were fitted on each side of her vast quarterdeck. This installation was unofficially referred to as 'Clapham Junction', and the projecting ends of the rails can clearly be made out in this photograph. *BfZ*

Courageous and *Glorious* were used as gunnery training ships for a time after the war, but they were converted into aircraft carriers in 1924. In the early 1930s they were the most successful carriers of their time; this is remarkable, since they were decided failures as cruisers. This photo shows *Glorious* in 1935. Five years later she was sunk by salvoes from the German battlecruisers *Scharnhorst* and *Gneisenau* in the North Sea. Her sister-ship *Courageous* had already been sunk a year earlier by U-boat torpedoes. *BfZ*

Furious

The third 'large light cruiser' was *Furious*, but in contrast to the other two, each with their 15in (38.1cm) guns, *Furious* was intended to be fitted with two 18in (45.7cm) guns – the heaviest calibre yet carried by a warship. However, the design was modified even before the ship was completed: she retained the 18in turret aft, but a flying-off deck was fitted forward with a hangar below it, and a lift connected the two. Between eight and ten floatplanes could be carried on board. For launching, they were mounted on a light carriage which ran on a rail, the latter having a gentle downward slope; when the aircraft had landed on the water near the ship, a derrick hoisted them back on board. Here *Furious* is shown in July 1917, shortly after completion, with her 18in turret well in evidence. *BfZ*

This broadside view of *Furious* makes her hybrid design obvious. The ship remained in this configuration for only six months. *BfZ*

From November 1917 to March 1918 *Furious* was back in dockyard hands. The after 18in turret was removed, and she was fitted with a landing deck. This idea was a notable advance, although there were still considerable technical problems. *Furious* was supposed to carry a normal complement of 16 aircraft, but at times there were up to 26 on board. This photograph shows how *Furious* appeared when she attacked the German airship base at Tondern on 19 July 1918 – the first carrier operation in the history of warfare. The 'framework' behind the funnel, with manila ropes stretched vertically between it and the deck, is a crash barrier for stopping aircraft which miss the arrestor wires. *BfZ*

Hood

◀ It was not long before *Furious* was converted to a 'real' carrier. In 1922 she was returned to the dockyard, and when she emerged again in 1925 she looked utterly different: now she had a completely flush flight deck and a full-length hangar deck below, enabling about 33 aircraft to be accommodated on board. She did not have an island initially, only being fitted with one in 1938–39, as can be seen in this photograph. *Furious* survived the Second World War, but was reduced to scrap soon afterwards. *BfZ*

When news reached Britain that the Germans were preparing the construction of the *Mackensen* class in 1914, the decision was taken to build vessels in response, ships which could also outclass the *Derfflinger*s by a wide margin. In order to achieve this, only one calibre could be adopted: 15in (38.1cm). In March 1916 the final designs were authorised: they proposed 36,000-ton ships with eight 15in guns and a speed of 32–33kts. A few weeks after the contracts had been signed, the Battle of Jutland took place, and the loss of three battlecruisers made the Navy aware of the errors that had been perpetrated in battlecruiser design up to that time. Doubts were expressed about the design of this new class of battlecruiser, since here too protection had been given low priority. The result was an extensive revision to the designs: the armour thickness was increased by an average of 50 per cent, which added about 5000 tons to the weight. The degree of urgency involved in the evolution of the design into hardware is evident from the hectic building rate: the ship's keel was laid in September 1916, even though the design changes were not completed until well into 1917. *Hood* was the resulting ship: she was commissioned in 1920, and came to be the symbol of Britain's sea power for almost two decades. She was not the most powerful ship for long, but she was the largest warship of her time. *Hood* is seen here in the final stages of fitting-out, on 9 January 1920; she was commissioned two months later. Her three sister-ships, incidentally, were never built, as it became known that work on the new German capital ships had ceased. *Author's Collection*

Hood's machinery was very powerful; its total output was 144,000shp – the highest ever achieved with a warship at that time. The large amount of hull volume taken up by the machinery meant that the main turrets had to be fitted very far apart and relatively close to the ends of the ship, which in turn meant that the very long hull had to withstand heavy bending loads. This photograph was taken on 31 May 1929, immediately before the ship entered dock for two years for her first refit. The quarterdeck was considered to be very 'wet' and was often submerged when the ship was at operating high speed. *Author's Collection*

In the immediate prewar years *Hood* was stationed in the Mediterranean, but joined the Home Fleet as soon as hostilities began. She was not able to take part in the operations around Norway in early 1940, as she was undergoing a refit; her first full operation was on 3 July 1940, when she was temporarily seconded to Force 'H'. On that day an attack was mounted against the French naval base at Mers el Kebir, Oran. After the capitulation of France, many of the French Navy's major warships had been moved there, and Britain now demanded that they be handed over, to avoid their falling into the hands of the Axis powers. The French declined, however, so the British opened fire, causing considerable damage. This was the first time for 125 years that the French and British had fired at each other – the first time, in fact, since Waterloo. A year later, *Hood* was no more. On 24 May 1941 she sank under salvoes from the German *Bismarck*. Her loss was preceded by an enormous explosion, which tore her in two, caused by one 38.1cm (15in) shell which detonated in the 4in (10.2cm) shell room, taking one of the after 15in shell rooms with it. Only three men survived. The ship thus shared the fate of her predecessors *Invincible*, *Indefatigable* and *Queen Mary*. The *Hood* disaster showed again that despite the design changes made after the Battle of Jutland, her protection was still inadequate. This photo was taken in the final years of peace when the ship was in the Mediterranean. *BfZ*

Nelson was the first battleship in the world to be built within the qualitative restrictions of the Washington Treaty. Her firepower was as impressive as her ruggedness: nine 16in guns in triple turrets, all of them concentrated forward, and armour 14in (356mm) thick on vertical surfaces and $6^1/_4$in (159mm) thick on horizontal surfaces. The price paid for these attributes was a top speed of only 23kts, since weight had had to be saved through the machinery. This photograph dates from 1941, after mine damage which *Nelson* suffered on 4 December 1939 had been repaired. For protection against future magnetic mines, the ship was fitted with a de-gaussing coil, clearly visible on the hull, although this was replaced by a different system later. *Author's Collection*

Early in 1941 the German battlecruisers *Gneisenau* and *Scharnhorst* were waging a successful 'tonnage war' in the Atlantic, and during this period they made contact with British battleships on three occasions, but each time the German ships were able to escape. One of the battleships was *Rodney*. A few weeks later, in May 1941, *Rodney*, in company with other units, succeeded in destroying the German battleship *Bismarck*. This picture probably dates from that year, and shows *Rodney* with a striking camouflage scheme. 'C' turret still retains its catapult, together with a Walrus aircraft. *Author's Collection*

Following the Allied landings in Normandy, the battleships *Nelson* and *Rodney* joined in the land campaign, using their heavy guns to support the troops' advance. This was especially effective in the Caen area, where German resistance had been strengthened. The Allied ground forces thus received not only the obligatory air support from bombers and fighter-bombers, but also assistance from offshore: battleships, cruisers and destroyers, and *Rodney* in particular, pounded the German positions almost non-stop, and made troop movements on the German side virtually impossible. This photograph of *Rodney* was taken at that period, and shows her firing her main armament. *BfZ*

By the close of World War II the day of the battleship was finally over. The two great Anglo-Saxon navies dispensed with their oldest units first, but soon afterwards it was the turn of the more recent vessels, amongst them *Nelson* and *Rodney*. *Nelson* was broken up at Inverkeithing; she is shown here in February 1949 being helped to her final berth at the breakers' yard by tugs. She is already high in the water, as all her supplies and most of her equipment and fittings have been removed. Some of the armament is also missing. *BfZ*

King George V class

Anson, Duke of York, Howe, King George V, Prince of Wales

The actions of *Prince of Wales* were the subject of some very severe criticism when she withdrew from the engagement with the German battleship *Bismarck*, but this was without justification: *Prince of Wales* had been commissioned only eight weeks before this encounter, and was by no means fully worked-up, and there were recurrent problems – especially concerning her guns. If the ship had persevered, she would possibly have met her end, and hence the decision to withdraw was the best course of action under the circumstances. However, in the eyes of many Britons, the honour of this ship was only restored when she was sunk. This photo shows *Prince of Wales* shortly after she was commissioned. *Author's Collection*

When the British resumed building battleships in 1937, they had long since settled on a 14in (35.6cm) main calibre. A gun of this type was already in production, and the development of a heavier calibre would have delayed the building of the ships by several years. Another important reason for opting for this calibre was that the weight saved could be used to increase protection, ie provide thicker armour. This unilateral decision to limit battleship main calibre was not followed by any other navy, and a strong difference of opinion about these new ships arose in Great Britain: to conservative eyes they were a definite mistake, but this view was shown to be unjustified as the class proved itself extremely well during the war. This is *King George V*, the name-ship of the class, in South-East Asian waters, photographed around the beginning of 1945. The erosive effects of a long period at sea are unmistakable. *Author's Collection*

Duke of York was the third *King George V* class ship, and was completed towards the end of 1941. Her first voyage – with Prime Minister Winston Churchill on board – was to the USA, where the Allied War Council met for the first time. She remained part of the Home Fleet until early 1945 (apart from a short period with Force 'H' in the Mediterranean during Operation 'Torch' in November 1942), and during these years she was used in many sorties against Northern Norway, and as a convoy escort. At the end of 1943 she engaged the German battlecruiser *Scharnhorst*, which, after stubborn resistance, was sunk. *Duke of York* spent the last part of the war with the British Pacific Fleet, only returning home in the summer of 1946. Eleven years later she was stricken and soon afterwards broken up. This photo shows *Duke of York* shortly after the end of the war. *Author's Collection*

Events that took place on 10 December 1941 demonstrated conclusively that the battleship was no longer the supreme instrument of naval power. On that day, land-based Japanese naval bombers attacked the British capital ships *Repulse* and *Prince of Wales*, out from Singapore, with torpedoes and bombs, and sank them. That *Repulse* succumbed to this attack was not surprising in view of her weak protection, but the fact that so modern a ship as *Prince of Wales* did not survive must have caused a lot of rethinking: from now on it was obvious that the battleship had lost its original significance, and could be annihilated from the air like any other warship. If it was to be used in the future, then it should only be under the protective 'umbrella' of friendly aircraft. The Americans and the British immediately took the necessary measures dictated by this experience: from then on aircraft carriers always accompanied battleships. The painting shows the attack on the two ships as envisaged by a British artist; *Prince of Wales* is in the foreground. *Author's Collection*

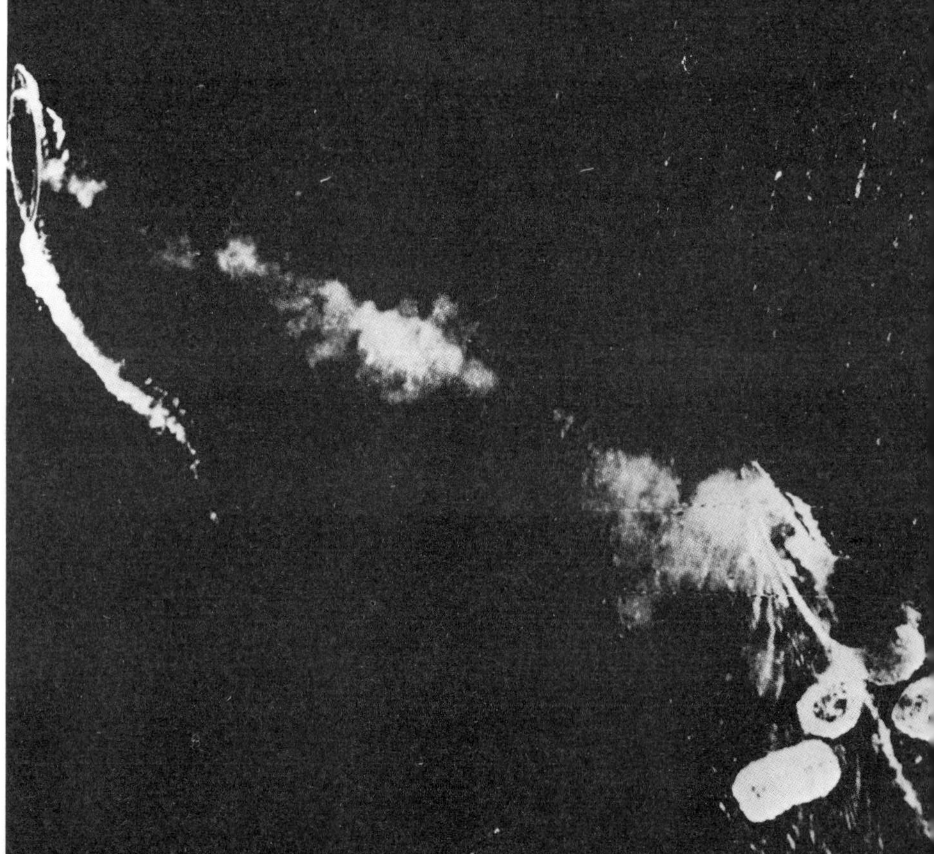

This aerial photo was taken by a Japanese aircraft during the attack on *Prince of Wales* (top left) and *Repulse*; it shows the two ships under bomb attack. Shortly afterwards both vessels sank. *Author's Collection*

At the summit conference in November 1943, the British and Americans agreed that the focal point of the war was going to be in the Pacific, and that after the defeat of Germany, British forces should be used there against the Japanese; these forces should include a sizeable battle fleet. The time soon arrived: early in 1945 the British Pacific Fleet was formed, exclusively from modern units, including the battleships *King George V* and *Howe*, and later also *Duke of York* and *Anson*. The photo above shows *Anson* in August 1945 in drydock in Sydney, Australia, where she was being refitted. *BfZ*

Units of the British Pacific Fleet, with *Duke of York* nearest the camera. *Author's Collection*

Salvoes from these gun barrels sank the German battlecruiser *Scharnhorst* on 26 December 1943, but at the time this photograph was taken – September 1958 – the first of them were lying on deck as scrap. Shortly before this the breakers had begun their work, and *Duke of York* was taken apart, piece by piece, with their cutting torches. When the ship was placed in the reserve in early 1949, she had been in active service for the relatively short period of $7^1/_2$ years. *Author's Collection*

Vanguard

Work on the two battleships *Lion* and *Temeraire* had been started in the summer of 1939 but was stopped shortly after the start of the war, because the 16in (40.6cm) guns and their turrets could not be manufactured in time. The decision was therefore taken to order another ship, and equip it with the 15in (38.1cm) guns which had once been fitted on the cruisers *Courageous* and *Glorious*. The result was a modern battleship, with an obsolete, but still thoroughly serviceable, main armament. The ship was named *Vanguard*. She was the largest British warship that had ever been built; this remains so today, and all the indications are that no future British warship will approach her size. The aerial photo shows *Vanguard*'s two after turrets very clearly. *Author's Collection*

The British had originally planned to have *Vanguard* completed by 1943, but they had to wait until early 1946 and so the ship was too late to serve in World War II. However, there had been no great urgency when the war situation changed so fundamentally from 1944 on; the building rate was slowed down considerably, as other projects assumed higher priority. The first major event for *Vanguard* was a symbol of peace: it was a tour with the British Royal couple from February to May 1947, taking them as far as South Africa. The photograph dates from that time. *Author's Collection*

When *Vanguard* was delivered to the breaker's yard, in 1960, the era of the British capital ship was finally over – an era which had begun 55 years before, and during which a series of ever mightier vessels had evolved. All of them, once the pride of a great sea power which dominated the world, have disappeared – not a single example has been retained as a monument. *Sic transit gloria mundi ... BfZ*

Germany

Shortly after the turn of the century the Germans produced their last pre-dreadnought design: the result was the five units of the *Deutschland* class. Other great sea powers had adopted a 'medium-heavy' armament in addition to the main and the secondary batteries, but the Imperial Navy did not follow this trend, since simultaneous fire control with the means available at the time appeared to be too difficult. The only concession in this respect was an increase in calibre of the secondary armament from 15cm (5.9in) to 17cm (6.7in). One of the five units of the class was *Pommern*, seen here on 18 July 1911 passing beneath the Levensauer Bridge on the Kaiser Wilhelm Canal, in an east-west direction. She met her fate on 1 June 1916 during the Battle of Jutland. British destroyers attacked in the night, and she was hit by a torpedo. In a gigantic explosion she broke apart and sank, taking more than 800 men with her. *BfZ*

This 12 July 1910 photo of *Westfalen*, the Imperial Navy's first dreadnought, shows the ship still featuring her characteristic wireless gaffs on the masts. In 1911 these were removed. Apart from *Westfalen*, only *Nassau* had this type of fitting, but she kept hers only until 1915. Note the absence of torpedo nets. *BfZ*

The first German capital ships had their main armament arranged in a 'hexagonal' pattern: one turret was sited at each end, and two further turrets were located on each beam, thus enabling up to eight barrels to be brought into action on either side. The weight of a broadside in the *Nassau* class totalled 2416kg (5326lb). The four barrels not in use were intended to serve as 'lee fire reserves', according to the tactical ideas of the time. This aerial photograph shows *Westfalen*, and was taken towards the end of the war. The white circles on the roof of the two centreline turrets were for recognition purposes. *BfZ*

The bridge structures on the larger warships of the early years of the twentieth century were as simple as possible, and occupied little space. Usually a *Friedenssteurstand* (lit: peacetime steering position) was built around the armoured control position (easily recognisable here by its vision slits), and the ship was normally conned from the former; only in battle did the ship's commander move to the conning tower which, with its very thick armour, was virtually impregnable. The other essential components of the bridge structure were one or two signal decks, searchlight platforms, a compass platform, and of course the mast, used for hoisting signals. This photo of *Rheinland*, dating from 1911, shows the typical bridge layout of German ships at that time. *BfZ*

The well-designed underwater protection systems of German capital ships made it necessary to adopt a broader beam than previously (as is apparent in this 26 April 1910 photo of *Rheinland*), and this provided the opportunity to raise the ships' stability substantially. The three aftermost turrets are clearly visible here, with two 28cm (11in) guns each. The *Westfalens* were the last German capital ships to be fitted with 'gooseneck' cranes. *BfZ*

Blücher

The heavy cruiser *Blücher* was by no means the German 'reply' to the enormous technological advance represented by *Invincible*, despite the assumptions and claims of the time; she represented the ultimate development in German armoured cruisers. As such, she had important advantages over foreign ships of the same type, especially British vessels. Her twelve barrels had obvious benefits because of her uniformity of calibre – rate of fire, fire control, spotting, logistics – compared with the dual calibre main battery of British armoured cruisers, and she was also faster. Hence *Blücher* was well suited for her role as a battlefleet reconnaissance unit, and also as a long-range cruiser. However, *Blücher* was just not equal to the very different tasks of the battlecruiser; the ship was nevertheless classed as such, and joined a battlecruiser unit. On 24 January 1915, she met her fate at the Dogger Bank: she was sunk by gunfire from British battlecruisers, having withstood them for one and a half hours. *Blücher* was the first German warship with a tripod mast, which was only fitted in 1913 as an experiment. *BfZ*

Von der Tann

Von der Tann was the German response to the Royal Navy's *Invincible*. She was inferior in gun calibre to the British battlecruisers, but the German ship's protection was far superior. At Jutland *Von der Tann*'s 28cm (11in) guns destroyed the British battlecruiser *Indefatigable*. This photo dates from 26 May 1910 and was taken during trials; the ship was commissioned on 1 September 1910. *BfZ*

Compared with the *Invincible* class, *Von der Tann* had a slightly improved main armament layout: the midships turrets on the British ships were quite close together, so that the turret on the disengaged 'lee' side only had a small arc of fire across the deck, but the German design offered the two midships turrets a much wider arc, to starboard and to port. The German vessel also carried a secondary armament of 150mm (5.9in) guns, as against the lighter 4in weapons on board the *Invincibles*. *BfZ*

Up to and during the First World War, it was considered essential to equip German capital ships with torpedo tubes. All ships down to heavy cruisers were fitted with fixed tubes below the waterline, usually five in number. Four of them fired on the beam, the fifth being arranged as a bow tube. This photo, taken in 1912 in a floating dock at Kiel, shows *Thüringen*, with her bow torpedo tube clearly visible. *BfZ*

With capital ships of the prewar era the length-to-beam ratio (which dictates the slimness of the ship's hull and therefore its speed) was still not ideal. However, no speed requirements above 20kts were laid down, so existing ratios, averaging around 5.8:1, were considered satisfactory. In the *Helgoland* class the ratio was 5.52:1; the squatness of the resulting hulls is shown in this aerial photograph of *Helgoland* taken on 17 June 1918. *BfZ*

With the design of the *Helgoland* class, the main armament was arranged in a hexagonal layout as in the *Nassau* class, but by now the gun calibre had been increased to equal that of the British ships. This photo of *Helgoland* was taken well into the war, as evidenced by the absence of torpedo nets, the liferafts stowed on the main turrets, the lack of a compass platform above the after control tower, and the mast platforms. *BfZ*

The Americans carried out some startling experiments with a German capital ship: after the First World War, *Ostfriesland*, the third ship of the *Helgoland* class, was ceded to the United States, and was taken over as 'Battleship H' on 7 April 1920. In the summer of 1921, a series of bombing tests was begun off the Virginian coast, not far from Cape Henry, their purpose being to gain information about the future of the battleship in view of the increasing effectiveness of military aircraft. The experiments began on 20 July 1921 with a number of bombing attacks, during which 13 hits were recorded. On the following day three further hits were made, but even so the ship was not fatally damaged. However, some leakage occurred, leading to flooding, and the ship gradually settled lower in the water. After further bombs had been dropped, most of which were near-misses, the ship sank within 10 minutes. Here was the first hint of what battleships could expect from the air in future. The photo shows *Ostfriesland* en route to the USA with an American crew. Note the US flag at the mainmast and, on the bow, the letter 'H', representing the ship's designation from that time on. *BfZ*

◀ With their three funnels, the *Helgoland*s really stemmed from the design era which produced the pre-dreadnoughts of the *Braunschweig* and *Deutschland* classes. Of the four ships of the *Helgoland* class only one was built in a Navy yard, the other three being laid down by private shipbuilders. *Thüringen* was one of the latter, built by AG Weser in Bremen; this photo, taken in the winter of 1910–11, shows her being fitted out. The secondary armament and main turrets are already fitted, although the barrels are missing from some of the latter. *BfZ*

All German battlecruisers up to *Mackensen* were named after army generals; *Goeben* recalled the Prussian General August von Goeben (1816–1880), who had achieved the rare honour of being awarded the Grand Cross as well as the Iron Cross for his services in the Franco-Prussian War of 1870–71. *Goeben* was part of the Mediterranean Division from 1912, and played an important part in Turkey entering the war on the side of the Central Powers. She was finally transferred to Turkey permanently in 1918, where she served for more than five decades before being scrapped there. A Turkish offer to return the ship was turned down by West Germany, despite a number of moves to preserve her. This photo was taken in the Dardanelles in 1915. *BfZ*

This picture conveys the relaxed nature of peacetime service: a large proportion of *Moltke*'s crew has assembled for the photographer wherever there is any space – even on the narrow funnel rim. The bridge is virtually invisible, although it was not a prominent feature in any case. Stowed along the hull are the ship's torpedo nets and the booms from which the nets were hung to form a complete 'curtain' around the ship; this protection only possible of course when the ship was at anchor. *Moltke* already features a cap on her forefunnel – this was only fitted in 1913. *Author's Collection*

The battlecruiser *Moltke* the morning after the Battle of Jutland en route to her home port, photographed from another ship of the High Seas Fleet. In the background is an escorting torpedo boat. Having received only four hits, the ship escaped relatively unscathed compared with most of the other German units. One year earlier, *Moltke* had been hit forward by a torpedo from the British submarine *E1*; she returned home with over 400 tons of water on board, and was repaired in Hamburg. In April 1918 she was again torpedoed, this time by the British submarine *E42*; more than 2000 tons of water entered the ship on this occasion, although she still managed to make port. *Author's Collection*

Although *Goeben* was mined three times during World War I, there was no opportunity to carry out extensive repairs owing to the unavailability of dockyards, and the damage could only be temporarily patched up. It was not until May 1918 – more than three years later – that a dock became free; this was after Russia's withdrawal from the war, when the ship paid a visit to Sevastopol and the drydock there could be used. However, the damage could still only be inspected, since a shortage of skilled labour and materials made repairs out of the question. It was eight years later, after Turkey herself had constructed a floating dock, that the damage could finally be made good. This photo of *Goeben* was taken whilst she was in drydock at Sevastopol, May 1918. *BfZ*

Kaiser class

Friedrich der Grosse, Kaiser, Kaiserin, König Albert, Prinzregent Luitpold

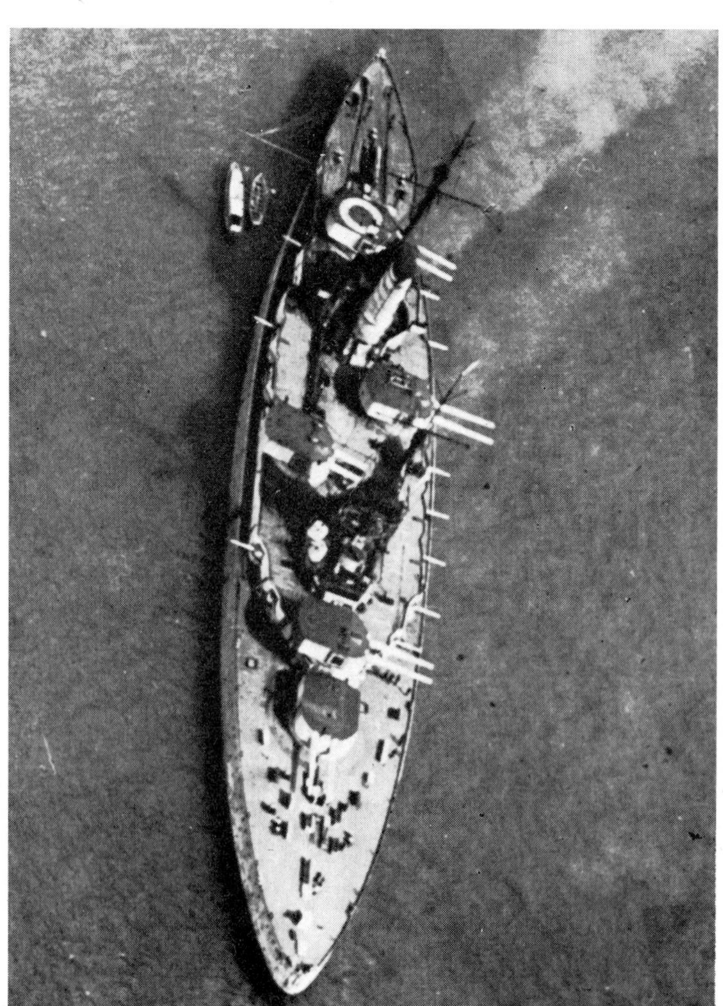

The *Kaiser* class represented a fresh approach in the arrangement of main armament: the two midships turrets were laid out *en echelon*, enabling them to fire on either beam; with a superfiring arrangement aft, this meant that ten (instead of eight) barrels could be brought to bear to starboard or to port, despite the fact that the number of turrets was reduced. This aerial photograph of a *Kaiser* class vessel makes the advantages of the layout particularly evident, as all the turrets apart from that right aft are trained to starboard, even the port side mounting. *BfZ*

The *Kaiser* class battleships, with their widely-spaced funnels and masts, had a well-balanced, imposing appearance. From a distance, the only real means of distinguishing the bows from the stern was the fact that there were two turrets aft. This is *Kaiserin*, photographed on 4 May 1914. *BfZ*

Before the war, the High Seas Fleet would split up after its summer manoeuvres and spend a short period in the Norwegian fjords, to allow the crews to rest. This happened in 1914, when the manoeuvres coincided with a tour by Kaiser Wilhem II on board the Imperial yacht *Hohenzollern*. On 25 July the attitude of Russia, Serbia and Austria-Hungary caused him to interrupt this tour and order the High Seas Fleet to return to their home ports. Only a few days later, war broke out. This photo shows the fleet flagship *Friedrich der Grosse* and other units in a Norwegian fjord. *BfZ*

Friedrich der Grosse was the German fleet flagship from the time of her commissioning. She was the only representative of her class to have spreader yards on the masts forward and aft. In 1913–14 there was another obvious distinguishing feature: the aft bridge superstructure was much larger than those of the other ships in her class, and this was used as a signals and reviewing bridge. In this photo *Friedrich der Grosse* is at a review which took place in Kiel harbour on 4 July 1913. *BfZ*

König Albert was the only completed German dreadnought which was not present at the Battle of Jutland, as she had suffered condenser failure. She had been built in the Schichau yard at Danzig, where this picture was taken in a floating dock. The side armour is clearly visible; the 8.8cm (3.5in) guns – the forward starboard mounts can be seen here – were later removed and their casemates sealed up. *BfZ*

Seydlitz

The battlecruiser *Seydlitz* was an improved variant of the *Moltke* class. The calibre and distribution of her armament were unchanged, but speed was increased by 1kt. However, a far more important aspect was her significantly enhanced protection – events were to prove that this stood her in good stead. The other area where *Seydlitz* differed from her predecessors was the forecastle, which was raised one deck and thus brought about an improvement in her sea-going qualities. At the same time the forecastle length could be increased, since it proved possible to accommodate the forward turrets in a wider, and therefore more effective, part of the protective belt. In the *Moltke* class this distance was 42m (137ft 9in), rising to 46m (150ft 11in) for *Seydlitz*. This peacetime photo dates from 4 July 1913. *BfZ*

For *Seydlitz* the Battle of Jutland produced an inferno: she was hit by 21 heavy and 2 medium shells, and also a torpedo. Ablaze, with 98 dead on board and having taken on more than 5000 tons of water, she toiled home under her own steam, full astern as she was well down by the bows. Judging by the devastation, it was a considerable achievement by her crew to hold the ship and bring her back. This photo was taken on 13 June 1916: *Seydlitz* is seen being moved from No 3 Dock – where she had been patched up and lightened – into a floating dock. *BfZ*

Seydlitz shortly after her arrival at No 3 Dock at Wilhelmshaven, with her bows lying very low. The 28cm (11in) barrels of 'A' turret have been removed to lessen the ship's displacement. *BfZ*

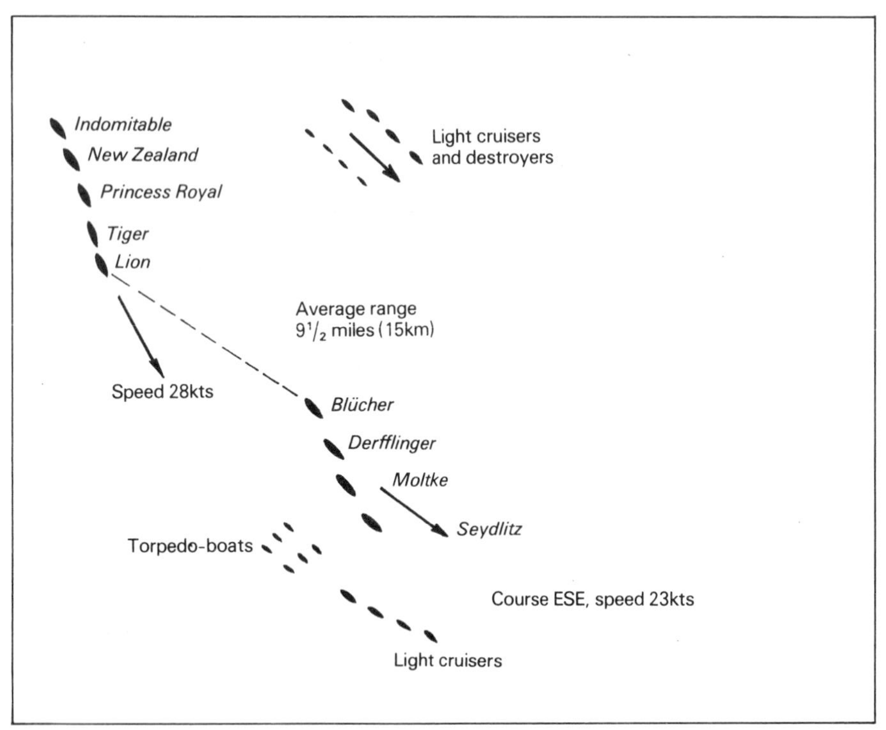

On 24 January 1915, German and British capital ships faced each other for the first time. The engagement came about when German scouting forces, covered by the battlecruisers *Derfflinger*, *Seydlitz* and *Moltke*, and the cruiser *Blücher*, came upon a British formation. The Germans were trying to drive off some enemy light forces around the Dogger Bank, and fishing vessels acting as patrol boats. The British forces consisted of five battlecruisers escorted by light cruisers and destroyers. The British ships opened fire on *Blücher* and hit her several times, reducing her speed considerably; the cruiser became detached from the group, and was eventually sunk under concentrated enemy fire. *Seydlitz* was also severely damaged, as was *Lion* on the British side. This map shows the position of the engaging forces at the height of the battle.

König class

Grosser Kurfürst, König, Kronprinz, Markgraf

The *König* class represented the next stage in the development of armament layout for the German Navy. These units also had five heavy turrets, but the beam positions in the midships area were abandoned; instead, all the turrets were arranged along the ship's centreline, with only one amidships and two at either end in superfiring positions. This photo shows *Markgraf*; her tubular mast was only fitted in 1917, replacing the previous simple pole mast. *BfZ*

Grosser Kurfürst was completed one day before the war broke out, and she is shown here leaving her shipyard – AG Vulcan at Hamburg (the later Howaldtswerke). This ship did not come through the war undamaged: she was hit by eight shells at Jutland, on 5 November 1916 the British submarine *J1* found her with a torpedo, on 5 February 1917 she collided with her sister-ship *Kronprinz*, and in October 1917 she struck a mine, suffering considerable damage. *BfZ*

The fourth ship of the *König* class originally carried an impersonal name – *Kronprinz* – as did her sister-ships. On 27 January 1918, the 59th birthday of Kaiser Wilhelm II, the name of the successor to the throne was added: from then on the ship was called *Kronprinz Wilhelm*. At the Battle of Jutland she was the only ship of her class to escape damage. This picture shows *Kronprinz* around 1915, lying at anchor in Kiel harbour. At this time the ship already featured the tubular mast with spotting top; the latter was slightly altered again in 1918. *BfZ*

One of the shells which hit *Markgraf* at Jutland landed at the base of the funnel close to the bridge, but only caused local damage, as shown by this photograph. *BfZ* ▶

Grosser Kurfürst and *Markgraf* sustained considerable damage at Jutland and were out of action for several weeks. *Grosser Kurfürst* was hit eight times, *Markgraf* five times. Both ships were repaired by AG Vulcan at Hamburg, and were declared ready for action again in the second half of July 1916. Crew losses on the two ships were fortunately very low: fifteen on *Grosser Kurfürst* and only eleven on *Markgraf*. This photo, taken in drydock, shows the effect of a near-miss on *Grosser Kurfürst* – a shell landed close to the armour belt, but caused only superficial damage. *BfZ*

The *Derfflinger* class were the first German battlecruisers to be fitted with 30.5cm (12in) guns, and the arrangement of the main and secondary armament was also revised: it was decided to adopt just eight barrels in four twin turrets, two at either end in superfiring positions. The usual arrangement of the secondary armament in casemates was retained, but was moved for the first time to the upper deck instead of the battery deck as had been the case previously. This photo of *Derfflinger*, taken just before the outbreak of the war, shows these developments clearly. The ship is undergoing final fitting out at the Blohm & Voss yard, Hamburg. *BfZ*

Of the seven battlecruisers in service with the Imperial German Navy, five were built by Blohm & Voss at Hamburg; the last, *Derfflinger*, is shown here leaving the shipyard. After the Battle of Jutland the ship was fitted with a well-spread tripod foremast to replace the original pole mast. Every German capital ship from the *Helgoland* class onwards carried two port and one starboard anchor, at the bows, as shown here. In the background on the left is the large Blohm & Voss building gantry which was demolished after 1945. Today the remaining slipways are served by much more powerful cranes. *Blohm & Voss*

Whilst undergoing trials, *Lützow* suffered severe turbine damage and was therefore not fully operational until early 1916, although commissioned in August of the previous year. The only pre-Jutland operation in which she took part was the bombardment of Yarmouth and Lowestoft in April 1916. The chief differences between *Lützow* and *Derfflinger* were the funnels: *Lützow*'s were of equal height though cased to different levels, the forefunnel being fully cased and the after one only to half height. *BfZ*

Lützow was the only battlecruiser of the Imperial Navy to be lost during the war. The ship's broadside torpedo room was flooded, after being hit many times; this eventually led to serious flooding forward, altering the trim to such an extent that the screws were out of the water. The reserves of buoyancy were by no means exhausted, however; many experts believe that *Lützow* could certainly have remained afloat, but the prevailing situation tipped the scales, and the order was given to scuttle. *BfZ*

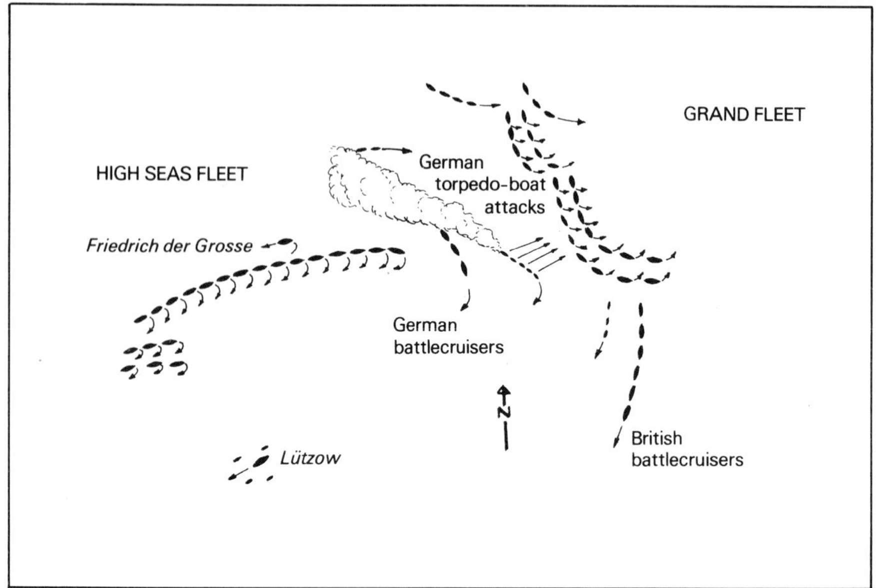

The Battle of Jutland was the greatest naval action in history for neither before nor after – not even in the Second World War – has there been such a gathering of forces at sea. On 31 May 1916 the German High Seas Fleet – 16 capital ships and 6 pre-dreadnoughts, 5 battlecruisers, 11 light cruisers and 61 torpedo boats – was steaming on a northerly course and came upon the British Grand Fleet off Jutland, approaching from the west. The British Fleet was numerically far superior, comprising 28 battleships, 9 battlecruisers, 8 armoured cruisers, 26 light cruisers, 77 destroyers and 3 support ships.

A sharp engagement took place between both sides' battlecruisers, but then the main body of the High Seas Fleet caught up, finally meeting the British battle fleet. The Germans proved their skill and power, but they were not able to alter the strategic situation, even though their ships inflicted more damage than the British vessels; Great Britain's naval superiority was unimpaired, but the High Seas Fleet's sorties were thereafter few and far between.

This drawing conveys the situation on the evening of 31 May 1916: the Grand Fleet had opened fire at 18.17, which was returned by the main force of the High Seas Fleet. This phase ended at 18.33 with the now famous *Gefechtskehrtwendung* ('battle about-turn') by the main body of the German fleet. At 18.55 the German main force turned again, and at 19.13 Scheer, the German Fleet commander, ordered: 'Battlecruisers, at the enemy! Give them everything!' In spite of their damage, which was considerable in some cases, the German battlecruisers steamed towards the Grand Fleet lying in a broad arc before them, and simultaneously the German torpedo boats attacked, in order to ease the load on the heavy units. At this the British fleet turned, and at 19.18 the main body of the High Seas Fleet steered a new course and retreated from the enemy. Thus contact between the two fleets ended. The severely damaged *Lützow* had been limping home since 18.37, and was scuttled shortly afterwards.

The battlecruiser *Derfflinger* on 2 June 1916, in dock at Wilhelmshaven for temporary repairs to the damage sustained at the Battle of Jutland. The ship was among the four most severely damaged German capital ships: she was hit by 17 heavy and four medium calibre shells, about 3000 tons of water was taken on board, and 157 of the crew had perished. By mid-October 1916 the ship was operational again, after a period at Kiel where final repairs were carried out by Howaldtswerke. *BfZ*

When the battlecruiser 'Ersatz *Hertha*' (lit: '*Hertha* replacement') was laid down on 2 October 1913, it could not be foreseen that she would one day bear the name of a general who at that time was scarcely known, having lived in retirement since 1911. Paul von Hindenburg (1847–1934), later to become *Generalfeldmarschall* von Hindenburg, emerged from retirement shortly after the outbreak of war. He defeated the Russians at Tannenberg, East Prussia, and again in Poland, Masuren and Lithuania. This series of victories made him the most popular German army leader of the First World War. In recognition of his services this new battlecruiser was renamed *Hindenburg* when she was launched on 1 August 1915. The photo, taken on 14 July 1917, shows her a few weeks after being commissioned. *BfZ*

Derfflinger and her successors were justifiably considered to be fine-looking vessels, particularly when viewed broadside on. This is *Hindenburg*, showing her long forecastle and equally long quarterdeck, the angular turrets, the well-proportioned funnels and the heavy tripod mast (not, incidentally, fitted in *Lützow*). *BfZ*

The battlecruiser *Hindenburg* only ever used her guns for target practice: she never had an opportunity of firing at the enemy, although she took part in two sorties, in November 1917 and April 1918. This photograph was taken during a gunnery practice and shows the ship at high speed and belching black smoke. *BfZ*

A few months later, *Hindenburg* was scuttled in shallow water at Scapa Flow, together with the other interned units of the High Seas Fleet. *BfZ*

The *Bayern* class were the Imperial Navy's most powerful battleships; with them the transition to 38cm (15in) guns was effected, following the British lead, and at the same time the number of barrels was again reduced. The trend had started with the twelve barrels of the *Nassau* and *Helgoland* classes, continued with the ten of the *Kaisers* and *Königs*, and ended with the eight barrels of this class, disposed in the most effective way – superfiring positions in two turrets forward and aft. This permitted both a reduction in the length of the citadel and thicker armour. *Bayern* was the first ship of this class to be completed, and she is shown here at Wilhelmshaven in 1917. In the background is the Kaiser Wilhelm bridge. *BfZ*

Bayern (pictured) and *Baden* only received their mainmasts in 1917; before that they had just two antenna spreaders with a gaff between. At the time this photograph was taken only two 8.8cm (3.5in) AA guns were carried; the planned eight guns of this calibre were not fitted to any ships from then on. This class made it quite obvious that basic battleship design had reached perfection: in the following two decades the only improvements that were made concerned specific details, not the form of the ship itself. *BfZ*

Baden, which was launched in October 1915 at the Ferdinand Schichau yard at Danzig and joined the fleet one year later, was the Imperial Navy's last fleet flagship. In March 1917 the fleet commander ran up his flag for the first time; this view shows *Baden* shortly before she was commissioned. The new system for handling the launches is clearly visible, as are the torpedo nets (which were, however, soon removed). The davits on the searchlight platforms forward and aft were used to lower the lights and stow them below deck before an engagement – except in the case of night actions. *BfZ*

The *Bayern* class *Linienschiffe* were the first in the German Navy to have a tripod mast as original equipment; its location is shown in this 1915 picture of *Bayern*, taken at the Howaldtswerke yard at Kiel. *BfZ*

The third *Bayern* class ship, *Sachsen*, was built by the Freidrich Krupp Germania shipyard at Kiel, and was launched in November 1916; however, she was never completed and was scrapped in 1921. She was 3m (10ft) longer overall than her sister-ships and her funnels were 4m (13ft) taller. This photo was taken at Kiel in 1919 and shows the stage at which the ship's construction was halted. The hut-like buildings on the forecastle are the forward turrets, whose roofs had not yet been fitted – temporary wooden roofs had been erected to prevent water and damp getting inside. The 38cm (15in) guns planned for her and her sister-ship *Württemberg* were used on the Western front. *Author's Collection*

Scapa Flow became the graveyard of the German High Seas Fleet. Under the conditions of the Armistice the fleet was to be interned, and taken to a neutral port for this purpose; if a neutral port was not available, then an Allied port was to be used. The internment took place in November 1918; the ships' destination was not to be a neutral port but Scapa Flow, the anchorage of the Grand Fleet. After months of waiting, as the situation grew more and more confused, Vice-Admiral von Reuter gave the order to scuttle all ships, and this was carried out on 21 June 1919. The once feared German High Seas Fleet had ceased to exist. For decades after this the British were engaged in salvaging the wrecks. The photo shows *Bayern* and in the background on the left the light cruiser *Emden*, and was probably taken early in 1919. *BfZ*

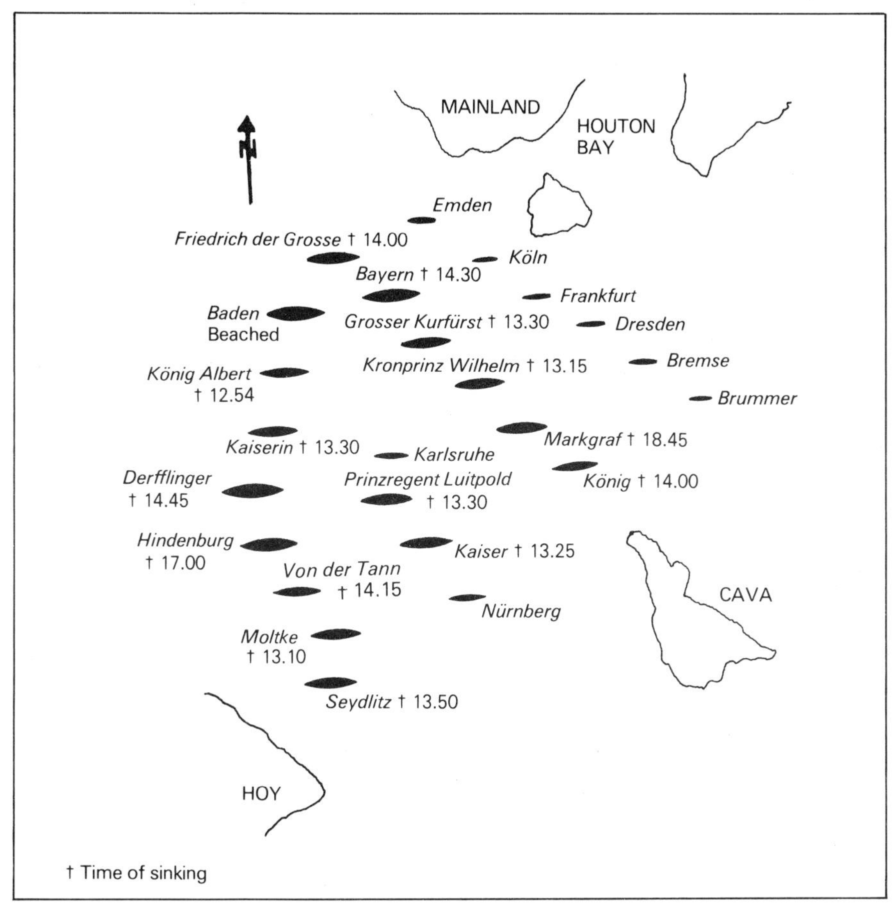

The final resting places of the larger units of the German High Seas Fleet on 21 June 1919 in Scapa Flow.

Mackensen

On 21 April 1917 the battlecruiser *Mackensen* was launched at the Blohm & Voss yard, but according to the original schedule the ship should have been finished a year earlier. This photograph shows that in 1917, the fourth year of the war, even the launching of a ship of this size had to be carried out without the usual pomp – no garlands, no smart paint scheme, not even a name plate or a few flags. The design of the bow is very apparent here: forefoot is cut away at an angle, and the opening for the bow torpedo tube is visible. *Drüppel*

Few naval enthusiasts will remember this model, which once stood in the *Museum für Meereskünde* (Museum of Marine Science) in Berlin. It represented the First World War battlecruiser *Mackensen*, which was never completed, a fate shared by her three sister-ships. *Author's Collection*

Deutschland class

Admiral Graf Spee, Admiral Scheer, Deutschland

The first *Panzerschiff* – later to be named *Deutschland* and subsequently renamed *Lützow* – became a truly 'political' ship even before she existed. Passionate arguments took place in the *Reichstag* about her, resulting in scenes which, as the *Panzerkreuzer-Debatten*, are indissolubly linked with the history of the Weimar Republic. On 16 November 1928 the decision was made to build the ship, and the keel was laid a few months later. *Deutschland* was launched on 19 May 1931. It was at this time that the term 'pocket-battleship' was coined, and the name was not without justification: *Deutschland* and the units which followed *were* a sort of 'stunted battleship', as indicated by their heavy armament, and their speed gave them the capability of running with cruisers. They were, indeed, more powerful than any cruiser and faster than any battleship – with the exception of three British and three Japanese vessels. This photograph shows *Deutschland* just leaving her slipway. *BfZ*

The armoured ship *Deutschland* was renamed *Lützow* in November 1939 and from then on was officially referred to as a 'heavy cruiser'. Evidently Hitler feared that should *Deutschland* be lost, the German people might think of it as a bad omen; at the same time the sale of cruiser 'L', which had already been launched and transferred to the Soviets under the name of *Lützow*, could be concealed. The day soon came when the former *Deutschland* might have been lost. On 11 April 1940, on a return voyage to Oslo, she was hit aft by a torpedo from the British submarine *Spearfish*, and the stern almost broke off, rendering her incapable of steering or manoeuvring. As she had no escorts at hand, she was in danger of being hit again, and that would undoubtedly have meant her end. However, luck was with her: a launch was quickly sent out which kept watch until escorts could reach her, and she was brought home with the assistance of tugs. This picture was taken on 13 April 1940 – shortly before *Deutschland* entered dock at Deutsche Werke, Kiel – and shows the quarterdeck, badly damaged and lying low in the water. Repairs took almost nine months. *Author's Collection*

The end of *Lützow*. On 16 April 1945 she was severely damaged by near-misses from 12,000lb (5443kg) bombs south of Swinemünde and was grounded. As a stationary battery, she repeatedly attacked the advancing Red Army with her guns, which were still operational. When all her ammunition was exhausted, her crew finished her off with explosive charges. In September 1947 the Russians salvaged the wreck and towed it away; it was broken up by 1949. This is a view of *Lützow* after the air attack of 16 April 1945. *Drüppel*

1 April 1933 represented a day of special significance for the *Reichsmarine*: the first event was the commissioning of *Deutschland*, the first *Panzerschiff*, and the second was the launching of *Admiral Scheer*, the second. This photograph was taken on the eve of the launch, and shows *Admiral Scheer* on Slipway I at Wilhelmshaven Navy Yard, ready for launch. The third armoured ship, *Admiral Graf Spee* is on the neighbouring Slipway II, where her keel had been laid in October 1932. *BfZ*

Admiral Scheer was originally very similar in appearance to her sister-ship *Admiral Graf Spee*, but after a major refit which lasted from February to September 1940 she had more in common with *Lützow* – at least as far as the changes to her superstructure were concerned. Soon after this she broke out into the Atlantic, and attacked merchant shipping, penetrating as far as the Indian Ocean. On 1 April 1941 she returned home safely, leaving behind her 17 sunken enemy ships totalling over 100,000grt. In early 1942 she was moved to Norway, and from there took part in various operations as far away as the Kara Sea. This photo dates from the autumn of 1942 and shows the ship leaving a fjord. Her camouflage scheme was later dispensed with. *BfZ*

The end came for *Admiral Scheer* on 9 April 1945. She was in Deutsche Werke's fitting-out bay at Kiel when she was hit by five bombs during an RAF attack, and she capsized. This photograph shows the wreck as it was found by British troops when they marched into the city. In the foreground are two bow sections for Type XXI U-boats. From the end of the war until 1948, *Admiral Scheer* was partially broken up where the wreck lay. The remains were then buried under rubble as the entire fitting-out basin was filled in. Today nothing remains to mark the ship's grave. *Drüppel*

Although built to the same general design, the third armoured ship, *Admiral Graf Spee*, looked very different from *Deutschland*. This was principally because of the unusual design of the turret mast, which *Admiral Scheer*, the second ship in the class, also featured. The deckhouse between the funnel and the catapult, which housed the bakery, was carried only at the beginning of the ship's career. This photograph probably dates from winter of 1937–38. The iced-up forecastle demonstrates the sorts of temperatures that were experienced around this time. It is also clear that the vessel must have shipped a lot of water when steaming against the sea; however, *Admiral Graf Spee* and her two sister-ships proved to be good sea boats. *BfZ*

A peaceful gathering: the pocket-battleship *Admiral Graf Spee* and the British capital ships *Resolution* and *Hood*, photographed at the Fleet Review off Spithead for the Coronation of King George VI in June 1937. There is no hint that only a little over two years will elapse before the start of a new war between the two nations. *Author's Collection*

The general public were scarcely aware of the somewhat unfortunate launch of the battlecruiser *Gneisenau* on 8 December 1936. The braking system was inadequate, and her stern struck the neighbouring Hindenburg Bank. The damage was repaired very quickly. This photo shows the force of the impact as the stern dug into the bank. *BfZ*

Machines can show beauty, as this photograph illustrates. This is the battlecruiser *Scharnhorst*'s funnel with the platform built around it which had become a characteristic feature of German warships. One of the two searchlights on the platform can be seen, covered by a tarpaulin, and on the left is the forward port boat crane. In the foreground is a 15cm (5.9in) gun in a single turret, above it a 10.5cm (4.1in) twin AA gun, and in the background one of four AA fire control towers, which were often called *'Wackeltöpfe'* ('wobble pots') as their triaxial stabilisation made them capable of movement in any direction. This picture was taken before *Scharnhorst*'s refit, as the mainmast is still stepped against the funnel. *BfZ*

Scharnhorst was a warship with exceptionally pleasing lines when she was first completed, with her straight stern, her mainmast close against the funnel, and the latter with its horizontal cap. The photo, taken in April 1939, shows these features clearly.

A few months later, when *Scharnhorst* finished her refit at Wilhelmshaven, the effect was even more pleasing, with her 'Atlantic' bow, her raked funnel cap and her mainmast well aft. *Scharnhorst*'s appearance after this refit is shown in this photograph of a builder's model, taken on 6 April 1940. *Author's Collection*

From 22 January to 23 March 1941 the battlecruisers *Scharnhorst* and *Gneisenau* carried out a successful raiding war in the Atlantic, accounting for 22 ships totalling more than 115,000grt. During their sortie they had to evade British battleships three times. Over these 61 days they steamed 17,800 nautical miles, and then docked at the French port of Brest, which they were not able to leave again until the following year. Here *Gneisenau* is seen shortly after entering Brest; the flags proclaim her success. In the foreground is a group of Japanese Navy officers, guests of the *Kriegsmarine*.

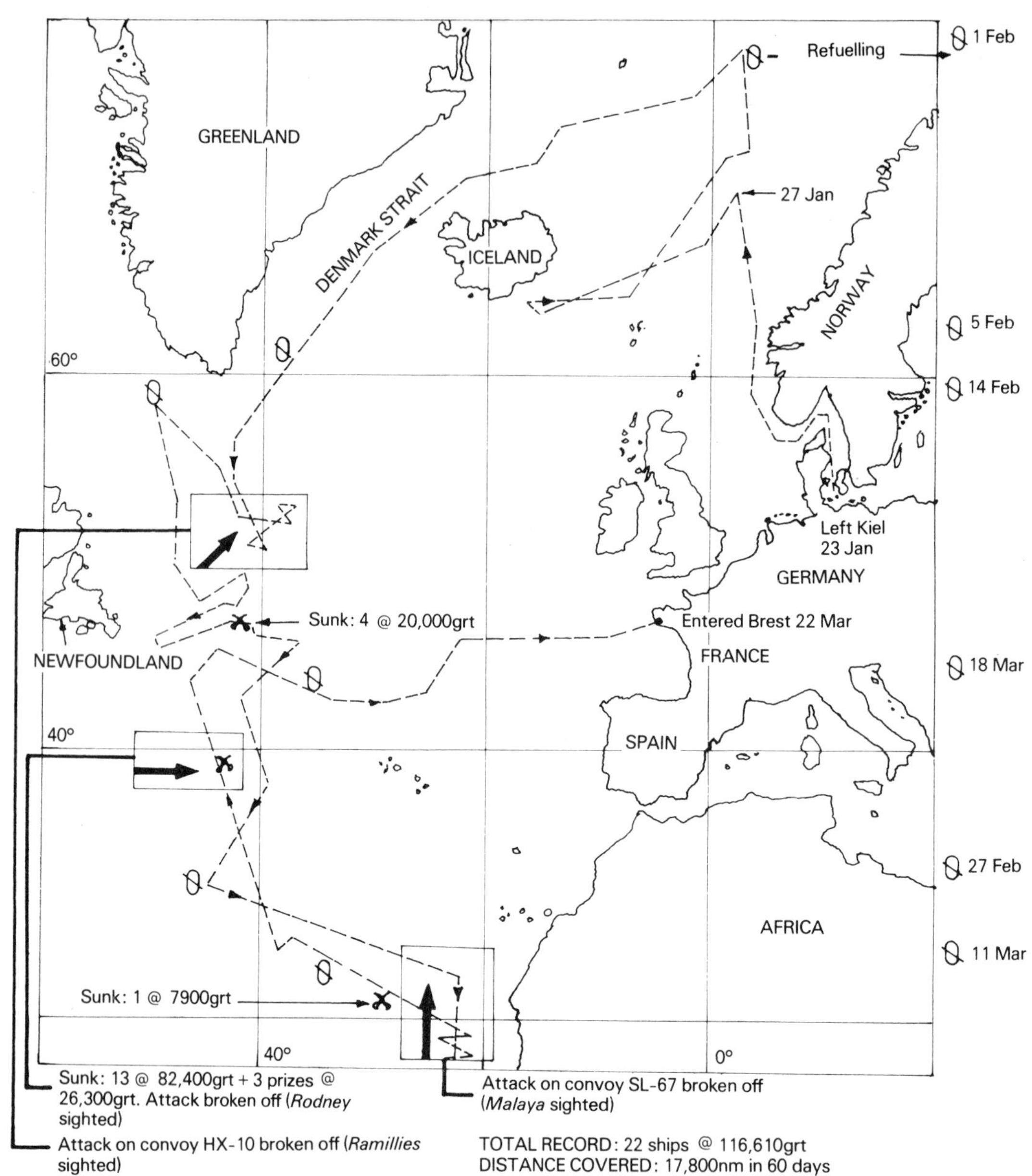

In the Second World War battleships were often used for tasks which had previously been the province of cruisers: on the German side it was the waging of the trade war, while on the British side the task was that of convoy protection. In January 1941 the battlecruisers *Scharnhorst* and *Gneisenau* left Kiel, broke out into the Atlantic via the Denmark Strait and attacked enemy convoy traffic. Three times they had to withdraw from engagements because British battleships came into sight, although these were elderly, slow units which the German ships could evade thanks to their higher speed. However, *Scharnhorst* and *Gneisenau* inflicted heavy losses on enemy merchant shipping. The map shows the area covered during this raiding sortie, which became known as Operation 'Berlin'. The ships returned to Brest in March 1941.

During her long stay at Brest *Gneisenau* was hit several times in air attacks. On one occasion the catapult was destroyed, and the ship was fitted with a completely new set of equipment which enabled aircraft to be launched from inside the hangar. In February 1942 *Gneisenau*, in company with *Scharnhorst* and other units, set off on her voyage home; preparations for this – for example gunnery and torpedo practice – were carried out while the ships were at anchor in Brest. The photograph shows *Gneisenau* firing a torpedo. Her new hangar/catapult system can just be made out. In the background, on the left, is *Scharnhorst*. *BfZ*

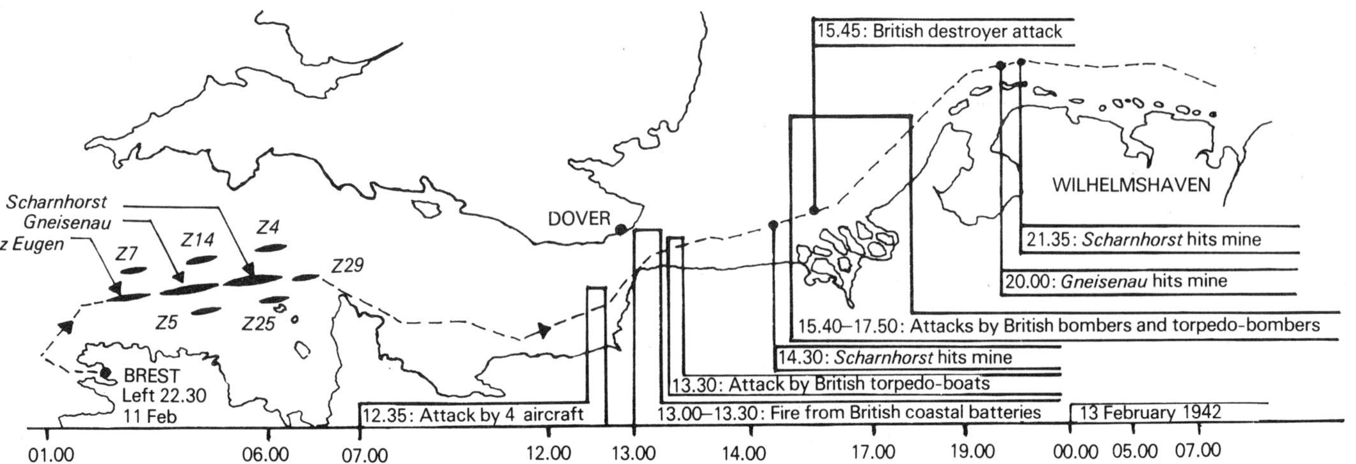

So serious was the problem of the ever-increasing number of air attacks on Brest that the German authorities deemed it prudent to move the ships elsewhere. Hitler decided that they should be brought home via the English Channel. This voyage was undertaken on 11 February 1942, and was known as Operation 'Cerberus'. The individual stages and events of this, the famous 'Channel Dash', are shown on the map.

Immediately after 'Cerberus', *Scharnhorst* made for Wilhemshaven, but she soon moved on to Deutsche Werke at Kiel, where her damage was made good. From October 1942 she undertook training voyages in the Baltic and was based at Gotenhafen, where this photo was taken in the autumn of 1942. *Scharnhorst* is raising steam, and her aircraft is parked on the quay. One of the two torpedo stowage lockers is clearly visible next to the starboard aft 15cm turret. A few months later *Scharnhorst* moved to northern Norway, never to return to Germany again. *Author's Collection*

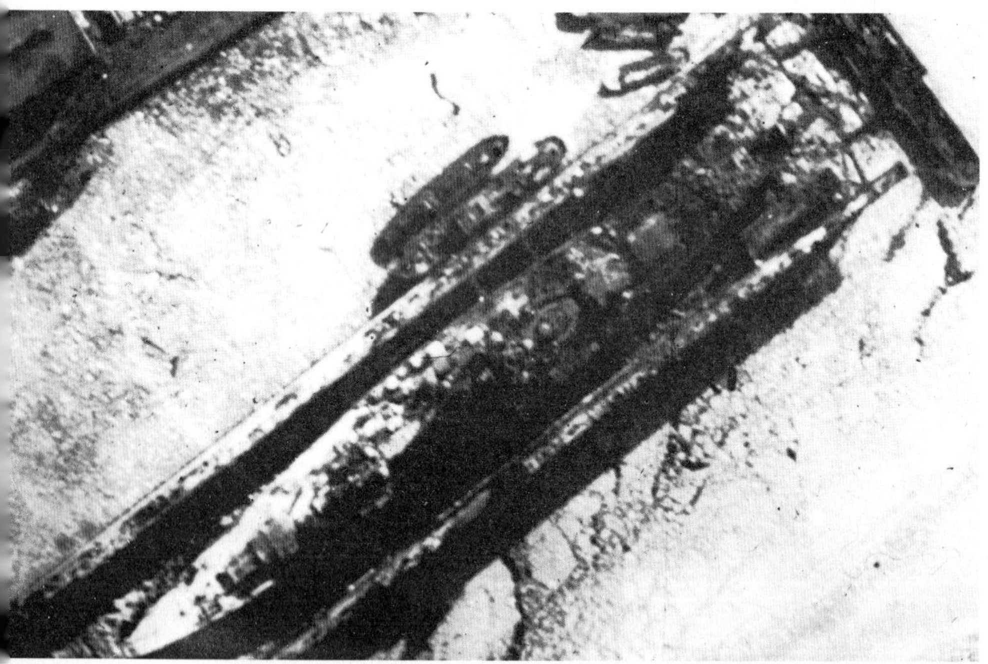

This aerial photograph of *Gneisenau* was taken by a British reconnaissance aircraft and shows Deutsche Werke's floating dock at Kiel, shortly before the disastrous bomb hit on 27 February 1942 which destroyed her forecastle, including the shell rooms and forward turrets. A few weeks later, at the beginning of April, the ship was towed to Gotenhafen, to be taken out of service there on 1 July. The conversion planned at that time was never begun (although preparations were made) as Hitler had ordered all capital ships to be taken out of service early in 1943.

Another photo taken by a British aircraft, this time showing *Gneisenau* in 1942 at Gotenhafen; the heavy turrets are now missing, the entire secondary battery has also been removed, and even the AA guns have been dismantled. *Author's Collection*

Slipway II in the Navy's own shipyard at Wilhelmshaven was its biggest. It was used to construct the battlecruiser *Hindenburg* among others, and in the 1930s it was used for the armoured ship *Admiral Graf Spee* and later the battlecruiser *Scharnhorst*. Four weeks after the latter was launched, *Tirpitz* was laid down; she is shown here during 1938. The new battleship is already complete up to and beyond the armoured deck and the barbettes are already in place. In the background on the left is one of the old pre-dreadnoughts, either *Schlesien* or *Schleswig-Holstein*. *Author's Collection*

Hamburg, 14 February 1939: in bright winter sunshine battleship 'F', just christened *Bismarck*, is launched at the Blohm & Voss yard, the first genuine battleship of the *Kriegsmarine*. Her official displacement was given as 35,000 tons standard, though in reality she was bigger, around 41,000 tons. A few weeks later her sister-ship *Tirpitz* was launched. In this picture *Bismarck* still has an almost straight stem; this was modified soon afterwards, before the ship was commissioned. *BfZ*

This picture dates from the early hours of 1 April 1939, and shows battleship 'G' ready for launch. The slipway is already partially flooded and the first spectators are already present (the crowd numbered 80,000!). It was not long before Adolf Hitler arrived with his full retinue, and the ship was christened *Tirpitz* and launched. Late that afternoon Hitler made a speech in the town square in Wilhemshaven before an enthusiastic audience, in which he railed against the Western 'policy of encirclement'. This condemnation was directed particularly at Britain; 28 days later Hitler made plain what he had hinted at in Wilhelmshaven – he denounced the Anglo-German Naval Agreement of 1935. *BfZ*

Bismarck in her fitting-out bay in the winter of 1939–40, beneath the gigantic 250-ton hammer crane. The main turrets are in place, and the funnel and mast have already been fitted. The ice forming in the basin show how hard the first winter of the war was. From launch to commissioning it took only about a year and a half for the battleship *Bismarck* to be ready for action; this period was unusually short, thanks to the application of the workforce. *BfZ*

The date 24 August 1940 was the high point of the Blohm & Voss warship construction programme. On that day the HAPAG passenger ship conversion *Vaterland* was launched (in order to vacate the slipway, not to complete the ship) and, immediately afterwards, *Bismarck*, the largest warship ever built by this yard, was commissioned. This photograph was taken shortly after the commissioning ceremony. *Author's Collection*

Bismarck left Gotenhafen on 18 May 1941, and entered Korsfjord near Bergen (Norway) on the 21st to take on fuel for Operation *'Rheinübung'*. She was still in the fjord when British reconnaissance aircraft discovered her, but she managed to slip out unnoticed in the evening. On 24 May the British battlecruiser *Hood* blew up under her fire – *Hood* was the largest, although not the most powerful, warship in the world at that time – but *Bismarck* met her own fate three days later. More than 3300 men, German and British, died in those few days. This picture was taken just after *Bismarck* had entered Korsfjord. By the time she left, that evening, her camouflage scheme was no longer in evidence. *Author's Collection*

Encouraged by the successful use of heavy units against British convoy traffic in the Atlantic, the battleship *Bismarck* set out on a similar operation (Operation *'Rheinübung'*) with the cruiser *Prinz Eugen*. During the attempt to penetrate through to the Atlantic via the Denmark Strait, the German units came upon heavy British forces. A battle ensued in which the British battlecruiser *Hood* exploded and sank, having been hit several times, and the battleship *Prince of Wales* withdrew after being damaged. This defeat caused the British to bring in forces stationed far distant in order to hunt down the German ships. A few days later they were able to locate *Bismarck* and eliminate her. This map shows how these operations developed, and how the 'net' closed in.

KEY

1 Heavy cruisers *Norfolk* and *Suffolk*
2 Battlecruiser *Hood* and battleship *Prince of Wales*
3 Battleship *King George V*, battlecruiser *Repulse*, aricraft carrier *Victorious*, light cruisers *Kenya*, *Galatea*, *Aurora* and *Hermione*, plus six destroyers
4 Battleship *Rodney*, plus three destroyers
5 Battleship *Revenge*
6 Battleship *Ramillies*
7 Light cruiser *Edinburgh*
8 Five destroyers
9 Heavy cruiser *London*
10 Battlecruiser *Renown*, aircraft carrier *Ark Royal*, light cruiser *Sheffield*, plus six destroyers
11 Battleship *Nelson*

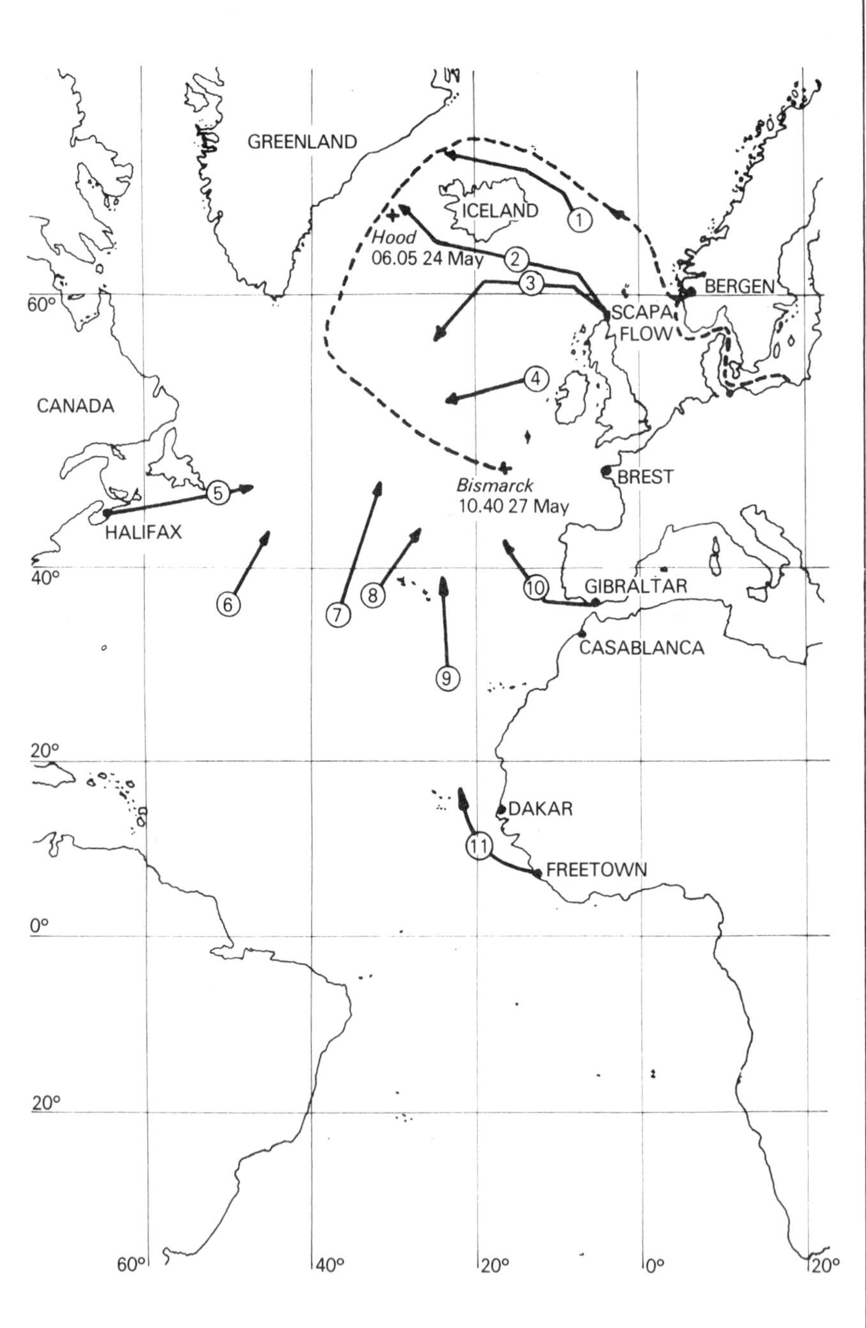

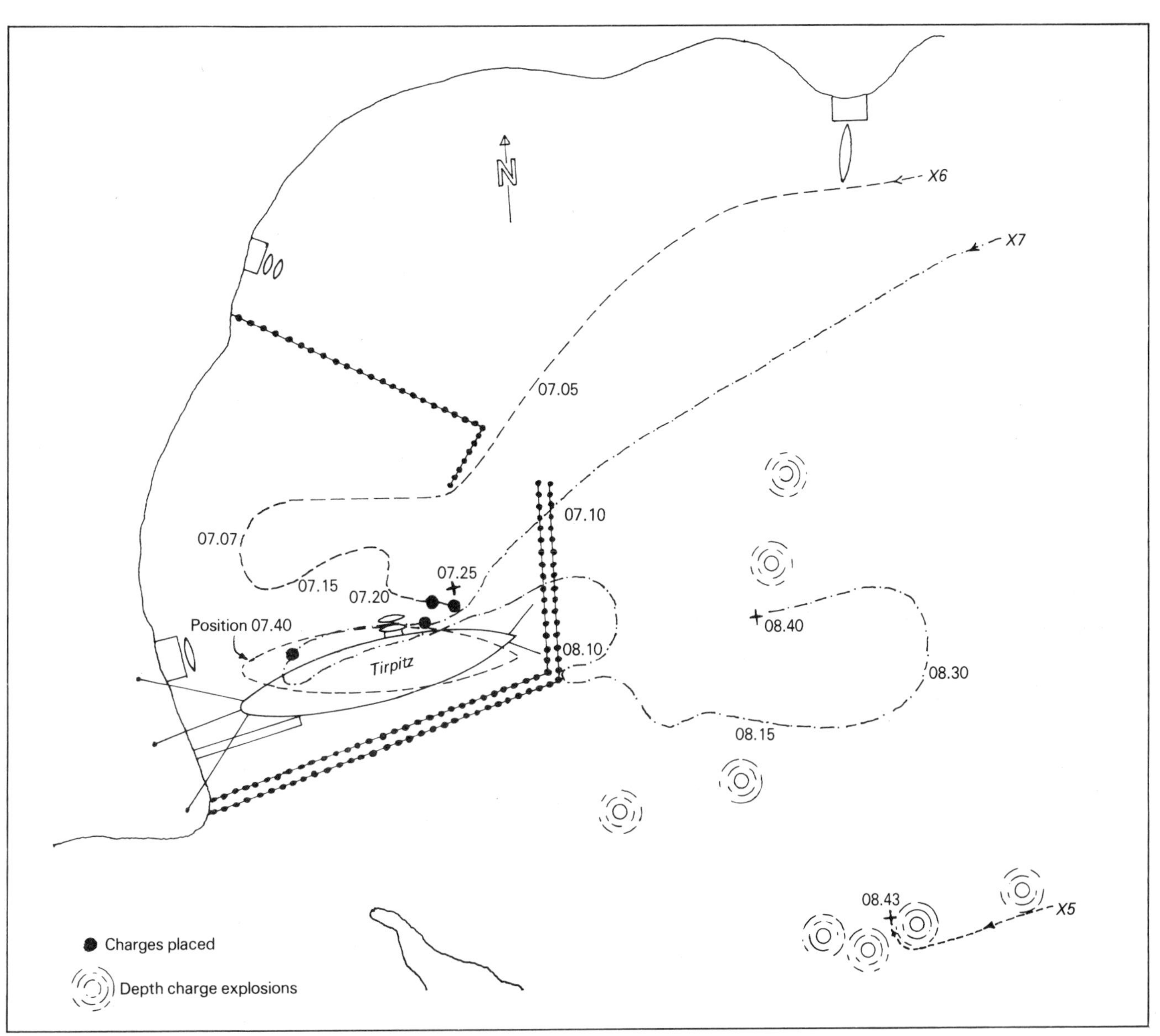

In September 1943 the British began Operation 'Source': its purpose was to eliminate the battleship *Tirpitz*, lying in Kaafjord in northern Norway. The miniature submarines *X5*, *X6*, *X7*, *X8*, *X9* and *X10* were used for this mission, towed to the entrance to the fjord by large submarines. *X6* and *X7* managed to penetrate the curtain of netting protecting *Tirpitz*, and laid their mines. When they detonated, *Tirpitz* was badly damaged and out of action for months. The drawing shows the routes taken by the miniature submarines, and when and where they were themselves destroyed; it also shows how *Tirpitz* tried to alter her position after the 'X'-craft had been detected.

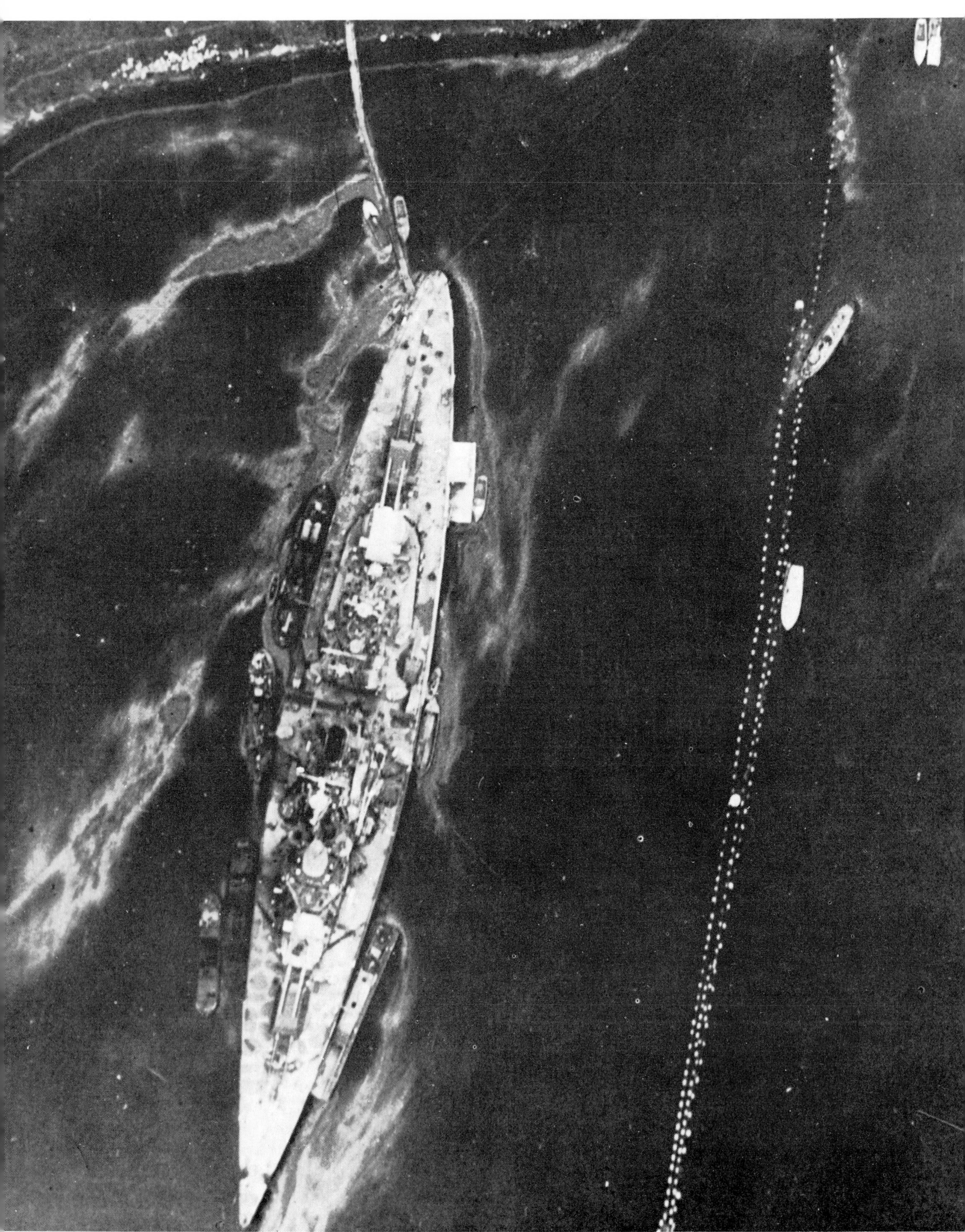

From January 1942 onwards, the battleship *Tirpitz* was stationed in northern Norway, from where she was never to return. Initially she stayed in the Trondheim area, but from early 1943 moved north of latitude 70°, near the Arctic Ocean and the enemy convoy routes. Whilst it is true that *Tirpitz* only took part in a small number of sorties, she at the same time tied up considerable enemy forces just by her threatening presence, to some extent acting as a 'fleet in being'. The British therefore made great efforts to render her harmless. At first they used air-dropped depth charges, then miniature submarines and mines, and finally carrier aircraft and bombs, but they were unable to administer the *coup de grâce*. In the end they sent land-based bombers. The first two attacks were unsuccessful, but the third, on 12 November 1944, had the desired effect: *Tirpitz* was hit or near-missed by several 12,000lb (5443kg) bombs and capsized, 1200 members of her crew losing their lives. The last German battleship was finally destroyed. The fact that the British had to work so hard to eliminate *Tirpitz* was due to the elaborate security measures taken on her behalf. This is *Tirpitz* in Faettenfjord (near Trondheim) in 1943. *BfZ*

This photo of *Tirpitz* dates from July 1944, when the ship was anchored in Kaafjord. The protective netting screens are clearly visible in both this and the previous illustration. *Author's Collection*

United States of America

In the years 1901 to 1905 a total of 13 capital ships were laid down in the United States, each equipped with eight guns of an intermediate calibre – 8in (20.3cm) – in addition to its heavy and medium battery. The culmination to this line of development was the six units of the *Connecticut* class (*New Hampshire* is shown here). Note the characteristic lattice masts, (popularly referred to as 'basket' masts), although the term 'lattice mast' is not technically correct. It was not in fact a grid design, but a multi-tubular mast, in which the top and bottom rings were rotated relative to each other, forming a 'spiral', as can be seen in the photograph. These masts were to remain a feature of American battleships into the Second World War. *USN (Author's Collection)*

When this picture of *South Carolina* was taken (April 1921) she only had a few months of active service remaining: she was decommissioned the following September, and soon stricken and scrapped. The US Navy dispensed with a total of 23 pre-dreadnoughts and four dreadnoughts immediately after the First World War. *USN (BfZ)* ▶

The *South Carolinas*, and not the *Dreadnought*, would have been the first 'all-big-gun' battleships had their construction been carried through at the same hectic pace as *Dreadnought*'s. The fact that *South Carolina* (BB26) and *Michigan* (BB27) were not completed until after the British ship was due to the much greater care applied to their design and construction. Compared with *Dreadnought* they were extremely advanced: the distribution and thickness of the armour plating was superior, and the main armament layout has not been improved upon right up to the present day. This photo shows *Michigan* on 10 April 1913, with signal flags hung out to dry behind the after funnel. The black bands around the funnels indicated the division to which the ship belonged within the battle fleet: *Michigan* belonged to the Third Division at that time (three bands around the forefunnel) and held second position within the division (two bands around the after funnel). *USN (Author's collection)*

The Americans first exceeded the 20,000-ton mark with the *Delaware* class, which was begun in 1907. The main calibre was unchanged, as was its excellent layout, but a fifth turret was added, following the trend of increasing the number of barrels. In contrast with the *South Carolinas*, these ships were fitted with a secondary armament, although they were not the usual 6in guns, but 5in (12.7cm) weapons – a calibre which was adopted for all subsequent battleships. This is an aerial photograph of *Delaware* (BB28), taken in 1918 or later since AA guns are already fitted on the circular platforms on top of the crane posts. An awning has been rigged right aft. *USN (BfZ)*

From November 1917, *Delaware* was seconded to the Sixth Battle Squadron of the British Grand Fleet, and was stationed at Scapa Flow; early in July 1918 she was moved to Rosyth, where this photograph was taken. At the end of July *Delaware* left her British base and returned to Hampton Roads, USA, escorted by the British destroyers *Restless* and *Rowena*. After the war, she was refitted at Boston Navy Yard, but was scrapped a few years later. *IWM (BfZ)*

Florida belonged to the first generation of US dreadnoughts. Her main armament was disposed in five turrets, following the same layout as her predecessors *Delaware* and *North Dakota*; the main external difference was the arrangement of the two funnels between the tall 'basket' masts. The illustration above shows *Florida* after her 1919–20 refit. A range clock is fitted on the after control position, and deflection scales are painted on the two superfiring turrets, whilst 3in (7.6cm) AA guns can be made out on the crane post platforms. In the background is the old hospital ship *Relief*. *USN (BfZ)*

Utah during World War I, fitted experimentally with rangefinding baffles – which were also fitted to a large number of British capital ships at that time. Their effect was supposed to be increased by the special paint scheme, which was designed to break up all horizontal lines. *USN (BfZ)*

Following their modernisation in the mid-1920s, the battleships *Florida* and *Utah* returned to the Atlantic Fleet; they visited Europe and called in at Kiel, where this picture of *Utah* was taken on 5 July 1930. Both ships were taken out of service shortly afterwards. *Florida* went to the breakers' yard, but *Utah* was converted into a remote-controlled target ship. One of the most characteristic features of American battleships of this period were the catapults fitted on the main turrets, on which up to two aircraft could be stowed, as can be seen in this picture. *Schäfer (BfZ)*

After *Utah* had been fitted out as a target ship, she also served (from 1935) as a training ship for gun crews on light AA weapons, and conducted experiments with various AA mounts. The successes of aircraft against warships during the first two years of World War II made it imperative for the US Navy to equip their warships with additional AA guns, and to provide the necessary training capacity for this *Utah* was sent to Puget Sound Navy Yard in the summer of 1941, where she was equipped with heavy AA weapons. This picture, dating from 18 August 1941, shows her being painted during this refitting stage. The remaining 12in (30.5cm) turrets can be seen here – although their barrels had been removed ten years earlier – and the barbettes of the other turrets are also visible; 5in (12.7cm) guns have been fitted on the turret tops forward and aft, and further 5in mounts are located on sponsons above the former secondary armament casemates. Only the aft 5in AA guns are shielded. A few months after this photo was taken *Utah* was sunk at Pearl Harbor, hit by two Japanese airborne torpedoes. *USN (Terzibaschitsch Collection)*

Wyoming and *Arkansas* were the last of the first generation US dreadnoughts; they also were equipped with 12in (30.5cm) guns, although the number of barrels had once more been raised by two, providing a total of twelve. The silhouettes of these ships were similar to those of *Florida* and *Utah*, but the cage masts and funnels, grouped closely together, were arranged further forward, which was the inevitable result of fitting in an extra main turret. From certain angles, as with this shot of *Arkansas*, these vessels gave the impression that the stern, with its two after turrets, did not belong to the ship at all. *Arkansas* is seen here evidently running trials, in connection with which the framework on No 5 turret may have been erected. *USN (BfZ)*

Wyoming on 25 July 1919 showing the modifications which had been carried out during the First World War. *USN (BfZ)*

◀ *Wyoming* served as a training ship from the beginning of the 1930s, and from that time she retained only three of her main turrets, giving a total of six barrels. From 1942 on the ship was called upon principally for training AA gun crews: for this reason more and more modern AA guns were installed. This 1942 photo shows *Wyoming* with 5in (12.7cm) single and twin turrets along the starboard side. *Terzibaschitsch Collection*

◀ *Wyoming* on 17 June 1943, in the same state as in the previous photo. *Terzibaschitsch Collection*

The longer the war lasted, the greater the threat from the air became, with the result that ships' AA gun capabilities were constantly being expanded; this in turn demanded the training of an ever-increasing number of AA gun crews. The outcome for *Wyoming* was that even the main turret positions were needed for fitting AA weapons, and so in 1944 the remaining 12in mounts were replaced by further 5in AA guns. At the end of her career the ship featured an asymmetrical arrangement: 5in mounts were fitted only on the starboard side, while there were none on the port side except for a few unshielded single 5in mounts. *Wyoming* is shown here after her final conversion, with no main turrets, and featuring only a simple pole foremast instead ◀ of the 'basket' mast. *Author's Collection*

Arkansas was the oldest American battleship to see action in the second World War, although she was by no means in an adequate state of repair; nevertheless she was considered worth modernising again. During this conversion she lost the old 'basket' mast above the bridge, in place of which a tripod mast was erected; in addition the secondary armament was reduced and the AA armament increased. This photo shows the ship around 1942. *USN (Terzibaschitsch Collection)*

Another photo of *Arkansas* after her final refit, this time on 1 July 1943 in the Atlantic, where she served for a long time on convoy duty. *USN (Author's Collection)*

New York class

New York, Texas

New York and *Texas* were the first in a new generation of American battleships: with these vessels the US Navy followed the European trend of increasing calibre. They were fitted with 14in (35.6cm) guns, but only ten in number, although a main armament of fifteen 12in (30.5cm) guns had been discussed. These two ships heralded the period of the 'super-dreadnought' in the USA. *Texas* is shown here during trials; the unfinished mainmast is very evident. *USN (BfZ)*

Texas and *New York* were the most modern and powerful US battleships at the outbreak of war in Europe. Following the USA's declaration of war against the Central Powers on 6 April 1917, six capital ships were despatched to Europe to join the British Grand Fleet, forming the Sixth Battle Squadron; three more capital ships were sent to the south of Ireland for the protection of the North Atlantic sea routes, and were based in Bantry Bay. *New York* and *Texas* were among those which served with the Sixth Battle Squadron. This is *Texas*, photographed probably at Rosyth in 1918. *IWM (BfZ)*

After World War I *Texas* was fitted with flying-off platforms on Nos 2 and 4 turrets, following British practice, tests being carried out using three different types of aircraft. The first launching took place on 9 March 1919, with a British Sopwith Camel. However, the system was not introduced as standard as the US Navy considered it inadequate, and the Americans went their own way and soon began to develop catapults. This photograph shows the flying-off platform on *Texas*'s No 2 turret; a Sopwith Camel is parked on it. Between the two searchlights above the bridge can be seen one of the ship's range clocks; these devices remained a feature of US battleships into the 1930s. *USN (BfZ)*

Texas, with a Camel on each of her flying-off platforms. *USN (Terzibaschitsch Collection)*

Texas and *New York* were completely modernised in the mid-1920s: their boilers were fitted for oil firing, protection was enhanced by the addition of torpedo bulges, the original cage masts were replaced by tripods, and a single funnel replaced the original two. In addition there were various improvements to the secondary armament and AA battery, and new fire control systems. All this involved a considerable increase in weight, to the detriment of the ships' sea-going qualities: they had not only become slower, but also more difficult to manoeuvre and extremely 'wet', and they rolled heavily, resulting in frequent incursions of water into the casemates. This photograph of *Texas* was taken before 1935, since the AA platforms on the masts are missing. *USN (BfZ)*

New York after 1935, with mast AA platforms in position. *USN (Terzibaschitsch Collection)*

New York was the first US battleship to be fitted with radar: in December 1938 a large XAF antenna, developed by the Naval Research Laboratory, was experimentally installed; it was fitted over the bridge, as indicated by the circle. *USN (BfZ)*

Apart from the fitting of additional AA weapons and radar equipment, *Texas*'s appearance hardly altered after her 1925–27 modernisation. The ship is shown here in the Atlantic on 15 March 1942, having been detailed for convoy escort duties since 1941. Note the two colour paint scheme. *USN (Author's Collection)*

A photograph of *Texas* dating from about the same time as the previous illustration. Clearly visible here is the SC radar antenna above the foretop. *IWM (Terzibaschitsch Collection)*

The ever-increasing effectiveness of heavy calibre guns, mainly due to improved fire control systems and firing methods, led the USA to consider to what extent future capital ships could be made immune to very severe attacks on their vitals. The solution to the problem was considered by the Americans to be an 'all or nothing' system of protection. The principle was that by reducing the area of armour plating, only those areas which were vital to the vessel's battleworthiness would be protected, but they would be protected as stoutly as possible, and the areas concerned included the horizontal surfaces. Naturally this system involved a massive increase in weight: the entire horizontal armour in *Texas* and *New York* amounted to 1322 tons; the figure for the first 'all or nothing' battleships – *Nevada* and *Oklahoma* – climbed to 3291 tons (ie nearly 2000 tons more), and the total weight of armour rose from 8120 to 11,162 tons. Nevertheless, the total displacement increased only slightly: for these ships, a return to the main armament layout of the *South Carolina* class was chosen, *viz* two turrets forward and aft, with Nos 1 and 4 positions having triple turrets (the first to be installed on American warships), thus providing ten barrels. The photograph shows the two *Nevada* class battleships in company with other capital ships, during manoeuvres in stormy seas. The photo was taken around 1919. *Author's Collection*

From August to December 1918 *Oklahoma* was stationed at Bantry Bay in Ireland for the protection of the North Atlantic sea routes; at that time she carried this peculiar camouflage scheme, which was very similar to that worn by *Utah*. The port forward 5in (12.7cm) gun has already been removed, although the 5in guns abaft it are easily distinguished. All these mounts were sited on the main deck and had no armour protection at all; they fired through openings which could be sealed by flaps (the last four are closed here). One of the 3in (7.6cm) AA guns fitted in 1918 can be seen on No 3 turret. *USN (BfZ)*

In the late 1920s all the older battleships up to and including the *Pennsylvania* class were modernised; amongst these ships were *Nevada* and *Oklahoma*. When they returned to the fleet after almost two years' absence, they were scarcely recognisable: their external appearance was no longer dominated by 'basket' masts but by massive, very widely based tripod masts. The ships had also been fitted with torpedo bulges, which had increased their beam by just 13ft (4m). This photograph of *Oklahoma* was taken during Atlantic manoeuvres in the 1930s. *BfZ*

Nevada off Cuba in the early 1930s. Both this and the previous photograph show the single aircraft derrick right aft still fitted – it was only later that this was changed for the characteristic crane. *BfZ*

Since they were modernised to the same design, *Nevada* and *Oklahoma* differed from each other only in detail: around the funnel, the bridge superstructure and also the masts. From 1935 to 1940, they could be distinguished by the fact that only *Nevada* had an AA platform on top of her mainmast; *Oklahoma* was fitted with such a platform only in 1940. This is *Nevada* in 1937, with *Oklahoma* in the background. *Author's Collection*

It was equally difficult to differentiate between the *Nevada* and *Pennsylvania* classes; this is *Arizona*, also in the 1930s. At greater distances, the only useful feature for deciding whether a ship belonged to the *Pennsylvania* class was the tripod foremast: the platform close up below the spotting top was not a feature of *Nevada* class ships. *BfZ*

Nevada looked entirely different after the damage sustained at Pearl Harbor had been repaired and the ship modernised. With the exception of the main armament everything above the upper deck had been replaced – the superstructure as well as the secondary armament. With her wide, raked funnel cap projecting from its casing she looked bizarre – interesting, to be sure, but also incredibly ugly. This photograph dates from 15 December 1942 and was taken at Puget Sound Navy Yard, a few weeks before the ship was recommissioned. *Nevada* was soon back in action, initially in Operation 'Landcrab' – the re-taking of the Aleutian island Attu – and then as an escort for the Atlantic convoys. *USN (Author's Collection)*

This June 1944 photograph of *Nevada* was taken off the Normandy coast, where the ship served as one of three American battleships supporting the landings with her heavy guns. *Nevada* alone fired 1216 rounds of 14in shells, plus 3531 rounds with her 5in guns. *USN (Terzibaschitsch Collection)*

The next two battleships, *Pennsylvania* and *Arizona*, were essentially similar to the *Nevada* class; however, they carried a complete set of triple turrets for the main armament, which allowed the number of barrels to be raised again to twelve. The calibre remained the same, and protection was basically unchanged. This photo shows *Pennsylvania*'s Nos 3 and 4 turrets, with the mainmast in the background. The small calibre weapons fitted on the barrels were used for gunnery practice. The photo may have been taken soon after the ship's commissioning, as the mainmast is still in its original condition. *BfZ*

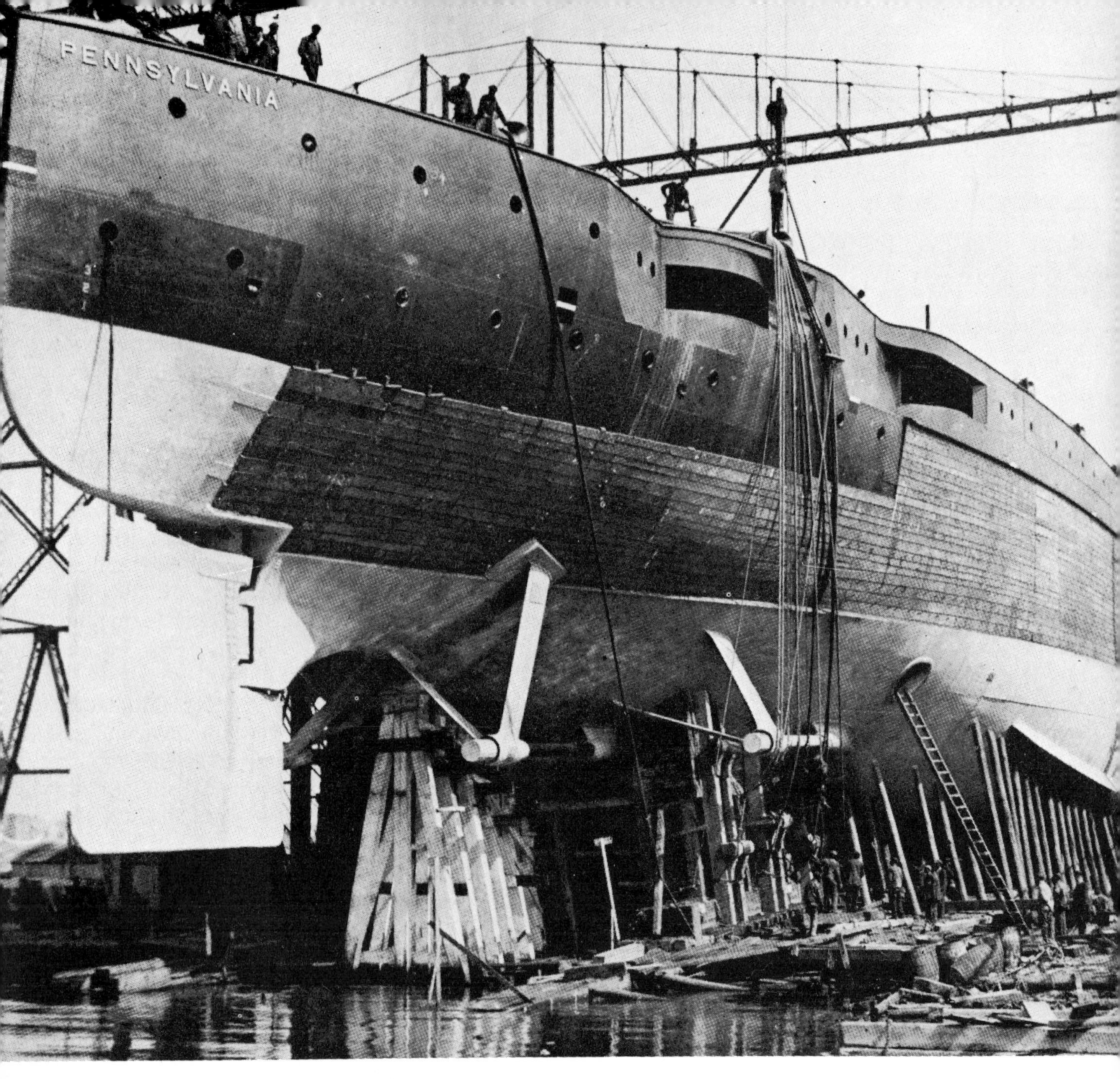

While the Newport News Shipbuilding and Dry Dock Co of Newport News, Virginia, was awaiting the granting of the building contract for vessel No 171 – the battleship *Pennsylvania* – the ship was referred to by the Press as 'the most powerful battleship of the world'. However, this view was mistaken, since in the meantime Great Britain had adopted an even heavier gun calibre, and had ordered the battleships of the *Queen Elizabeth* class; when *Pennsylvania* was launched on 16 March 1915, *Queen Elizabeth* had been in service for two months. This photo was taken a few hours before *Pennsylvania*'s launch; the propellers have yet to be fitted to the shafts, although the large balanced rudder is already in place. The external armour, as can clearly be seen, is yet to be fitted. Also visible is one of the underwater torpedo tubes, with a ladder leaning against its opening; just behind this the bilge keel begins. The blinds for the openings of the two aftermost 5in (12.7cm) guns on the starboard side are not yet fitted. *Author's Collection*

Pennsylvania escaped lightly during the attack on Pearl Harbor. She was actually in drydock, and was hit by only a single bomb, which caused no major damage. She was quickly repaired, and was ready for action again in April 1942; her external appearance remained largely unchanged, apart from the fitting of additional AA weapons. However, she was completely modernised in a refit lasting from the autumn of 1942 until February 1943, and when she left Mare Island Navy Yard she was almost unrecognisable. The foremast had been drastically shortened, the mainmast entirely removed, and the bridge superstructure modified, but the principal difference was her brand new secondary armament, and in addition new fire control systems and radar equipment had been installed. The work was carried out in record time – the whole job, which in peacetime conditions would scarcely have been completed in less than two years, took only a little over three months. This photo shows *Pennsylvania* probably in the summer of 1943 or later, as the mainmast was fitted with the large CXAM radar antenna around this time. *Author's Collection*

During the Second World War, a number of heavy ship's guns were transferred to the US Army for the defence of Oahu, the most important of the Hawaiian group of islands. Set up in coastal positions, they included the eight 8in (20.3cm) twin turrets removed from the aircraft carriers *Lexington* and *Saratoga*. These weapons were then considerably reinforced by the arrival of two 14in (35.6cm) triple turrets which had been salvaged from the sunken *Arizona*. Here one of *Arizona*'s turrets can be seen set up on land during gunnery practice in August 1945. *United States Naval Institute Proceedings*

During the World War II the Americans assembled their old battleships into Fire Support Groups: with their highly accurate gunfire, they literally ploughed up the enemy terrain yard by yard, before the troops landed. In most cases the troops then met little resistance, and could quickly gain a foothold. However, enemy resistance stiffened noticeably where the ships' guns could not reach – and then it had to be defeated from the air. The Fire Support Groups were an impressive sight as they steamed along. In the foreground here is the modernised *Pennsylvania* and, behind her, *West Virginia* and *Colorado*. *Author's Collection*

Pennsylvania held the record for the most ammunition used in a single mission by a US Navy ship: in the course of the attack on Guam she fired 1800 salvos from her main armament, and her secondary battery brought the total to 10,000. This was by no means the only operation of its kind for her: in further actions during the great 'island hopping' campaigns, her gunfire frequently smoothed the way for the attacking US troops. Of course, no gun barrel could withstand such heavy usage for a long period – the more it fired, the greater the reduction in range and accuracy. When *Pennsylvania* entered Puget Sound Navy Yard early in 1945 for a complete refit, she was fitted with 14in barrels that had been held in reserve for *Oklahoma* and *Nevada*; this photo, showing *Pennsylvania* in a floating drydock, dates from that period. In the foreground is the stern AA mount fitted during the refit. *Newport News Dry Dock Co*

With the three units of the *New Mexico* class the US Navy took the improvements incorporated into the *Nevada*s a logical step further; although protection, firepower and machinery were basically unchanged the main armament, which comprised twelve barrels in triple turrets as in the *Pennsylvania* class, featured longer barrels thus giving a considerably higher muzzle velocity compared with the previous model. The bow shape was also new, and this was retained until the end of the battleship building programmes and was even used for new cruisers for a time. This photograph shows *New Mexico* after 1922, as can be fairly easily recognised by the many detail changes from her original appearance, as for instance the platforms surrounding the masts and the presence of catapults. The forward 5in (12.7cm) casemate guns have already been removed – they were taken off in 1920; US vessels suffered from the same problem as many battleships of other nations – these casemate positions were too wet, and the problem grew worse as speed increased. The large 'E' on the side of the conning tower stands for 'efficiency', a distinction accorded to ships whose crews had achieved a particularly high level of competence. Clearly visible are the ship's aircraft secured to their catapults, a characteristic feature of US battleships in the 'between wars' period, and to some extent right up to the end of World War II. Incidentally, the turret catapults could only be trained together with the turrets themselves. *Author's Collection*

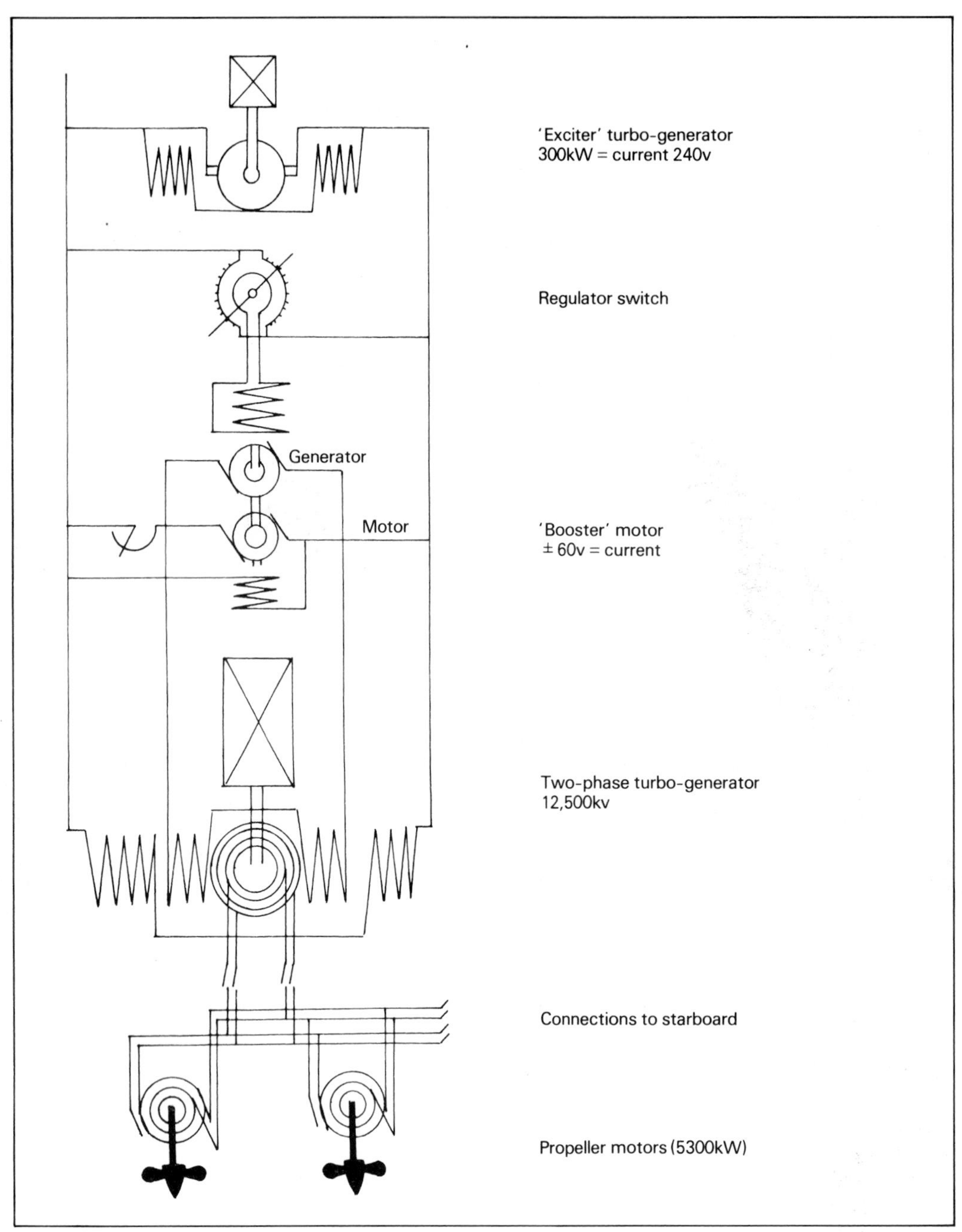

It was originally intended that *New Mexico* should have direct-acting turbine machinery, as indeed should her sister-ships. However, by the time the vessel was ordered, highly satisfactory results had been achieved with the Melville-Mecalpine electric reduction system, and therefore it was decided to install turbo-electric drive. This diagram shows the circuit used for the system, and is based on a drawing which appeared in an American publication of the 1920s.

A photograph of a typical US Fleet Review of the 1930s; such events usually took place in connection with naval manoeuvres. The photo dates from 31 May 1934 and shows part of the battle fleet; *Mississippi* is in the foreground, her crew lining the decks. A few supply ships, together with the aircraft carriers *Lexington* and *Saratoga*, can be picked out in the background. A comparison of this illustration with the earlier shot of *New Mexico* will show the extent of her reconstruction. *USN (Terzibaschitsch Collection)*

The older battleships up to and including the *Pennsylvania* class had been modernised in the second half of the 1920s, and they were followed by the three *New Mexico*s in the early 1930s. Tripod masts were not a feature of the reconstructions (although they were probably included in the original proposals), and the ships were distinguishable by a very tall, compact bridge superstructure and new pole mainmast. This photo dates from the summer of 1937, and shows two ships of the class lying at anchor off San Pedro, California (*Idaho* in the foreground). In the far background is *Texas*, identifiable by her AA platform over the foretop, fitted in 1935. *BfZ*

In July 1941, US forces relieved the British units stationed in Iceland. Among the American warships which gathered in Hvalfjord near Reykjavik were the aircraft carrier *Wasp*, three cruisers, a number of destroyers, and the battleship *Mississippi*. Their task was to guard the Denmark Strait against German surface vessels attempting to break through. This is a photo of the battleship taken during those weeks, against a typical Icelandic backdrop. The 5in (12.7cm) AA guns are already protected by splinter shields, which can be clearly seen here; the external appearance of the battleship is otherwise little changed. *BfZ*

Idaho on 24 December 1942 off Puget Sound Navy Yard, shortly before the completion of a refit, showing her new fire control equipment fore and aft, various AA additions and No 3 turret's catapult replaced by a platform with a few light AA mounts. The 5in casemate secondary battery is also missing, as are the heavy cranes either side of the funnel, and the numerous small boats, whose places have also been taken by AA weapons. This picture also shows well the unusually tall funnel, which was supposed to ensure an unobstructed and swift escape for the exhaust gases, and thus prevent any obstruction to the bridge and spotting top. *BfZ*

The final 'classic' naval battle – battleships versus battleships – was fought in October 1944. The action developed during the operations at Leyte, when two Japanese battle groups steaming from the south were attacked by American aircraft. Against the Japanese, the Americans had concentrated a powerful force, which included six old battleships, at the northern entrance of the Surigao Strait. During the engagement the Japanese battleship *Yamashiro* sank under concentrated fire. This was the last occasion that battleships exchanged fire. Amongst the six American 'battlewagons' was *Mississippi*, shown here at anchor off Manus (Admiralty Islands) in October 1944, shortly before the battle. In the background are two escort aircraft carriers and a large number of amphibious transports and support ships. By this time *Mississippi* had a raked funnel cap. *BfZ*

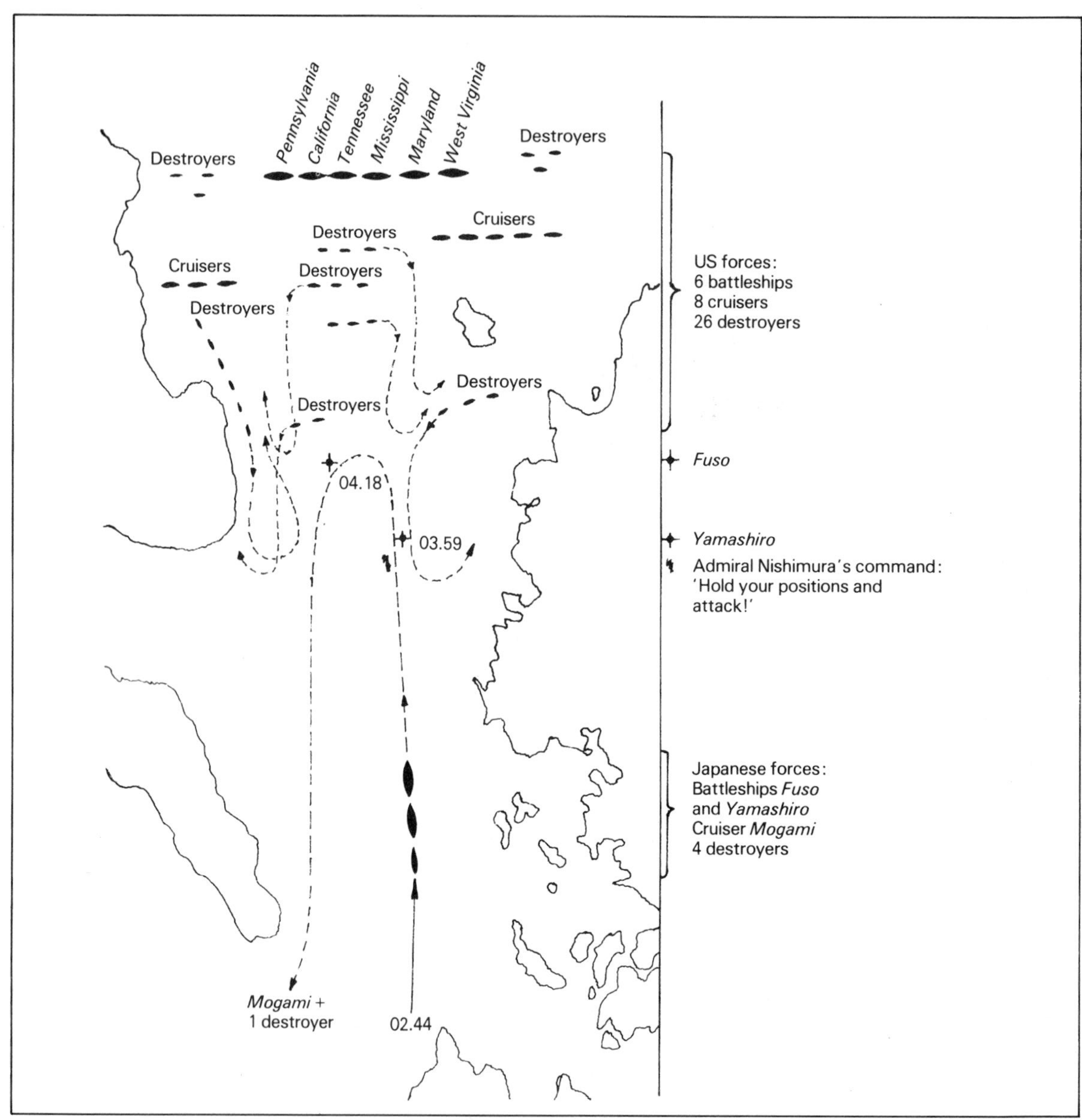

The course of the naval battle in the Surigao Strait. To the north is the Support Force of the US Seventh Fleet, with eight cruisers and 26 destroyers, with six old battleships in reserve; in the south are two approaching Japanese battle groups, one under Vice-Admiral Nishimura with two battleships, one cruiser and four destroyers, the other under Vice-Admiral Shima with three cruisers and seven destroyers. At 02.44 the Japanese reached the southern entrance to the Surigao Straits and were soon attacked by numerous American torpedo-boats, although they were able to evade most of them. US destroyers then attacked and achieved torpedo hits on both Japanese battleships, and Vice-Admiral Nishimura gave the order 'Hold your positions and attack!' One of his stricken battleships, *Fuso*, began to sink at 03.59, shortly after being engaged first by the US cruisers and then by the battleships. US gunfire was then concentrated on the remaining Japanese battleship, *Yamashiro*, which sank at 04.18. The surviving Japanese forces withdrew. By about 05.00 *Fuso* had disappeared beneath the waves.

Soon after the end of the Second World War the US fleet was drastically reduced in size; hundreds of ships were taken out of service, and many of them were stricken and scrapped, especially those that were obsolete, although some of the latter were retained for experimental purposes. The scrap metal industry experienced a massive boom, as can be seen in this photograph, which shows three capital ships in the process of being broken up. The picture dates from early 1946 and was taken at Port Newark, New Jersey. In the foreground is *New Mexico* (already down to her armour deck); behind her is her sister-ship *Idaho*, with *Wyoming* opposite. *Author's Collection*

For *Mississippi*, the postwar period brought a new role. She was converted to a gunnery training/experimental ship in 1946–47, and thus followed in the steps of *Wyoming*. With the exception of No 4, her heavy turrets were removed, and in their place were fitted a number of 5in (12.7cm) AA guns in single and twin mounts, arranged asymmetrically. The photo shows the ship around 1947, still under conversion in the shipyard; note the barbettes of the forward 14in triple turrets, one 5in/38 twin turret to starboard and two staggered 5in/54 single mounts to port. Later, one of the new 8in/47 twin turrets was fitted in the position once occupied by No 1 turret; these guns were intended for the *Worcester* class cruisers. Some time afterwards *Mississippi* was fitted out as a test ship for the Terrier guided missile system. It was in this role that she completed her period of service on 31 July 1956, almost 40 years after she had been originally commissioned. *Author's Collection*

The Americans returned to twin funnels with the *Tennessee* class – this was the most important visible difference from previous battleship classes. *Tennessee* and *California* had a great deal in common with their predecessors, the *New Mexicos*, principally as regards armament and protective system. One feature which had been considered a prototype system in *New Mexico* was fitted to these new ships as standard: the turbo-electric drive. This system had been chosen despite considerable disadvantages: greater weight and space required, difficulty in insulating against moisture, and dangerously high voltages. However, these drawbacks were considered to be outweighed by the advantages: separate reversing turbines were not necessary, performance astern was equal to that ahead, the ship was able to change over rapidly from ahead to astern drive, and so on. This is *Tennessee*; on the turret catapult are two Curtiss SOC-3 floatplanes. *BfZ*

Tennessee was severely damaged by the Japanese attack on Pearl Harbor, although not to the same extent as her sister-ship *California*. Repairs were begun without delay, and in March 1942 she was ready for action again. The cage mast was removed and replaced by a 'turret' shaped structure with a simple pole mast behind it. The top picture shows *Tennessee* in this state, and her appearance was unchanged until late summer 1942. No 3 turret is trained to port, and the 5in AA guns are behind splinter shields. *Author's Collection*

In contrast to her sister, *California* was not salvaged until March 1942, and after temporary repairs she was transferred to Puget Sound Navy Yard in June, travelling under her own steam. In this photograph she is seen leaving Pearl Harbor, with both her 'basket' masts missing. The signal mast erected over the bridge was only a temporary fitting. *Terzibaschitsch Collection*

Had she been given a new bow shape during her reconstruction, *Tennessee* would have been completely unrecognisable; even so, it was difficult to tell that the ship, when she left dock for the first time after her modernisation in 1943, was in fact *Tennessee*. The Americans had taken some very radical steps with the reconstruction – out of an old 'battlewagon' they had created what was virtually a new battleship, in which only the hull, the machinery and the main armament were original. *Tennessee* and *California* – which was modernised to the same design – emerged with an appearance slightly reminiscent of the *South Dakota* class battleships, as is evident in this photo of *Tennessee*, which was taken on 8 May 1943. *USN (Author's Collection)*

Tennessee on active service. Some of her radar equipment is still not fitted. *USN (Terzibaschitsch Collection)*

The older battleships were able to give valuable service after the Americans had recovered from the shock of the initial Japanese attack and had moved from the defensive to the offensive: with the massed fire of their accurate gunnery, they pounded one enemy stronghold after another. In order to subdue a particular target area prior to invasion, naval shellfire was often employed, especially if aerial bombardment did not have the desired effect; it is therefore indisputable that the old battleships made a valuable contribution to the success of American amphibious warfare in World War II, playing out a role for which they were never designed. Only a few years earlier, naval officers would have given a sympathetic smile to anyone who dared predict such a change: coastal bombardment was considered to be a task which would be carried out only under exceptional circumstances. The photograph shows *Tennessee* in action, with her main armament trained to port. *BfZ*

The *Colorado* class was the first US *ne plus ultra* battleship design, and represented a reaction to a Japanese challenge. In that increasingly powerful Far East island empire a more powerful naval gun – 16in (40.6cm) – had been developed, to be fitted to two battleships. This was the heaviest calibre that had appeared so far on a dreadnought, and the United States felt it had to match the Japanese vessels. Externally, the *Colorado*s were exactly the same as the *Tennessee*s, and originally consisted of four units, but only three of them were completed. The photograph dates from the early 1930s: *West Virginia* is entering port escorted by tugs. In this view the ship is dominated by her angular twin 16in turrets. *Author's Collection*

The fourth ship of the *Colorado* class – *Washington* – was a victim of the 1922 Washington Treaty and, although already launched, was not completed. She nevertheless served as a useful platform for explosive trials, and in these she proved to be extremely resistant. She was first subjected to shock waves from a series of detonations at close range, but these had virtually no effect; after this, 14 hits by 14in shells ended her existence. This 5 April 1922 photograph shows how far *Washington* had progressed when her construction was halted: the funnel and bridge superstructure are already in place and the cage mainmast is under construction; the barbettes of the 16in turrets are temporarily sealed off, and the heavy side armour is clearly visible. In the background is a covered slipway. *BfZ*

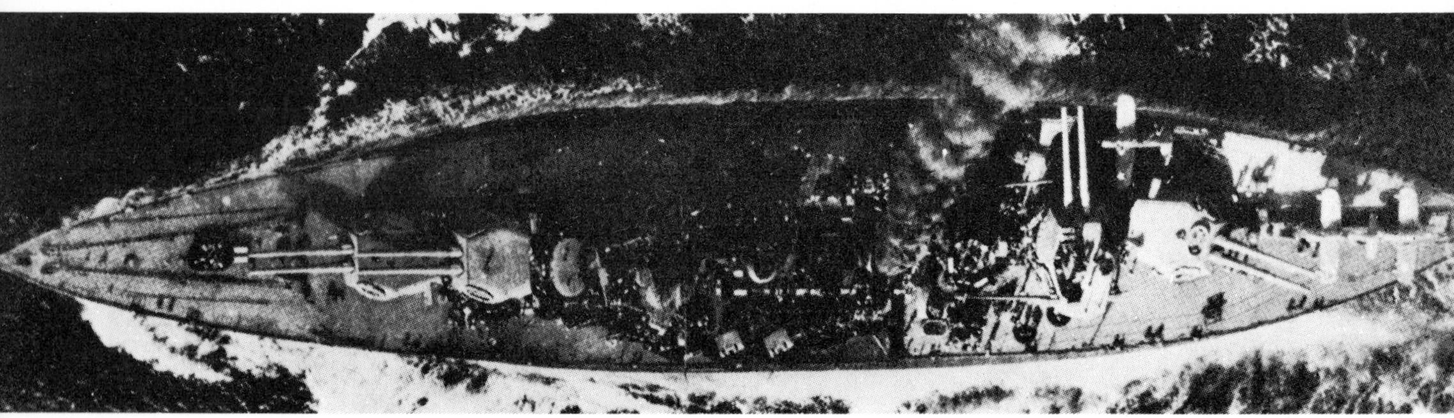

At the end of December 1941, after the attack on Pearl Harbor, *Maryland* steamed under her own power to Puget Sound Navy Yard at Bremerton, Washington, for repairs, where *Colorado* had been refitting since the summer. Early in 1942 both ships were ready for action again, but their external appearance had now altered: the top half of the mainmast had been struck, and a large number of additional AA weapons had been installed. In 1943 both ships were modernised again: this time they lost the bottom half of their mainmast, and a tower with a simple pole mast was substituted. Additional stiffening was also worked in, and some regrouping of the AA armament took place. Here are three photos of these ships, all dating from 11 August 1942: *Maryland* (top), *Colorado* (centre) and *Colorado* again. *Author's Collection*

West Virginia was salvaged early in 1942 and was reconstructed along the lines of *Tennessee* and *California*. She was ready for action again by the summer of 1944, and from then she could only be distinguished from *Tennessee* and *California* by her twin turrets, and by minor differences to her light AA armament. The ship is seen here shortly after being recommissioned, in the vicinity of Puget Sound Navy Yard at Bremerton. *USN (Terzibaschitsch Collection)*

The censor has obliterated the radar antennae in this 22 July 1945 photo of *West Virginia* – a very rare instance of such practice in the US Navy, which was very free with its information, even in wartime. *USN (Terzibaschitsch Collection)*

Maryland showing her configuration at the end of World War II. This particular ship had not been extensively modernised because the damage suffered at Pearl Harbor was not so serious that she had to spend a long period in dock for repairs, which, as in other cases, would have allowed a complete reconstruction to be carried out at the same time. Hence the ship differs little from her appearance prewar. *Colorado* was similarly little altered. *USN (Terzibaschitsch Collection)*

South Dakota class

Scarcely had the First World War ended when a menacing arms race erupted between Japan and the United States, and this began to involve other nations as well. The American move was a series of six battleships, which would have outclassed every other warship in existence: at 43,000 tons design displacement, they were intended to have twelve 16in (40.6cm) guns in triple turrets as well as extremely thick armour; in addition, after a break of more than twenty years, they were to be fitted with a full strength secondary battery consisting of 6in (15.2cm) guns. In the event, these 'super battleships' were never completed: they fell victim to the terms of the Washington Naval Treaty of 1922. Amongst this class of six – the South Dakota class – was *Montana*, whose keel had been laid on 1 September 1920 at Mare Island Navy Yard. When work on her was halted, she was 28 per cent complete. The photo was taken early in 1922, when work had already ceased; the following year the hull was broken up on the slip. *Author's Collection*

An artist's impression of how a ship of the *South Dakota* class might have looked. *Author's Collection*

Lexington class

The US Navy was not at first enthusiastic about the battlecruiser type of ship; it was only when evidence was shown of their claimed effectiveness in battle that the decision was made to build such vessels – a decision encouraged by the fact that both Britain and Germany had been working on new battlecruiser designs in the meantime. The programme of 1916 authorised six such ships, each displacing around 35,000 tons, having a top speed of 34kts, and armed with ten 14in (35.6cm) guns. Following the Battle of Jutland, in which the Royal Navy lost three battlecruisers and the German Navy one, the decision was made to increase the ships' armament and therefore redesign the vessels: now they were to be equipped with eight 16in (40.6cm) guns, whilst protection was to stay essentially the same as in the original design. However, these revisions never materialised; instead, a completely fresh design was prepared, since a thorough analysis of the lessons learned in the war had shown unequivocally that the swift end of the three British battlecruisers could be blamed on fatally weak protection and inadequate strength. The new, third design was completed in 1920, and the six ships were ordered without delay. Their displacement had now risen to over 43,000 tons. How they would have looked in their final version is shown by this contemporary artist's impression. *Author's Collection*

The 16in Mk 2 guns ordered for the *South Dakota* class and the battlecruisers of the *Lexington* class were stored for years in arsenals before a decision was made on their use. The Harbor Defense Programme of 1940 called for the building of 38 new batteries using these guns, most of them on the American continent, with a few at Pacific bases, in the Atlantic and in the Panama Canal area. Their range was around 25 miles (40km) and each shell weighed about 1 ton (1000kg). Shown here is the installation of one of the guns in a bunker. *United States Naval Institute Proceedings*

As a result of the Washington Naval Treaty of 1922 the United States had to dispense with the six battlecruisers under construction, but she was permitted to complete two of these vessels as aircraft carriers – *Lexington* and *Saratoga*, whose construction was the furthest advanced – and in 1927 they were completed as such. Until World War II they remained the largest aircraft carriers in the world, and they were also the fastest. This photograph shows *Lexington* in the early 1930s. A characteristic feature of the two ships was the unusually large funnel. The four 8in (20.3cm) twin turrets at either end of the superstructure were a failure from the start, and were of no practical use: it obviously had not been realised when they were installed that an aircraft carrier could not permit herself to become involved in a gunnery duel with other warships, since a single, medium-calibre shell could be enough to immobilise her main weapon – her aircraft – if the flight deck suffered damage. Moreover, if the vast quantities of aviation fuel which had to be kept on board were ignited, the results would have been catastrophic. *BfZ*

Lexington was an early casualty of the Pacific war, but her sister-ship *Saratoga* survived, although by no means undamaged. Twice she was hit by submarine torpedoes, three times by bombs and three times by Kamikazes. However, she did not meet her end until 1946, off Bikini Atoll, where she was used as a target ship for the atom bomb tests 'Abel' and 'Baker'. Here she is seen with a $9^1/_2$-degree list to port after being hit by a torpedo on 31 August 1942, fired from the Japanese submarine *I26* near the Solomons. The carrier was towed to Tongatabu by the cruiser *Minneapolis*, and emergency repairs were carried out; from there she went to Pearl Harbor for full repairs, and by early 1943 the carrier was ready for action once more. Note that the 8in turrets have already been replaced by twin 5in (12.7cm) mounts. *BfZ*

In 1933 the United States began intensive preliminary design work and project studies on battleships; by 1935 more than fifty designs had been prepared in detail. A design which kept within the standard displacement limits of the Washington Treaty stipulations – *viz* no more than 35,000 tons – was decided upon, and at the same time there was a requirement that the external dimensions and draught were to be kept within the limits dictated by the Panama Canal locks. The contract design initially called for a main armament consisting of twelve 14in (35.6cm) guns in three quadruple turrets, two forward and one aft; however, because of the secrecy surrounding the new battleships then being built in Japan, the decision was made on 21 June 1937 to install new 16in (40.6cm) guns. By the end of October 1937 the keel of the first ship, *North Carolina*, was laid at New York Navy Yard, and nine months later that of her sister-ship, *Washington*, was laid at Philadelphia Navy Yard. Despite the time difference, both ships were launched within days of each other: *North Carolina* on 13 June 1940 and *Washington* two weeks earlier on 1 June 1940. The launch of *Washington* is recalled in these two photos. First, the most critical moment of the launch: the stern is already afloat, but the forward half of the ship is still on the slipway, subjecting the vessel to very considerable bending loads which will never be reached again no matter how rough the sea. A ship has to pass an extremely demanding test at this moment. The second photo shows the hull now completely afloat. The barbettes of the heavy turrets are clearly visible here, as are the rudiments of the superstructure. *BfZ*

In March 1942 one of the new US battleships, *Washington*, together with the aircraft carrier *Wasp*, two heavy cruisers and a few destroyers, had been moved to Europe, where they were based at Scapa Flow, in order to give the Royal Navy the opportunity to move Home Fleet units for the operations against Madagascar which began on 4 May 1942. The high points of these first American 'visits' were the operations mounted to guard two valuable convoys (PQ-15 and QP-11), from 26 April to 12 May 1942. *Washington* was allocated the task of long-range escort, and she is seen here in company with the British battleship *King George V* during this period. The cruiser *Kenya* leads. *USN (BfZ)*

From 29 January 1944, Task Force 58, under the command of Vice-Admiral Mitscher, attacked Japanese bases in the Marshall Islands in preparation for the landing on Kwajalein Atoll. On 1 February *Washington*, attached to TF58, rammed the battleship *Indiana* in total darkness, penetrating 20ft (6m) into the latter's starboard side and causing a 200ft (60m) gash along her hull. *Washington*'s bows suffered considerable damage for a length of 60ft (18m) and were severely distorted. Both battleships were made watertight temporarily in Majuro Lagoon, and then steamed to Pearl Harbor, where *Washington*'s damaged stem was cut off and replaced by a temporary fitting, which can be seen in this 4 March 1944 photograph. Final repairs were carried out in Puget Sound Navy Yard, and *Washington* was ready for action again by the beginning of June. *BfZ*

Washington on 20 April 1944, with her new stem already fitted, undergoing trials during her Puget Sound Navy Yard refit. The hull is painted with two-colour scheme of Measure 22, which was standard at that time. The large SK radar antenna can be made out on the foremast. *BfZ*

North Carolina saw only two years of active service after World War II and was stricken in 1960. The following year she was transferred to the Historic Naval Ships Association, for preservation as a floating memorial. Since 2 October 1961 she has been anchored in a dredged out creek of the Cape Fear River at Wilmington, North Carolina, which is where this photo was taken. The only feature which differentiated her from her sister-ship *Washington* was the platform half way up the turret foremast, which could be seen from a long distance. On top of the foremast is the SK-2 radar antenna, and on the turret mast the Mk 38 director for the main armament, in front of which is a Mk 37 director. Further aft, at the same height, is one of the ship's 40mm quadruple AA gun tubs. On either side of the forefunnel is a Mk 37 director for the 5in guns; beneath them, and on the superstructure deck beside the forward 5in twin turret, are further 40mm tubs. *USS North Carolina Battleship Commission.*

South Dakota class

Alabama, Indiana, Massachusetts, South Dakota

Compared with the units of the *North Carolina* class, the *South Dakota* 'short-hull battleships' were 50ft (15m) shorter for the same displacement and beam, this was made possible by extensive space-saving measures, chiefly in the drive system, which meant that the armoured citadel could be shortened by a good 56ft (17m). Protection could thus be improved, in particular by thickening the armour deck. On the other hand, the armament was virtually unchanged. Output was raised by 9000shp, yet speed decreased by 1kt against the *North Carolina*s; this was due to a less efficient length-to-beam ratio – 6.16:1 compared with 6.82:1. The class ship, *South Dakota*, was laid down in July 1939 and launched on 7 June 1941 at the New York Shipbuilding Corporation's yard at Camden, New Jersey (see photo); she was commissioned just ten months later and considered operational by the following August. She was soon to prove the truth of this: during the campaign at Guadalcanal in November 1942, while steaming with *Washington* and four destroyers, she was attacked by a Japanese force which included the battleship *Kirishima*, two heavy and two light cruisers and nine destroyers. The Americans were taken by surprise and were attacked on two sides; they lost three destroyers, and the fourth was severely damaged. *South Dakota*, whose radar was no longer intact, tried to escape, but came up against *Kirishima* and the two Japanese heavy cruisers, and a fierce gunnery duel developed. The American battleship was hit 27 times, (some sources quote 42 hits), mainly from 8in (20.3cm) shells. Some of the hits were serious and *South Dakota*'s superstructure suffered badly, but she was still able to avoid a torpedo attack by Japanese destroyers. She was relieved by *Washington*, which had crept up unnoticed by the Japanese and now mounted a surprise attack. Within seven minutes *Kirishima* had been devastated from a range of less than 9000yds (8000m): the ship went up in flames and sank soon afterwards. *Washington* herself had suffered neither damage nor casualties, but *South Dakota* had lost 38 men, with another 60 wounded. She required 68 days in dock to repair the damage. *USN (BfZ)*

The building of *South Dakota* went back to Scheme V of the design studies which had evolved in 1935–37 during preliminary work on the *North Carolina* class. This design covered a ship of around 650ft (200m) length and 107ft (32.7m) beam, with a main armament of ten 16in (40.6cm) guns in two triple turrets forward and two twin turrets aft. Her machinery, of 130,000shp, would provide a top speed of 27kts. The final design of *South Dakota* evolved from this basis, but the main armament was reduced to nine 16in guns. The three subsequent ships – known unofficially as 'Battleships 1939' – differed in detail from their predecessor: externally, the difference was in the secondary battery, which comprised twenty barrels as against *South Dakota*'s sixteen. The 'Battleships 1939' series began with *Indiana*, which was commissioned only a few weeks after *South Dakota*; she is seen here off Hampton Roads on 8 September 1942, the day before she steamed out on her first mission. She set course for Guadalcanal, where her arrival was well timed, since she could close the gap left by the temporary loss of *South Dakota*. At this time *Indiana* still had her two cranes; the unit installed on the port side was later removed. *USN (BfZ)*

The outbreak of war in the Pacific forced the Americans to accelerate their construction of new battleships. This photograph was taken at Norfolk Navy Yard in early 1942 and shows *Alabama* fitting out. She had been laid down on 1 February 1940, was launched two years later, and was commissioned in August 1942 – a building time of $30\frac{1}{2}$ months, ie eighteen months less than would normally have been necessary. Here her superstructure is in place and her main turrets are installed, although the barrels for the latter are not yet in place. The opposite is true of the secondary battery: the twin 5in mounts are already in place, but the shields are missing. The smoke escaping from the funnel indicates that boiler testing is probably in progress. Alongside *Alabama* is *Craneship No 1*, whose task was to hoist the 16in gun barrels on board; the former pre-dreadnought *Kearsarge*, she had been converted to a crane ship in 1920 and was capable of lifting weights of up to 250 tons. *BfZ*

The *South Dakota*s were considered to be the best possible battleship design conceived within treaty limitations: their attributes were great strength, brought about by a well-designed system of underwater protection and strong armour, optimum firepower regarding calibre and number of barrels, and an acceptable top speed. Even so, the 35,000-ton limit was not respected, as was the case with virtually all the navies which had taken up battleship building again in the 1930s. In general, it was only Great Britain that had kept within the treaty limits, but only in the case of the *Nelson* class, in which the 35,000-ton limit had not even been reached. In the case of the *South Dakota* class the actual standard displacement amounted to between 38,900 and 39,600 tons when the ships were completed. Externally these battleships looked extremely compact, as is particularly clear from this aerial view of *Alabama* taken on 1 December 1942, a few months after the ship was commissioned as the final unit of her class. Part of the light AA armament is still missing. *BfZ*

Massachusetts made her combat debut in the European theatre of war: she was assigned the role of flagship of the Western Naval Task Force, made up of US Navy units, to which four escort carriers, three heavy and four light cruisers, 38 destroyers, three minelayers, eight minesweepers, one flying boat tender, four submarines, 23 troop transporters, eight supply transporters and five tankers were allocated, together with the old battleship *Texas* and the aircraft carrier *Ranger*. This fighting force was sent to the west coast of Morocco, with the main target as Casablanca, as part of Operation 'Torch' – the Allied landings in French North Africa. An action developed with the French warships at anchor in Casablanca harbour, amongst which was the incomplete battleship *Jean Bart*. *Massachusetts* fired 786 16in and 221 5in shells and was herself hit by a few light shells which, however, caused no major damage. The photo shows *Massachusetts* in 1944, already featuring the tall mainmast behind the funnel and SK radar on the foremast. *BfZ*

Less well-known is the diversionary operation carried out by the British Home Fleet in July 1943, in which an American Task Force comprising the battleships *South Dakota* and *Alabama*, two heavy cruisers and five destroyers also took part. The ships headed for northern Norway, which was intended to divert attention from the imminent landings in Sicily, but since they were not picked up by German reconnaissance the operation was valueless. British forces consisted of the battleships *Anson*, *Duke of York* and *Malaya*, the aircraft carrier *Furious*, and several cruisers and destroyers. The photograph was taken during this mission: to the left is *South Dakota*, and behind her *Alabama* and *Furious*. *USN (Terzibaschitsch Collection)*

Both the *North Carolina* and *South Dakota* classes were considered to be handicapped by their limited speed, although this was only true in the latter stages of the war, when they were used in combined operations with fleet aircraft carriers, which were as a rule 5–6kts faster. For this reason, thoughts were turned in 1954 towards the possibility of raising their speed. The space required could basically only be provided by removing the aft 16in turret, and it was calculated that the performance would have to be raised to 256,000shp to achieve a top speed of 31kts. There were two possible ways of achieving this: a completely new high performance system of the normal type; or a system of gas turbines as a 'booster' for high speed running. The latter would have had to be 'switched in' to the existing steam turbines when they were running at full speed, but in either system a very large number of modifications to the hull, the shafts, the propellers and in other areas would have been necessary. The cost of a conversion of this type was estimated at around $40 million per ship, a sum which did not include the cost of the necessary changes to the electronics and the ship's system of protection. However, this figure could not be countenanced, so the Navy had to abandon the project. This photo was taken during the Letye operations in October 1944 in the Pacific: battleships and aircraft carriers are in formation, with *Alabama* ahead, the light carrier *Cowpens* on the right, and *South Dakota* in the background. *BfZ*

From the end of 1937 the US Navy began working on projects for 45,000-ton battleships, initially purely as an academic exercise. The chosen starting point was the battleship *South Dakota*, the first version having a fourth 16in (40.6cm) triple turret and increased performance of 170,000shp in order to achieve 27kts. However, the concept of the 'high-speed battleship' was too attractive to the US Navy for them to agree to continue building 'treaty' battleships without at least studying the former. Hence a series of designs for high-speed battleships was drawn up from early 1938 onwards, vessels almost 1000ft long (300m) and with an unusually high speed of 35.5kts. Their protection was, however, only designed to withstand shells of 8in (20.3cm) calibre of less, which meant basically that the British battlecruiser concept had emerged again; such a development did not meet with the approval of the US Navy. For a time the Navy returned to the idea of a very strong 'slow' battleship, even considering a rise in calibre to 18in (45.7cm) In the meantime political developments regarding the treaties led the Navy to expect that the development of battleships, which had up till then been restricted, would shortly be allowed a freer rein; before this actually happened, the Navy finally decided on the 45,000-ton high speed battleship (May 1938), but insisted upon an acceptable protection scheme. The result was the *Iowa* class: six ships were authorised and begun, and four were completed, the last of which was *Wisconsin*, launched on 7 December 1943 at Philadelphia Navy Yard. This photo shows her shortly before being launched. *BfZ*

Iowa was the first ship of her class to be commissioned, on 22 February 1943. She was declared operational on 27 August 1943, but it was before this, on 16 July, that she suffered her first damage when she touched the bottom on her way from New York to Casco Bay, Maine. Sixteen fuel cells were ruptured, and eighteen bottom plates had to be replaced. *Iowa*'s first mission was to convey President Roosevelt to the Cairo and Teheran conferences, and she set sail on 13 November 1943. She was close to being torpedoed on the way to North Africa, not by the enemy, but by one of her own escort destroyers: a torpedo was launched as a result of a technical fault, and the ship was only just able to avoid it. She is shown here a few weeks later, on 24 January 1944, on course for the West Pacific, where she was to take her place in the US Fifth Fleet. *BfZ*

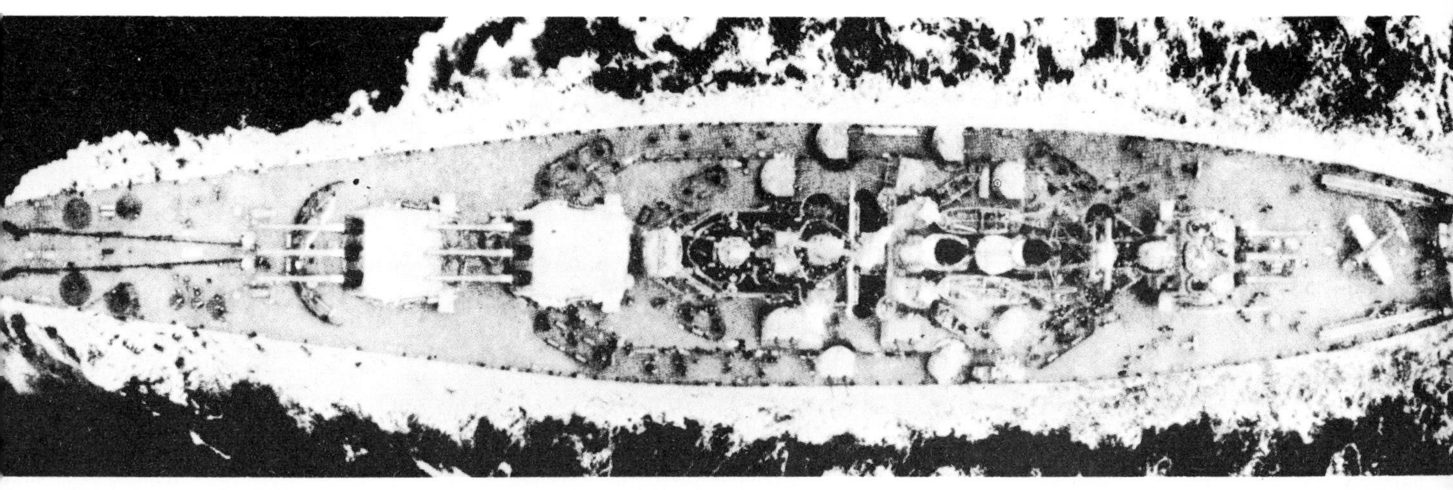

New Jersey, the second ship of the *Iowa* class, in company with the French battleship *Richelieu* in the summer of 1943, during her working up period. The photo was taken off New York or Philadelphia; *Richelieu* was on the East Coast at this time for a refit. From this angle the almost completely flat surfaces of *New Jersey*'s hull are evident, in contrast to the sloping side armour usually associated with battleships; with the *Iowa* class, however, the heavy side armour was not attached externally, but internally at a certain distance from the outside plating, where it fulfilled the function of a torpedo bulkhead, since it was angled outwards at 19° from the vertical. The *Iowa*s' side armour was scarcely thicker than on the 'treaty' battleships of the *North Carolina* and *South Dakota* classes, and was probably arranged the way it was in order to reduce drag to achieve the 33kts top speed demanded. *BfZ*

These aerial photos show that the armament and superstructure layouts for the *North Carolina*s and *Iowa*s were virtually identical. Their hulls, however, were very different: the *North Carolina* hull was of 'classic' design, whilst that of the *Iowa* class was much slimmer and to some extent built for speed, as evidenced by the shape of the bows, for which optimum sea-going characteristics were the top priority. The *Iowa*s' length-to-beam ratio – 7.97:1 – corresponded to that of the very fastest ships; with the *North Carolina* class this ratio was only 6.82:1. The first photo shows *North Carolina* (4 June 1942) and the other *New Jersey* (mid-1943). Note that in both cases the maximum beam is not exactly amidships, but further aft, a feature influenced by the arrangement of the powerplant. The numerous light AA positions are evident: it is not difficult to pick out the circular tubs of the 40mm quadruples, nor the 20mm weapons grouped together, also provided with splinter protection. *Author's Collection*

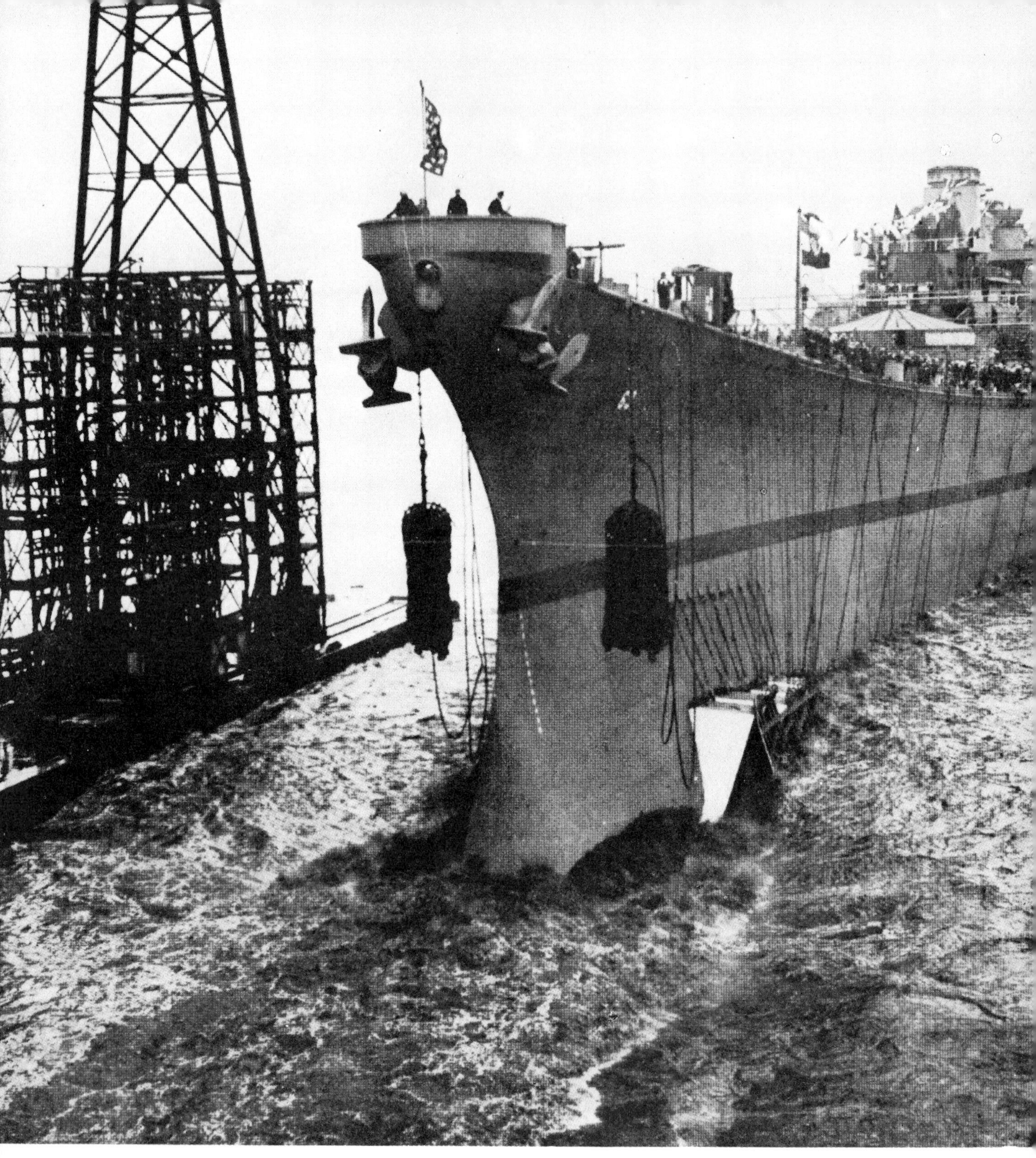

When *Missouri* was launched at New York Navy Yard on 29 January 1944, nobody could have imagined that only a year and a half later she would be playing out a unique role in world history. On 2 September 1945 the Japanese negotiators signed the surrender of their nation on board this ship – and with that the Second World War finally came to an end. This picture shows exceptionally well the elegant, harmonious lines of the hull shape of this class: at the bottom the stem ends in a 'Taylor bulb', and at the top it is bell-shaped, capped by an AA platform projecting slightly over both sides. *Author's Collection*

After being commissioned on 11 June 1944, *Missouri* remained on the American East Coast, to work up ship and crew, and also so that minor adjustments could be attended to in the shipyard. This photograph was taken on 22 October 1944 from an aircraft over Chesapeake Bay, and clearly shows *Missouri*'s circular SK-2 radar antenna, which the ship carried from the beginning. Her camouflage scheme is Measure 12. In the background is an escort carrier. *BfZ*

Wisconsin immediately after launch. Most of her superstructure is already in place, and the engines and boilers are obviously already installed. Exactly 1046 days (just under three years) had been required from keel laying to launch, and after that it was only 130 days to commissioning – a total construction time of 1176 days or slightly more than 39 months. Compared with the building times of other battleships, for example *Alabama*, this was a long time, but at this stage of the war aircraft carriers already had priority. At the same time as *Wisconsin* was being built, Philadelphia Navy Yard was also involved in building two large aircraft carriers (and soon after those a third one), as well as two heavy cruisers, fifteen escort destroyers and some smaller vessels. *BfZ*

The *Iowa*s were the fastest battleships in the world: their engines produced a maximum output of 212,000shp and their designed top speed was 33kts. Their screw arrangement was also unusual: the inboard five-bladed propellers were 17ft (5.18m) in diameter, whilst the outboard units were four-bladed and 18ft 3in (5.56m) in diameter. With their high speed they were designed to work in conjunction with fast aircraft carriers, forming battle groups with them. Here *New Jersey* is shown accompanying an *Essex* class carrier at high speed on 18 December 1944. The spray thrown up by the bows covers the forecastle and appears to be flooding it. *BfZ*

ship USS New Jersey, which lobbed one-ton shells from its 16-inch guns a
rcraft positions in Syrian-controlled mountains of eastern Lebanon yester
ndergoes sea trials in 1982 before its reactivation last January. AP PHOTO

JOSEPH DAVIS . . . "I'm taking all bets" GLOBE PHOTO BY JOHN BLAN

The contents of the northern lights box make u
a physics lab's shopping list: electron gun,
turbine, generator-alternator, bearings,
capacitors, composite pressure containers,
cathodes and anodes, radio frequency shield,

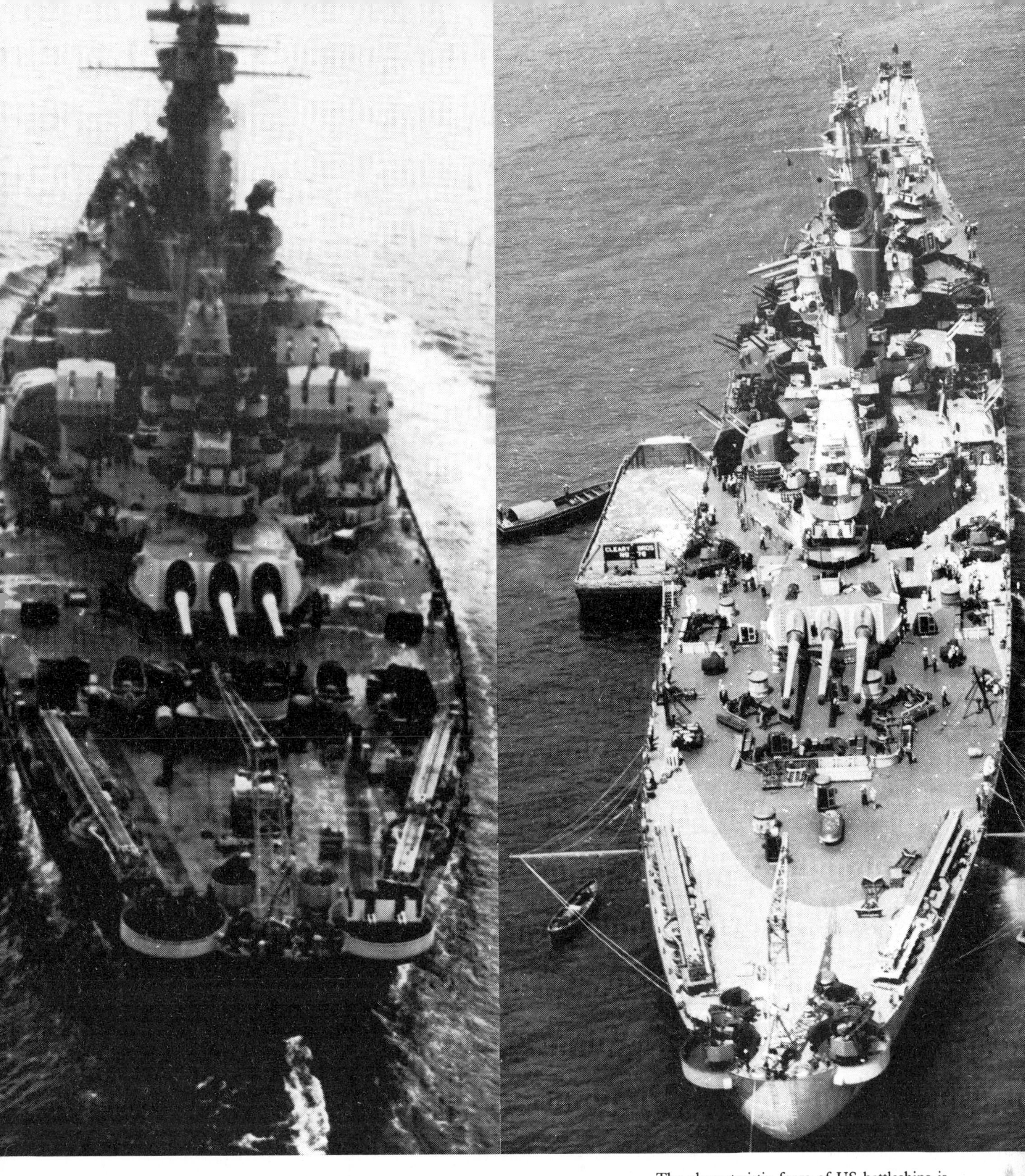

The characteristic form of US battleships is evident in these two photographs: two catapults right aft, behind them a gun tub each side with a 40mm quadruple mount, in between a crane for hoisting aircraft on board, then the aft 16in triple turret, behind that the wedge-shaped superstructure block running up to amidships, and on either side of this the 5in twin turrets – all the ships were of a similar layout. On the left is *Alabama*, and on the right is an *Iowa* class unit, probably *Missouri*. The photo of *Alabama* dates from 12 March 1945 and was taken at Puget Sound Navy Yard. *BfZ*

As the war moved ever closer to their island empire, the Japanese adopted a new form of attack: pilots – the so-called Kamikaze flyers – dived their aircraft on to US and British warships, for preference on to large units like battleships and aircraft carriers. The aircraft were usually loaded with explosives or, more seldom, with a bomb. Virtually all the old American battleships were hit by them, sometimes repeatedly: in November 1944 *Colorado* and *Maryland*, in January 1945 *New Mexico*, *Mississippi* and *California*, in March *Nevada*, in April *New York*, *Tennessee*, *Maryland* again and *West Virginia*, in May *New Mexico* again, and in June *Mississippi* again; however, only one of the new battleships was hit – *Missouri*. On none of the battleships was the damage so severe that a substantial loss of fighting efficiency occurred, and all the affected vessels were repaired in a short time. The large number of old battleships hit in contrast to the single new vessel can be explained by the fact that the former belonged to the Fire Support Groups and always stayed close to the coast, allowing them to fire as far as possible inland with their heavy guns; here the Kamikaze aircraft had plenty of worthwhile targets within their very limited radius of action. On the other hand the new battleships usually stayed out at sea, out of range for that type of aircraft. This photo was taken fractions of a second before the Kamikaze struck *Missouri* on 11 April 1945; despite an intensive AA barrage, the hit could not be prevented. *USN (Author's Collection)*

The last two ships of the *Iowa* class were not completed; one of them was *Kentucky*, which had been laid down shortly before the end of 1944. There is a curiosity here: it was one of the very rare instances where the same ship's keel was laid twice. The first occasion was early in 1942, but the keel had to be dismantled, because the yard received a mass contract for landing vehicles, and these had absolute top priority, requiring the entire capacity of the yard. When the situation eased the construction of the battleship was restarted, and the second keel-laying took place on 6 December 1944 in a building dock at Philadelphia Navy Yard. After the end of the war, in August 1946, work on the ship was stopped once more, only to be resumed on 17 August 1948. The intention then was to advance the ship just far enough to permit it to be launched. The photo shows the vessel still in her building dock. *BfZ*

On 20 January 1950 *Kentucky*'s hull was finally pumped dry, rather more than 5 years after the final keel-laying. The first photo shows her apparently very low in the water, but this impression is deceiving, as the ship had only been completed up to her armour deck and so the upper deck is missing. The openings in the armour deck for the barbettes etc are clearly visible, and, lying on the deck immediately in front of No 1 barbette, is the bell-shaped bow section (a shape characteristic of the *Iowa* class), which has been pre-fabricated and stored on deck for convenience. The smaller photo shows the *Kentucky* hull six years later, without her bows. These had been removed and fitted to her sister-ship *Wisconsin*, after the latter's bow had been damaged in a collision. Early in 1959 work started on breaking up *Kentucky*'s hull. Her engines were removed, and today power the fast combat support ships *Sacramento* and *Camden*, which have been in service since 1964 and 1966 respectively. *Author's Collection*

Of the *Iowa* class battleships, only *Missouri* ▶ was kept in service after the war; the other three ships were taken out of service in 1948 and 1949 and placed in reserve. When the Korean conflict developed into open war, the three ships in reserve were reactivated, first *New Jersey*, then *Wisconsin* and finally *Iowa*. All took part in continuous close support missions against strategically important targets on the Korean coast, and placed these targets under accurate fire, with the usual effect. The photograph shows *Iowa* on 15 December 1952 during one such mission off the east coast of Korea. Aerial identification marks are painted on the forward turrets: *Iowa*'s hull number '61' on No 1 turret and a stylised US flag on No 2. *Terzibaschitsch Collection*

The excellent logistics which the US Navy had developed in the Second World War were used to good effect for Korea. Part of this system was the dockyard facilities in the vicinity of the mission area, and such a facility was available at Guam, about 1600 nautical miles from the southern tip of Korea. This was a floating dock, big enough to take even the *Iowa*s, and it allowed repairs and work to be carried out which would otherwise have had to be done three times further away, on the American West Coast. *Wisconsin* is seen here in this floating dock, in April 1952. *Terzibaschitsch Collection*

With the end of the Korean War, the four *Iowa*s remained in service; *Wisconsin* and *Missouri* were operational for the longest periods, both of them only returning to the 'mothball fleet' in 1958, where they remain today, over twenty years later. Various modifications were made to all the ships during their second period of service, mainly in the area of electronics, as part of which the masts had to be altered. However, the catapults were also removed, and two helicopters replaced the ships' aircraft. In 1955 *Iowa* and *Wisconsin* were fitted with a massive 'portal' mast abaft the second funnel, with loading machinery on either side, and the old aircraft crane was also removed. The planned rearmament of AA guns to thirty 3in (7.6cm) barrels in place of the 40mm quadruples was, however, not carried out on any of the ships. This photo of *Wisconsin*, taken on 22 January 1956, shows the changes very clearly. *BfZ*

The final battleship salvoes were fired in the Vietnam War: in 1968, after more than ten years in reserve, *New Jersey* was reactivated for operations off the coast of Vietnam. The US authorities made this decision because air attacks were in far too many instances proving ineffective, especially on pin-point targets. They hoped to have more success with the accurate gunnery that could be provided by a battleship, which could reach far into enemy territory. After *New Jersey* was commissioned in April 1968 – for the third time in her career – she spent 120 days in action off Vietnam, and during this period she achieved a record 47 days in continuous operation. She expended 6200 16in shells, 5688 of which were at targets in Vietnam, and the 5in battery raised this figure to more than 15,000; during the Second World War, in contrast, she fired only 771 sounds of 16in, and in the Korean War and the period immediately following 667 rounds. Political and military developments led to *New Jersey* being withdrawn from front-line operations off Vietnam, despite the successes she had achieved. Her flag was hoisted for the last time on 17 December 1969. The photo shows *New Jersey* leaving Philadelphia harbour for trials, 26 March 1968. *BfZ*

The US Navy laid great emphasis on the importance of her warships – battleships and aircraft carriers – being able to negotiate the 110ft (33.5m) wide locks of the Panama Canal, which determined the maximum permissible beam of these vessels. The battleships of the *Iowa* class had a beam of 108ft 2in (32.97m) – leaving just enough room for the fenders in the lock chambers which were used to secure the ships. The largest battleships ever to see service with the US Navy were thus able to pass through the Panama Canal. This photo shows *New Jersey* on her canal passage, not during World War II, but at a later point in time – en route for Vietnam in 1968 after her reactivation. *BfZ*

The high speed and enormous range of the *Iowa*s made them the subject of a number of conversion studies in the postwar period; at 12kts they could cover 18,000 nautical miles, whilst at 17kts they could still manage 15,900. The battleship had long lost its dominant role in naval warfare, and for this reason the US Bureau of Ships investigated the possibilities of converting the *Iowa*s into 'high-speed missile monitors': the proposals involved removing all three main turrets and replacing them with two twin launchers for Talos and Tartar surface-to-air missiles, one ASROC launcher for eight missiles and a Regulus II system with four missiles; a bow dome enclosing a high-efficiency sonar system was also planned, as well as accommodation for two ASW helicopters; Talos and Tartar weapons systems were to be installed; and the vessels were to be equipped to function as command ships. The removal of the 16in turrets would bring about such a reduction is weight that fuel bunkerage could be doubled, enabling a much greater range to be achieved as well as permitting the ships to supply other vessels. The cost of such a conversion was calculated at $178 million per ship, plus a further $15 million for the twin Tartar launcher. However, the sums involved were much too high, and the proposals never had a chance. In view of this, a further study was conducted into the possibilities of a 'semi-conversion': the forward turrets were to remain, and only one Talos and one Tartar twin launcher were to be fitted, plus ASROC, but with the addition of two Regulus II weapons systems with a total of six missiles. This would not have allowed the fuel capacity supply to be doubled, but even at the new level of 11,600 tons, a range of about 26,000 nautical miles could be achieved at 12kts. It was considered essential to carry out modifications to the superstructure, especially the fitting of 'macks' instead of the previous funnels and masts, to provide better accommodation for the antennae and sensors. The armoured control tower was also to be removed. It was estimated that this conversion would cost $84 million, and the total would be only slightly lower if the ASROC weapons system and the bow sonar bulge were not included. The rapid development of missiles systems – in particular the adoption of ballistic missiles launched from submarines – caused these projects to be abandoned and work was stopped, but in 1962 yet another conversion plan was drawn up, which had been worked out collectively by the Navy and the Marine Corps. This proposed converting the ships into 'force bombardment and assault ships', and also meant the removal of the aft 16in turret, in order to provide space for a large helicopter flight deck which was to extend from abaft the superstructure to the stern. One Marine Corps battalion would be assigned to each ship, for whose transport to the area of operation twenty helicopters and sixteen landing craft were to be taken on board. The two forward 16in turrets were intended to provide covering fire. The cost of this conversion was estimated to be between $5 million and $20 million per ship, which was considered very reasonable; nevertheless, approval was not granted. The illustration is an artist's impression of how the *Iowa*s would have looked after conversion to 'force bombardment and assault ships'. *United States Naval Institute Proceedings*

The building of the *Alaska* class was much more the result of the personal intervention of President Roosevelt and his interest in the German 10,000-ton 'pocket-battleships' than of the requirements of the Navy itself; it was also rumoured that similar ships of a superior design were under construction in Japan. The *Alaska*s had many of the characteristics of battlecruisers of earlier periods, but they were designated 'large cruisers' within the US Navy, a term which by no means conveyed their true character: as 'cruisers' they were considerably too large and expensive, but on the other hand they were too vulnerable to be able to operate in conjunction with the battleships. Originally, the Americans considered building twelve ships in this class but only six were ordered, and of these only two – *Alaska* and *Guam* – were completed. However, the end of the war was already in sight when they were ready for service, and they spent only 32 and 29 months respectively with the fleet. For years they were 'mothballed', but were eventually scrapped. This photograph was taken on 22 September 1944 and shows *Alaska* during trials. *BfZ*

An unusual photo of *Alaska* dating from 5 June 1944 and taken at the New York Shipbuilding Corporation's yard at Camden, New Jersey, a few days before the ship was commissioned. Instead of having the usual catapult arrangement right at the stern, *Alaska* returned to the system adopted for heavy cruisers up to the *New Orleans* class, in which the catapults were located on either beam amidships. Here the starboard catapult is clearly visible on its high mounting; to launch an aircraft, it had to be slewed round sideways. Also visible here is one of the two aircraft hangars, incorporated into the bridge superstructure; these are located either side of the turret mast, and finish virtually flush with the after edge of the mast. The two aircraft handling cranes are situated by the smokestack. These hoisted the aircraft, which landed on the sea nearby, on to the ship and placed them on the deck, from where they could be stowed in the hangars, after their wings had been removed. *USN*

The third *Alaska* class ship, *Hawaii*, was laid down relatively late – December 1943 – and was supposed to be completed by 1 December 1945. This did not prove possible however, since priorities in warship building were changed in favour of other types shortly after the contract was signed. By the time *Hawaii* was launched, late in 1945, the war was over and ships of this type were virtually useless; nevertheless, work on her continued until April 1947 – in fact planning work had been in progress since the autumn 1946, with the intention of completing *Hawaii* as a trials ship for guided weapons systems. However, these plans were not approved by the authorities, nor was a design study of 1951 which envisaged the vessel's completion as a Tactical Command Ship. The photograph shows *Hawaii* being launched at the New York Shipbuilding Corporation yard at Camden on 3 November 1950. The chains hanging down by the anchors are designed to have a braking effect on the hull as soon as it is afloat. *BfZ*

Montana class

Between 1938 and 1939 an important change of direction was made by the US Navy: the concept of the 'high-speed battleship' had been consolidated in 1938, and had been realised in the *Iowa* class, but it was considered necessary just one year later to build more strongly protected and even more heavily armed battleships in the future, which would thererfore not need to be so fast. Initial design work began in the summer of 1939, and the aim was evidently to keep the ship within the 45,000-ton limit; however, early experiences in the war in Europe indicated the need to increase the displacement substantially to achieve optimum strength – when the project was abandoned early in 1942, a standard displacement of more than 63,000 tons had already been decided on. Five ships, the *Montana* class, were included in the programme; their building contracts had been awarded by mid-1940, but not one vessel was laid down, since the US Navy had already come to the conclusion that the battleship had been superseded by the aircraft carrier as the decisive naval weapon, no matter how powerful and well protected the former might be. Incidentally, the *Montana* class represented the United States' first break with their basic rule that a ship's maximum beam must be dictated by the need to navigate the Panama Canal – and when the first 'super carrier', *Midway*, was laid down, the rule was broken again. *Midway* and her five sister-ships were ordered as a kind of substitute for the *Montana*s. Every new American aircraft carrier commissioned since has had to choose the sea route round one of the two Capes in order to travel from east to west, or *vice versa.* The first photo is of a model representing the *Montana* class at the 1940 design stage, and the other illustration is an artist's impression of the final design. *USN/ United States Naval Institute Proceedings*

Japan

When *Satsuma* and *Aki* were laid down early in 1905, they were the first two 'all-big-gun' battleships in the world – or they would have been, had they been completed to the original plans. In fact, their armament was intended to comprise twelve 12in (30.5cm) guns, grouped as follows: one twin turret forward and one aft, plus another twin turret on either beam with singles forward of and aft of each of these. As these 12in guns still had to be purchased in Great Britain, and the funds required had been used up in the war with Russia, it was decided to adopt a smaller calibre – 10in (25.4cm) – in the beam positions instead of the 12in weapons; these guns also had to be bought in Britain, but they were cheaper, and the savings made it possible to pay for the *Aki*'s turbines, which had been ordered in the United States. Whilst only two funnels were needed for *Satsuma*'s twenty boilers (the ship was powered by expansion engines), *Aki* needed three funnels for her three boilers; the reason for this was the arrangement of the boiler rooms, which differed on each ship. Here *Aki* is seen at Kure on 26 December 1915, with one 3in (7.6cm) gun on each of the end turrets. After she was taken out of service, *Aki* was used as a trials ship for experiments with the new 60.9cm (24in) torpedoes, and after that as a bombing target. *BfZ*

Japan's first step in the direction of the 'all-big-gun' battleship was thwarted by financial difficulties, and as a result her navy found itself left behind after the war with Russia: by this time Great Britain, the United States and Germany were engaged in building dreadnoughts, and other naval powers were on the point of ordering them. To confirm and secure her predominance in East Asia, which she had achieved by winning the war, Japan had to join in the race and take up the construction of these ships. Her limited funds only allowed two units to be built initially, *Kawachi* and *Settsu*, which were laid down in the first quarter of 1909. They were based on plans drawn up independently by Japanese designers; only the heavy guns had to be ordered in Great Britain, as the necessary licences had been obtained for building the turbines. This is *Kawachi*, on 6 February 1912. *BfZ*

Externally, *Kawachi* and *Settsu* resembled *Aki*, but their second funnels were further aft in relation to the other two stacks, and they could also be distinguished by their tripod masts – *Kawachi* and *Settsu* were the first Japanese warships to be so fitted. The photo shows *Settsu* at anchor off Kure. *BfZ*

One curious fact relating to the main armament on the two *Kawachi*s was that although all twelve barrels were of the same calibre they were of two different models: the beam turrets had shorter barrels than did the rest, and their performance was correspondingly different. The explanation is that the original design called for a main armament consisting of identical guns, but improved finances subsequently made it possible to buy a newer model of higher performance, although only in limited numbers. Here *Settsu* fires her main battery soon after commissioning. *BfZ*

Settsu opens fire during gunnery practice, 25 October 1915. *BfZ*

A variation in main armament was not the only notable feature of the *Kawachi* class, for their secondary armament was also out of the ordinary. The latter comprised guns of two different calibres: ten 6in (15.2cm) guns in casemates on the battery deck, plus eight 4.7in (12cm) guns, some of the latter behind shields on deck, the rest on the battery deck – a unique arrangement. The photograph shows *Kawachi* at anchor off Kobe. The ship sank in Tokuyama Bay on 12 July 1918 following a massive explosion on board. Investigations showed that her cordite had spontaneously ignited, leading to the explosion which completely destroyed the ship and killed more than 500 of her crew. The remains of *Kawachi* were later broken up where she had gone down. *Author's Collection*

Settsu, taken from the same angle as the previous photograph and showing the most important characteristic which distinguished her from her sister-ship – the curved stem. *Author's Collection*

Settsu had to be withdrawn from service under the terms of the Washington Treaty, but the Japanese were permitted to use her as a target ship when she had been disarmed. She served in this capacity for more than two decades, almost to the end of World War II. Most of the time she was used by the Japanese Navy Air Force as a bombing target, and was largely responsible for the high standard of training attained by carrier pilots who were to meet with such success during the opening stages of the war. At the end of July 1945 *Settsu* was hit by a bomb and grounded off Tsukumo; soon after this she was broken up on the spot. The first photo shows *Settsu* as she appeared at the end of the World War I; in the second she is seen as a target ship, photographed on 1 April 1940 at Kure. She remained in this condition almost until the end. *BfZ*

In recent literature *Kurama* and *Ibuki* have occasionally been referred to as battleships, but this is incorrect: the decisive factor is the type of ship as which they were ordered, ie *Soko-Junyokan*, or armoured cruisers; later, when they had been completed, the Navy designated them *Junyo Senkan*, or battlecruisers. However, this should not detract from the fact that these ships remained what they had been from their conception: well protected cruisers, not especially fast, although having an armament similar to 'transitional' battleships, ie consisting of two heavy calibres. Bearing in mind their moderate armour thickness – 178mm (7in) maximum – they could not be considered battleships; neither, with their low top speed of only a little over 22kts, could they be described as battlecruisers, yet they were known as such within the Japanese Navy, and this was probably to equate them with the Royal Navy's *Invincible* class. From this hair-splitting exercise, the only definite fact to emerge is that *Kurama* and *Ibuki* represented the final development of the Japanese armoured cruiser, or, alternatively, the forerunners of the 'real' battlecruiser. *Kurama* is shown here at anchor in Spithead Roads, in company with British battleships; the photo was taken in June 1911 during a European cruise. *BfZ*

Kurama in Kure harbour, 18 June 1913; in the background to the right is the battleship *Settsu*. *Ibuki* differed from *Kurama* in that her masts were not fitted with bipod legs. *BfZ*

Hiei, the first of the three *Kongo* class battlecruisers to be built in Japanese shipyards, was laid down on 4 November 1911, and commissioned on 4 August 1914, her design closely following that of her sister. These three units could be distinguished from *Kongo* by their forward funnels, which were grouped more closely together, as can be seen by comparison with the photo of the model of *Kongo*. This photograph of *Hiei*, dating from 26 April 1914, shows her on trials. The structures between the two after turrets are probably measuring devices. *Hiei* still features funnels of identical height; however, even before she was commissioned, the forefunnel was raised by a good 6ft (2m). *BfZ*

Kongo class

Haruna, Hiei, Kirishima, Kongo

Even before details about the British *Invincible* class had been made known, the Japanese had begun design studies for a new type of capital ship. They settled on a displacement of just 19,000 tons, with an output of 44,000shp for a top speed of 25kts, whilst the main armament was intended to be four 12in (30.5cm) and ten 10in (25.4cm) guns. When the actual specifications for *Invincible* became public it was considered necessary to adopt ten 12in guns to gain an advantage; these guns were originally arranged as in the German *Moltke* class, but eventually the British *Orion* class layout was copied. Great Britain then ordered her *Lion* class vessels, and gained a further advantage; Japan was thereby forced to ask for assistance from a foreign country to gain access to Western technology. The best route here seemed to be to order a pattern ship. A building contract was signed with the British Vickers shipbuilding company, who produced a design. When *Kongo* was delivered, she represented the most powerful battlecruiser of the period, even overshadowing the British *Lions*, although she still suffered from the same problem as her British antecedants in that her protection left something to be desired. Shown here is the model of *Kongo* produced by the builders. *Author's Collection*

The speed with which Japan's shipbuilding industry was able to free itself from its decades of dependence on foreign aid and catch up with modern technology is shown by the four *Kongo* class battlecruisers. Although the name ship had to be ordered from another country, it was possible to build the three subsequent units in Japan's own yards, and in the case of *Hiei* only 30 per cent of the materials had to be purchased abroad. For the next two ships, *Haruna* and *Kirishima*, even this was not necessary: no materials had to be imported – and the Japanese warship industry had achieved independence. This is *Hiei* off Kobe, dressed overall to celebrate the birthday of Tenno, with *Kongo* in the background on the right, *Kirishima* next to her, and the armoured cruiser *Aso* (ex-Russian *Bajan*) in the background on the left. The photo was taken on 30 October 1915 on board *Haruna*. *BfZ*

Kirishima, with the armoured cruisers *Azuma* and *Iwate* on the right behind her, taken around 1919. If one compares this with the previous illustration, *Kirishima*'s very high bridge superstructure is apparent – a result of new fire control systems. *BfZ*

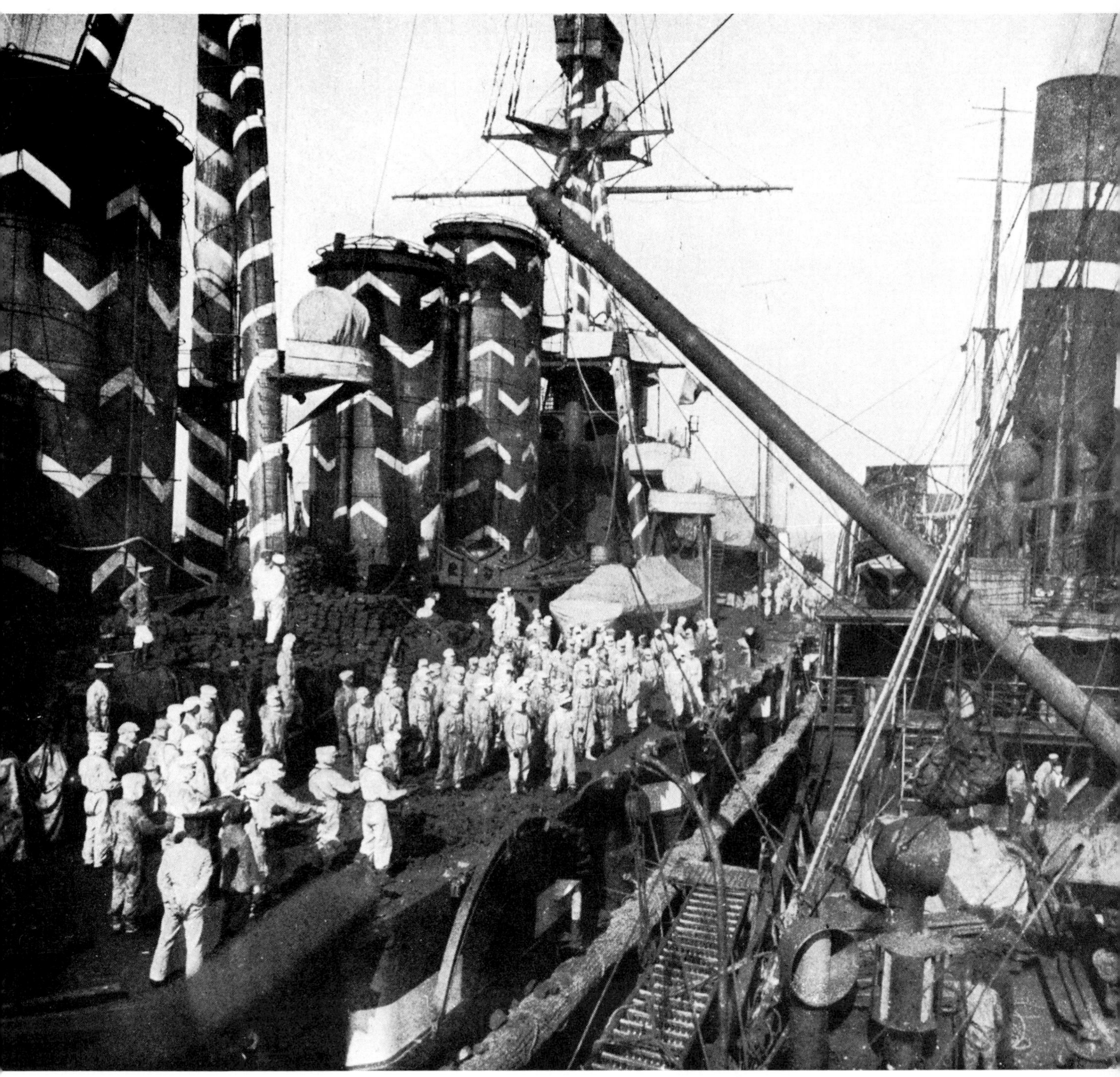

Although Japan's navy took part in the war against the Central Powers, it suffered few losses, and none of these was due to enemy action: in four instances ships were stranded and in three internal explosions occurred. However, *Haruna* was almost lost: in the summer of 1917 she struck a mine, probably laid by the German auxiliary cruiser *Berlin*, and was seriously damaged. This 21 October 1915 photo shows *Haruna* in camouflage, alongside the freighter *Kaga Maru*, during coaling operations. *BfZ*

Kongo and *Hiei* were the only ships to be fitted with a tall cap on the forefunnel in the early 1920s, the intention being to keep smoke away from the bridge. The ships could be distinguished from one another in that *Kongo*, shown here in 1926, had her forefunnel closer to the bridge superstructure, and between the first and the second funnel was a tall searchlight platform. *BfZ*

Hiei at Sasebo in August 1925; note that, in contrast to *Kongo*, the forefunnel is further away from the bridge superstructure, leaving room for another searchlight platform. Japanese capital ships retained their torpedo nets long after all other navies had abandoned them, and it was not until 1929 that they were finally removed. *BfZ*

Kongo around 1928, seen from the air, showing that her torpedo nets have been removed. The derrick installed aft of No 3 turret indicates that the ship already carries aircraft on board, although without catapult launching facilities; the aircraft had to be lowered down to the water, and they took off from there. *BfZ*

The *Kongo* class battlecruisers underwent their first reconstruction in the 1920s, the main objective being to increase protection, including the fitting of torpedo bulges. However, new boilers were also installed, as is evident from the fact that there were now only two funnels. *Kongo* is shown here in drydock at Yokosuka on 24 December 1929; her forefunnel has been removed and may be seen in the background on the quayside. *BfZ*

Kongo on 20 March 1931, her reconstruction not yet complete. The two funnels are now bulged at the top, a design intended to prevent flying sparks, which might otherwise betray the ship's presence at night or in fog. The forefunnel was now considerably taller than the second, giving the ship an unmistakable silhouette. *BfZ*

After their first reconstruction, the *Kongo*s were designated *Senkan*, or battleships; the reason for this new designation was evidently the lowering of the top speed from 27.5 to 25.9kts as a result of the modifications made. This, together with improvements made in protection, meant that the ships had more in common with battleships than with battlecruisers, at least in the eyes of the Japanese Navy. *Haruna* is shown here on 25 May 1928 – a few weeks before she was recommissioned – probably on trials. *BfZ*

The London Naval Treaty of 1930 required that one *Kongo* class battleship should be withdrawn from service, although it could be maintained as a training ship after appropriate demilitarisation. The choice fell on *Hiei*. She entered the dockyard in September 1929, and when she left again three years later she had no armour belt and only six 14in guns; there were no 6in guns and 25 boilers fewer than before, providing her with a top speed of only 18kts. A quite narrow tubular smokestack had been fitted in place of the two forward funnels, along with a system of multiple searchlight platforms. The forward tripod mast had been replaced by a structure which resembled a pagoda, so many platforms and projections had been fitted around it. The first photo shows *Hiei* around 1924; awnings have been rigged over large areas of the upper deck. The other illustration dates from October 1936 and shows *Hiei* as a training ship. She is off Kobe and Tenno's standard is fluttering from the maintop, indicating that he was on board at the time. Incidentally, the 6in guns can be seen once more – they had been re-fitted shortly before this photo was taken. The ship is very high in the water, owing to the reduction in weight as a result of her conversion. *BfZ*

One result of the London Naval Conference was that the building of new battleships could not be contemplated, and so the Japanese Navy decided on a complete reconstruction of their three operational *Kongo* class battleships. The main aim of this exercise was to raise the top speed so that in future the ships would be able to operate with fast aircraft carriers, and thus help protect them. *Haruna* was the first ship to enter dock (summer 1933), followed by *Kirishima* and finally *Kongo*. All were fitted with completely new machinery and in addition they were lengthened by roughly 26ft (8m) to maintain the optimum length-to-beam ratio for the high speed required. When they emerged, the *Kongo*s could achieve 30kts, although 136,000shp – more than double the original power – was necessary. These reconstructions altered the external appearance of the class considerably: from now on the two funnels were of equal height, and a more compact 'pagoda mast' was substituted for the tripod foremast (which had scarcely been recognisable as such anyway). *Haruna* is shown here after her reconstruction; note that her second funnel is in fact a little taller than her forefunnel – this was probably the most obvious feature which distinguished *Haruna* from her sister-ships. *BfZ*

Hiei functioned as a training ship for only four years. When she returned to dockyard hands in November 1936 – ostensibly for routine work – there was no hint to the rest of the world that the Japanese were about to break the existing treaties and provide themselves with an additional battleship 'by the back door'. Under a cloak of secrecy, *Hiei* was refitted with everything which had been removed from her a few years earlier and carefully stored, including her heavy belt armour and the fourth 14in turret. At the same time she was completely modernised, as had been her sister-ships in the 1930s, and received additional protection and new machinery. *Hiei* was recommissioned on 31 January 1940 after three years of reconstruction work, and she was now of very similar appearance to her three sister-ships, but with one exception: in place of the 'pagoda' foremast she had been fitted with a compact superstructure unit which had been developed as a prototype for the *Yamato* class. This photo shows *Hiei*'s silhouette after her conversion. *Author's Collection*

The modest funds of Japan's 1911 programme were only sufficient for the building of a single battleship, *Fuso*, whose construction was begun early in 1912; a second ship, *Yamashiro*, could not be ordered until 1913, her keel being laid at the end of that year. *Fuso* was completed towards the end of 1915, and *Yamashiro* early in 1917. Armament consisted of twelve 14in (35.6cm) guns in six twin turrets – two of which were arranged amidships, one behind each funnel. No 4 turret was at the same height as No 5, and this was a special feature of this class. *Fuso* is shown here at Kure in her original condition, 25 June 1919; the old battleship *Satsuma* is in the background on the left. *BfZ*

Yamashiro, also in her original state, in 1917 at Yokusuka. On close examination it can be seen that the distance between the tripod foremast and the forefunnel is slightly less than with *Yamashiro*; the latter was fitted with an enlarged conning tower and thus the mast had to be moved roughly 3ft (1m) further aft. *BfZ*

During the 1920s the external appearance of *Fuso* and *Yamashiro* altered: more and more platforms were added to and around the foremast, so that the basic structure of the mast was hardly visible. The forefunnel was fitted with a raked cap, while a multi-storey searchlight platform was erected forward of the second funnel. An aircraft was carried, as can be seen here, although it would have had to take off from the water. This photo of *Yamashiro* dates from 1930. *Author's Collection*

Yamashiro on 20 October 1934 at Yokosuka Navy Yard; she is also in drydock undergoing modernisation. *BfZ*

Fuso and *Yamashiro* were modernised in the early 1930s. Apart from having additional protection worked in – they were given torpedo bulges and thicker horizontal armour – their speed was also increased: from now on they could achieve 24.7kts instead of the original 23, thanks to completely new machinery which almost doubled the original output, a move which could never be justified on economic grounds. Fighting efficiency was improved by installing modern fire control systems, increasing the elevation of the guns and fitting new AA weapons, and range was also increased. The photo shows *Fuso* on 28 April 1933, just prior to the completion of her modernisation, still in the great drydock of the naval yard at Kure, in which, four and a half years later, *Yamato* would be built. *BfZ*

Fuso after her recommissioning in 1933. Whilst this vessel initially had her catapult located on No 3 turret, *Yamashiro*'s was fitted on the starboard side of the quarter-deck; from 1938, however, *Fuso*'s was also located towards the stern. *BfZ*

At long range, the two *Fuso*s could only be distinguished by the different shapes of their towering bridge superstructure. This is *Yamashiro*, at anchor off Yokosuka on 25 January 1935, shortly before her modernisation was completed. *BfZ*

The installation of new fire control equipment was amongst the most important features of the Japanese Navy's battleship modernisation programmes. This is a view of *Fuso*'s 'pagoda' foremast, on top of which is a rangefinder whose similarity with contemporary German equipment is obvious. These 'pagoda' structures had relatively narrow bases, as can be seen here. The photo was taken on 21 May 1936. *BfZ*

Apparently because of a lack of suitable positions on the upper deck, half the heavy AA guns on board *Fuso* and *Yamashiro* were located on platforms high up on either side of the mainmast. This view of *Fuso*, taken from the quarterdeck, shows two 12.7cm (5in) twin AA guns in these new positions; the asymmetrical shields were a characteristic feature of this particular model. This photograph also dates from 21 May 1936. *Author's Collection*

The Battle of Surigao Strait proved fatal for the two *Fuso* class battleships. They were part of a battle group which was engaged against amphibious units of the US Navy and which was due to join up with another battle group in the Sulu Sea. When the Japanese tried to enter Surigao Strait, they came upon a far superior American force, and the result was the last 'classical' naval battle: battleship against battleship. *Fuso* was badly damaged and sank a few hours later, whilst *Yamashiro* was pounded by American battleships and cruisers and eventually sank after suffering massive explosions. This is one of the last photographs of *Yamashiro* – taken early on 24 October 1944 by an aircraft from the American carrier *Enterprise* – as she and her group approached the southern entrance to the Surigao Strait and were attacked by US shipboard aircraft. The bomb plumes can be seen all around her, but on this occasion she was lucky, suffering only moderate damage. However, catastrophe struck a few hours later. *BfZ*

Hyuga and *Ise* were essentially improved *Fuso*s and had the same fighting value; in contrast to their predecessors, however, *Hyuga* and *Ise* had Nos 3 and 4 turrets grouped together and superimposed behind the after funnel, thereby allowing the boiler rooms to be arranged more effectively, the funnels to be set closer together and the magazines for these turrets to be better protected. This is *Hyuga*, around 1919–20. *BfZ*

Hyuga class

Hyuga, Ise

The 1914 Programme provided for the construction of the next two Japanese battleships, *Hyuga* and *Ise*. The contracts were again awarded to private shipyards, to ensure the continuity of the building policy followed up till then: the first two battleships, together with one battlecruiser of the *Kongo* class, had been built in Navy yards, the next two battlecruisers in private yards, and the *Fuso* class battleships again in Navy yards. *Hyuga* is seen here leaving her slipway on 27 January 1917; the keel of the battleship *Tosa* would shortly be laid on the same slip. *BfZ*

▲ A close-up of Nos 3 and 4 turrets on board *Hyuga* or *Ise*; in the background can be seen some of the new 14cm (5.5in) guns, which *Hyuga* and *Ise* were the first capital ships to receive. *BfZ*

An aerial photo of the battleship *Hyuga*, taken around 1929, showing numerous boats, large and small, on the upper decks. The wave-like outline of the forecastle deck is clearly in evidence; this increased the arcs of fire of the forward secondary guns to such an extent that they could even fire directly ahead. *BfZ*

The modernisation of *Hyuga* and *Ise* took place between 1934 and 1937 and followed the pattern set by the *Fuso* class. *Hyuga* is seen here on 10 May 1937 in the Bay of Sukumo, a few weeks after completion; her new torpedo bulges are clearly visible. The ships were lengthened by several feet, one funnel was removed, and top speed was increased by 1.7kts. *BfZ*

The Japanese lost four aircraft carriers at the Battle of Midway, and in order to make up for these losses as quickly as possible a series of emergency measures was decided upon; one of these was the conversion of *Hyuga* and *Ise* to 'battleship-carriers'. The two after turrets were removed and a flight deck with a hangar below was substituted. This is *Ise*, photographed after her conversion on 24 August 1943. *Ships of the World*

Hyuga (shown here) and *Ise* could never of course be described as 'real' aircraft carriers after their conversion, since although aircraft could take off from them they could not land back on board. Each ship was scheduled to receive 22 dive-bombers, operating from two catapults, but by the time the conversions were complete dive-bombers were no longer available and so the work had been in vain. *Ships of the World*

Together, in the same place, and on the same day, *Hyuga* and *Ise* both perished, just as their predecessors *Fuso* and *Yamashiro* had done. *Hyuga* and *Ise* met their fate at Kure on 28 July 1945, where they were both hit by numerous bombs during heavy attacks by US carrier aricraft, and both settled to the bottom. The two ships are seen here after the end of the war; *Hyuga* (above), photographed in August 1946, and *Ise* pictured around early 1946. *Fukui/Author's Collection*

The Royal Navy's decision to adopt a 15in (38.1cm) gun at first brought no apparent reaction from the Japanese Navy; however, when war broke out in Europe, the Japanese Naval Command thought the time ripe to consider an increase in calibre, and by going for a 16in (40.6cm) weapon they secured a substantial advantage over every other naval power. The first battleship to be equipped with this new gun was *Nagato*; when commissioned in the autumn of 1920, she was the most powerful battleship of her time, and remained so until the autumn of 1927, when the British *Nelsons*, which had the same calibre but more barrels, were completed, although admittedly she had rivals as early as 1921 in the American *Colorados*. *Mutsu*, commissioned one year after *Nagato*, is shown here in the autumn of 1921. Both ships were fitted with torpedo nets, even though other navies had long since abandoned them. *BfZ*

Following World War I the Japanese Navy conducted a number of experiments with shipboard aircraft. In 1922 the battleship *Yamashiro* was fitted with a 62ft (19m) long flying-off platform on No 2 turret after the British pattern, from which a wheeled aircraft (a British Gloster Sparrowhawk) could be launched. The next tests were carried out in 1925–26 with a 59ft (18m) platform supplied by the German aircraft manufacturer Ernst Heinkel. From this a floatplane could be launched, by placing it on a dolly which ran on rails to the end of the slightly inclined platform. *Nagato* was the only ship to be fitted with the Heinkel system, as shown in the photograph. *Author's Collection*

Nagato at Yokosuka on 12 April 1922, without torpedo nets and with a tall, curved cap on her forefunnel. Note that the foremast is no longer of tripod design, but had six legs. *Author's Collection*

Smoke discharging from the forefunnel proved a great hindrance to bridge operations on board *Nagato* and *Mutsu*, and since the clinker screen fitted subsequently did not improve the situation more radical measures were taken: the forward stack was curved back in an 'S' shape from the bridge to the mast, and this greatly improved matters. The silhouette of the two battleships was so dramatically altered that from then on they could not be mistaken for any other warships. This was by no means an advantage, since identification by an enemy was made that much easier. This is *Mutsu* in 1929. *BfZ*

A view from *Mutsu*'s bridgework looking aft, with the 'S' shaped smokestack in the foreground. The photo dates from 1933. *BfZ*

Nagato and *Mutsu* were not only exceptionally powerful battleships, they were also faster than any comparable battleships of foreign navies at this time (including the British *Nelson*s which were superior to them by one 16in gun), although this situation only became clear after the end of the Second World War. To the last the Japanese had claimed the speed of *Nagato* and *Mutsu* to be 23kts, or at least had never attempted to correct this erroneous information. In fact the ships achieved a speed of 26.7kts, which was exceptional for the time. This photo shows *Mutsu* around 1924–25. *BfZ*

Nagato and *Mutsu* were 'rejuvenated' in the 1930s by means of a major reconstruction following the same general scheme as the battleships modernised beforehand. The work was begun in 1934, and in the course of 1936 both ships rejoined the Fleet, considerably stronger and more powerful than before. They had been increased in length; their new machinery still allowed them to make 25kts; the elevation of their heavy guns had been increased to a maximum 43° (which improved their range substantially); and modern fire control equipment had improved the accuracy of their gunnery. Their external appearance had also changed considerably, especially since they now only had one funnel, a feature which helped to make their silhouettes much less recognisable. The photograph shows *Mutsu* on 20 May 1936 at Yokosuka Navy Yard, at an advanced stage of her reconstruction. The torpedo bulge is very obvious. *BfZ*

Mutsu after reconstruction, 30 January 1937. Her new silhouette is very evident. *BfZ*

At the news of the American landings in Leyte Gulf on 20 October 1944, a large number of Japanese naval units were sent into action; amongst these were seven battleships, which steamed from Lingga Bay near Singapore to Brunei on the north-east coast of Borneo for refuelling, where this picture was taken on the morning of 20 October 1944. *Nagato* is in the foreground, with (behind her) *Musashi* (with the heavy cruiser *Mogami* in front), whilst right in the background is *Yamato*. Four days later *Musashi* fell victim to US carrier aricraft in the Sibuyan Sea, yet the Japanese advanced and met a group of American escort carriers east of Samar on 25 October, sinking one carrier and three destroyers. This was *Nagato*'s last wartime operation. *BfZ*

Nagato was the only Japanese battleship to survive the war: after returning from the south-west Pacific in the autumn of 1944, she remained in Yokosuka, seeing no further action owing to lack of fuel. This is how the Americans found the ship at the end of the war: her funnel and parts of the mainmast had been removed in the interests of camouflage. In the background the US battleship *South Dakota* lies at anchor. *BfZ*

On 20 September 1945 the Americans seized *Nagato* as 'spoils of war'. Little more remained for her as her fate had already been decided: she was to become a target ship for the atomic bomb tests planned for Bikini Atoll. This photo dates from the first days after the Japanese surrender; note the US personnel on the forecastle deck. *Author's Collection*

Tosa class

Japan's reaction to the acceleration in American capital shipbuilding was her so-called '8–8' programme of 1918, but the fact that this acceleration occurred at all on the other side of the Pacific was plainly the result of the Japanese adopting a 16in (40.6cm) gun calibre, a move considered in the USA to be an indication of Japanese expansion. This '8–8' programme included the building of eight battleships and eight battlecruisers: Nos 1 and 2 were *Nagato* and *Mutsu*, to be followed by the 'high speed battleships' *Tosa* and *Kaga*. The latter can be thought of as further developments of the *Nagato* class, just as fast as their predecessors, but with a main armament increased by two barrels. The first ship to be laid down at the Mitsubishi yard at Nagasaki was *Tosa*, in February 1920, and she was launched on 18 December 1921, from the very same slipway, incidentally, on which the 'super battleship' *Musashi* would be built two decades later. Here *Tosa* is seen immediately before being launched. *Mitsubishi*

Before the renewed naval arms race had reached its peak, the Washington Naval Treaty of 1922 was concluded: understanding had prevailed, and with it the good sense that the realisation that these new fleet building programmes would in no way make peace more secure but only place new burdens on the nations concerned after a war that had enormously depleted their resources and had only just ended. The treaty partners agreed that none of the capital ships which had been begun – with a very few exceptions – could be completed, and none of those planned could be laid down. This affected *Tosa* and *Kaga* – and Japan had to dispose of both these ships. *Tosa* was therefore to be used as a test ship for explosives trials which were carried out in several series in June 1924; the results gained were so useful that for years they served as the basis for calculating the measure of protection required for heavy warships, right up to the 'super battleships' of the *Yamato* class. After this series of tests had been completed, *Tosa* was sunk in the Bungo Strait on 9 February 1925, a target ship for gunnery practice by Japanese warships. The photograph shows *Tosa* fitted out as a test ship. The covered opening for No 3 barbette can just be seen, right in the foreground, in front of the relatively small superstructure deck. There is no funnel as such, but a narrow exhaust pipe is fitted for the ship's heating system. The bridge superstructure with its light signal mast is also a temporary fitting. Just abaft the rear edge of the superstructure deck can be seen the locations for the mainmast. *Author's Collection*

Kaga would have been broken up, but before this could happen Japan was struck by the earthquake disaster of 1 September 1923. As a result of this the battlecruiser *Amagi*, which had been scheduled for conversion into an aircraft carrier, was so severely damaged that the plans for her had to be abandoned. As Japan, under the terms of the Washington Treaty, had been granted the right to convert two capital ships under construction into aircraft carriers, the decision was made to rebuild *Kaga* instead of *Amagi*. Work on her was begun in November 1923, not at the Mitsubishi yard in Nagasaki, but at the Navy yard at Yokosuka, since the yard already had a considerable fund of experience as a result of the preparatory work carried out there on *Amagi*. She is shown here in the early stages of her conversion: the photo was taken on 20 September 1927, and shows the original battleship stern with the Admiral's walk, which was later removed. *BfZ*

Kaga's appearance in 1928 on completion. The 'stepped' outline forward is easily discerned: first the flying-off deck extending right forward as an extension of the lower hangar deck, then the upper hangar deck with its flanking 8in (20.3cm) turrets, and finally the completely flat flight deck. In the 1930s *Kaga* was given a complete refit. *BfZ*

Amagi class

After the fast battleships of the *Tosa* class, the Japanese ordered four battlecruisers: *Amagi*, *Akagi*, *Takao* and *Atago*. Following these, a class of four capital ships was planned which differed only in detail from each other: *Owari*, *Kii* and Nos 11 and 12, for which the names *Kinko* and *Shunka* had been allotted, probably speculatively. Whilst the four *Amagi*s were classified as *Junyo Senkan* – ie battlecruisers – the *Owari*s were classified as *Kosoku Senkan*, or fast battleships. The difference lay in the 1/4kt higher speed of the *Amagi*s and in the *Owari*s' 38mm (1 1/2in) thicker side armour – although the *Amagi* class had 28mm thicker horizontal armour. Only the four battlecruisers were laid down; even they could not be completed, certainly not in the planned form, but the conversion of two of them to aircraft carriers was allowed. The choice fell upon the two most advanced battlecruisers, *Amagi* and *Akagi*, especially as they were designed for high speed, which would be required of an aircraft carrier. The rebuilding of *Amagi* was not possible because of the damage caused by the earthquake on 1 September 1923; *Kaga* was therefore converted to an aircraft carrier in her place. *Akagi*, laid down in the naval dockyard at Kure in December 1920, was finished at Sasebo Navy Yard after floating out – the photograph shows her on 7 April 1925 as she was first floated in her dock. Two weeks later, on 22 April 1925, *Akagi* was moved out of the dock and this date is taken to be her official launching. *Ships of the World*

Akagi as she appeared when completed; the similarity with *Kaga* is obvious. However, *Akagi* only had an exhaust duct on the starboard side, which projected sideways but was not canted towards the stern. The photo dates from 1930. *BfZ*

Kaga and *Akagi* were completely modernised in the mid-1930s. Amongst other things, they were fitted with torpedo bulges, new machinery and new boilers, an extended flight deck and an island. *Akagi*'s island was erected on the port side, in contrast to the general carrier practice of using a starboard location. The 8in (20.3cm) turrets were removed, but the Navy, not wanting to lose these guns, installed four new casemates on *Kaga*, two either side aft and with one 8in gun in each, thus bringing the total to ten barrels again, the same as before. *Akagi*'s six remaining casemate guns were considered adequate, although this was certainly not because the Japanese had realised the ineffectiveness of fitting heavy guns on board aircraft carriers. The reason was purely technical, with space limitations probably being the crucial factor. During the war these guns were never fired against enemy targets, although to be fair they had little opportunity: both carriers were sunk in June 1942 during the Battle of Midway, *BfZ*

The Japanese '8–8' programme was intended to be completed by Nos 13 to 16: 47,500-ton 'super battleships' with 18in (45.7cm) guns, a maximum speed of 30kts, and armour that would offer protection against hits by shells of the same calibre; hence they would have been the most powerful capital ships in the world. The highly talented British expert Oscar Parkes, who died in 1958 after many years of work producing drawings on paper and canvas, immortalised these and the other Japanese projects of the time in his personal style. Amongst them were the design studies begun in 1930 for the replacement vessels for *Kongo* and *Fuso*, the former conceived by a team under the leadership of Admiral Hiraga, the latter designed by Captain Fujimoto. They were both designed as 'treaty' battleships, ie their displacement and main calibre were within the qualitative limits of the 1922 Washington Treaty; however, they did not come to fruition any more than the designs of the '8–8' programme, since Japan was forced by a variety of circumstances to be a signatory to the 1930 London Naval Treaty, which extended the moratorium on battleship building until the end of 1936. Top left is a *Tosa* class battleship; top right, a battlecruiser of the *Amagi* class; centre left, one of the 47,500-ton No 13–16 battleships; centre right, the battleship design by Hiraga; and at the bottom the design by Fujimoto. *The Navy*

What Japan had not been able to produce in the early 1920s was made up for fifteen years later: the construction of 'super battleships' which would put all others in the shade. The Japanese had never really been able to accept the fact that international treaties had placed severe restrictions on the expansion of her fleet during the period after World War I, and even considered them humiliating. Hence the voices of those who demanded an unconditional expansion of the Navy grew ever louder, and eventually this lobby prevailed. In 1934 preparations were made for the resumption of battleship building, and in 1937 the first ship, *Yamato*, was laid down; *Musashi*, the second, followed in 1938, and in 1940 the third and fourth ships were ordered. *Yamato* was the first to be commissioned, late in 1941, and *Musashi* followed the next summer, a few weeks after Midway, a battle which ironically had provided very obvious indications that the final arbiter at sea was no longer the battleship but the aircraft carrier. This photo dates from 20 September 1941 and shows *Yamato* at Kure Navy Yard. Routine dockyard work is in progress. Here can be seen one of the mighty 46cm (18.1in) triple turrets, two secondary battery triple turrets, and several 5in (12.7cm) twin AA guns. The secondary turrets on either beam were later removed to make space for additional AA weapons. Aft of the 46cm turret, on the quarterdeck, can be seen a few wooden huts, which would have been used as temporary workshops, stores, etc. The vessel to the extreme right of the photograph is an aircraft carrier. *BfZ*

Yamato successfully completed her builder's trials in October 1941, and it was then only a few weeks before she was commissioned – 16 December 1941, exactly one week after the attack on Pearl Harbor. These photos were taken during her trials, between 20 and 30 October. *BfZ*

Truk Atoll in the Carolines served as Japan's main base until early 1944, and was heavily defended. This photo dates from the summer of 1943, and shows both *Yamato*s at anchor. Awnings have been rigged on board *Musashi* (foreground) because of the heat. *Author's Collection*

Great size, strength, power – these virtues were not enough to ensure the battleship's survival, and by no means enough to withstand attack by aircraft; the latter proved to be the battleship's mortal enemy. The Japanese 'super battleships' were no exception: both were lost to aerial attack. These two photographs (taken on 24 October 1944, the day *Musashi* went down) show *Yamato* from different viewpoints. On this occasion she was fortunate and survived, but the final hour was merely postponed. Both photos were shot by American carrier aircraft during their attacks. *Author's Collection*

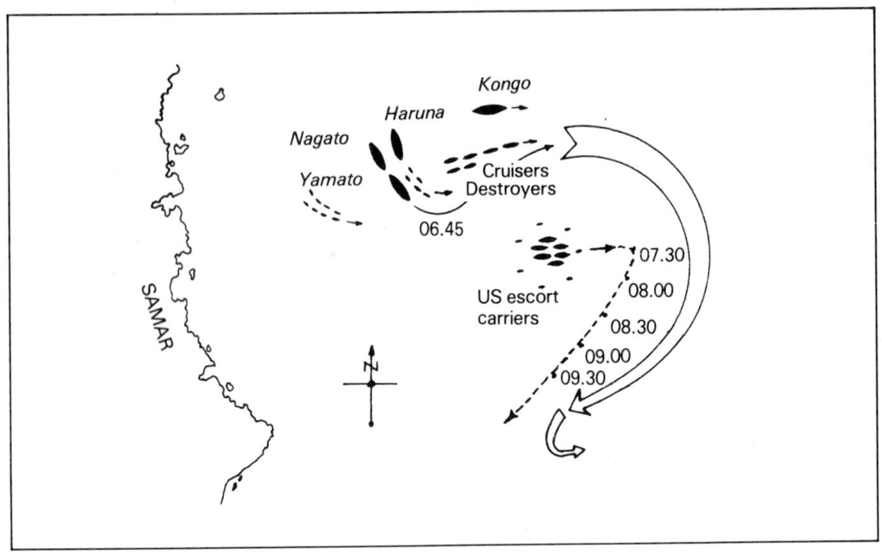

The Battle of Leyte Gulf saw the demise of the 'super battleship' *Musashi*. Together with her sister-ship *Yamato* she tackled the enemy landing fleet; they were accompanied by the battleships *Nagato*, *Haruna* and *Kongo*, and also cruisers and destroyers, but not a single aircraft carrier was on hand. *Musashi* was attacked by large numbers of American carrier aircraft, was hit by about thirty bombs and torpedoes, and finally sank. The Japanese force carried on and came upon a group of American escort aircraft carriers, with a destroyer escort, to the east of Samar. The carrier aircraft immediately took off and attacked. Although the Japanese were forced to take evasive action again and again, their cruisers eventually managed to get within range of the escort carriers, and opened fire; the battleships then joined in, and *Yamato* fired 104 salvoes from her main armament. This was the only time that she had an enemy in her sights. The Americans lost the escort carrier *Gambier Bay* and three of her escorting destroyers. The map shows the course of the engagement from the time the Americans came into sight until the Japanese force retreated before the unrelenting aerial attacks and turned towards the San Bernardino Strait.

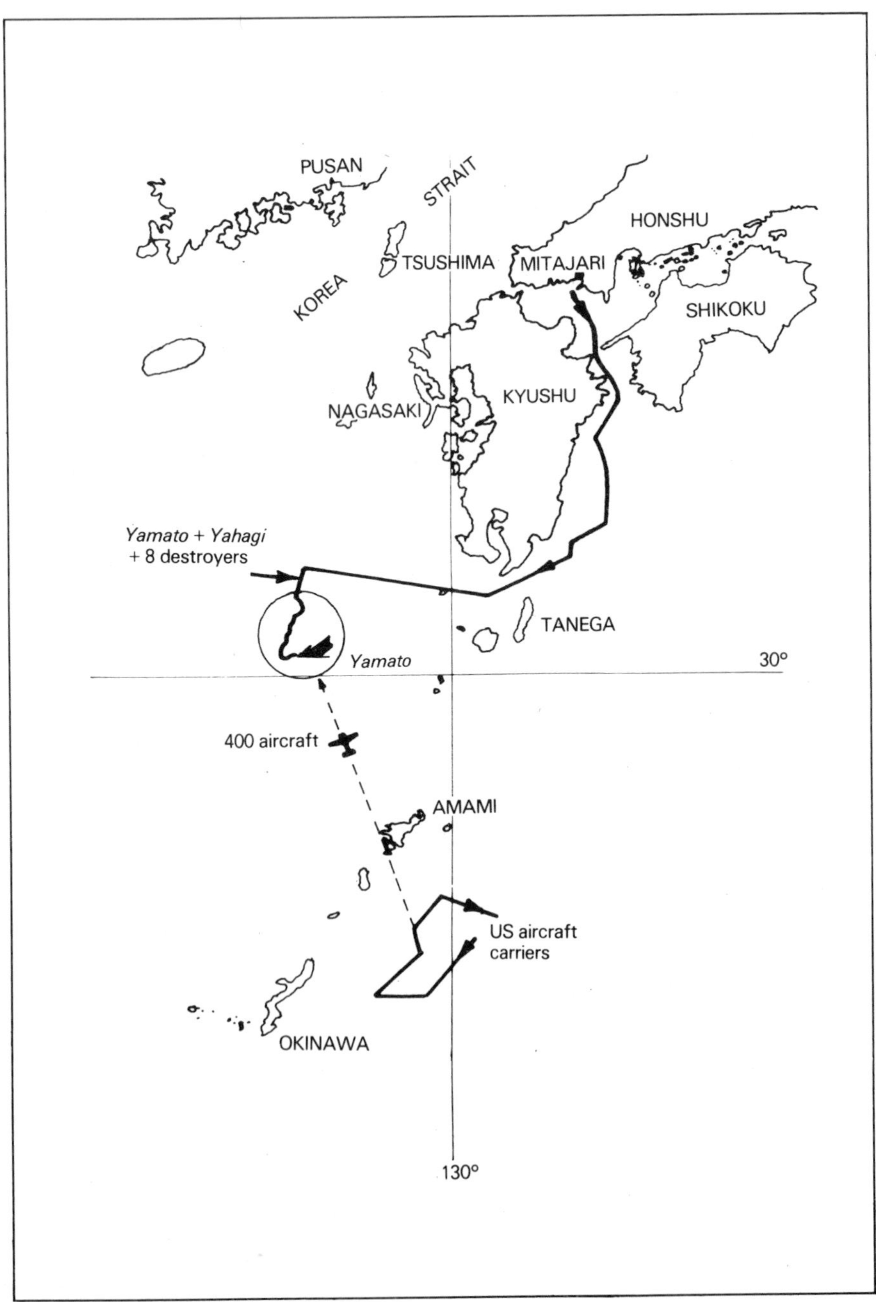

On 6 April 1945 the Americans landed at Okinawa and brought the war precariously close to the Japanese homeland. The Japanese used large numbers of Kamikaze aircraft in an attempt to weaken the enemy and force him to abandon the operation, and to this end they sent a naval force consisting of the battleship *Yamato*, the light cruiser *Yahagi* and eight destroyers – but no aircraft carriers – into action. However, the group was quickly picked up by American reconnaissance, and on the morning of 7 April, when the group was south-west of Kyushu, a large number of American carrier aircraft from Task Groups 58.1 and 58.3 attacked, sinking the cruiser and one destroyer, and hitting *Yamato* with two bombs and one torpedo. Early in the afternoon US aircraft attacked again and finished off *Yamato* with nine torpedoes and three bombs. She sank taking most of her crew – nearly 2500 men – with her, and the Japanese had lost their last 'super battleship'. The Americans, for their part, had used 386 aircraft against the enemy force. The map traces the course of *Yamato*'s final voyage.

The third *Yamato* class battleship, *Shinano*, was laid down at Yokosuka early in 1940, but was completed as an aircraft carrier; the Japanese decided on this move to compensate for the carrier losses sustained during the Battle of Midway. *Shinano*'s career was short, and had a tragic end: ten days after being commissioned she crossed the path of an American submarine during trials, and was hit by six torpedoes. She could not be prevented from sinking. Not a single photograph of the ship has been discovered, but Shizuo Fukui, the well-known Japanese naval writer and artist, has provided this masterly portrait. *Fukui*

In their Fifth Naval Expansion Programme, which was drawn up before the war, the Japanese had included two battlecruisers (Nos 795 and 796). They developed a 31cm (12.2in) gun for these ships, and trials with this began in 1941. However, when details of the American *Alaska* class cruisers became known, a heavier calibre was decided on: instead of the nine 31cm guns originally planned, six 36cm (14.2in) weapons were substituted, to be disposed in twin turrets instead of the original triple turrets. Neither of these two battlecruisers was built: the plans were shelved after the successes of Pearl Harbor, since the building of further aircraft carriers now had priority. The photograph is of a model representing this class. *Author's Collection*

It was not the *Yamato* class that was intended to be the *ne plus ultra* of Japanese battleship design, but Nos 798 and 799 of the Fifth Fleet Expansion Programme. These 70,000-ton giants were to be fitted with 50.8cm (20in) guns, six in number and grouped in twin turrets. No details or plans of the ships have ever come to light; whether this model of a super *Yamato*, based largely on the *Yamato*s themselves, does justice to the designs cannot be said with certainty. *Ships of the World*

France

In 1902, when capital ship development was leading towards the 'all-big-gun' battleship, the new French Navy Minister, Pelletan, took office. He was a strong advocate of the *Jeune Ecole* and a powerful opponent of battleship building. Under his influence there were considerable delays in the building of the *République* class battleships, which had been laid down shortly after the turn of the century, and they only joined the fleet in 1906–08. It was only after Pelletan's departure that a change of direction took place – mainly as a result of the naval battle at Tsushima: France's naval high command began to free itself from the Utopian teachings of the *Jeune Ecole* and found its way back to the attitudes prevalent in other navies. By that time, however, the difficulties of French internal politics had become an important factor in the drawing up of a naval construction programme, as had the inadequate capacity of her industry. For these reasons the 1906 budget once more included the old type of battleships (*Danton* class), although these did feature a heavy intermediate calibre. There were six *Danton*s, and it seems as if the French wanted to catch up as fast as possible on what they had missed, and had therefore given priority to quantity rather than quality. The ships were not only inadequate, they grew to be quite a problem: outmoded even before they were completed, they occupied a major portion of France's shipbuilding capacity for years. It would have been more sensible – and not only with the benefit of hindsight – to order only two ships instead of the six, and make the funds saved available for future capital ships. Judging by their displacement and dimensions, it would have been entirely possible to equip these ships with two or four extra 30.5cm (12in) guns instead of the twelve secondary 24cm (9.4in) guns. The fact that this simple solution was not adopted may indicate the insecurity that the teachings of the *Jeune Ecole* had caused. There was certainly no shortage of proposals and discussions which should have shown the right direction: even in 1907 alternative ideas had been put forward which envisaged future battleships as having a uniform main armament consisting of a large number of barrels. For the *Danton* class, it would even have been better to have twenty 24cm guns than the four 30.5cm and twelve 24cm weapons, if only from the point of view of having a uniform fire control system, and this possibility was also discussed at the design stage. The *Danton* class – typified by *Voltaire* (shown here) – had an unmistakable silhouette, thanks to its five funnels in two groups. *BfZ*

It was not until five years after the British *Dreadnought* was laid down that France managed to make the transition to 'all-big-gun' battleships; for this the French had their energetic new Navy Minister, Delcassé, to thank – it was he who, together with the newly appointed Commander-in-Chief, Admiral de Lapeyrère, gradually managed to raise the fighting efficiency of the fleet. The first French dreadnought was *Courbet*, shown here immediately after being launched on 23 September 1911 at the navy yard at Brest. The closely grouped secondary armament casemates can be clearly made out. *French Navy (Author's Collection)*

The third unit of the *Courbet* class was *France*, laid down in November 1911 at Atéliers et Chantiers de la Loire (St-Nazaire) and launched one year later. The characteristic bow shape had been introduced by French designers in the *Danton* class, and represented advanced thinking: every other navy which had adopted dreadnoughts persisted in fitting a ram bow, which was in reality a relic of a form of battle which had long since been left behind. The French had correctly realised that ramming, although once a decisive tactic, was a thing of the past, outmoded by the much greater ranges at which battle was now sought thanks to the developments in naval gunnery and armour plating. This picture dates from 7 November 1912 and shows *France* leaving her slipway. *French Navy (Author's Collection)*

Courbet as completed. The class still showed features reminiscent of the multi-funnel warship architecture which evolved in the previous century.

Another photo of *Courbet* in her original configuration. The positioning of the foremast abaft the foreward funnels recalls British practice with *Dreadnought*, *Colossus*, *Orion* and *Lion*. *Author's Collection*

France was commissioned the month the First World War broke out; a few days later she took part in a foray into the Adriatic from Malta (where the French fleet had assembled), with the intention of breaking the Austrian naval blockade of Montenegro. The greatly superior French force was met by the Austro-Hungarian cruiser *Zenta*, which sank under their fire, and one destroyer, which escaped. This is *France*, evidently soon after a wartime refit, with almost immaculate paintwork. The two bands around the second funnel indicate the division to which she belongs. The Triplex rangefinder above the bridge can also be seen, each of its three bases being 3.66m (12ft) long. The device was installed during the war, and was also to be found on board Italian capital ships. *BfZ*

On 26 August 1922 *France* ran aground on uncharted rocks in Quiberon Bay during a storm. Salvage was virtually impossible and the wreck (see photo) was left to her fate, although parts were later broken up on the spot. *BfZ*

Courbet after her first reconstruction, which was carried out between 1921 and 1922. Her external appearance was altered in several important respects: her two forward funnels were trunked together, and in front of this a tall, sturdy tripod mast was fitted, to carry her modern fire control systems. The mainmast was cut down in 1918 to allow sufficient freedom of movement for the tethered balloon that was carried; two outriggers projecting forward from the mast were used as antenna attachment points, as can be seen in the photograph. *French Navy (Author's Collection)*

Paris was taken in hand for a very similar modernisation to that of her sister-ship *Courbet* in 1923–24, the differences mainly concerning the forward funnels: *Courbet* now only had one stack whereas *Paris* retained two, although they were fitted so close together that they looked like one unit, especially from a distance. This photo was taken after *Paris'* second modernisation (1928–29), in which new boilers, fire control systems and AA weapons were installed. On this occasion the forward funnels were raised by about 2m (6ft); previously they had finished roughly flush with the top edge of the upper bridge platform. The base of the original mast, which was left in position during the refit, can be seen abaft the forward funnels. *French Navy (Author's Collection)*

Courbet also underwent a second modernisation, in which she too was fitted with new boilers, fire control systems and AA weapons, the boilers having originally been built for the *Normandie* class battleships. From then on she again featured a full mainmast. Range clocks, a feature of other nations' battleships in those years, can also be seen, at the foretop. The photo dates from before 1938–39, as the antenna stays which were fitted at this time on the after funnel are not yet in place. After their second reconstructions *Courbet* and her sister-ship *Paris* served only as training ships. *Author's Collection*

A rare sight: *Paris* flying the Union Jack, at Plymouth in 1942. Together with her sister-ship *Courbet*, she was moved to the south coast of England in June 1940, and both vessels were requisitioned by Britain on 3 July of that year after France's capitulation, as part of Operation 'Catapult'. *Courbet* was placed at the disposal of the Free French Forces (FNFL) in 1943, and after temporary use as an AA and radar training ship she was beached near Ouistreham to serve as a breakwater during the Normandy invasion, and was broken up there later; *Paris* served as an accommodation ship for Polish sailors and was not used in the war again. In August 1945 she returned to Brest, but never re-entered service, remaining there for another ten years until she was sold in December 1955. She was broken up the following year. The bow wave painted on the hull was intended to deceive the enemy but could hardly be taken seriously on this old ship as her engines could not even muster 18kts. *Author's Collection*

Jean Bart, the second unit of the *Courbet* class, was different from her sister-ships in that she featured 'gooseneck' cranes. She was the only French capital ship to be damaged by enemy action during the First World War. In December 1914 she crossed the path of an Austro-Hungarian submarine in the Otranto Straits during a sortie into the Adriatic, and she was hit by a torpedo forward, resulting in about 1000 tons of water being taken aboard; severely damaged, she had to be towed to Malta. This blow came as a shock to the French Navy, and from then on only cruisers were used in the blockade of the Otranto Straits. In 1937 the ship had to give up her name to a new battleship, and was rechristened *Océan*, serving as a training hulk (she had been used as a training ship since 1931). On 27 November 1942 she shared the fate of the principal ships of the French Navy at Toulon, where she was grounded, although the *Kriegsmarine* used the wreck as a gunnery target. This very early photograph shows *Jean Bart* as she was when first commissioned. *Author's Collection*

The building of the three *Provence* class battleships planned in the 1912 budget took place just at the time Great Britain was embarking on her 'super-dreadnought' programme. Following the example of Britain and other naval powers, France had increased the main calibre in her ships from 30.5cm (12in) to 34cm (13.4in), which involved a reduction in the number of barrels by two compared with the *Courbets*. This was no real disadvantage, as the wing turret arrangement of the *Courbet* class had been abandoned and replaced by a single turret on the centreline amidships, which could fire on either beam. The hull shape was almost unchanged from the *Courbet* class, and the overall dimensions were virtually identical, factors which allowed the building time to be slightly accelerated. *Lorraine* is seen here during fitting-out beneath the 150-ton crane at her shipyard, Atéliers et Chantiers de la Loire et Penhoët of St-Nazaire. This picture dates from around 1914 or 1915. *Author's Collection*

Provence, France's 'super-dreadnought', was commissioned in the summer of 1915, and she is shown here at high speed. The dense black smoke is indicative of coal-fired boilers, although the ships had additional oil firing. The booms for the Bullivant torpedo net system are also visible here; the system was removed in 1917, as it proved virtually useless in practice, as was discovered by all the other navies. In the same year the elevation of the guns of No 5 turret was increased from 12° to 18°, thus extending their range from 14,500 to 18,000yds. *French Navy (Author's Collection)*

Lorraine was completed only after long delays caused by industrial problems due to the war: although her sister-ships took slightly more than three years to build, it was four years before her flag could be raised. This photograph demonstrates what fine, compact lines she possessed. A characteristic feature of French warships of the time was the funnel cap, where a plate-shaped section was mounted above the jacket. Note the height of No 3 turret – the same as that of No 2. The photo dates from 1916–17 since the torpedo net booms are still in place. *French Navy (Author's Collection)*

On 31 August 1918 it was decided to equip *Bretagne* with modern fire control systems during her next refit at Brest; this necessitated a tripod foremast in place of the previous pole mast. The modernisation was begun the same year, and completed in 1920. Here *Bretagne* is seen in drydock, still in her original condition. French capital ships carried their stern anchor hanging free, instead of in a hawsepipe. *French Navy (Author's Collection)*

In the development of shipboard aircraft facilities the French Navy trod its own path. In 1918 and 1920 the battleships *Paris* and *Bretagne* were equipped with a flying-off platform on No 2 turret for short-term experiments, and in 1924 a different system was tried on *Lorraine*. She was fitted with a suspended ramp roughly half way up her foremast (see photo); this projected forward and to starboard, and from it was hung a small aircraft, which was accelerated forward on a runner until it was released at the end of the ramp. This system had been developed by the US Navy for the airships *Akron* and *Macon*. It was not so much the difficulties in the launching procedure which caused the French to abandon the experiments, but rather the complicated method by which the aircraft had to be manoeuvred to the foremast and hoisted up to the launching ramp. *Author's Collection*

A detail view of *Lorraine*'s experimental aircraft ramp, to which the aircraft has just been hoisted. After it had been secured the aircraft had to be pushed back to the mast before it could take off. *Author's Collection*

Lorraine's boilers were given additional oil-firing capability in the late 1920s, as were those of her sister-ships, and new fire control equipment was also fitted, but these alterations made virtually no difference to her external appearance – *Lorraine* looks here exactly as she did after her first reconstruction, when she had been fitted with, amongst other things, a tripod mast. *French Navy (Author's Collection)*

Bretagne looked almost exactly the same as *Lorraine* after her conversion; to differentiate between the two ships one had to look very closely, but one distinguishing feature was the thick steam pipe behind the forefunnel, which was fitted only to *Bretagne*. Both ships had had their forward 13.8cm (5.4in) guns removed during the first reconstruction because water entered the casemates when the ships were travelling at high speed. *French Navy (Author's Collection)*

All three of the *Provence* class units underwent further reconstruction in the early 1930s. As part of this they were given modern, high-performance boilers, exclusively oil-fired and six in number – eighteen less than previously, but with a combined output that was nevertheless much higher. Fed by the new boilers, the engines produced 43,000shp instead of the original 29,000. In addition, new fire control equipment was once more installed, the AA defence was reinforced again, and the main armament was fitted with new barrels; protection was also improved to a limited extent. *Bretagne* is seen here during her reconstruction, at La Seyne around 1934. *BfZ*

During their third reconstruction, all three *Provence* class vessels were fitted with the 34cm (13.4in) guns originally intended for the *Normandie* class battleships, and their secondary armament was reduced by a further four barrels (the two aftermost weapons on each side), allowing the heavy AA armament to be doubled. From now on the after funnel was the same height as the forward one. This is *Provence* in about 1935, after her modernisation. *Author's Collection*

Bretagne in about 1938, also after her reconstruction. Note the antenna outriggers on the after funnel and the long 'lattice' type yardarms on the tripod mast. *Author's Collection*

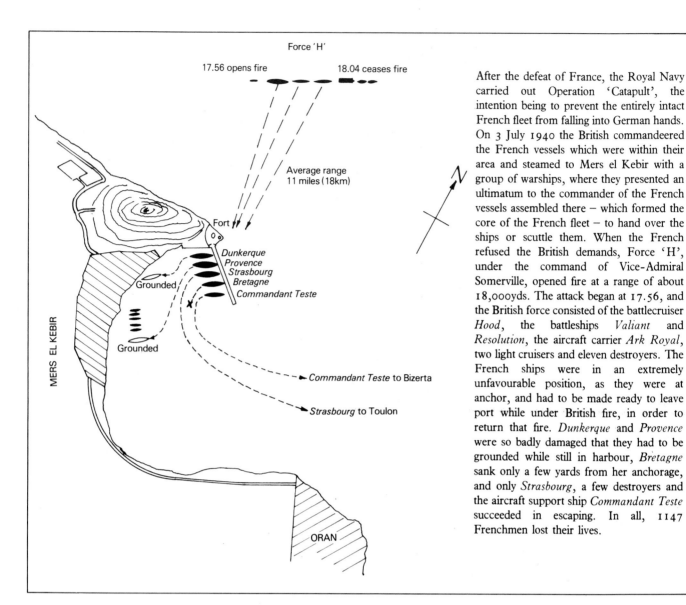

Force 'H'

17.56 opens fire

18.04 ceases fire

Average range
11 miles (18km)

Fort

Dunkerque
Provence
Strasbourg
Bretagne
Commandant Teste

Grounded

Grounded

MERS EL KEBIR

Commandant Teste to Bizerta

Strasbourg to Toulon

ORAN

N

After the defeat of France, the Royal Navy carried out Operation 'Catapult', the intention being to prevent the entirely intact French fleet from falling into German hands. On 3 July 1940 the British commandeered the French vessels which were within their area and steamed to Mers el Kebir with a group of warships, where they presented an ultimatum to the commander of the French vessels assembled there – which formed the core of the French fleet – to hand over the ships or scuttle them. When the French refused the British demands, Force 'H', under the command of Vice-Admiral Somerville, opened fire at a range of about 18,000yds. The attack began at 17.56, and the British force consisted of the battlecruiser *Hood*, the battleships *Valiant* and *Resolution*, the aircraft carrier *Ark Royal*, two light cruisers and eleven destroyers. The French ships were in an extremely unfavourable position, as they were at anchor, and had to be made ready to leave port while under British fire, in order to return that fire. *Dunkerque* and *Provence* were so badly damaged that they had to be grounded while still in harbour, *Bretagne* sank only a few yards from her anchorage, and only *Strasbourg*, a few destroyers and the aircraft support ship *Commandant Teste* succeeded in escaping. In all, 1147 Frenchmen lost their lives.

Operation 'Catapult' took the French vessels by surprise. *Provence* (foreground) was badly hit and had to be beached in the shallows; she was salvaged, and was taken to Toulon in November 1940. *Bretagne* had an even harder time, capsizing under the British fire after suffering major explosions. In 1952 she was salvaged and then scrapped. She is seen in the background here, already ablaze; between her and *Provence*, *Strasbourg* is trying to escape. *Author's Collection*

Lorraine's third reconstruction was much more extensive than that of her sisters. It began in the summer of 1934 and was completed by early 1936. No 3 turret was replaced by aircraft equipment: a large hangar was erected, housing four aircraft, and a 22m (72ft) long fully revolving catapult was installed on its roof. The machines were stowed in the hangar via one of two cranes, entry being at the side. To make space for the hangar, the after funnel had to be moved back 5m (16½ft). *Lorraine* was at anchor in Alexandria on 3 July 1940 and fell into British hands in Operation 'Catapult'; she was transferred to the Free French Forces on 31 May 1943, who raised steam and moved her to Dakar. In the following two years *Lorraine* took part in active operations again: firstly in August 1944 in the Allied invasion of southern France, later in the blockade of the Gironde estuary, and in April 1945 in the attack on the German 'Atlantic fortress' of Royan-Gironde Nord, in all instances bombarding German-held positions. After the end of the war she was retained as a training ship and then a hulk up to 1953. The photo shows her on 13 September 1944 during the return voyage of the French fleet to Toulon, which had just been liberated. Her aircraft equipment has already been removed. *BfZ*

Normandie class

The French Navy's main contribution to the development of capital ships was the introduction of the quadruple turret for the main armament, although the recently adopted 34cm (13.4in) calibre was not increased. The first ships scheduled to be fitted with such mountings were the four units of the *Normandie* class, which were authorised under the 1913 Programme. A second class of four battleships, also to be fitted with 34cm quadruple turrets, was planned – the *Lyon* class. The four *Normandie* class ships were all laid down in 1913 and were launched in 1914–15. This is *Languedoc* leaving her slip, 1 May 1915. *French Navy (Author's Collection)*

Work on the *Normandie*s was hampered by the outbreak of war and finally stopped altogether in the summer of 1915, initially because many of the yard's workmen were called up into the Army although later the reason became the critical state of the country brought about by the war effort. In the end, work only progressed far enough to enable the slipways to be cleared. After the war ended, all the hulls were scrapped, although a purely academic study was carried out in 1919 on the possibility of completing the ships as battlecruisers. They would have had a top speed of 32kts and a modified main armament – six 43.2cm (17in) guns were considered. The illustration, taken from an oil painting, shows how the ships were intended to look according to the original plans. *French Navy (Author's Collection)*

Normandie on 19 October 1914, immediately after being launched. *French Navy (Author's Collection)*

In December 1913 a fifth *Normandie* class battleship was authorised, the reason being that after the four ships of the *Courbet* class only three *Provence*s had been built; the *Normandie*s were then increased by one unit – *Béarn* – in order to maintain divisional strength at four ships each. The new ship was intended to operate with the three *Provence* class vessels. *Béarn* was laid down early in 1914, although work on her was also stopped in the summer of 1915; work resumed in December 1918, but only in order to clear the slipway. She was able to leave the dockyard early in 1920, but she escaped the fate of her sisters: instead of being scrapped she was converted into an aircraft carrier, and was commissioned as such in the late summer of 1926. This photograph was taken on 1 February 1933. *French Navy (Author's Collection)*

Another view of *Béarn*. In comparison with British, American and Japanese carriers that had also been converted from capital ships, *Béarn* was less successful, not least on account of her inadequate speed. *French Navy (Author's Collection)*

In June 1940 *Béarn* was able to escape to Fort de France (Martinique), where she was decommissioned; four years later she was completely overhauled and re-armed at New Orleans, although she was only able to operate as an aircraft transport because of her low speed. She saw out the rest of the Second World War in this role, carrying troops and supplies to French Indo-China as the situation deteriorated. For the rest of her years she served as a training ship and later a hulk at Toulon. She was broken up in Italy in 1967. This photo, from 1945–46, shows how *Béarn* appeared in her role as an aircraft transport. *French Navy (Author's Collection)*

France received the German battleship *Thüringen* as part of her war reparations, but did not really know what to do with her. Delivered to Cherbourg in April 1920, she was used for a time as a target ship before being scrapped at Gâvres-Lorient in 1923–24. This picture shows her at Lorient, her breaking-up just under way. *Author's Collection*

The second capital ship which France received as reparations after the end of the First World War was *Prinz Eugen* of the former Austro-Hungarian Navy. She was transferred to Toulon in the summer of 1920, disarmed and largely stripped of her fittings, and then served as a bombing target. She was used finally as a gunnery target ship and for various experimental purposes. She is shown here beached after explosives trials; she sank soon afterwards under fire from the battleships *Bretagne* and *France*, south of Toulon. *BfZ*

The Washington Naval Treaty had given France the right to build one capital ship in 1926 and one in 1927 as replacements for her old battleships, which were no longer suitable for the needs of the time, and in addition she could claim a replacement ship for *France*, which had been lost in 1922. France only took up this option when Germany's first 10,000-ton 'pocket-battleship' was built. As their 'response' to the German armoured ships, the French laid down *Dunkerque* late in 1932, followed by *Strasbourg* two years later. Neither the displacement limit of 35,000 tons nor the permitted calibre of 16in (40.6cm) was reached, the French settling for a much lighter design of slightly over 26,000 tons with 33cm (13in) guns. Their advantage lay in their relatively high speed of over 29kts, which had basically only been possible by doing without thicker armour. By the usual standards the two *Dunkerque*s were really in the battlecruiser category, although this term no longer officially existed as the units concerned had been classed as 'capital ships' since the 1922 Naval Treaty. This is *Dunkerque*, shortly after being commissioned on 1 May 1937. In 1939 she was fitted with a taller funnel cap. *Author's Collection*

With the *Dunkerque* class the French were able to install the gunnery technology which they had been planning since before the First World War, initially for the *Normandie* class and later for the *Lyon* class. The choice of two quadruple turrets could be justified from a simple calculation: four 33cm twin turrets would require 6240 tons; two quadruple turrets weighed only 4520 tons – a total saving of 1720 tons. In order to prevent the diameter of the barbettes from assuming vast dimensions, the barrels had to be supported as pairs in a common cradle, and not in individual cradles. The turrets were grouped forward to keep the citadel as short as possible; the consequent savings in weight were used in improving protection in other areas. The turrets were arranged a considerable distance apart – 27m (88ft 6in), measured between the centres of each barbette – to make it less likely that a single hit would knock out both at once. Certain problems had to be coped with: for one thing there was the absorption of recoil by the ship's crew – the ships were relatively lightly built – and for another the conning tower was so badly affected by noise and smoke that the full arcs could not be exploited. Here *Dunkerque*'s No 1 turret is trained to starboard and seen shortly after firing a salvo. The photo was taken on 21 September 1936. *BfZ*

The French Navy originally wanted four *Dunkerque*s – at least, that number was considered necessary to keep a balance with the German 'pocket-battleships' – but in 1934, when Italy was preparing to exploit to the full the qualitative limits of the existing treaties by ordering two new battleships, the French altered their original plans and completed the *Dunkerque* class with *Strasbourg*, which was ordered in late autumn 1934. From then on they accelerated their design work on 'replies' to the Italian ships. This sequence of armament, counter-armament and 'response' armament is a typical example of how one wedge drives the next in the machinations of power politics. Here the half-completed *Strasbourg* is seen after her launching in December 1936. Hut-like buildings can be made out covering the secondary barbettes; these were intended to prevent damp and dirt entering the ship. The photo dates from 1937. *Author's Collection*

Strasbourg was commissioned late in 1938 and was only slightly different from her sister-ship. The main points of variance were in the bridge and foremast area: *Dunkerque* had a rotating rangefinder on top of the conning tower projecting from the bridge block, *Strasbourg*'s was located much higher up, on top of the tower bridge block. Her conning tower was therefore fully integrated into the bridge superstructure, which was increased in size. This photo very clearly shows the massive, multi-storey bridge. Note the three rangefinders mounted one on top of another, which were fully rotatable around a common axis. However, they caused an enormous amount of topweight, with consequent effects on the ship's stability. *Author's Collection*

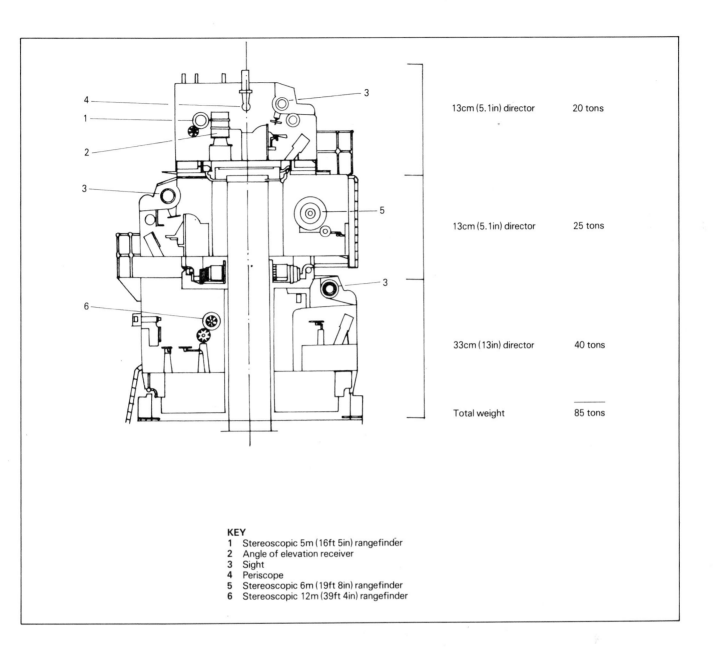

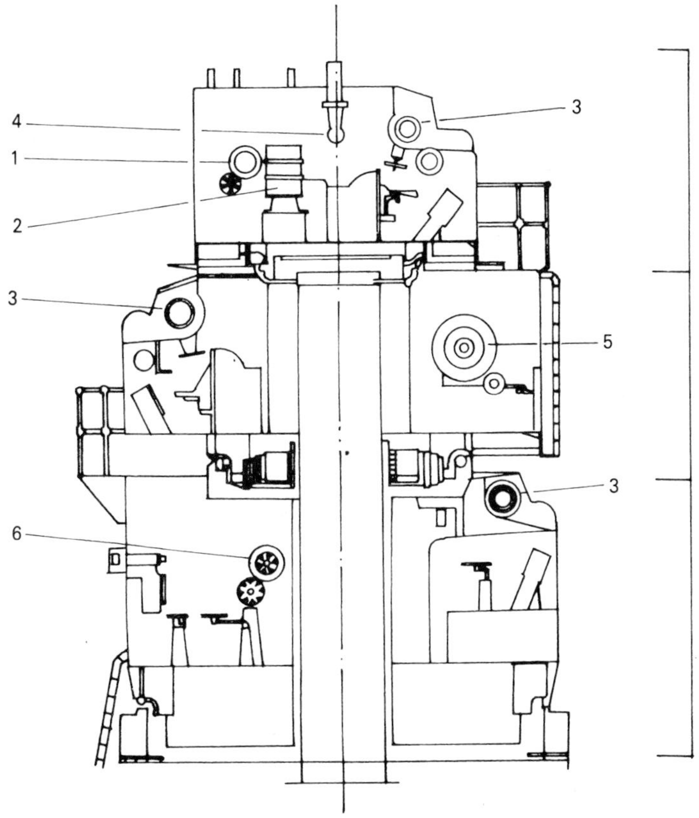

4
1
2
3
3
5
3
6

13cm (5.1in) director	20 tons
13cm (5.1in) director	25 tons
33cm (13in) director	40 tons
Total weight	85 tons

KEY
1 Stereoscopic 5m (16ft 5in) rangefinder
2 Angle of elevation receiver
3 Sight
4 Periscope
5 Stereoscopic 6m (19ft 8in) rangefinder
6 Stereoscopic 12m (39ft 4in) rangefinder

A diagram showing the composition of *Strasbourg*'s rangefinder complex, together with data on the weight of its components.

Neither of the *Dunkerque*s was outstandingly successful, although each took part in several wartime operations: *Strasbourg* was sent out to hunt the German 'pocket-battleship' *Admiral Graf Spee* soon after the outbreak of the war, and *Dunkerque* followed shortly afterwards, searching for the German battleships *Scharnhorst* and *Gneisenau*. In the period following this, both took part in convoy escort duties. In April 1940 they were transferred to the Mediterranean, which they were never again to leave. Both ships are seen here at Brest shortly before the war began; *Dunkerque* is almost hidden in the background. *BfZ*

The *Dunkerques* were the first capital ship design to have aircraft equipment from the outset, and this consisted of a 22m (72ft) long high performance catapult, which could revolve through 360°, and a hangar 15 × 7.5 × 5m (49ft × 24ft 6in × 16ft 6in). There were four Loire Nieuport 130 flying boats permanently on board, although only two could be accommodated in the hangar, even with their wings and tailplanes removed. The third flying boat was carried on the catapult, the fourth was probably stowed on board in a dismantled condition. This photo of *Strasbourg* shows the hangar, its sliding door open. *Author's Collection*

A Loire 130 which has just been catapulted from *Strasbourg*. In the background the destroyer *Volta* is at anchor. *BfZ*

When German troops entered Toulon on 27 November 1942 as part of Operation 'Lila', the French fleet commander, Admiral de Laborde, gave the order to scuttle the large number of French vessels at anchor there, amongst which were the battleships *Dunkerque*, *Strasbourg* and *Provence*, four heavy and three light cruisers, thirty destroyers, three torpedo-boats, sixteen submarines and eleven gunboats and smaller vessels. The water was too shallow throughout for the ships to become completely submerged, but additional explosive charges and onboard fires made most of the ships virtually irreparable. This photo shows *Strasbourg* sunk in about 8 fathoms (14m) of water. *BfZ*

Another view of the damaged *Strasbourg*, with the heavy cruiser *Colbert* to starboard. Early in 1943 *Strasbourg* was raised under the direction of the Italians, and was cut up piece by piece: superstructure, armour plating and even the catapult were taken away to Italy for scrap. In May 1944 the wreck was handed over to the French for 'conservation', who moved her to an out-of-the-way berth. There she was hit by heavy bombs during a USAAF attack in August 1944, and sank again. In August 1945 the wreck was salvaged, after which it was used in underwater explosives experiments until 1951. It was not finally sold for scrap until 1955. *BfZ*

Richelieu passed the Armistice period at Dakar, whence she had been transferred when the French collapse seemed imminent in June 1940. Shortly after this, she was damaged by the British: at Dakar, the French declined similar conditions to those laid down at Mers el Kebir, and a British motorboat got through the boom defences and dropped several depth charges under *Richelieu*'s stern. Immediately after this six Swordfish from the carrier *Hermes* attacked and hit her with a torpedo, but the damage was by no means so severe that *Richelieu* could be considered eliminated. In September 1940, when a powerful British force attacked Dakar to prepare the way for Gaullist troops to land, she was ready for action again. She returned fire with her 38cm guns and scored a hit on the British battleship *Barham*, and the vigorous French defence forced the British to break off their attack. This photo shows *Richelieu* anchored at Dakar, protected by booms. Her aircraft equipment can be seen here – exactly the same installation as on the *Dunkerque* class. *BfZ*

The Italians ordered two *Vittorio Veneto* class battleships in 1934, to which the French responded with two more new ships. They were originally intended to be called *France* and *Verdun*, but the final names chosen were *Richelieu* and *Jean Bart*. Superficially, they bore a strong resemblance to the *Dunkerque*s, but they were much more powerful, much stronger, and also faster. Their external similarity resulted from the fact that their design concepts were identical: the location of the main armament forward to achieve the smallest possible citadel, with improved protection for the citadel itself. The guns were again to be arranged in quadruple turrets; the French decided upon a 38cm (15in), calibre after considering twelve 34–35cm (13.4–13.75in) barrels – the latter would have involved such an extension of the citadel that thinner armour would have had to be accepted. This rare photo of *Richelieu* was taken in May or June 1940 in the roads at Brest, shortly before being moved to Dakar. *Author's Collection*

Jean Bart was launched at St-Nazaire in March 1940. Early that year, when France's collapse had begun to appear inevitable, the ship was only 77 per cent complete: she was still in the newly installed fitting-out basin of her shipyard, which was separated from open water by an earth dam, and according to the building schedule the ship was not due to begin trials until October, which would have left enough time for the dam to be dug away. However, France's precarious position made swift action necessary. At the end of May the French began dredging away the dam and the task was finished at 02.00 on 19 June 1940; only 90 minutes later the ship was towed out of the fitting-out basin, ran aground, freed herself, and finally reached open water. At that moment German aircraft attacked and managed to hit her with one small bomb, but gradually all her systems came into operation, even though they had never been tested before. Under her own steam the ship reached Casablanca on 22 June, where she remained for the rest of the war. *Jean Bart* is seen here with her forecastle torn open by the bomb. *Author's Collection*

Jean Bart was by no means battleworthy when she was transferred from St-Nazaire; only the forward turret had been fitted with guns – but these were not operable yet – and the secondary armament was absent entirely. In the ensuing months the French succeeded in making the forward 38cm quadruple turret serviceable, and this proved useful in November 1942 when the Allies landed in French North Africa, enabling the ship to return fire when the Allies appeared off Casablanca. However, she herself drew the fire of the American battleship *Massachusetts*, and was severely damaged. After the French had ended their resistance they worked in conjunction with the Allies, and plans were prepared in British design offices for the *Jean Bart*'s conversion and completion as a 'battleship-carrier'. The 38cm quadruple turrets were to be retained, but behind them a 130m (426ft 6in) long flight deck was to be added with an island on the starboard side; for self-defence, sixteen 4.5in (11.4cm) AA guns were to be installed in twin turrets. Fortunately, this highly controversial hybrid design came to nothing. The photo shows *Jean Bart* with a severely damaged quarterdeck: note the aircraft hangar. *BfZ*

▲ The third unit of the battleship programme begun in 1935 was *Clemenceau*, which was laid down by the French in the Salou building dock at Brest on 17 January 1939, right after *Richelieu* had been launched from the same slipway the same day. When German troops entered Brest, they found the *Clemenceau*'s citadel, 133m (436ft) long, 20m (66ft) wide and 10m (33ft) deep – in other words the ship was about 10 per cent complete. The unfinished hull was declared German booty, although it was virtually inconceivable that building would continue under German direction. The German military authorities had the hull made buoyant, so that it could be launched and thus leave the slip clear for their own uses; it was then towed to an isolated anchorage nearby. Shortly after the start of the Allied invasion, the German defenders at Brest considered towing the incomplete hull and sinking it to block the harbour entrance, but this did not come about since in August 1944 it was sunk by bombs dropped during a US air raid. In 1948 the French salvaged it and by 1951 it had been scrapped. This photograph, dating from 1943, shows *Clemenceau*'s box-shaped citadel after it had been floated out of the building dock: at the top, the citadel is flush with the lower armour deck, part of which has been removed. *BfZ*

After the Allies had obtained a foothold in French North Africa, the FFL (Forces Françaises Libres), in which French patriots had banded together, were greatly strengthened. Amongst these were *Richelieu* and her crew, but the ship's decrepit condition meant that she could not be made ready for action, and so she sailed for the US East Coast in January 1943, where she was overhauled and modernised at New York Navy Yard. By August the work was essentially complete, and the ship spent the following months with the British Home Fleet, mainly to work herself up and prepare her and her crew for battle. This picture shows *Richelieu* entering New York early in 1943. *BfZ*

Richelieu as she appeared after her New York Navy Yard refit: her aircraft equipment had already been removed at Dakar, and three of her 38cm guns, which had been irreparably damaged in action at Dakar in 1940, were replaced by intact barrels from *Jean Bart*; in addition she was fitted with numerous AA weapons, radar and other equipment. She did not keep her brightly coloured chequer-board (US Measure 12) camouflage for long. From the beginning of 1944 *Richelieu* took an active part in the war, initially with the British Home Fleet, and then in the British Eastern Fleet in the Indian Ocean. Whilst with the Home Fleet she took part in a sortie against Norway in February 1944, in which she operated as long-range escort to the British carrier force. She remained in the Indian Ocean until late 1945, and then returned to Europe. In early 1946 she entered Cherbourg, six years after leaving Brest. The photo shows her during operations in the Indian Ocean in 1944. *BfZ*

This stern view of *Richelieu* shows the grouping of her secondary armament aft; it comprises three 15.2cm (6in) triple turrets. Originally two more had been planned amidships, high up between the forward superstructure and the funnel, but these were never installed – *Richelieu* was fitted with the appropriate barbettes, but *Jean Bart* was not. With the third ship, *Clemenceau*, a different arrangement was designed for the AA guns, with the purpose of increasing their arcs of fire. This is a postwar photo of *Richelieu*. *BfZ*

Jean Bart entered Brest in October 1945 to be repaired and finally completed. Funds were desperately short, and work progressed only very slowly – there was some debate for a time about halting completion work altogether. However, this caused such public indignation that construction did proceed, but it was not until early 1949 that first trials could be held. The missing 38cm guns were replaced by the weapons that had been manufactured for the third and fourth ships, some of which had fallen into German hands and had been incorporated in bunkered positions as part of the Norwegian coastal defences, only being returned to France after the war. The fitting of AA weapons had to be postponed so frequently that they could not be installed until 1951–52. The ship was finally commissioned in May 1955, more than fifteen years after her keel had been laid. The consequent great expense incurred – and this at a time when the battleship had long since lost its position of prestige – was by no means justified. The ship did take part in the Anglo-French Suez adventure in the autumn of 1956, but her heavy guns were not used to support the landings, as it was realised that this course of action would have resulted in unacceptable casualties among the civilian population. This photograph shows *Jean Bart* in the early 1950s, still without AA armament, although the positions for these mountings are clearly visible. *BfZ*

This detail photograph of *Richelieu* dates from the early 1950s and shows the arrangement of the superstructure, the AA armament and especially the unique funnel design. In the original design, *Richelieu* and her sister-ships had funnels of a shape and position (separate from the after control position) similar to *Dunkerque* and *Strasbourg*. However, during construction work the designs were changed: the control position was moved on to the funnel, the opening of which was canted towards the stern. In adopting this arrangement the French anticipated a development which was taken up by American warships in the form of 'macks' (*m*ast *a*nd sta*cks*), although the French design was adopted not in order to solve problems of space or weight but rather to move part of the after control position away from obstructive exhaust gases, which in the earlier arrangement were bound to pass over it; the greater optical horizon thus gained was a bonus. The two forward 10cm (3.9in) AA twin turrets are located in the position that was to have been occupied by the port forward 15.2cm turret. Between the tower bridge (in which a lift was fitted) and the funnel can be seen the upper deck boat platform; the starboard derrick is raised, the port unit in its neutral position. *BfZ*

Another close-up of *Richelieu*, showing the funnel and the rotating rangefinder hood close up beneath its opening; two more rangefinders can be seen on the tower bridge. *BfZ*

This is how *Richelieu* appeared postwar. She spent only ten years on active service after the war, and she spent more of this time as a training ship. In 1956 she was placed in reserve, and in 1968 she ended up in the breakers' yard at La Spezia, Italy. This photo dates from 1954. *BfZ*

Jean Bart looked rather more attractive than did her sister-ship *Richelieu*, the main reason for this being the cut down forward superstructure, making the ship appear more compact. What cannot be seen in this photo are the torpedo bulges added subsequently below the waterline. These had a twofold purpose: they were intended to balance out the increased displacement which had resulted from the additional equipment that had been fitted (mainly AA guns), and they were also designed to improve underwater protection. *Jean Bart*'s AA armament was the most powerful ever fitted on a capital ship, consisting of 52 barrels of between 57mm and 100mm calibre. In theory she was capable of firing 3832 rounds per minute, and thus throw up a curtain of fire around the ship which would be very difficult to penetrate. *Author's Collection*

Jean Bart once more, seen from the starboard quarter at Toulon, where she remained as a stationary gunnery training ship after being decommissioned in the summer of 1961. Seven years later she was stricken, and in 1969 she was scrapped – the last French dreadnought. Her demise signified the end of the battleship in Europe, apart from the Turkish *Yavuz*. *Author's Collection*

Italy

The *Regina Elena* class, a battleship design which was ordered by Italy shortly after the turn of the century, represented a unique type of transitional ship. Her creator was the energetic designer Vittorio Cuniberti, who was destined to have a strong influence on the development of battleships. These last 'classical' Italian ships-of-the-line were produced under the guiding principle that they should be 'more powerful than any faster ship, and faster than any more powerful ship'. In this the Italians were anticipating something that was practised by the German Navy in the 1920s when they built their 10,000-ton *Panzerschiffe*. For this new class Cuniberti reduced the main armament to two 30.5cm (12in) guns, in single turrets, and then fitted in a 'semi-heavy' battery of twelve 20.3cm (8in) guns, the latter not, however, in casemates, as was usually or even exclusively the case elsewhere, but in twin turrets on either beam, so that eight heavy barrels were available for a broadside. He raised the top speed to over 21kts, which made the ships clearly superior to all other vessels at the time; that this involved sacrificing heavy armour goes without saying. Had these ships been built before the British *Dreadnought*, they would certainly have commanded a position of respect, but their construction took far too long – some of the ships took seven years – so that they had lost much of their impact by the time they were delivered. This photo shows *Regina Elena*, probably shortly after being commissioned. Incidentally, none of the four ships of the class looked alike; *Vittorio Emanuele* bore most similarity to *Regina Elena*, although her funnels were 2.5m (8ft 3in) taller. *Italian Navy (Author's Collection)*

Dante Alighieri

On 27 June 1909, an amendment was made to the Fleet Act of 1905 which permitted the building of capital ships, and this gave chief designer Cuniberti the opportunity to change his plans. He had published his ideas in the 1903 edition of *Janes' Fighting Ships*: he made clear his attitude towards future battleship building and recommended the adoption of the 'all-big-gun' battleship. His views, vindicated by the experiences of the Russo-Japanese war of 1904–05, took visible form in *Dante Alighieri*, which was laid down in 1909 as the first Italian dreadnought. She was not only the fastest ship of her type and time (23kts), she was also equipped with triple turrets (invented in Austria-Hungary), which were disposed in the 'Cuniberti arrangement': one turret forward and one aft, and two turrets amidships, all along the centreline. He had arrived at this scheme because he had no faith in superimposed turrets. By arranging part of the secondary armament in twin turrets, he anticipated a development which was only continued after the First World War, and then became established throughout the world in battleship building. The arrangement of the machinery was largely dependent on the armament: the turbines were installed between the two midships turrets, while the boilers were grouped together behind the forward and in front of the aft turret. All these features can be deduced from the photograph. The ship had much individual character, her scant superstructure appearing to be in the nature of an afterthought, but the design was chosen very deliberately by Cuniberti: the result was that the artillery had ideal arcs of fire. *BfZ*

Dante Alighieri was by no means a good-looking ship – her superstructure was small and not particularly imposing. The four narrow funnels display little idea of harmony of line, standing close together in pairs with a mast between each pair. In retrospect, it is barely comprehensible why each pair was not joined to form single units. On the bridge can be seen the Triplex rangefinder, with which French capital ships of the time were also equipped. *Italian Navy (Author's Collection)*

Dante Alighieri's only modernisation was carried out in 1923: the pole foremast was replaced by a tripod mast with a two-storey foretop, and the forefunnels were also raised by about 3m (10ft). From 1925 a floatplane was occasionally carried, parked on No 3 turret when not in use. *Barilli*

The Italian Navy made a notable breakthrough when they produced the three battleships of the *Conte di Cavour* class, (which were laid down in 1910), taking the supposed risk of building superimposed turrets. The number of barrels was unusual at thirteen, but this number evolved naturally, since only twin turrets could be installed in the raised positions, while triple turrets were fitted on the upper deck. From the point of view of stability this was an absolutely correct decision. The photo, taken on 11 November 1913, shows *Giulio Cesare* undergoing engine trials: the black smoke belching from the funnels indicates that forced draught is being applied to the boilers. Also clearly visible are the torpedo nets, rolled up with their booms below the battery deck. *Ansaldo, Genoa (Author's Collection)*

For the third ship of the *Conte di Cavour* class, the Italians chose the name of one of their greatest artists: *Leonardo da Vinci*. This was one of the very rare cases in which a warship was not named after a sovereign, a statesman or a commander-in-chief. *Leonardo da Vinci* differed from her sister-ships in that her derricks were attached to the support legs of the two tripod masts and not the masts themselves, and she thus had twice as many as her sister-ships; the bridge superstructure was also somewhat different. Here *Leonardo da Vinci* is seen during main gunnery trials; the photo was taken before the ship was commissioned. *BfZ*

The background to the sinking of *Leonardo da Vinci* at Taranto on 2 August 1916 has remained unclear to this day: in the opinion of some – mainly the Italians – an Austrian sabotage unit had a hand in it, while others consider that an internal explosion or enemy action is more likely. The idea of an internal explosion cannot be excluded, for the Italian Navy was using British cordite propellant, and the three navies – Japanese and Italian, as well as British – who had used the substance had suffered serious losses in capital ships through its igniting. Two hundred and forty-nine members of *Leonardo da Vinci*'s crew died in the incident. The photo shows the wreck of the ship during salvage operations which took place three years after her loss. *BfZ*

Leonardo da Vinci in dock at Taranto, keel uppermost. A repair was considered, but on inspection the damage proved to be too severe to warrant such a course of action. After being sealed, the wreck was removed from the dock and broken up in 1923. *BfZ*

Conte di Cavour was modernised between 1924 and 1926, and as part of this the tripod mast behind the forefunnel was replaced by a four legged mast in front of it; this new mast was fitted with the foretop which had become so important for fire control. The abbreviated main leg of the tripod mast was retained, serving as a derrick. *BfZ*

Giulio Cesare, seen here, was modernised the same way as her sister, but the measures were not enough to keep these ageing ships in a satisfactory condition. In 1928 their status was changed: *Conte di Cavour* was placed in reserve, and *Giulio Cesare* became a gunnery training ship. *BfZ*

From the outset the Italian Navy was very receptive to ideas about the introduction of shipboard aircraft; this is apparent from the many tests carried out such as this one on board *Conte di Cavour*, which had been fitted with a fixed catapult on the port side of the forecastle. This photograph dates from 1926 and shows the launch of a Macchi M18 floatplane. The forward turret has had to be trained away to starboard to facilitate take-off. *Author's Collection*

As their 'answer' to the French *Dunkerque*, the Italians decided to reconstruct completely their old battleships, not wanting to undertake any new construction at first. *Conte di Cavour* and *Giulio Cesare* were taken in hand in October 1933. With the exception of the barbettes of their main turrets fore and aft (the centre turret was completely removed), they were stripped of all their superstructure, and then their engines and boilers, in order to renew everything from the bottom up. Here we see the gutted *Conte di Cavour* in her reconstruction dock at Trieste. The photo was taken on 3 March 1934, six months after work began. *BfZ*

Conte di Cavour (pictured here) and *Giulio Cesare* were scarcely recognisable after their reconstructions, which lasted 43 months for each ship; the extent to which they were rebuilt can only be compared with Japanese capital ships of the time. The hull was a typical example: it was lengthened, not at the stern as with the Japanese capital ships, but by adding a 10m (33ft) long bow section with a new style stem. This lengthening of the hull was necessary to achieve a better length-to-beam ratio to correspond with the increase in speed demanded. Completely new machinery was installed; its performance exceeding that of the old system by more than 60,000shp. The ships had become not only more modern, but they were aesthetically very pleasing, giving expression to that sensitivity to harmony which the Italian warship designers of the 1920s and 1930s achieved. *Author's Collection*

A further means of improving the capabilities of the *Cavours* was found by boring out the 30.5cm (12in) barrels to 32cm (12.6in). Compared with the 452kg (996.5lb) of the 30.5cm shell, a 32cm projectile weighed 525kg (1157.4lb), and the range also increased by more than 4000yds. Even the secondary battery was completely renewed: the 12cm (4.7in) calibre was retained, but in place of the old casemate guns modern turrets were fitted. The total weight of broadside was reduced, the previous 6074kg (13,391lb) having dropped to only 5382kg (11,865lb); however, this was primarily because the midships turret had been removed, in order to make room for the new, more powerful machinery. One cannot get something for nothing, especially in warship building. Here *Conte di Cavour* opens fire with her after 32cm turrets, early in 1937. *BfZ*

Conte di Cavour and *Giulio Cesare* received their baptism of fire just four weeks after Italy entered the war. Near Punta Stilo they came upon a detachment of the British Mediterranean Fleet, and a 105-minute battle ensued. The British battleship *Warspite* achieved a direct hit with a 15in (38.1cm) shell on *Giulio Cesare*, and this forced the Italian commander, Admiral Campioni, to order his destroyers to attack and provide a smokescreen. Contact between the two fleets was lost, and both retreated. Here the two Italian battleships are seen during the action, photographed from *Conte di Cavour*; *Giulio Cesare* has just opened fire. *Author's Collection*

A few months later the Italians suffered much more severely: during the night of 12 November 1940, twenty Swordfish torpedo-bombers took off from the British aircraft carrier *Illustrious* and attacked the main body of the Italian fleet at anchor at Taranto. Three battleships were hit by torpedoes, *Conte di Cavour* suffering the most damage: she sank to the bottom after being hit by a single torpedo – and that not even the usual 21in (53.5cm) weapon, but an 18in (45.7cm) aerial torpedo, which had 30 per cent less explosive power. It tore open the hull, well below the armour belt, and created a hole about 12m × 8m (40ft × 26ft), causing the ship to sink quickly. It was obvious that in terms of underwater protection this class left much to be desired, although the ships had been fitted with the Pugliese system during their reconstruction. This completely new underwater defence system consisted of a quadrant-shaped torpedo bulkhead curved to follow the outer skin. The sealed space thus formed was then used to store fuel oil, and in its centre was an empty cylinder 3.6cm (1.4in) in diameter, the purpose of which was to act as an expansion chamber and absorb the force of any underwater explosion. The Italians had hoped that their ships would be safe from airborne torpedoes whilst at anchor in the Mare Grande off Taranto, where the water was only $6^{1}/_{2}$–8 fathoms (12–15m) deep, as that type of torpedo usually ran more deeply. In this respect however, the British had adjusted their torpedoes very carefully, so that they kept to the required depth of 10m (33ft) and never sank deeper. The torpedoes also had magnetic and contact detonators, and hence not only struck the ships very low down but were very effective. This miscalculation may have been one of the reasons why the Italians did not take the sealing of their ships sufficiently seriously, thereby increasing the magnitude of the disaster. This is *Conte di Cavour*, grounded shortly after the attack. *BfZ*

Conte di Cavour after the start of her salvage operations, with some of her armament removed. *Author's Collection*

Conte di Cavour was raised in July 1941 and towed to Trieste for repairs; by the late summer of 1943, however, the work was still not finished. With the Italian capitulation the ship fell into German hands, but a continuation of the work was never considered. She remained at Trieste until 15 February 1943, when she was severely damaged in an American air raid, and was immediately scrapped. *Conte di Cavour* is seen here in early December 1941 – a year after the Taranto disaster – in her repair dock at Trieste. In the background can be seen the tower bridge of *Roma*, which is in the final stages of fitting out. *BfZ*

In the course of her repair work, *Conti di Cavour* was scheduled to be modernised, although this was to be restricted to her armament. The secondary 12cm (4.7in) guns were to be replaced by 13.5cm (5.3in) weapons, and instead of the eight 10cm (3.9in) AA guns twelve 65mm/64 AA guns were to be installed in single turrets. The former light AA armament was to be replaced by a total of twenty-three 20mm/65 guns in twin and single mountings. In addition, radar was to be added. The drawing makes it clear what was planned. *Author (from* Orrizonte Mare *No 1: 'Corazzate classe'* Conte di Cavour*)*

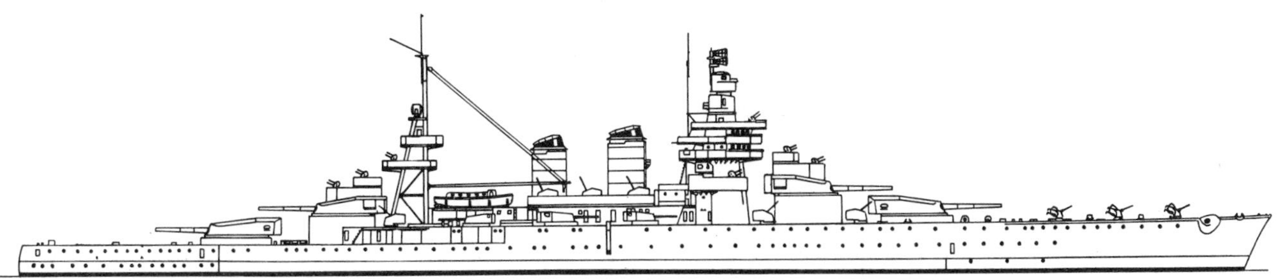

The battleships of the *Caio Duilio* class, which were designed and authorised in 1911, were basically descendants of the *Conte di Cavours*. They shared the same main armament – thirteen 30.5cm guns – the same armament layout, and the same machinery. With this new class, however, the Italians had reverted to a full-strength secondary battery, although some of the guns were in very unfavourable positions, being so far forward that they were obstructed by the bow wave when the ship was steaming at high speed; moreover, in contrast to the *Cavours*, the midships turret was located one deck lower, this being an attempt to counter the additional weight of the secondary armament. In appearance, the class was much more pleasing to the eye than its predecessors, not least as a result of the disposition of the tripod foremast in front of the forefunnel. This 1924 photograph depicts *Andrea Doria*. *BfZ*

Andrea Doria again, photographed in the early 1920s, with a Macchi M18 parked on the midships turret. There was still no catapult, so the aircraft had to be lowered to the water via a derrick before it could take off. *BfZ*

▲ *Caio Duilio* in the late 1920s, with a catapult on the port side of the forecastle. This was a fixed installation and projected about 5m (16ft 6in) beyond the deck. A derrick had been installed just in front of the forward 15.2cm casemate for hoisting the aircraft back on board after it had landed on the water. The derrick was folded forward at an angle when not in use, so as not to obstruct No 1 turret when the latter was trained. The arrangement of the bow anchors was similar to that of the British capital ships of the period: two to starboard, and only one to port. *Author's Collection*

Shortly before reconstruction work on *Conte di Cavour* and *Giulio Cesare* was completed, *Andrea Doria* and *Caio Duilio* went into dock to be 'rejuvenated', and the scale of the work was even greater than before. When *Andrea Doria* ran her machinery trials in February 1939 she was still unarmed, as shown in the photo. No 3 barbette is clearly visible here (behind the new mainmast), as are the new funnels and foremast. Two davits can be picked out to port; these were folded flat against the hull when not in use. ▼ *BfZ*

▲ *Andrea Doria* in 1940, probably shortly before being recommissioned after her reconstruction. From this angle it is evident that the appearance of this battleship and her sister-ship *Caio Duilio* was now very similar to that of the *Vittorio Veneto* class after they had been modernised. Seen from a distance, it was principally the presence of a fourth turret which served to differentiate these vessels from the *Vittorio Venetos*. *BfZ*

During reconstruction, *Caio Duilio* and *Andrea Doria* were also fitted with the new 90mm (3.5in) AA guns which could fire at 12 rounds per minute and were considered first rate weapons. Although Italian battleships possessed a sufficiently extensive and powerful AA armament, their success rate during World War II in terms of aircraft shot down was less than expected. This can only be a result of inadequate training for the gun crews, and one example will illustrate the problem: in the British attack on Taranto in November 1940 Italian shipboard AA crews brought down only two of the twenty Swordfish which took part. The aircraft were of an antiquated design and, with a top speed of around 135mph (220km/h), were extraordinarily slow. This view of *Caio Duilio* shows five of her 90mm turrets; the light cruiser *Guiseppe Garibaldi* can be seen in the ship's wake. *BfZ*

Caio Duillo and *Andrea Doria* were fitted with a different secondary battery from the modernised *Conte di Cavours*: the new 13.5cm (5.3in) gun had been developed in time for them, and an equal number of the new weapons were installed. These 13.5cm guns were grouped in triple turrets high up to either side of the bridge superstructure and No 2 turret; however, this amounted to a perilously heavy concentration of firepower in a confined area, which could be eliminated by a single unlucky hit. This photo of *Caio Duilio* was taken on 4 August 1947. Apart from the main turrets, some secondary guns and several light AA weapons can be seen. *BfZ*

After Italy's capitulation in September 1943, *Caio Duilio* and *Andrea Doria* were taken to Malta and interned there. Both were allowed to return home in Summer 1944, and formed the core of the Italian postwar fleet, although they were used principally for training purposes. Nevertheless, they continued to serve for more than a decade until they were stricken in 1956 and scrapped. This photograph was taken in 1948, and shows *Caio Duilio*'s bridge and forward turrets. The concentration of main and secondary turrets in a confined space is very obvious: the distance from the No 1 barbette to the aftermost of the secondary battery was only about 30m (100ft), measured between the vertical axes of these barbettes – surely too little to be able to localise the effect of a heavy calibre hit in this area. *BfZ*

Caio Duilio, in the well-known paint scheme of the postwar period, photographed in the early 1950s. *Author's Collection*

Francesco Caracciolo class

Italy's contributions to the 'super-dreadnought' programmes were the four 30,000-ton battleships of the *Francesco Caracciolo* class, which were laid down in 1914–15. They were to be as powerful in terms of armament as the British *Queen Elizabeths* which had been under construction since 1912 and had ushered in the era of the fast battleship. The designed speed of 28kts would have made them even faster than the British vessels, but this feature was in no way directed at Great Britain, rather at Austria-Hungary, as the ships represented an 'answer' to the latter's 'Ersatz Monarch' class. The high speed of the *Francesco Caracciolo* class demanded a substantial lengthening of the hull, firstly to provide space for the 105,000shp machinery, and secondly to raise the length-to-beam ratio to the optimum in order to achieve the required performance, although this could only be accomplished by restricting the armour to some extent. The Italians had planned the main armament very well: the turrets were placed in pairs forward and aft, and were far enough from each other to allow the effects of hits from heavy shells to be localised. The war delayed the ships' completion: work on them was stopped in favour of destroyers, submarines and smaller vessels, and was discontinued altogether after the war, with the exception of *Francesco Caracciolo* herself. She was the furthest advanced, and work was resumed in the autumn of 1919, though only in order to clear the slipway. She was launched on 12 May 1920, and a few weeks later she was sold to a large shipping company who wanted to have her converted into a 25,300grt fast freighter; however, this project also came to nothing because of the company's financial difficulties. *Francesco Caracciolo* is seen here at launch. Her bow shape is similar to that of French capital ships of the period. *Author's Collection*

Vittorio Veneto class

Impero, Littorio, Roma, Vittorio Veneto

After France declined to ratify the 1930 London Naval Treaty and resumed building capital ships with the *Dunkerque* class, Italy was no longer prepared to remain within the treaty limitations. The result was that two battleships were ordered in the autumn of 1934. According to official information of the time, they were within the limits laid down by the Washington Naval Treaty of 1922, the ships' standard displacement being quoted as 35,000 tons and their main calibre 38.1cm (15in). The latter figure was correct, but the actual displacement was more than 6000 tons greater than the stated figure. *Vittorio Veneto*, the first ship of the class, was named after the small town where in August 1918 the last great battle on the Alpine Front, which had seen the Italians victorious over the Austro-Hungarians, had taken place. This photo shows the ship just before her highly celebrated launch, 25 July 1937. *BfZ*

Vittorio Veneto, immediately after being launched. Painted on the bows are three bundles of fasces; these were the ancient Roman symbol for the administration of official power, which Italian Fascists often used at that time, and eventually adopted as their emblem. *BfZ*

A few weeks after *Vittorio Veneto* was launched, her sister-ship, *Littorio*, followed. The name derived from the Lictor, the Roman bearer of the fasces. On 30 July 1943, immediately after the collapse of the Mussolini regime, the ship was renamed *Italia* to underline the break with Fascism. *Littorio* is seen here on her slipway: her bulbous bow is particularly evident, as are the stylised fasces symbols mounted either side of the bows ready for the ship's imminent launch. *Ansaldo, Genoa (Author's Collection)*

At the end of 1939 *Vittorio Veneto* and *Littorio* began their sea trials. They looked scarcely real, since many important items had not yet been fitted, including their fire control, the entire AA armament and the ship's aircraft equipment. This photo of *Vittorio Veneto* dates from December 1939. *BfZ*

In 1938 two more battleships of the *Vittorio Veneto* class were ordered, *Impero* and *Roma*; they differed only in detail from their predecessors. The Ansaldo Yard at Genoa had been given the contract for *Impero*, and her keel was laid on the same slipway from which *Littorio* had been launched the previous year. *Impero*, shown in the photo, was launched on 15 November 1939. *Author's Collection*

The battleships of the *Vittorio Veneto* class had twelve 90mm (3.5in) AA guns for defence against high flying aircraft. These were accommodated in single turrets, and each group of six guns (one on each side) was supported by an optical director. The photograph shows *Vittorio Veneto*'s starboard 90mm mountings with their director mounted above them, and was taken on the occasion of the ship's commissioning. Leading representatives from the shipyard and the Navy pose for the photographer. *Author's Collection*

Roma was the last of the *Vittorio Veneto* class battleships, being laid down at Trieste in September 1938. She was launched the day after Italy joined the war on the German side, and was commissioned two years later. She is shown here in 1942 shortly before she was completed, during final fitting-out operations, and has already been camouflaged. Both photos show the armament particularly well. *Author's Collection/BfZ*

During the British attack on Taranto on 12 November 1940, *Littorio* was hit by three torpedoes: of these, the third proved to be particularly devastating: it tore a hole 15m × 10m (50ft × 33ft), flooding the bows, which hit the bottom. It was fortunate that the ship was at anchor in shallow water: if she had suffered this blow whilst at sea it would have been very difficult to prevent her sinking. In mid-1941, after months of repair work, the ship rejoined the fleet. The *Vittorio Veneto* had also been fitted with the Pugliese underwater protection system, and it was now clear that the system did not come up to expectations. This was a bitter disappointment to the Italian Navy, made worse by the fact that it was impossible to make substantial improvements to the ships' protection once they had been built: the work required would have involved design changes of a fundamental nature, for which there were neither the time, the materials, nor the labour available. The photograph shows *Littorio* with her bows grounded; the salvage vessel *Po* lies alongside. *BfZ*

Littorio, showing the location of the three torpedo hits received at Taranto, and the extent of the subsequent flooding. *Author*

Hardly had repairs begun on the severely damaged *Littorio* than *Vittorio Veneto* was herself badly damaged: on 28 May 1941, in a naval action off Cape Matapan, she was hit by two aerial torpedoes delivered by carrier aircraft from the British carrier *Formidable*, although, even with more than 4000 tons of water on board, she was able to be assisted back to Taranto. This photograph dates from the first days of April 1941, when *Vittorio Veneto* was being docked. The two empty cylinders placed temporarily on the forecastle had been fixed alongside the ship's hull, where they corrected her list and prevented the ship sinking further. *BfZ*

A new angle on shipboard aircraft equipment was the use of catapult-launched fighter aircraft on Italian battleships, using Reggiane Re 2000 single-seat fighters, capable of 330mph (530km/h) and armed with two 12.7mm (0.5in) machine guns. This was an emergency measure – the danger to the Italian fleet from Allied air superiority in the Mediterranean was growing ever greater, and the Italians had no aircraft carriers of their own whose aircraft could have provided cover for their ships. The Re 2000s were therefore only launched in the face of imminent air attack and then had to seek out a landing place on dry land, thus preventing them from carrying out the real job of a ship's aircraft – reconnaissance. *Vittorio Veneto* and *Roma* had two Re 2000s on board, *Littorio* only one; the only comparable vessels were the British 'CAM' ships of the Second World War with their Sea Hurricanes. This picture of *Vittorio Veneto*, showing one of her Re 2000s on the catapult, was taken in late October 1942. *Author's Collection*

A notable design feature of the *Vittorio Veneto* class was the unusually high position of the after 38.1cm turret, an arrangement intended to protect the ship's aircraft – parked on the quarterdeck when not required for action – from blast damage. The space available there would certainly have allowed a hangar to be built, in the same way as with the French *Dunkerque* class, but the Italians eschewed the idea, for reasons unknown: perhaps they considered weather-proof accommodation unnecessary on account of the good weather usually experienced in the Mediterranean. This is a May 1942 photo of *Roma*. *BfZ*

Another view of *Roma*, this time in August 1943, with her new camouflage paint scheme. *BfZ*

Vittorio Veneto and *Littorio* were originally fitted with a gently curving stem, but after their first sea trials a straight stem, which extended just below the waterline, was added; the flare could thereby be increased, thus making the forecastle drier. The modification increased overall length by about 6ft (1.8m). *Impero* was launched with the early-type bow, but *Roma* had the new bow when launched, and she was also nearly 5ft (1.5m) higher forward because her sheer had been increased. This is *Vittorio Veneto* fitting out in 1939, still with her original bow. *BfZ*

Roma in early 1942, showing her very different bow shape. This vessel also differed from her sister-ships in that she had only one starboard bow anchor. Both *Vittorio Veneto* and *Roma* were built by Cantieri Navali Riuniti dell'Adriatico at Trieste. *BfZ*

This and the following two photographs of *Roma* were taken during trials, and illustrate the Italians' natural talent for styling and for harmony of line, which was evident in their warship building from the 1920s onwards. The slender hull with its raked stem, the mightly triple turrets of the main armament the clearly delineated bridge tower and the two funnels, the taller one in front of the shorter, and the flat-topped, angled funnel caps – all these were characteristics of a type of warship architecture that was virtually unique in its day, and which was much copied. The battleships of the *Vittorio Veneto* class were justifiably considered to be among the best looking in the world, which only goes to make the circumstances surrounding the loss of *Roma* the more tragic. The Italian fleet left en route for Malta, where it was to be interned, under the terms of the surrender, but it was attacked by German aircraft in an effort to prevent the ships being transferred. *Roma* was twice hit by SD 1400-X glider bombs, which caused her to sink; over 1200 of her crew died. The first bomb struck the area between No 2 turret and the port forward secondary turret, while the second hit the starboard side abreast the second funnel, between the two aftermost 90mm AA mountings. The battleship *Italia* – the one-time *Littorio* – was also hit by one heavy bomb during this attack. In effect, the Italian fleet suffered the same treatment from its former allies as had the French at Mers el Kebir three years earlier. *BfZ*

Impero was not launched until the autumn of 1939, and was transferred from Genoa to Brindisi on 1 June 1940, because it was felt she would be less vulnerable there. Any resumption of building was unthinkable – in any case the shortage of steel made it impossible. In January 1942 she was towed to Venice, and later to Trieste, where she was seized by the Germans after the Italian surrender, serving as a stationary experimental and target ship. On 20 February 1945 she was hit so badly in a US air raid that she sank. She was salvaged, in the autumn of 1947, towed to Venice, beached, and then gradually broken up, the last remnants not until 1950. This photo was taken off Venice, on 14 August 1948. *BfZ*

A starboard view of *Impero*, also dated 1948, showing the hull grounded. No 3 barbette is visible, and the ship's wartime camouflage is still in evidence. Substantial parts of the hull have already been dismantled. *BfZ*

Vittorio Veneto and the renamed *Italia*, which had been transferred to Malta when Italy capitulated, were immediately moved on to Alexandria, and thence to the southern end of the Suez canal, where they remained for the rest of the war. At this time it was discussed whether the two ships could not be operated for the defence of carrier groups belonging to the British fleets in the Indian and Pacific Oceans; after her collapse and capitulation, Italy could not be considered an ally, but was accepted as a co-warring state against Germany. The idea was soon dropped however, owing the ships' insufficient range and other logistical inadequacies, and early in 1946 both were allowed home. This 1947 photo of *Vittorio Veneto* shows her after 38.1cm (15in) triple turret. *BfZ*

As a result of the peace treaty signed in February 1947 and its armament limitations (which were lifted again in 1951), Italy was allowed to keep two of her five remaining battleships, *Caio Duilio* and *Andrea Doria*; the third old battleship, *Giulio Cesare*, was ceded to the Soviet Union, while *Vittorio Veneto* and *Italia* were destined for the scrapyard in order to forestall any Soviet claim on them. In 1948 both were taken out of service, and by 1950 both had been scrapped at La Spezia. This is *Vittorio Veneto*, photographed on 5 September 1948, already showing obvious signs of being broken up. *BfZ*

On no occasion did the guns of Italian battleships inflict really serious damage on the enemy; the reasons for this were the decisions of the Italian Naval Command, who often used their capital ships half-heartedly or timidly. This view of *Vittorio Veneto*'s after turret, taken whilst the ship was being broken up, shows three of her powerful 38cm guns. *Author's Collection*

Austria-Hungary

Designs for the three *Radetzky* class battleships date back to 1905–06. The ships were launched between 1909 and 1910 and, following the example of other countries – in particular Italy, where the *Regina Elena* class had been completed only a short time before – they were fitted with a 24cm (9.4in) calibre secondary armament consisting of four twin turrets mounted on either beam; as such, they represented an important further development of the *Erzherzog Karl* class built in the early years of the century, which were the first Austrian battleships to be fitted with a heavy secondary battery, consisting of eight 19cm (7.5in) guns. With the *Radetzky*, the Austria-Hungarian Navy had reached a stage of development from which the only possible course was the transition to the 'all-big-gun' battleship. Externally, the ships bore a strong resemblance to the British *King Edward VII* class completed a little earlier; from a distance, the only identifying characteristics were the *Radetzky*s' distinctive cranes between the funnels. This is *Erzherzog Franz Ferdinand*, around 1916–17. *Stockinger Collection*

Viribus Unitis class

Prinz Eugen, Szent István, Tegetthoff, Viribus Unitis

The fact that Austria-Hungary was able to build dreadnoughts so early was due principally to Admiral Rudolf Montecuccolli, who had been C in C since 1904 and was thus the highest ranking officer. When the Stabilimento Tecnico Triestino shipyard made a personal approach to him in 1910, offering to begin building capital ships on the two slipways then becoming available, he immediately seized the opportunity: on his own responsibility the keels of two dreadnoughts, *Tegetthoff* and *Viribus Unitis* were laid that same year, and the building costs were initially covered by the yard. This was an extremely risky decision for Count Montecuccoli, since there was no legal basis for his action; on the other hand, his boldness also showed a great sense of responsibility towards the skilled workers of the shipyard, as a large proportion of them would otherwise have had to be laid off. His initiative was rewarded the following year when Parliament agreed to a long-term naval construction programme, which included sixteen battleships to be built by 1920; this move secured the future of the two units then being built, and two further ships were laid down soon afterwards. The first ship to be launched was *Viribus Unitis*, on 2 June 1911; this photo shows the moment of launch, her stern just afloat. Below the ram bow can be seen the opening for the bow torpedo tube. The guest of honour at the launching ceremony was the successor to the Austrian throne, Archduke Franz Ferdinand; almost exactly three years later, his body was takerr home on board this ship after the Sarajevo assassination. *BfZ*

The *Viribus Unitis* class (also known as the *Tegetthoff* class) had an unmistakable similarity to the *Radetzky* class pre-dreadnoughts; this similarity was not surprising, since only a few years separated the two designs, and the chief characteristics for each were laid down under the direction of Siegfried Popper, the chief of Austrian naval construction, who, despite having been in retirement since 1907, was still a major influence. If one compares the two classes, one gets the impression that the *Viribus Unitis* class were simple linear enlargements of the *Radetzky*s with superimposed turrets. This is *Tegetthoff* at anchor.

Viribus Unitis, photographed in July 1914; her flag is at half-mast since the ship is carrying home the coffin containing the body of the Austrian heir to the throne, Archduke Franz Ferdinand, who was murdered on 28 June 1914 at Sarajevo. *BfZ*

The fourth *Viribus Unitis* class ship was given a Hungarian name, *Szent István* (St Stephen), after King Stephen the Holy (977–1038), who became the patron saint of Hungary. By using this name, the Austrians took into account the feelings of Hungary, whose representatives had agreed to the great naval construction programme of 1911 with the proviso that the Danubius yard at Fiume – the only large Hungarian shipyard – should take part. This involved great expense, as the yard had hitherto only built fairly small vessels and therefore would have to be fitted out for the building of large ships. The first was to be *Szent István*, which was not commissioned until late 1915; she is shown here in company with *Tegetthoff* (centre) and *Viribus Unitis*, at Pola in 1916–17. *Stockinger Collection*

Szent István differed from her three sister-ships in that she had a platform built around the forefunnel which extended from the bridge to the after funnel and on which several searchlights were installed; a further distinguishing feature was the modified ventilator trunk in front of the mainmast. The ship is seen here again around 1916–17. *Szent István* was the only ship of her class not to be fitted with torpedo nets. *Stockinger Collection*

The Austro-Hungarian Navy was one of the first to adopt the triple turret; it was also the first to accept the supposed risk of mounting triple turrets in superimposed positions. However, these guns were not used in anger, except when *Tegetthoff* and *Prinz Eugen* bombarded Ancona in May 1915. Here *Viribus Unitis* is seen engaged in gunnery practice, not long after being commissioned. *BfZ*

From 1916–17 the *Viribus Unitis* class battleships carried hood-like frameworks on their funnel tops, over which wire mesh nets were stretched, apparently to offer protection against fluke bombs since the uptakes were not fitted with armoured gratings. At first the mesh was stretched flat across the funnels, but later it was attached to tubular frames with a raised centre, the exact shape varying with each ship; these fittings can be clearly seen in this photograph of *Viribus Unitis*. Note the Lohner flying boat of the Austro-Hungarian Naval Air Arm. *BfZ*

The battleships of the *Viribus Unitis* class were fitted with a battery of eighteen guns to ward off torpedo-boats, although this number was later reduced to twelve; these guns were mounted on the turret roofs and on the upper deck amidships, and were known officially as '7cm anti-torpedo-boat guns L/50 K10' although, curiously, their calibre was only 6.6cm (2.6in). Two of these guns are seen here on board *Prinz Eugen*, whose No 4 turret has just fired. Two auxiliary boat davits can be seen in front of the capstan, having been removed from their sockets and laid on deck in order to provide clear arcs of fire for the anti-torpedo-boat guns. The photograph dates from the summer of 1914. *BfZ*

'Ersatz Monarch' class

From 1913 on, more and more signs began to appear that shifts in the balance of power in the Mediterranean area were imminent, and the Austro-Hungarian Navy found it necessary to ask for replacements for four obsolete pre-dreadnoughts. However, parliamentary difficulties led to long delays in the legal processes required to order these ships, and the contracts for the four replacements were not awarded until the summer of 1914, immediately before the outbreak of World War I. The first ship should have been laid down on 8 August, but the date was first postponed and the whole project later completely abandoned as a result of political developments and the mobilisation which followed. In overall conception, these new ships were improved versions of the *Viribus Unitis* class, with their main calibre increased to 35.5cm (14in). The guns were arranged in two triple and two superimposed twin turrets; apparently only one gun was manufactured, and this was eventually used by the Army. This 1/100 scale model of a capital ship of the 'Ersatz Monarch' class was built by Hartmut Franke and Ludwig Lohberger, and was based on the third design. *Franke/Lohberger*

Russia

In 1903, the Russians began building two classes of battleships which for the first time had a heavy secondary armament of 20.3cm (8in) guns, as well as their main battery of four 30.5cm (12in) guns. The number of 20.3cm guns, however, varied: the *Svyatoy Yevstafi* class, which were built on the Black Sea and were intended for the Black Sea Fleet, had four of these weapons, all in casemates, whilst the ships built at St Petersburg and destined for the Baltic Fleet – the *Imperator Pavel I* class – had fourteen, six of them in casemates and the other eight in turrets on the upper deck. The ships of the two classes, which were also of very different size, were not completed until 1910; the war with Japan had led to considerable delays, not least because of the design changes found necessary – relatively few in the case of the *Svyatoy Yevstafi*s but considerably more with the *Imperator Pavel I* class. Of the two classes, the *Imperator Pavel I* vessels were undoubtedly the more advanced in concept and therefore represented the last stage in the development of Russian pre-dreadnoughts; even so when the ships were finally commissioned, $7^{1}/_{2}$ years after the first keel had been laid, they were obsolete. This photo shows *Imperator Pavel I*, not long after she was commissioned *BfZ*

Another view of *Imperator Pavel I.* The masts, the construction of which recalls contemporary US practice, were cut down drastically during the winter of 1916–17. *Author's Collection*

Gangut class

Gangut, Petropavlovsk, Poltava, Sevastopol

A contemporary painting showing a *Gangut* class battleship fitting out. In the background can be seen another battleship hull, and behind that a covered slipway with a further unit under construction. *Sudostroeyne*

After her serious defeat at the hands of the Jananese it was extraordinarily difficult for Russia to make the transition to dreadnought-type designs while they were rebuilding their fleet, but in 1907 the materials were authorised for such a programme, and tenders were invited for the design of a dreadnought. A total of 51 designs from Russian and foreign design offices and shipyards were submitted; ten were short-listed (only one of which was Russian), and that produced by the German yard of Blohm & Voss was accepted. However, the design could not be followed up since the Russians demanded that the ships be built in Russian yards. Under the direction of chief designer Krylov, a new design, strongly influenced by the Italian chief designer Cuniberti, was drawn up. Triple turrets were adopted for the main armament, and these were arranged in the same manner as those of *Dante Alighieri*, a ship designed under Cuniberti's direction; moreover, following the Italian example, above average speed was also a requirement. The design led to the ordering of a class of four units, which were laid down early in 1909 at St Petersburg, two at the Baltic Yard, and two at the Admiralty Yard. The class took its name, unusually, from the last ship to be launched – *Gangut*; she was built on a covered slipway at the Admiralty Yard and launched in October 1911. The photo shows her shortly before being launched. *Author's Collection*

The *Gangut* class battleship *Poltava*, as completed, at high speed; the photograph dates from around 1916–17. A comparison of this class with the Italian *Dante Alighieri* will indicate their similarities. *Author's Collection*

Petropavlovsk at anchor, also around 1916–17. *BfZ*

In 1925 *Sevastopol* was renamed *Parizskaya Kommuna* and in the winter of 1929–30 was transferred to the Black Sea. On the way, severe weather in the Northern Atlantic caused serious damage, and she had to put in to Brest for emergency repairs, where this picture was taken. The flag of the host country is flying from the foretop. The top of the forefunnel is angled back to protect the bridge crew from smoke. *Author's Collection*

This mid-1930s photo of *Parizskaya Kommuna* has rarity value since it shows a catapult installed on No 3 turret; trials conducted with this equipment led to the installation of similar systems on new cruisers, and it was also intended to fit them on the new battleships. Otherwise *Parizskaya Kommuna*'s appearance is still the same as in 1929–30, when she was transferred to the Black Sea; her new curved stem, fitted some time earlier, is well shown. The fact that the ship is dressed overall can probably be ascribed to the celebration of a Communist state holiday. *Author's Collection*

The debut of the first modernised battleship to fly the Soviet flag took place in September 1934, when *Marat* entered the Polish port of Gdynia on a courtesy visit. *Marat* was the renamed *Petropavlosk*, and had undergone a thorough refit in 1926–28 which included the fitting of new boilers and gun barrels. In 1931–34 the Baltic Yard of Leningrad carried out a further refit, from which the ship returned considerably altered. The forecastle was raised by about 3ft (1m), and a sickle-shaped stem was incorporated; other measures concerned principally the bridge and foremast areas, mostly necessitated by the adoption of new fire control systems. The top half of the forefunnel was angled aft to help keep the bridge and conning tower free of smoke interference. This photo was taken in May 1937 at Spithead during King George VI's Coronation Review of the Fleet, at which *Marat* represented the Soviet Union. *Author's Collection*

In 1925 *Gangut* was renamed *Oktyabrskaya Revoluciya*. After undergoing an initial basic refit, she entered dock in October 1931 to be modernised, and when she reappeared three years later she looked completely different. Although she had undergone the same sort of treatment as *Marat*, everything was more strongly emphasised externally: a larger bridge superstructure, a much larger mast, the S-shaped forefunnel, and the much enlarged superstructure around the mainmast with its two heavy girder cranes for hoisting and lowering the ship's aircraft (and occasionally also torpedo-boats). The photograph shows *Oktyabrskaya Revoluciya* around the mid-1930s. *Author's Collection*

The *Luftwaffe* carried out repeated heavy dive-bombing attacks in September 1941 on the Soviet Baltic Fleet at anchor in Kronshtadt and Leningrad, with the intention of eliminating the fleet entirely, since it was blocking the German advance along the coast with its long-range fire. During these attacks the battleships *Oktyabrskaya Revoluciya* and *Marat* were seriously hit, *Marat* particularly so, since her forecastle, including her bridge and forefunnel, were destroyed by a direct hit by a 1000kg (2200lb) bomb. The ship sank to the bottom by the harbour entrance. There she remained for the rest of the war, but the Russians gradually managed to get Nos 3 and 4 turrets into working order again, followed by No 2, and *Marat* was employed as a stationary battery and provided very effective support to the Red Army's attack on the German defence lines at Oranienbaum in 1944; in 1943 she had been given back her old name *Petropavlosk*, and she was later renamed *Volchov*. *Oktyabrskaya Revoluciya*, hit by several 15cm (5.9in) shells from German artillery on 16 September 1941, was outside Kronshtadt harbour on this occasion, and was able to evade a large number of dive-bomber attacks, but she was caught by a few bombs (between three and six) which did less damage than on *Marat*. The following October she was transferred to the Baltic Yard at Leningrad, where her damage was repaired, although, she was hit again, this time by four bombs, in April 1942, during these repairs. She supported the land offensive with her heavy artillery until Leningrad was liberated, and in June 1944 she backed up the Red Army's push against the Karelian Isthmus and the Finnish-held islands. *Oktyabrskaya Revoluciya* is seen here during the aerial attack on 21 September 1941, under a hail of bombs; her stern is turned towards the harbour entrance. *Author's Collection*

Parizskaya Kommuna was in dockyard hands for a major refit from 1938, and she was modernised to virtually the same extent as *Oktyabrskaya Revoluciya*. The two ships were almost indistinguishable, but one difference was the shape of the crane system fitted on the mainmast, *Parizskaya Kommuna* (shown here around 1940) having support struts to hers. *Author's Collection*

Marat, which had been given back her old name of *Petropavlosk* in 1943, remained wrecked off Kronshtadt until the early 1950s and was then broken up *in situ*, but *Oktyabrskaya Revoluciya* remained in commission until the mid-1950s, keeping her name to the end, despite reports to the contrary. This photo was taken postwar and shows the ship in a slightly altered condition: the two girder cranes on the mainmast are now missing, and additional heavy AA guns are positioned on the after battery deck and on the forecastle. *Author's Collection*

This photograph of *Oktyabrskaya Revoluciya* was published in the *Illyastrivovannya Gazeta* of 10 August 1948, and shows obvious signs of the censor's activities: the two twin AA turrets on the forecastle have been touched out, as have the 37mm twins on No 1 turret. This deceit is hard to understand in the context of military secrecy, since the radar antenna (a British device, apparently) on the foretop has not been tampered with. A glance further aft reveals another interesting fact: the cranes on either side of the mainmast bear a striking resemblance to those fitted on board large surface vessels of the *Kriegsmarine*. The solution to the puzzle is that they are the cranes which were fitted previously to the cruiser 'L' (ex-*Lützow*), which had been handed over to the Soviet Union early in 1941, first under the name *Petropavlosk* and later *Tallinn*. The irreparable damage she suffered in the war precluded any ideas of completing her and so everything possible was utilised for other purposes. The battleship *Oktyabrskaya Revoluciya* was fitted with the German cranes to replace the old girder units, which might have restricted the arcs of fire of the AA weapons too severely. *Author's Collection*

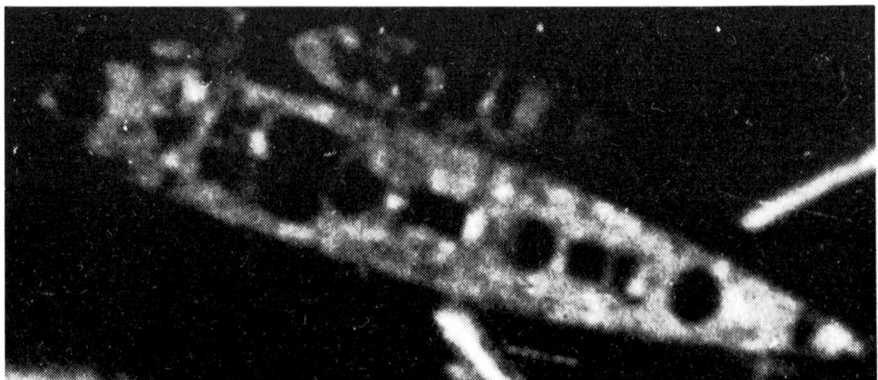

Poltava was renamed *Mikhail Frunze* in 1920 but was not recommissioned since she was gutted by fire soon afterwards. This aerial photograph was taken during World War II and shows her in the coal harbour at Leningrad in 1942. Although the picture is of poor quality it is evident that the 30.5cm (12in) turrets are no longer fitted. The hull was broken up after the end of the war. *Author's Collection*

Khrushchev, who took over power on Stalin's death, was very sceptical about the value of large warships; thus it was that in the mid-1950s the bell tolled for the two surviving Russian battleships. They were broken up in 1956, *Oktyabrskaya Revoluciya* (seen here) at Kronshtadt. *Author's Collection*

Sevastopol was probably broken up at the port from which she took her name. She is seen here at an advanced stage of scrapping. *Author's Collection*

Imperatrica Mariya class

Imperator Aleksandr III, Imperatrica Ekaterina II, Imperatrica Mariya

As a counterweight to the Turkish shipbuilding programme, three battleships of a design related to the *Gangut* class were ordered by Russia in 1911 for the Black Sea Fleet. The calibre and disposition of the main armament were the same as that of the *Gangut* class, yet despite all the superficial similarities between the two classes there were considerable differences in concept. With this new class the Russian Navy had turned away from the concept of the fast battleship – symbolised by the *Gangut*s – and had returned to the more traditional type, a better protected, but slower, vessel. The name ship of the class was *Imperatrica Mariya*, which joined the Fleet in the summer of 1915; she is seen here at anchor off Sevastopol late in 1915. The marked external similarity to the *Gangut* class is very obvious. *Author's Collection*

This photo was taken early in 1918 after the Russo-German treaty, and shows a group of German naval officers together with a few Russian seamen standing on the upturned *Imperatrica Mariya*. The cross indicates Admiral Hofmann, the highest ranking officer of the Imperial German Navy in the Black Sea area at that time. The wreck was not salvaged until 1922, and it was then broken up in drydock at Sevastopol Navy Yard. *BfZ* ▶

After several thrusts against the Turkish and Bulgarian coasts, and an action involving the light cruiser *Breslau* (Turkish *Midilli*), *Imperatrica Mariya* was the victim of an accident: on 20 October 1916 there was a violent explosion on board, followed by a second, as she lay at anchor in Sevastopol Roads; her forward magazine had ignited, and the fire spread to a shell room and caused the explosion. The ship was severely damaged, capsized, and sank. *BfZ*

The third ship of the *Imperatrica Mariya* class was named *Imperator Aleksandr III*, and was laid down at Nikolayev in the autumn of 1911 at the Russian Shipbuilding Co yard (known before and during World War II as Nordwerft, and today as the 61 Kommunar Yard), and did not join the Fleet until the summer of 1917. She is seen here during final fitting-out; to the right, in the background, is the slip on which she was built. Even before she was commissioned, two 13cm (5.1in) guns had been removed (the two forward mountings) and their casemates sealed, because experience with *Imperatrica Mariya* had shown that they flooded when the ship was steaming at high speed. *Imperatrica Mariya*, however, retained these guns until the end; *Ekaterina II*, the second ship of the class, had an overall length 6ft 6in (2m) greater, which meant that the forward casemates were that distance further aft and were therefore less 'wet'. *BfZ*

The battleship *Imperator Aleksandr III*, probably shortly after being commissioned, and in a spotless condition. *BfZ*

After the Russian Revolution the battleship *Imperator Aleksandr III* bore the name *Volya* (='Freedom'). When the ship was taken over by a German crew at Sevastopol in the autumn of 1918, the name was loosely transliterated as 'Volga'. But neither this name nor any other was ever given to the ship by the German authorities; she was never even commissioned under the German flag. The ship was transferred from Sevastopol to Novorossiysk in April 1918, and only returned to Sevastopol in August as a result of a German ultimatum. She is seen here off the Crimean coast. *BfZ*

The collapse of the German Empire in November 1918 resulted in a withdrawal from the occupied areas of Russia where by then the Civil War between the White Russians and the Bolsheviks had broken out. The Germans gave up the battleship *Volya* to the White Russian military authorities, who renamed her *General Alekseyev*, after the Army commander who was leading the fight against the Bolsheviks with a few thousand Cossacks and other volunteers. For the following two years the ship represented a sort of 'fleet in being', whose presence alone was intended to act as a deterrent to the Bolshevik troops in their advance and probably did indeed do so. When the White Russian forces could no longer resist Bolshevik pressure in 1920 and evacuated the Crimea, *General Alekseyev* and other White Russian Fleet units left Sevastopol, steamed to Constantinople, and reached Bizerta, French North Africa, in December, where they were interned. *General Alekseyev* and the other vessels officially remained in commission, until on French orders their flags were lowered in October 1924, never to be raised again. The French wanted to return the ships, but the Soviet Union was not interested. A Soviet committee had earlier been sent to Bizerta and had found the ships in a decrepit condition; there seemed no hope of ever making them serviceable again. Between 1926 and 1937 *General Alekseyev* was broken up piece by piece. The French stored her 30.5cm (12in) guns at the fortress of Sidi Abdullah, near Bizerta; a few of the weapons are supposed to have reached Finland during the Winter War of 1939–40, whilst others fell into German hands in the Second World War and were then built into bunkers on the Channel coast. The photograph, taken only a few years after the previous one, shows *General Alekseyev* (ex-*Volya*, ex-*Imperator Aleksandr III*) already in an advanced stage of decay. *Author's Collection*

Borodino class

In the autumn of 1912, four battlecruisers – the *Borodino* class – were ordered, representing part of an all-embracing naval construction programme which included the building of 24 battleships and 12 battlecruisers. These were all destined for the Baltic Fleet, and could therefore be used only with difficulty against any power other than Germany. This class of ships also had some features in common with the *Ganguts*, especially with regard to the disposition of the main armament, but the design featured a raised forecastle to improve seakeeping at the high speeds envisaged. A notable feature was the arrangement of a part of the secondary battery in two-storey casemates.

All four battlecruisers were laid down on 1 January 1914 at St Petersburg, two in the Baltic Yard and two at the Admiralty Yard. This print, which was published in the Soviet press, shows the launching of one of these battlecruisers: the artist has captured particularly well the shape of the hull and the secondary casemates. *Sudostroeyne*

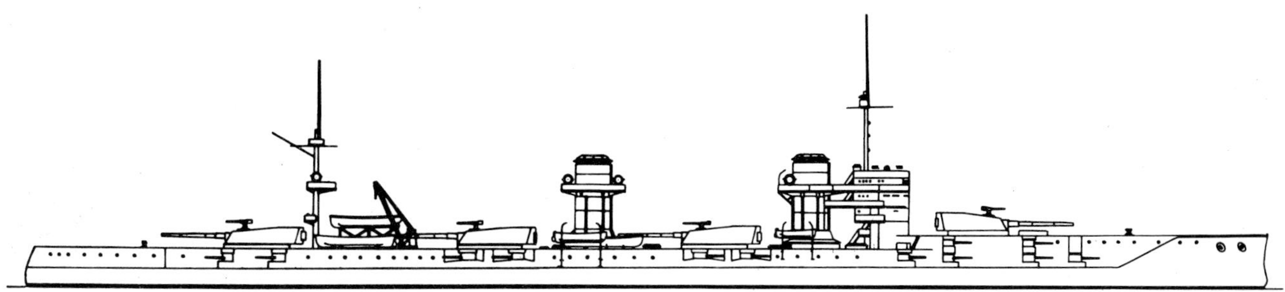

The designed final appearance of the *Borodino* class, according to more recent information. *Author*

None of the *Borodino* class battlecruisers was completed; all were launched, but after the Russians towed them around from place to place for a time work on them was halted early in 1917. *Izmail* was the furthest advanced, and her machinery is said to have been ready for fitting; for this reason, her completion was evidently considered after the end of the Civil War and may account for the fact that she was not broken up until 1931. Her three sister-ships had been scrapped as early as 1923–24, not in the Soviet Union but in Germany. This rare picture shows *Izmail* being launched on 22 June 1915 at the Admiralty Yard. *Author's Collection*

Sovetskiy Soyuz class

It was only many years after the end of World War II that the Russians published any material about the *Sovetskiy Soyuz* class. Admiral Gorshkov published a report on the role of navies in war and peace in a wide-ranging article which appeared in the official journal *Morskoy Sbornik*; shortly afterwards the same journal carried this artist's impression of one of the super battleships. The *Sovetskiy Soyuz* class, together with other Russian projects, are covered in more detail in the Appendices. *Morskoy Sbornik*

◀ Another rare photo of a *Borodino* class battlecruiser, this time *Kinburn*; she was launched on 30 October 1915, and is shown here in the early stages of fitting out at the Baltic Yard. *Author's Collection*

The only reports available on the construction of Soviet battleships up to 1939–40 are imprecise and somewhat contradictory, as even at that time the Soviet Union published no details at all about her armament programmes or the strength of her forces, and the expansion of her armed forces took place (and is still taking place) in the strictest secrecy. It was known at that time, however, that the Soviets had made tentative representations to the Western world with a view to securing assistance with the building of new battleships; what was also known was that a battleship was under construction in the Baltic Yard at Leningrad, although knowledge of this was limited to a displacement estimate of about 35,000 tons. Details only became known after the start of the German invasion. When German forces approached Nikolayev in August 1941 they were met with an impressive sight, visible from a considerable distance: on a slipway of the Marti Yard they found the hull of a battleship, almost ready for launching. On closer examination it proved to be substantially larger than had been supposed – this new battleship was of the same order of size as that picked up by German reconnaissance over Leningrad. They were not 35,000-ton vessels, but 60,000-ton 'super battleships', similar to those which had already been laid down in Japan and Germany. The photo shows the hull of the battleship on the slipway, as seen by German troops outside Nikolayev. *Bestermann*

Archangelsk

Following the capitulation of Italy, the Soviet Union claimed one third of all the Italian warships that had fallen into Allied hands, all of which were thoroughly modern vessels, but the British and Americans were very reluctant to agree to this. The reasons given for their refusal concerned the impossibility of transferring the ships to the Soviet sphere of influence in the middle of the war, and as substitutes they offered vessels from their own navies, a proposal to which the Soviets agreed. Amongst the ships transferred in the summer of 1944 was the British battleship *Royal Sovereign*, which, renamed *Archangelsk*, was moved from Rosyth to Murmansk from 20 to 29 August 1944, serving in the Soviet Northern Fleet until 1948. This photo was taken at Rosyth, shortly after the ship had been taken over by her Soviet crew. *BfZ*

Another view of *Archangelsk*, also at Rosyth. Early in 1949 the ship was returned to Great Britain, and soon afterwards scrapped. It is worth noting that the return coincided step for step with the transfer of the Italian battleship *Giulio Cesare*, which had been allocated to the Soviet Union under the peace treaty signed with Italy. The priority that the German High Command – unjustifiably – placed on *Archangelsk* is shown by the fact that several German submarines were sent to attack her early in January 1945; their *Biber* mini-submarines were to penetrate the Kola Inlet and eliminate *Archangelsk* and other worthwhile targets using torpedoes. However, the *Biber*s malfunctioned and the operation had to be abandoned. *Author's Collection*

This is the only photograph ever found showing the former Italian *Giulio Cesare* as the Soviet *Novorossiysk*; it was taken in the Black Sea, probably off Sevastopol. On 3 February 1949 the ship was delivered to the Soviet Union as part of the 1947 peace treaty, her transfer taking place at the same time as the return of *Royal Sovereign*. The Russians did not keep *Novorossiysk* for long: during the preparations for the celebration of the 38th anniversary of the October Revolution – on 3 or 4 November 1955 – she suffered an internal explosion and was so severely damaged that she sank. *Author's Collection*

Argentina

Rivadavia class

Moreno, Rivadavia

Following the actions of Brazil, Argentina ordered two dreadnoughts, not from British yards (which had been counting on these contracts), nor from the Germans (where prospects had seemed good initially), but from the Americans. The battleships *Rivadavia* and *Moreno* were laid down in 1910 and commissioned soon after the outbreak of the war in Europe. The division of the main armament into six turrets, and also its layout, reflected both British and American influence: American in the superimposed turrets, and British in the *en échelon* wing turrets. Here, *Rivadavia* is shown at her builders' yard, ready for trials and still under the US flag. *BfZ*

With their widely spaced funnels and the main armament spread out between them, *Moreno* and *Rivadavia* were somewhat reminiscent of the Italian *Dante Alighieri* and the Russian *Gangut* class, whilst the cage mast was typical of American practice; the full-strength secondary battery, on the other hand, showed German influence. A characteristic feature of these ships was the pair of tall, diagonally offset columns, connected by a footbridge, on each of which two searchlights were mounted. Both these columns also supported a boat crane. Here *Moreno* is being towed into port; the date of the photo is not known. *BfZ*

Rivadavia in 1937. Note the modifications made to her mainmast. *Barilli Collection*

Brazil

Minas Gerais class

Minas Gerais, São Paulo

When Great Britain took up the building of 'all-big-gun' battleships, Brazil saw the opportunity to secure her maritime supremacy over Chile and Argentina for years to come by immediately following Britain's action and ordered *Minas Gerais* and *São Paulo* even before *Dreadnought* had been commissioned. Construction started one year later, and both vessels were delivered in 1910. They were of a very similar design to the *Dreadnought*, although the wing turrets were arranged *en échelon* instead of being exactly opposite; Nos 2 and 5 turrets were superimposed. *Minas Gerais* is seen here undergoing initial trials; she is already fitted with torpedo nets. *Author's Collection*

From this angle, the *Minas Gerais* class' line of descent from the British *Dreadnought* is obvious: the positioning of the forefunnel between the bridge superstructure and the tripod mast and the wide space between the mast and the after funnel are as typical as the shape of the funnel casings. Rotating rangefinders of American manufacture are fitted on the two superimposed turrets; these were installed during a refit in the USA, which *São Paulo* underwent from 1917 to 1920 and *Minas Gerais* from 1920 to 1921. This photo shows *São Paulo* in early 1927; a range clock can be picked out below ◀ the foretop. *BfZ*

Brazil joined the war against the Central Powers on the side of the Allies in 1917, and offered to send her two dreadnoughts to Europe to be integrated into the British Grand Fleet. The plan was not, however, carried out, as it was felt that the Royal Navy no longer needed reinforcements. This is *São Paulo* in 1918; she has been camouflaged in preparation for her proposed transfer to the Grand Fleet. *BfZ*

As time passed, both *Minas Gerais* and *São Paulo* needed modernising, but only the former was taken in hand for such work. It lasted from 1934 to 1937, although the improvements and alterations involved were not very extensive. New, exclusively oil-fired boilers were fitted, but the old engines were retained and protection and main armament were untouched. The same measures were planned for *São Paulo* but were not carried out because she was in too poor a condition to justify such a programme. This is the modernised *Minas Gerais*. *Barilli Collection*

Brazil hoped to make further progress in her effort to gain naval supremacy among the South American nations by acquiring *Rio de Janeiro*, which was ordered from Britain in 1911. The ship proved to be a monster, her main armament being arranged in seven twin turrets to give a total of fourteen 12in (30.5cm) guns, a number not equalled by any other dreadnought. However, as the general trend towards heavier calibres became established, Brazil lost interest in *Rio de Janeiro* and she was happy to find an interested party in Turkey, who acquired the ship, half completed, and provided funds for the work to be continued. This is the ship from which the Brazilian flag was never flown – but not under Turkish colours: she flies the Union Jack. With the outbreak of World War I, the new vessel, on the point of completion, was requisitioned by Great Britain; soon afterwards she joined the Grand Fleet under the name *Agincourt*. *Author's Collection*

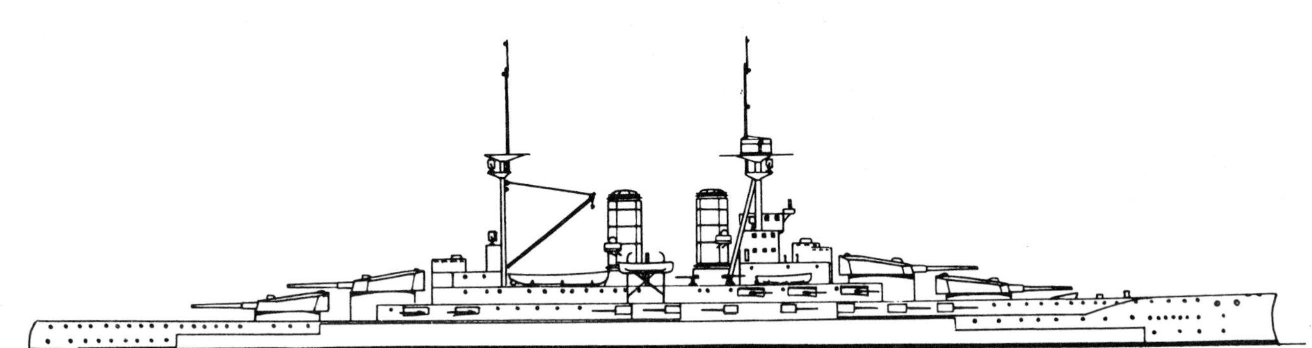

Brazil's ambitious naval construction programme culminated in *Riachuelo*, designed in 1913–14 as a replacement for *Rio de Janeiro*. She was to be a battleship roughly equivalent to the British *Queen Elizabeths*, the *ne plus ultra* in capital ship design at the time. The ship was authorised by Brazil in February 1914, but the project was never realised: financial difficulties delayed the keel laying and the outbreak of the First World War finally put an end to it. This drawing shows the final design of *Riachuelo*, as Vickers' 'Design No 781'. *Author*

Chile

Almirante Latorre

The third and last South American state to acquire dreadnoughts was Chile, when in 1911 she awarded building contracts for two ships to Great Britain. In general concept they were similar to the British battleships of the *Iron Duke* class which were laid down around the same time, although the main armament was fixed at 14in (35.6cm) instead of the 13.5in (34.3cm) then being fitted to British vessels. The two ships were originally named *Libertad* and *Constitution*, then *Valparaiso* and *Santiago*, and finally *Almirante Latorre* and *Almirante Cochrane*. In the event, only one ship was delivered, and even that not immediately: with the outbreak of war Great Britain requisitioned both ships, *Almirante Latorre* joined the Grand Fleet under the name of *Canada*, and work on the second ship was halted. Work on *Almirante Cochrane* was resumed towards the end of the war, but she was not completed to the original design and emerged as the Royal Navy's aircraft carrier *Eagle*. Chile was able to raise her flag on *Almirante Latorre* in 1920, five years after her completion, and the ship was not stricken from service for nearly four decades. Shortly after this she made her last voyage, towed by tugs to Yokohama, where she was scrapped. This photograph was taken shortly after the ship arrived there. *BfZ*

Another view of *Almirante Latorre* at Yokohama. Note the prominent anti-torpedo bulge. *BfZ*

Greece

Salamis

The Greek *Salamis* was planned as a '13,000-ton armoured ship', and the building contract for her was awarded to the German Vulcan shipyard at Hamburg in the summer of 1912. However, a few weeks later, war broke out against Turkey, and when the Greeks succeeded in thwarting an attempted breakout into the Aegean by the Turkish fleet, a remarkable change of plan took place: the Greek Naval Command decided that a fully-fledged dreadnought was required. The contract and the designs for *Salamis* were changed accordingly, involving an increase in displacement of 7000 tons. *Salamis* was laid down in the summer of 1913 and launched towards the end of 1914, although work then stopped owing to the exigencies of the war. With the end of

the war, Greece refused to accept the unfinished ship, the completion of which had been made impossible by the armament limitations laid down by the victorious powers. Agreement was not reached, and in 1923 the shipyard began legal proceedings against Greece which were not brought to a conclusion until ten years later. Greece was required to make a payment in settlement and the unfinished ship became the property of the yard, who had the vessel scrapped. These two photos show *Salamis* shortly after her launch. *Author's Collection*

During World War I there was some talk in Germany about the possibility of completing *Salamis* and commissioning her with the High Seas Fleet, but the idea had to be abandoned since it was not possible to produce the necessary guns in less than two years. The story that *Salamis* would have borne the name *Tirpitz* had she been completed and commissioned cannot be verified, and in any case the name would not have been appropriate for a variety of reasons. These two photographs of the ship date from the immediate postwar period and were taken at Hamburg. Alongside is the battlecruiser *Mackensen* which was broken up at Hamburg in 1923–24. *Author's Collection*

The Netherlands

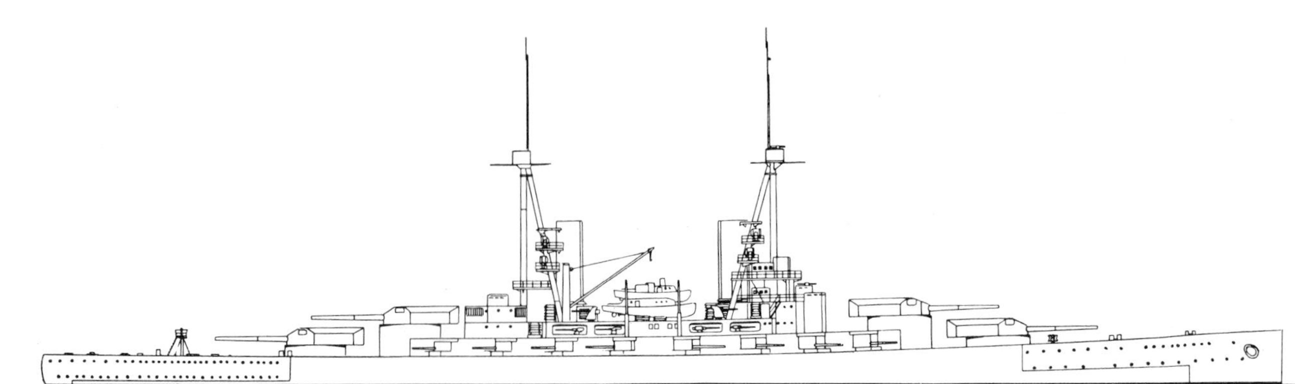

Twice in her history the Netherlands planned the acquisition of dreadnoughts, and on both occasions a war broke out shortly afterwards and put an end to her ambitions. In 1913 a long-term naval construction programme was decided on which included battleships, but they shared the fate of the three battlecruisers planned in 1939. In both instances the Netherlands had to rely on assistance from other countries as her industry lacked the capacity to produce heavy guns and armour plate. The Dutch always hoped to receive this support from their German neighbours. In 1913–14 one British and two German shipbuilding companies submitted designs, and although no decision was actually taken it seems that the design produced by Germaniawerft of Kiel (shown here) was closest to the Dutch specifications. *Author*

The battlecruisers planned in 1939 were of a type which bore at least a superficial similarity to the battlecruisers 'O', 'P' and 'Q' which were at the design stage in Germany at the same time, although with regard to their main armament and its layout they were identical to the German *Scharnhorst* class. The similarity with the battlecruisers 'O', 'P' and 'Q' was purely coincidental since these designs were being drawn up at exactly the same time and were kept secret – as happened without exception for every new vessel planned by the old Imperial Navy – so that it would have been impossible for the Dutch to study them and base their own ideas on them. This is an artist's impression of one of the proposed battlecruisers. *Nautica*

Spain

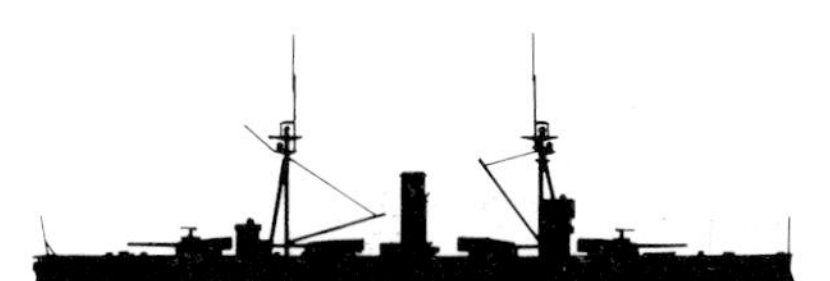

España class

Alfonso XIII, España, Jaime I

Spain responded to the building of ▶ *Dreadnought* with the Fleet Building Act of early 1908, which envisaged the construction of three battleships. British assistance was needed: the designs were prepared by Armstrong and most of the materials required also came from Britain. Only two ships were originally contracted for, *España* and *Alfonso XIII*, and these were laid down in 1908 and 1920 respectively. The design was remarkable in that an attempt was made to double the number of heavy guns whilst keeping the ships to pre-dreadnought dimensions. The attempt was successful, without a doubt, although only at the expense of protection: the ships proved to be the smallest and weakest dreadnoughts built and the concept was not copied anywhere else. This is *Alfonso XIII*, seen from astern. From 1931 this ship carried the name *España*, after the first ship of that name had been lost. *BfZ*

The name ship *España* ran aground at Cape Tres Forkas, Morocco, in August 1923, resisted all attempts at salvage, and had to be abandoned, although it proved possible to save parts of the ships, including the heavy guns, which were later used in coastal batteries. The ship is seen at the beginning of salvage operations; her shadow can be made out on the surface of the water. *Author's Collection*

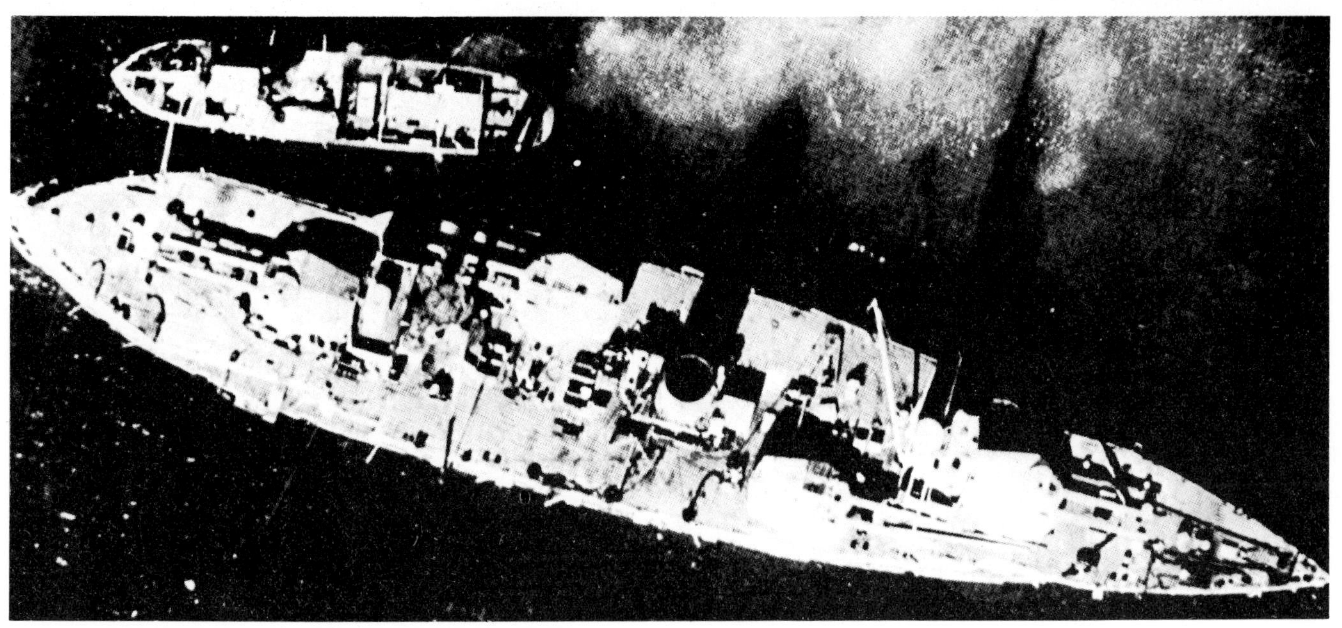

The third Spanish battleship authorised by the 1908 Act was originally intended to be built as a modified *España*: the designs were worked out in 1909–10 and included an increase in displacement to 17,000 tons and a speed of 21kts, and whilst the armament was to stay the same the range was to be greater. However, Spain's economic difficulties led to the plans being abandoned and the third ship, which was named *Jaime I*, was laid down to an unchanged design in 1912. Her completion was considerably delayed since supplies of materials from Great Britain were not forthcoming owing to the war, and work did not resume until 1919. *Jaime I* was finally able to join the Spanish Fleet in 1922. She was on the Republican side during the Spanish Civil War and was so badly damaged in battle that she had to be scrapped in 1939. This aerial view of *Jaime I* clearly shows the layout of her main and secondary armament. *BfZ*

Turkey

Yavuz Sultan Selim

Turkey made strenuous efforts to achieve maritime supremacy in the Black Sea – over her traditional enemy Russia – by acquiring dreadnoughts, but her plans foundered as a result of Great Britain's offhand attitude: at the start of the First World War both units ready for delivery to Turkey were requisitioned, and they joined the Grand Fleet a little later. In this situation the Germans, who had been exercising an ever stronger influence over Turkey for some years, suggested that they should supply replacement vessels; the offer was based on the fact that the battlecruiser *Goeben* and the light cruiser *Breslau* were in the Mediterranean, and both of them would have had difficulty reaching home after the outbreak of war. The two ships were henceforth moved to Turkish waters, where a sham sale was arranged (in fact both ships remained under German command and even kept their German crews), and these developments gave Turkey good reasons for joining the war on the side of the Central Powers. Four years later, shortly before the Armistice, *Goeben* was formally transferred. For the next few decades the newly named *Yavuz Sultan Selim* – renamed simply *Yavuz* in 1936 – remained the core of the Turkish fleet. She spent her last 22 years as a stationary ship at Gölcük; she is seen there in this photo, which was taken in 1952 or later since her pennant number, allocated to her by NATO, to which Turkey has belonged since 1952, is worn on her hull. *Yavuz* was scrapped in the mid-1970s, having had the longest existence of any dreadnought; with over sixty years of 'life', she achieved an exceptionally high age for any warship. *BfZ (Author's Collection)*

◀ Another view of *Jaime I* showing the ship's boats stowed on Nos 2 and 3 turrets. *BfZ*

Appendices

Appendix 1

German 'super-battleships'

The conclusion of the Anglo-German Navy Treaty on 18 June 1935 gave the *Reichsmarine* the opportunity to free itself of the constraints to which the Treaty of Versailles had committed it. By the terms of the 1935 treaty, the Reich's government was obliged never to allow the total tonnage of the German Fleet to exceed 35 per cent of the actual British tonnage, and this proportion was also to hold true in each individual category of ships (battleships, aircraft carriers, cruisers, destroyers and submarines). In the battleship category, this meant initially a permissible tonnage of 183,750, based on the 525,000 tons that the Royal Navy had been allowed for battleships under the terms of the Washington Naval Treaty of 1922[1]. Of these 183,750 tons, 30,000 were already 'used up' for the three *Deutschland* class 'pocket-battleships', so that for the construction of 'real' battleships 153,750 tons were available[2]; hence four battleships were laid down in 1935 and 1936 – *Scharnhorst* and *Gneisenau* at 26,000 tons each and *Bismarck* and *Tirpitz* at 35,000 tons each, leaving 31,750 tons remaining of the available tonnage[3].

On 4 March 1939 the British government sent a communiqué advising the intended total tonnage for British battleships up to the end of 1943, *viz* 711,000, for a total of 21 units. Working from this, Germany was permitted exactly 248,000 tons, which had to include the ships then available and those already under construction (7, with a total of 152,000 tons), leaving another 96,500 tons available; accordingly the *Kriegsmarine*'s 1938 budget provided for two further battleships, 'H' and 'J'. The standard displacement for battleships based on the current treaty situation had also become binding on the German Reich in respect of the so-called 'qualitative' limitations, and therefore the size of the ships was laid down at a maximum of 35,000 tons; however, this was raised by a special report to 45,000 tons on 30 June 1938 and meant that the revised limit could be fully exploited with the new units 'H' and 'J' then under construction.

The standard displacement of these ships was officially supposed to be as shown in the accompanying table, figures for the actual and the specified standard displacements being given in an OKM report dated 18 February 1938. Reports of this kind were made out as part of the exchange of information agreed upon in the Treaty. It is obvious that three different designs of 'H' were considered[4].

'H' CLASS SPECIFICATIONS

	Length (m)	Beam (m)	Displacement (t) Actual	Displacement (t) Specified	Draught (m) Actual	Draught (m) Specified
H-I	254.0	41.0	56,200	46,850	9.60	8.40
H-II	254.0	41.0	56,200	45,000	9.60	8.15
H-III	254.0	41.0	56,200	45,000	9.60	7.85

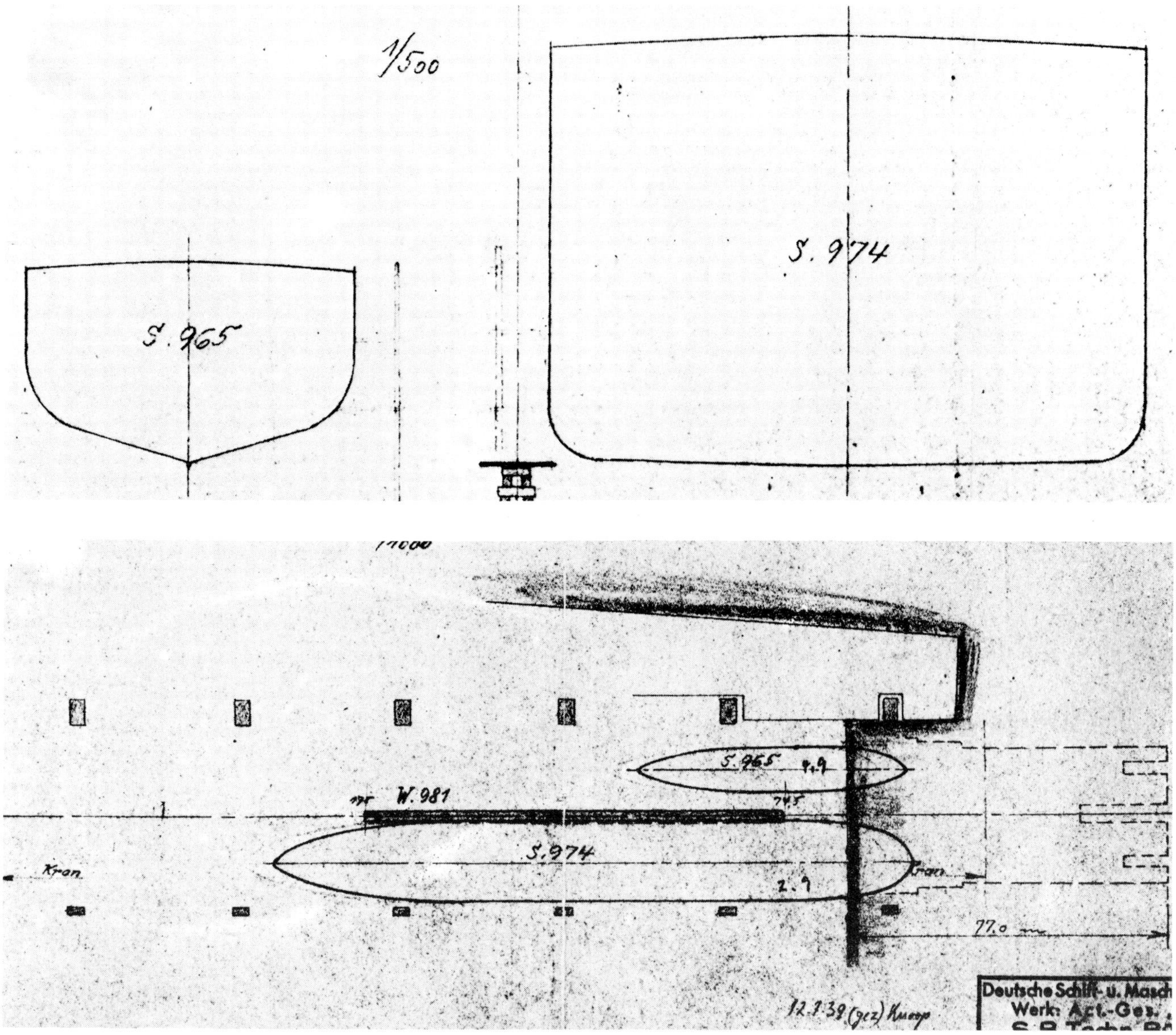

This general drawing from the joint stock company Weser, dated 12 July 1939, shows the use to which Slipway V was put at that time. It includes two ships: the smaller one (hull no 965) was the tug *Atlantik*, intended for the Navy; the larger (hull no 974) was *Rheinfels*, a motor freighter. Between them a section of the keel, around 330ft (100m) long, of battleship 'J' (hull no 981) has been drawn in. In the top picture the situation on the slipway is seen in section. It can be easily understood that this slipway, with its length of about 660ft (200m) would not have sufficed for the battleship; just as with the *Bremen*, the supplementary 77m (250ft) slipway also had to be used. *Author's Collection*

As relations between Germany and Britain began to come to a head at the end of 1938, the 'Z-Plan' was drawn up, the core of which was to be a number of heavily armed, long-range capital ships. This programme was the natural development of the strategic thinking which had already led to the building of the *Deutschland* class *Panzerschiffe*, although until then Hitler had hoped to reach a political agreement with Great Britain. However, his policies were met with ever sharper rejection by the British, whom he therefore had to count among his possible enemies from the end of 1938 on. An examination of any future naval war against Great Britain led to two alternative courses of action. The first proposal was a pure trade war involving submarines and 'pocket-battleships', and would have been relatively quick and inexpensive to carry out, but it seemed to be too one-sided; the alternative was long-term, and could only be carried out at great cost, but offered much wider potential, even though in retrospect it ignored the threat of the aeroplane. This plan was based on building a small but well-balanced and very powerful fleet which could not only wage a trade war but could also operate successfully against enemy warships. Although *Grossadmiral* Raeder, as commander-in-chief of the Navy at that time, emphasised that this long-term plan would result in a '*Flottentorso*' (lit: 'naval torso' = 'headless body') if it should happen that war broke out with Great Britain before the programme had been completed, Hitler persisted: in his opinion, the fleet would not be needed for his political ends before 1946.

The *Kriegsmarine* estimated that about ten years would be necessary in order to bring the 'Z-Plan' to fruition, ie until 1948–49. By then the fleet would consist of the following (including the units already in existence): 10 battleships, 3 battlecruisers, 3 *Panzerschiffe* ('pocket-battleships'), 4 aircraft carriers, 5 heavy

cruisers, 22 light cruisers, 22 scout cruisers, 68 destroyers, 90 torpedo-boats, 249 submarines, 10 minelayers, 75 S-boats and 227 escorts, plus minesweepers, submarine-chasers, etc. The aim was to have a total of 800 ships in service and a strength of 201,000 men; 33,000 million marks were set aside for the purpose.

Hitler approved the 'Z-Plan' on 17 January 1939, but he demanded that it be completed within six years instead of ten as the *Kriegsmarine* had intended; ten days later he gave absolute top priority to naval rearmament, over the expansion of the Army and *Luftwaffe*, and over the demands of the economy.

Nearly all the new warships were to be driven by diesel engines or mixed diesels and turbines to achieve the maximum possible range: war against Britain's lifelines could only be waged in the Atlantic, because it was directed at her overseas supplies, and thus maximum range was the prerequisite for a successful campaign there. Hence the diesel engine became the *Kriegsmarine*'s great hope.

German naval strategy was founded on:

1 The use of mines in British waters and the waging of a trade war by submarines further out around the British coast

2 A commerce war in the ocean lanes, to be waged by 'pocket-battleships', cruisers, auxiliary cruisers and submarines

3 Keeping British warships close to the island empire by creating a German 'fleet in being'[5]

With a commerce war being waged in all the oceans the Royal Navy would be forced to escort British convoys with powerful surface units. These well defended convoys were then to be attacked by powerful battle groups, consisting of several of the new capital ships, one aircraft carrier and a strong escort of scout cruisers and destroyers. Their aim was to be to hunt down the convoys and destroy them, but especially to defeat their heavy escorts.

Quite apart from its military value, this fleet – above all the capital ships – was intended to have a political role to play. The purpose of building them was not only to gain a considerable military superiority, but also to force Great Britain to accept a settlement when the new fleet was completed – especially the capital ships, since Britain had no equivalents at the time. Hitler evidently also hoped that by building a new fleet he would gain an instrument that would not only serve to keep the peace with Great Britain but would also compel her to adopt a different policy towards Germany; in this, Hitler's old desire to form an alliance may have played a not inconsequential part. Such an alliance would have meant that he could help to safeguard the British Empire with his fleet, in order to gain for himself a free hand for his own political ambitions on the European continent.

The stipulations of the 1935 Treaty, however, still stood in the way of the realisation of the 'Z-Plan', and for this reason political negotiations were planned in good time with the aim of extending the treaty. It never came to this, since the occupation of Czechoslovakia in March 1939 greatly increased tension between Germany and Great Britain. From this time on it was absolutely inevitable that Great Britain would be a future enemy, at least, so long as the Reich maintained its position of maritime weakness, a position which it had adopted of its own volition. The German reaction to this was the denouncement of the Anglo-German Naval Treaty on 28 April 1939. This was only of formal significance however, as by then the path for re-equipping the fleet had already been prepared.

In the summer of 1939 the keels were laid for the first two 'super-battleships' of the 'Z-Plan'. The vessels were due to be completed in the second half of 1943, but the war, which broke out soon after work began, delayed the realisation of this programme. The energy put into carrying out the programme can be illustrated with reference to the second ship ('J'), which was allocated to the Deschimag yard at Bremen. On Slipway V was the freighter *Rheinfels*, belonging to the Hansa shipping company of Bremen, and the naval tug *Atlantik*, when on 15 August 1939 the 'super-battleship' was laid down, although only after *Rheinfels* was launched on 2 September 1939, followed by *Atlantik* on 9 September, was this slipway available for the exclusive occupation of the new vessel. This photo dates from the first days of September 1939, and shows her keel being built (centre); to the right, *Atlantik* is still on the slipway. Only three weeks later the contract for the 'super-battleship' was stopped, the materials being taken away not long afterwards. *Rheinfels* had in the meantime vacated the slipway to the left. *Author's Collection*

THE TIME PROBLEM

In view of the changes in the political situation by that time, it was probably necessary to begin building the battleships at once in any case, and accelerate their construction schedule as much as possible. The details and characteristics of the ships had to be kept secret for as long as possible, in much the same way as in the case of *Dreadnought* over thirty years earlier. To this end contact had been made at an early stage with the private yards that were capable of building such large ships: Blohm & Voss (Hamburg), AG Weser (Bremen), and Deutsche Werke AG, (Kiel). The first task was to enlarge dockyard installations as necessary. Blohm & Voss and Weser declared their willingness to erect larger construction docks, for which considerable subsidies were provided in the 1938 Naval Budget: Blohm & Voss received 65 million marks, Weser 48 million. In addition, two large building docks were built at Wilhelmshaven[6].

Of the very greatest importance was the time required to build the ships, which was estimated differently by the individual shipyards. The problem was discussed on 12 July 1938 by the OKM and representatives from Weser. To the question of when the construction plans had to be delivered, the following information was conveyed: the outline drawings were expected on 1 December 1938 and by 1 March 1939 the main bulkhead outlines, building specifications main bulkhead drawings and the fittings plans. Assuming availability of materials, the Weser representative named 1 June 1939 as the earliest possible date for keel laying, and the building time as 30 months – hence the first of the battleships to be built by the company could be expected to be launched on 1 December 1941, and to be delivered 20 months later after fitting-out. The second ship allocated to them, if it had to be built on a slipway, would then by laid down on 1 January 1942, ie four weeks after the launch of the first ship; this meant that it would be launched on 1 March 1944 and delivered on 1 November 1945, assuming identical building times. However, should the building dock be finished in time, the dates for the second ship could be advanced by three months in each case, ie keel laying on 1 October 1941, launch on 1 April 1944 and delivery on 1 December 1945. The OKM considered these building times too long, and brought to bear the fact that the other private yards had quoted faster schedules: Blohm & Voss had indicated 28 months and the Deutsche Werke at Kiel 22 months slipway building time; both had estimated 20 months for fitting-out. During these negotiations the OKM made it abundantly clear that all new battleships had to be finished by the end of 1944, and that everything was to be done to achieve this goal.

THE FORCING OF THE BUILDING PROGRAMME

If the six new battleships were to have their desired political effect, then, as mentioned earlier, they had to be built as quickly as possible, wide-ranging measures needed to be taken to deliver materials within the prescribed time limits, and the decision was taken to give one man the sole responsibility for overseeing the entire battleship programme and to give him all the necessary powers. Rear-Admiral Werner Fuchs was entrusted with this task; he had been the head of the Fleet Department in the OKM since March 1938.

The measures which were taken were almost without precedent:

1 Blohm & Voss were made responsible for overall design work and had to supply the other yards with the plans they needed

2 The *Kriegsmarine* set up its own office in Hamburg, where the design work was to be carried out in collaboration with Blohm & Voss. Every essential decision was to be made there in the space of three days; any decisions made there could not be altered or reversed

3 Orders for materials were to be made via Blohm & Voss alone so that they could be shared out equally; to this end Blohm & Voss alone were to make out the order lists with all instructions regarding urgency, the range of materials required, delivery time and suppliers

4 At the same time Blohm & Voss had to work out schedules for the supply of ship-building materials, armour plate, engines, etc. All yards had to make storage space available when required, as the delivery of KC armour plate and the secondary turrets could be expected very early on

5 The steelworks were to nominate a co-ordinator, whose task was to divide up the shipbuilding material contracts among the individual steelworks in the most efficient way. Unusual sections were to be ordered together for all the ships

6 All material supplies had top priority over the other demands of the armament programme, and of the economy

7 Top priority was also given to extending the facilities of the shipyards concerned

8 Never more than two ships were to be mentioned together on order forms etc, as a means of maintaining secrecy

9 At the same time the supply of the necessary skilled workers had to be provided for (AG Weser alone needed 5000 men, although this included the labour force necessary for extending the dockyard complex and building the docks) and an extensive building programme was to be started to provide accommodation for these men, a programme calling for 1000 apartments with rents of around 20 Reichmarks

On 21 February 1939 Blohm & Voss suggested the following schedule for building the individual ships, based on their own provisional calculations:

A considerable expansion of Wilhelmshaven Navy Yard was planned, with the aim of facilitating the construction of the largest warships. This map shows the building basin (lower left) with the old dockyard and above it the planned extensive Nordwerft (North Dockyard). Three large building docks were planned for this area (VII, VIII and IX), and they were to be used for building the super battleships programmed under the 'Z-Plan'. Work on Docks VII and VIII was begun, but they were never finished. Their foundations are still there today, in an area which is used mainly for recreational purposes. *Drüppel*

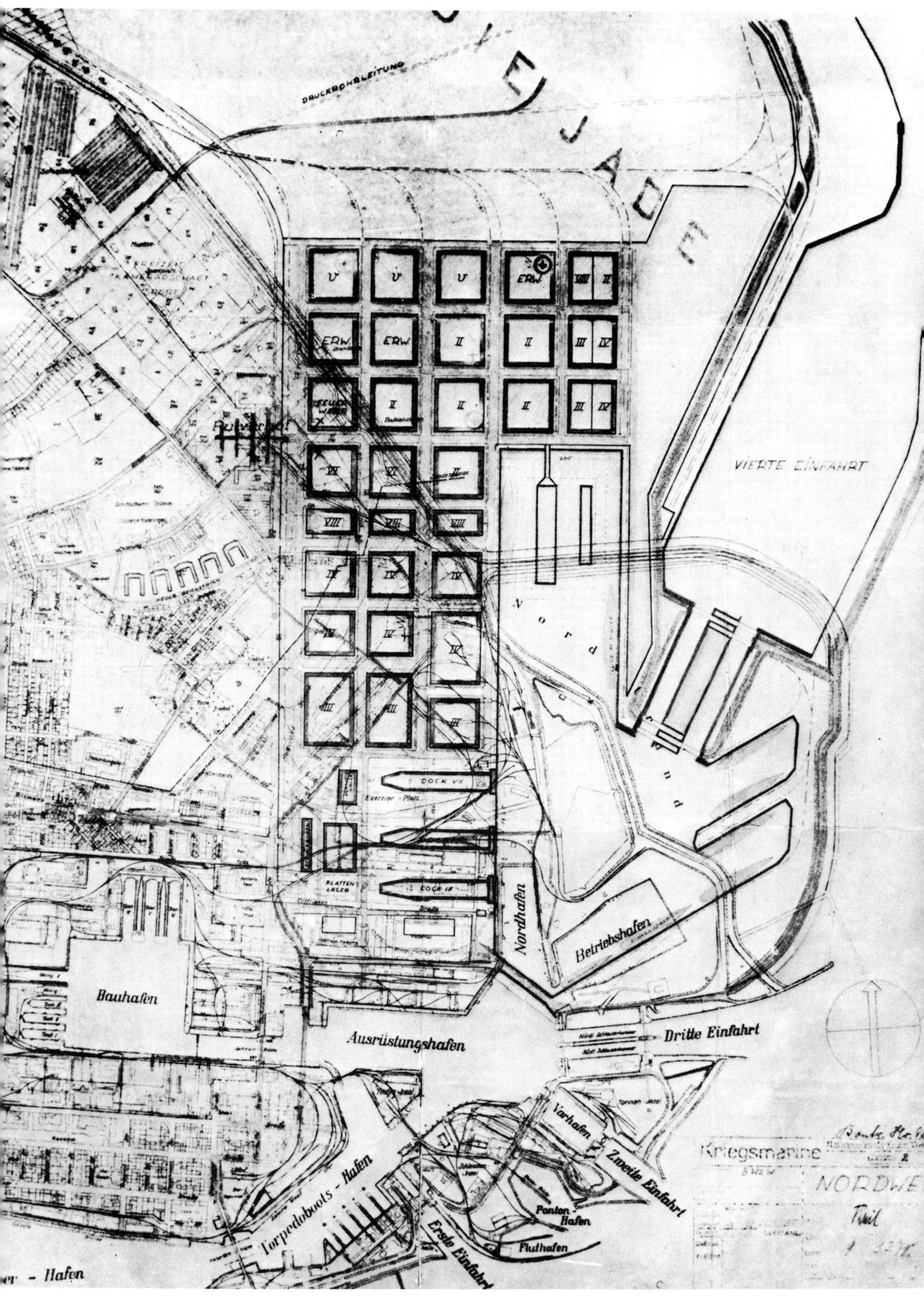
DRUCKROHRLEITUNG
VIERTE EINFAHRT
DOCK VII
DOCK IX
Exerzier - Platz
Nordhafen
Betriebshafen
Bauhafen
Ausrüstungshafen
Dritte Einfahrt
Vorhafen
Zweite Einfahrt
Torpedoboots - Hafen
Ponton-Hafen
Fluthafen
Erste Einfahrt
Kriegsmarine
NORDWE
- Hafen

Ship 'H' (Blohm & Voss, hull no 525): keel laying 1 September 1939, launch 15 July 1941

Ship 'J' (AG Weser, hull no 981): keel laying 1 September 1939, launch 1 September 1941

Ship 'K' (Deutsche Werke, hull no 364): keel laying 1 October 1940, launch 1 October 1942

Ship 'L' (Wilhelmshaven Navy Yard, hull no 130): keel laying 1 March 1940, launch 1 March 1942

Ship 'M' (Blohm & Voss, hull no 526): keel laying 1 October 1940, launch 1 October 1942

Ship 'N' (AG Weser, hull no 982): keel laying 1 March 1940, launch 1 March 1942

Ships 'J' and 'M' were to be built in the new large building docks, which had yet to be finished; in their case 'launching' meant the date on which the ships would be floated out.

The principal factor affecting the launch schedules was the delivery of machinery, transmission and electricity generators for the side shafts, as these had to be brought in and installed in their respective compartments before the ships were launched, and before the armour deck over the engine rooms was sealed.

AG Weser soon had to admit that it would not be possible to build its second battleship within the proposed schedule as its new building dock could not be brought forward to the stage where the building of such a ship could be begun, even with all the help they could muster, by the planned keel laying date, 1 October 1940. As a result, a compromise solution was considered which involved altering the direction and construction of another large slipway so that a ship of this size could be laid down[7].

After the end of the Second World War the Western Allies obtained full details of German warship building from the officers and officials concerned and thus gained concrete information about the 'Z-Plan' battleships for the first time. The illustrations relating to *Schlachtschiff H* (Battleship 'H') and dating from June 1945 came from the ministerial adviser of the time, Dipl Ing Otto Riedel, who from early 1939 to mid-1940 was head of the special design office set up for the construction of the new battleships. *BfZ*

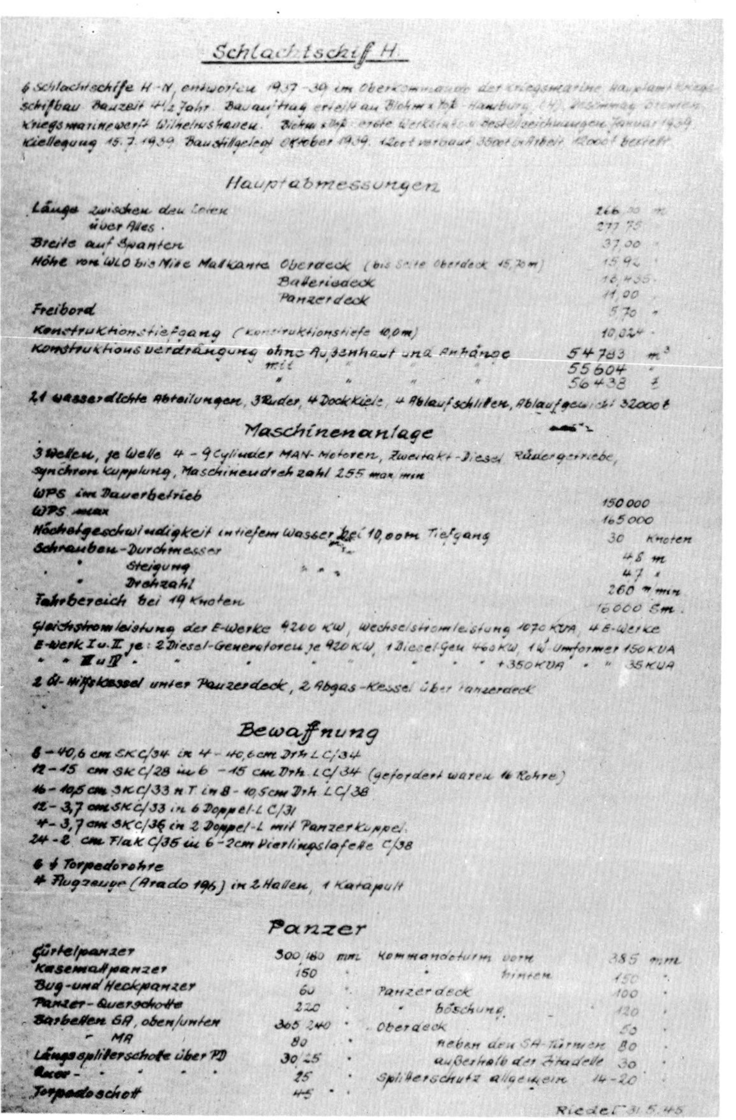

Schlachtschiff H.

6 Schlachtschiffe H–N, entworfen 1937–39 im Oberkommando der Kriegsmarine, Hauptamt Kriegsschiffbau. Bauzeit 4½ Jahr. Bauauftrag erteilt an Blohm & Voss Hamburg (H), [illegible] Bremen, Kriegsmarinewerft Wilhelmshaven. [illegible] Werkstatt- u. Bestellzeichnungen Januar 1939. Kiellegung 15.7.1939. Baustillgelegt Oktober 1939. [illegible] verbaut, 3500 t in Arbeit, 12000 t bestellt.

Hauptabmessungen

Länge zwischen den Loten		266,00 m
über Alles		277,75
Breite auf Spanten		37,00
Höhe von WLO bis Mitte Malkante	Oberdeck (bis Seite Oberdeck 15,70 m)	15,92
	Batteriedeck	16,435
	Panzerdeck	11,00
Freibord		5,70
Konstruktionstiefgang (Konstruktionstiefe 10,0 m)		10,024
Konstruktionsverdrängung ohne Außenhaut und Anhänge		54783 m³
mit " " "		55604 "
" " " "		56438 t

21 wasserdichte Abteilungen, 3 Ruder, 4 Dockkiele, 4 Ablaufschlitten, Ablaufgewicht 32000 t

Maschinenanlage

3 Wellen, je Welle 4–9 Cylinder MAN-Motoren, Zweitakt-Diesel, Rädergetriebe, Synchronkupplung, Maschinendrehzahl 255 max/min

WPS im Dauerbetrieb	150 000
WPS max	165 000
Höchstgeschwindigkeit in tiefem Wasser bei 10,00 m Tiefgang	30 Knoten
Schrauben-Durchmesser	4,8 m
" Steigung	4,7 "
" Drehzahl	260 ¹/min
Fahrbereich bei 19 Knoten	16000 Sm.

Gleichstromleistung der E-Werke 4200 KW, Wechselstromleistung 1070 KVA, 4 E-Werke
E-Werk I u. II je: 2 Diesel-Generatoren je 920 KW, 1 Diesel-Gen. 460 KW, 1 W-Umformer 150 KVA
" " III u IV " " " " " " + 350 KVA " " 35 KVA
2 Öl-Hilfskessel unter Panzerdeck, 2 Abgas-Kessel über Panzerdeck

Bewaffnung

8 – 40,6 cm SK C/34 in 4 – 40,6 cm Drh. L C/34
12 – 15 cm SK C/28 in 6 – 15 cm Drh. L C/34 (gefordert waren 16 Rohre)
16 – 10,5 cm SK C/33 n.T. in 8 – 10,5 cm Drh. L C/38
12 – 3,7 cm SK C/33 in 6 Doppel-L C/31
4 – 3,7 cm SK C/36 in 2 Doppel-L mit Panzerkuppel
24 – 2 cm Flak C/38 in 6 – 2 cm Vierlingslafette C/38

6 ⌀ Torpedorohre
4 Flugzeuge (Arado 196) in 2 Hallen, 1 Katapult

Panzer

Gürtelpanzer	300/180 mm	Kommandoturm vorn	385 mm
Kasemattpanzer	150 "	" hinten	150 "
Bug- und Heckpanzer	60 "	Panzerdeck	100 "
Panzer-Querschotte	220 "	" böschung	120 "
Barbetten SA, oben/unten	365/240 "	Oberdeck	50 "
" MA	80 "	neben den SA-Türmen	80 "
Längssplitterschotte über PD	30/25 "	außerhalb der Zitadelle	30 "
Quer- " " "	25 "	Splitterschutz allgemein	14–20 "
Torpedoschott	45 "		

Riedel 31.5.45

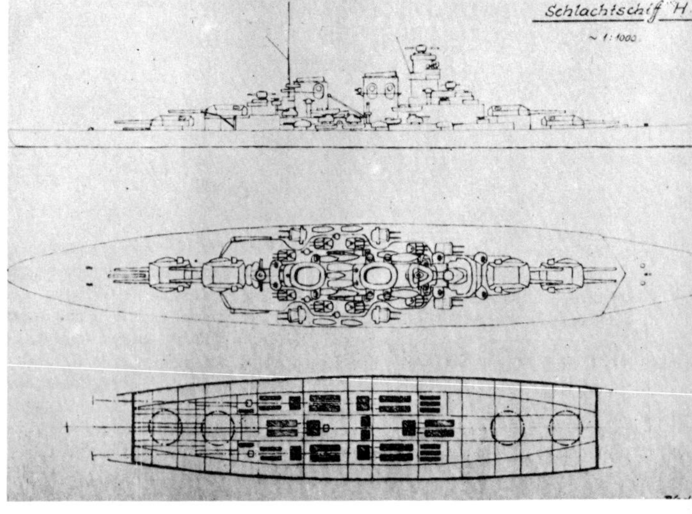

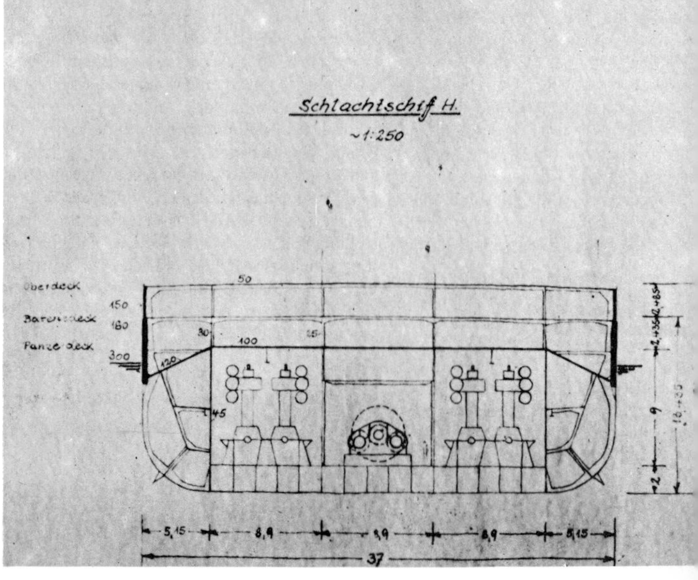

If there proved to be certain difficulties in the provision of machinery, the position with regard to the supply of armour plating was much better. The Krupp company was able to present a fixed schedule, which foresaw the following delivery dates:

1 First large armoured transverse bulkhead 13 months before launch
2 Second large armoured transverse bulkhead 12 months before launch
3 First small armoured transverse bulkhead 10 months before launch
4 Second small armoured transverse bulkhead 8 months before launch
5 Last main barbette[8] 5 months before launch
6 Last secondary barbette 5 months before launch
7 Last heavy side armour plate[9] 9 months after launch
8 Last citadel armour plate 12 months after launch
9 Forward control position 18 months before delivery
10 After control position 16 months before delivery
11 Forward control position shaft 17 months before delivery
12 After control position shaft 15 months before delivery
13 Rangefinder hoods 6 months before delivery

The provisional building costs were 240.5 million Reichmarks for 'H' and 237.6 million for 'J'; similar sums may be assumed for the other ships, so that the total expenditure for all these 6 ships must have been around 1500 million Reichmarks.

TECHNICAL PROBLEMS IN THE SHIPYARDS

Special preparations had to be made for the four ships to be built on the slipways with respect to their launching, as their launch weight was calculated at around 32,500 tons – after the British passenger liner *Queen Mary*, launched in 1936, the second highest launch weight ever. Two load-bearing carriages and two support carriages were necessary for this, each of them 2m (6ft 6in) wide, with a loading of 260 tons/m² (375psi). At the front edge of the slipway each carriage supported a maximum pressure of 12,500 tons, whilst the buoyancy pressure was calculated to be 7,500 tons; the depth of water needed at the front edge of the slipway was estimated to be 2.8m (9ft 2in). All this meant considerable alterations to the slipways in question, which were far from finished when the ships were, or should have been, laid down. The urgency with which the slipways were needed for building the battleships is evident from Weser's example. On Slipway V, which was intended for the construction of battleship 'J', the navy tug *Atlantic* and the motor freighter *Rheinfels* were already being built. While work continued on these two vessels, the keel of battleship 'J' was laid between them, and it was only on 9 September 1939 that the slip was available exclusively for 'J', ie three weeks after her keel had been laid[10].

SPECIAL PROBLEMS

The fact that the basic design of these ships was so different from that of turbine-driven vessels meant that the normal constructional sequence had to be revised. Representatives of all the shipyards concerned agreed on the procedure to be followed in two general meetings on 17 and 21 February 1939. The design of the main engines, which had no base plates of the usual type, made it necessary to break from the usual method of starting from the middle and working towards the ends and meant that the building of the stern half of the hull had to progress to such an extent that it could be termed self-supporting after 15 months of building; assembly and welded joints had to be advanced to the stage that the engines could be installed without risking distortion. The principle was based on connecting the engine frame, which carried the cylinders above it, directly to the completed longitudinal members (longitudinal ribs). For the installation of the main engines, openings in three decks, each 3m × 8m (10ft × 26ft), were made[11].

The engines were to be positioned in a dismantled state, involving individual component weights of 25 to 30 tons; this necessitated the acquisition of correspondingly powerful slipway cranes. It was planned to install the side engines first and assemble them temporarily[12], because final adjustments could only be made when the ship was afloat. This temporary assembly did include the final fitting of the cylinder block to the main frame, so that a compact block was available to facilitate the final adjustments. Six weeks after fitting the side engines the sealing of the armour deck was due to begin; the openings above the central engine rooms were to be sealed only after the ship had been launched. It was planned that the armour deck would be sealed up to the central installation openings 5½ months before launch. Alignment rails were to be fitted to the carriers, which took the form of frames, and these were used for the alignment of the shaft centres, and also served as a level for the main engines and the transmission. The level surface which resulted was intended to carry the main engines on their substructures, and the transmission.

CONSTRUCTION BEGINS

The by-passing of all the usual formality and layers of responsibility, combined with the unprecedented authority vested in Blohm & Voss, was highly successful. If it seemed at first that Blohm & Voss would only be able to lay down battleship 'H' on 15 September 1939 at the earliest, and AG Weser that of battleship 'J' three months later – ie on 15 December 1939 – what would have seemed scarcely possible under normal circumstances now became feasible: 'H's keel was laid in mid-July and 'K's one month later. This squeezed the time difference between the two ships down to only one month, instead of three months as had been estimated originally. If the war had not broken out soon afterwards, the keel of the third ('L') could have been laid in September, and that of the fourth ('N') in October. These were much earlier dates than Blohm & Voss had proposed even on 21 February 1939!

Blohm & Voss had received the contract for 'H' on 14 April 1939, and in July 1939 the contract for 'M' followed. In the same six summer months the contracts for the other ships were sent out: to AG Weser for 'J' and 'N', to Wilhelmshaven Navy Yard for 'L', and to Deutsche Werke at Kiel for 'K'. The keel of 'M' was laid on 15 July 1939 and that of 'J' on 15 August 1939.

With the outbreak of the war, the 'Z-Plan', and with it the building of these battleships, came to an abrupt end, since the war had taken the *Kriegsmarine* by surprise and pitted it against the Royal Navy at a time when the German fleet was thoroughly inadequate. Now the top priority became the building of the submarines, for the submarine was the 'only effective operational naval weapon in our time of weakness'[13].

In order to free the available shipyard capacity for the building of submarines it was essential to halt work on all heavy ships, unless their completion was possible in the foreseeable future, and this concerned principally battleships 'H' and 'J'. When work on them was stopped on 10 October 1939 they were at a stage which would have been reached in 6 to 8 months under normal circumstances; but further work on them could not be justified in view of the changed situation. In the case of 'H' 1200 tons of materials had been assembled, 3500 tons were under construction, and 12,000 tons had been ordered. 'J' had not progressed so far[14]. A total of 15,000 tons of materials had been assembled at the shipyards for the three ships by the time war broke out, and a further 30,000 tons had been rolled. Contracts for the ships which had not been laid down were cancelled: 'M' and 'N' on 10 October 1939 and 'K' and 'L' in the course of 1940.

However, some of the 40.6cm (6in) guns intended for these ships were completed, if not their turrets – at least so it appears[15]. These guns were installed in fixed positions as coastal defences, where they came to be known under the nickname '*Adolf-Kanonen*'. Four of them were sited at Trondenes near Harstad in northern Norway from 1942–43, where they guarded the access to the strategically important iron ore port of Narvik. In 1945 they were taken over by the Norwegians, and they fired their last practice salvoes in 1954. In the late 1960s they were offered to scrap companies at a unit price of the equivalent of £4,000. Three more guns were located on the Channel coast at Cap Griz Nez as '*Batterie Lindemann*', and presumably did not survive the war.

Notes

1 The Washington Naval Treaty finally lapsed in 1936, and for the signatories – Great Britain, USA, Japan, France and Italy – this ended the self-imposed moratorium on battleship building. The 'qualitative' limitations governing the construction of battleships – no standard displacement above 35,000 tons, no gun calibre greater than 16in (40.6cm) – remained in force up to 1938.

2 Despite their small size of officially 10,000 tons, these were regarded as true battleships because their main calibre exceeded 8in (20.3cm), which had been adopted as the maximum calibre for category 'A' cruisers of 10,000 tons maximum displacement (generally designated 'heavy cruisers') under the terms of the treaty.

3 It was not originally intended that these ships should be enlarged at some later stage: this came about when dictated by the requirements of the war.

4 OKM A-21-1: *'Typfragen, Schiffbauplan'* (*International Military Tribunal* Vol XXXIV, p188)

5 The core of this 'fleet in being' was intended to be the capital ships of the *Scharnhorst* and *Bismarck* classes.

6 The Blohm & Voss dock was finished during the war and survives to this day; in contrast, the Weser dock was never completed and was demolished after the war on British orders. Of the Wilhelmshaven building docks (Dock VII and Dock VIII), one was completed by the end of the war, but the other was still under construction. By the end of 1943, 25 and 8 million Reichmarks respectively had been spent on these, and the investment in the all-new Nordwerft (North Dockyard) had been 40 million. Dock VII at Wilhelmshaven is used today as an open-air swimming pool.

7 Slipway IV was referred to here, from which the heavy cruiser 'L' (*Lützow*) had been launched on 1 July 1939; battleship 'J' was meant to be built on Slipway V, from which the heavy cruiser 'K' (*Seydlitz*) had been launched on 19 January 1939.

8 The maximum weight of a single plate was 46 tons.

9 The maximum weight of a single plate was 25 tons.

10 *Rheinfels* was launched on 2 September and *Atlantik* on 9 September 1939.

11 Openings of 3m × 6m (10ft × 20ft) were planned for the fitting of the transmission.

12 MAN estimated 71 days each for this job.

13 Ruge: *Der Seekrieg 1939–1945* (Tübingen, 1954) p29.

14 AG Weser is not able to state how far 'J' had progressed in terms of materials.

15 The Soviet Union tried to acquire the turrets for 'H' and 'J' towards the end of 1939 as part of the economic treaties signed between her and the Reich. Hitler refused this on 8 December 1939 (IMT Vol XXXIV, p682).

Sources

US Naval Technical Mission in Europe, Technical Report No 526–45: 'Projected Battleships of the German Navy'

Various discussion minutes, figure summaries, constructional drawings etc from the shipyards included in this programme, principally AG Weser of Bremen (Deschimag)

International Military Tribunal (*IMT*), Volumes XXXIV & XXXV

Führer Conferences on Naval Affairs 1939–1945, in *Brassey's Naval Annual* (1948)

Raeder: *Mein Leben*, Vol II (Tübingen, 1957)

Bensel: *Die deutsche Flottenpolitik 1933–1939* (Frankfurt-am-Main, 1958)

Bidlingmaier: *Seegeltung in der deutschen Geschichte* (Darmstadt, 1967)

Fuchs: 'Der deutsche Kriegsschiffbau von 1939 bis 1945', *Wehrtechnische Monatshefte* 2/1959

Ruge: *Der Seekrieg 1939–1945* (Stuttgart, 1954, 1962)

Düffler: *Weimar, Hitler und die Marine* (Düsseldorf, 1973)

Wagner: *Lagevortrage des Oberbefehlshabers der Kriegsmarine vor Hitler 1939–1945* (Munich, 1971)

Salewski: *Die deutsche Seekriegsleitung 1939–1945* (Munich, 1973–75)

Appendix 2

Pearl Harbor, 7 December 1941

A 'DAY OF INFAMY'

Japan had twice used the ploy of a surprise attack in 'peace time' without any formal declaration as a means of starting a war: the first occasion had been in the summer of 1894 against China, the second exactly ten years later at Port Arthur as the first stroke of the war against Russia. The United States must have included the possibility of such an action in their political calculations, when the Japanese were making ever stronger claims to the island realms of the East. There was certainly no shortage of warning signs. Nevertheless the Americans were taken by surprise, and suffered a humiliating defeat.

In complete secrecy the Japanese had assembled a battle group, commanded by Vice-Admiral Nagumo, in a remote bay in the Kurils. On 26 November 1941 this battle group left their anchorage and steamed for eleven days, initially on an easterly course through storm and fog, then on south-eastwards under better weather conditions. Complete radio silence was maintained. Their target lay 3500 nautical miles distant: Pearl Harbor in Hawaii, the largest American naval base, and the base for the vessels operating in the Pacific. The audacity of this operation is almost without equal in history: the attackers were compelled first to cross an ocean, and then to take up a position from which to attack without being noticed. The Americans had to be completely unprepared, their ships at anchor in the harbour and their aircraft parked on the nearby landing strips, if the attack was to have the desired success. The Japanese plan succeeded: when the attack came, in the early hours of 7 December (a Sunday) and launched about 275 nautical miles north of Oahu, the Americans were in the middle of their weekend, which the majority of them intended to enjoy thoroughly.

At 06.00 the first wave of aircraft took off from the Japanese aircraft carriers: 50 level bombers, 51 dive-bombers, 40 torpedo bombers and 43 fighters; a little later, the second wave followed: 54 level bombers, 81 dive-bombers and 36 fighters. A total of 355 aircraft were involved in the one mission. The attack began shortly before 08.00, and the Americans suffered considerable losses.The battleships *Arizona*, *Oklahoma*, *Nevada*, *California* and *West Virginia* were sunk and *Maryland*, *Pennsylvania* and *Tennessee*[1] suffered moderate damage; the cruisers *Helena* and *Raleigh* were severely damaged, the cruiser *Honolulu* less so; the destroyers *Cassin*, *Downes* and *Shaw* and the repair ship *Vestal* were severely damaged; the minelayer *Oglala*, the aircraft tender *Curtiss* and the naval tug *Sotoyomo* were sunk; and the target ship *Utah* – a former battleship – capsized. The Japanese paid for these successes with the loss of 29 aircraft (exactly 8.17 per cent of aircraft launched), 55 crew, and also five miniature submarines. The latter were transported by fleet submarines and attempted to penetrate Pearl Harbor; all were lost without inflicting damage.

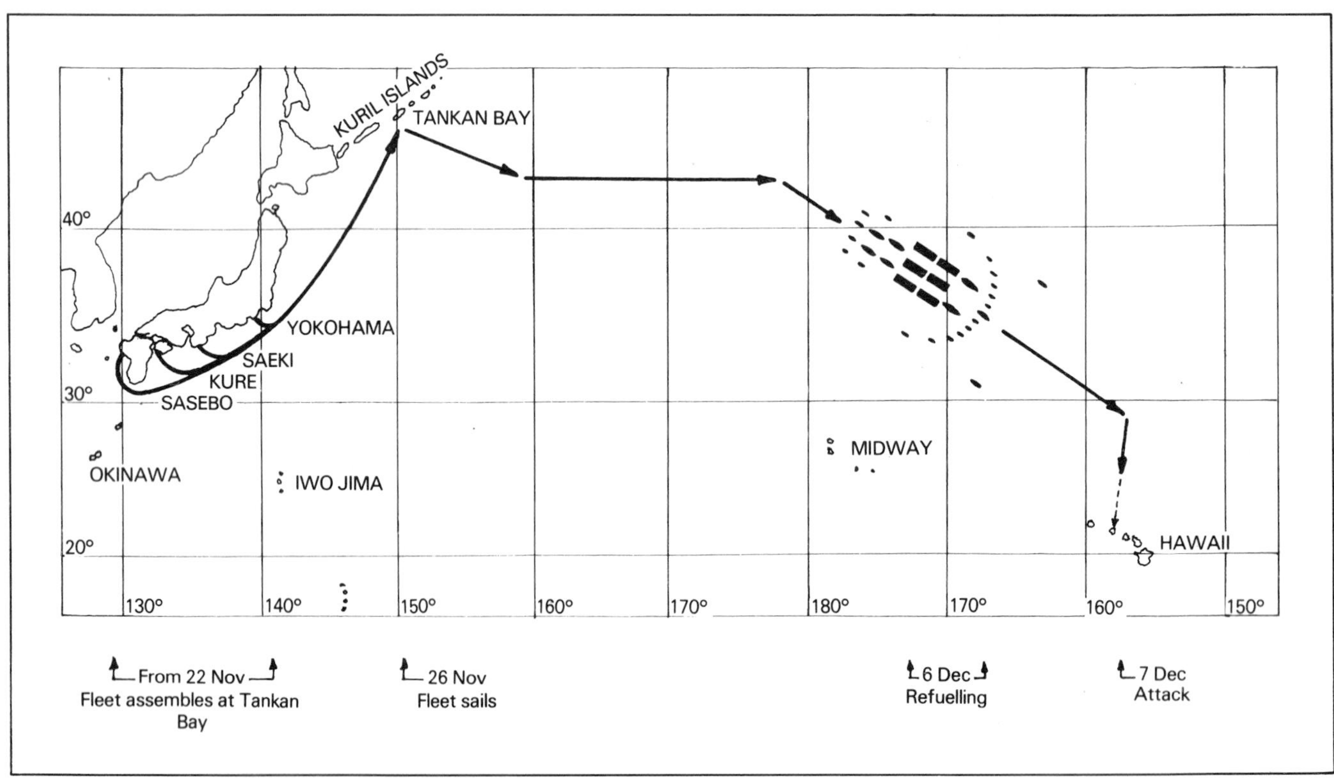

The route taken by the Japanese Pearl Harbor battle group. The units allotted to it had assembled at Tankan Bay on 22 November 1941 after leaving their home ports, and left on 29 November, initially on an easterly course, and then south-easterly, hampered by fog and storms. When the weather improved, the group replenished its fuel supplies. In the early hours of 7 December, an attack position north-west of Hawaii was reached. The war in the Pacific was about to erupt.

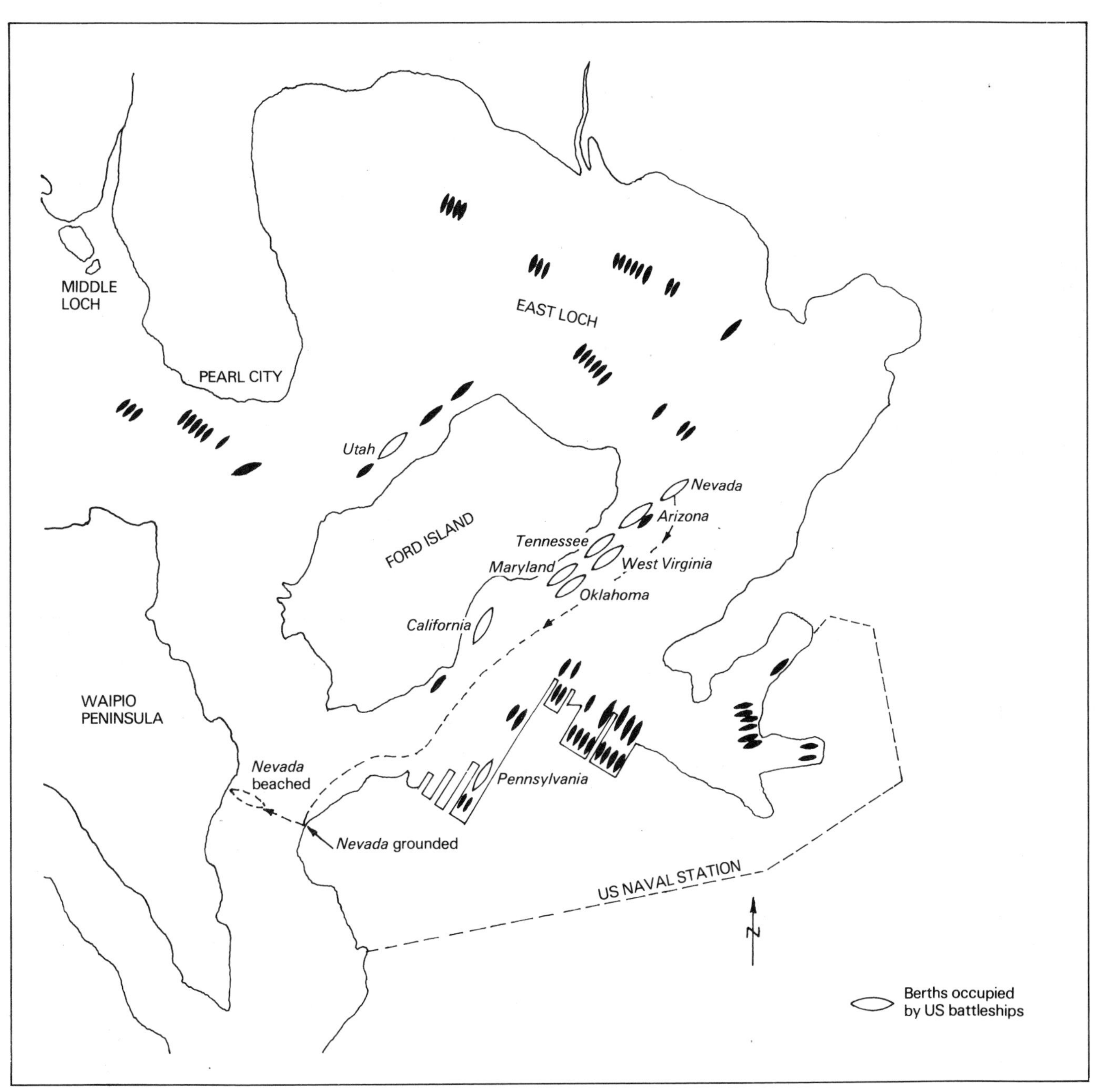

The attack on Pearl Harbor took the US fleet completely by surprise, although there had been no shortage of danger signals. Some of the battleships were at their berths, their crews were preparing for the weekend. Few lookouts were posted. However, not a single aircraft carrier was present – some were at sea, the others at other bases or in dock – and so it was the battleships that took the full force of the attack, and they suffered correspondingly high losses in terms of both damage and personnel. This map shows the positions of the battleships at the time of the attack.

California suffered a fate similar to the other seriously damaged battleships. She was hit by two torpedoes, and grounded because flooding could not be contained. A few weeks later was was salvaged, but the repairs took so long that she was not ready for action again until early 1944, although by then she was in a much better fighting condition than before. To port is the tanker *Neosho* and behind her the capsized *Oklahoma*; in the background the masts of *Maryland* and *Tennessee* can be made out. *USN (BfZ)*

Pennsylvania was in a drydock when the Japanese attack came; in front of her, in the same dock, were the destroyers *Downes* (left) and *Cassin*. A bomb fell between the two and destroyed the slipway, causing *Downes* to fall against *Cassin*. Nevertheless, both destroyers were reparable: *Cassin* was ready for action early in 1944, *Downes* by November 1943. *Pennsylvania* was only hit by one bomb and was repaired by April 1942. *USN* (*Author's Collection*)

Nevada was surprised least of all: she rapidly had her AA guns ready for action, shot down several attackers, and was hit only by one torpedo and a few bombs. When the ship threatened to capsize, her crew, in the midst of the inferno, managed to prepare her to get under way and make for the harbour exit; in doing this, however, she was hit by more bombs and finally began to burn. Fortunately, the water was so shallow that the ship was allowed to settle on the bottom, her stern sinking deeper and deeper. It proved possible to keep her there, which made repairs feasible. This photo was taken shortly before she was grounded; in the background to the left is *Pennsylvania* in drydock. *USN (BfZ)*

Arizona was particularly severely damaged at Pearl Harbor: a bomb went clean through her funnel, landed in the boiler area and detonated there with devastating results. The boilers exploded, together with some of the forward shell rooms, the force of the explosion tearing the ship in two. She had been hit by a total of eight bombs and one torpedo. This photo was taken immediately after her attackers had flown off, and shows *Arizona* grounded, with furious fires raging inside her. In this ship alone 1177 crew members perished. *Author's Collection*

The Japanese success against the US Fleet was, however, mitigated by three circumstances:

1 The arsenal and workshops suffered no serious damage and thus repair work could be maintained

2 Even more importantly, the attackers had not managed to hit the fuel supply tanks on land – the destruction of over 100 million gallons of fuel would have crippled the US Fleet for weeks

3 Most importantly, not a single American aircraft carrier had been at Pearl Harbor at the time of the attack: *Enterprise* (CV6) was with Task Force 8 about 200 nautical miles west of Hawaii, *Lexington* (CV2) was with Task Force 11 about 400 nautical miles east of Midway, *Saratoga* (CV4) was at San Diego, *Yorktown* (CV5) and *Ranger* (CV4) at Norfolk, *Wasp* (CV7) was involved in tests in the Atlantic, and *Hornet* (CV8) had not yet been commissioned.

The Americans were therefore able to compensate for the destruction of their battle fleet by adopting the policy which they had viewed, at best, with much scepticism, and which had been rejected by the older generation of naval commanding officers – but which they were now forced to accept: this policy required that battleships be replaced with aircraft carriers and that the latter should

West Virginia was also severely hit, sinking to the bottom on an even keel: she had been struck by six aerial torpedoes, which killed over 100 men, and intense fires raged inside her. The photograph shows *West Virginia* immediately after the attack. She already has her new AA fire control on either side of the foremast, and a small slanting cap to her forefunnel. The 5in (12.7cm) AA guns are protected by splinter shields; the large SK radar antenna on the foremast is not visible in this picture, although *West Virginia* was the first American battleship to be equipped with a radar system. In the background is *Tennessee*. *USN (Author's Collection)*

Oklahoma had to be completely written off: she was hit by five aerial torpedoes and capsized. She settled on flat seabed, admittedly, but salvage proved to be extremely difficult and complicated. The Navy itself had considered the task impossible, but a private company – Pacific Bridge, a firm that had already successfully dealt with a large number of difficult tasks of this type – achieved the apparent miracle: 21 electric winches were set up on land, and their hauling power of about 20 tons each was multiplied seventeen times by using an ingenious system of blocks and 1in (2.5cm) thick steel cables. On 8 March 1943 the winches took up the load, inch by inch, then foot by foot. Divers had temporarily sealed off the wreck and lightened it by about 3000 tons by removing fittings and supplies. Eight months later – on 3 November 1943 – the job was done: the wreck was refloated and could eventually be docked. This 1944 photo shows *Oklahoma* after the salvage work: the starboard anti-torpedo bulge has already been removed, and the heavy turrets are soon to be unshipped. In 1947 the ship was scheduled to be broken up at San Francisco, but the tow cable broke en route, and after fruitless attempts to save her, she finally sank. In the final reckoning her element had been victorious. *The Sphere* ▼

operate as the principal fighting ships. The events in the Pacific in 1942 and in the following years up to the end of the war provided a complete vindication of this policy: the aircraft carrier had become the principal fighting ship – and has remained so to the present day, at least as far as surface forces are concerned. The battleship became its subordinate; after the end of World War II there was no denying the fact that not only had it forfeited its leading role, but there was no place for it at all in the fleet. At Pearl Harbor the die was finally cast.

COMPOSITION OF THE JAPANESE BATTLE GROUP

6 fast aircraft carriers: *Akagi*, *Kaga*, *Soryu*, *Hiryu*, *Shokaku* and *Zuikaku* (total 423 aircraft)
2 fast battleships: *Hiei* and *Kirishima*
2 heavy cruisers: *Tone* and *Chikuma*
2 light cruisers: *Katori* and *Abukama*
12 destroyers: *Isokaze*, *Tanikaze*, *Hamakaze*, *Kasumi*, *Arare*, *Kagero*, *Shiranui*, *Akigumo*, *Urukaze*, *Akebono*, *Ushio* and *Sazanami*
8 Fleet tankers and supply ships: *Kyokuto Maru*, *Kenyo Maru*, *Kokuyo Maru*, *Shikoku Maru*, *Akebono Maru*, *Toho Maru*, *Nihon Maru* and *Toei Maru*
3 submarines: *I19*, *I21* and *I23*

The following submarines were also operating in the area around Hawaii: *I1*, *I2*, *I3*, *I4*, *I6*, *I7*, *I8*, *I9*, *I10*, *I15*, *I16*, *I17*, *I18*, *I20*, *I22*, *I24*, *I68*, *I69*, *I71*, *I72*, *I73*, *I74* and *I75*. *I16*, *I18*, *I20*, *I22* and *I24* each carried a miniature submarine.

US BATTLESHIP LOSSES AT PEARL HARBOR

Name	No of hits		Effect	No of dead	Result
	Bombs	Torpedoes			
Arizona	8	1	Explosion, sunk	1177	Total loss; wreck still in *in situ*
Oklahoma	1	5	Capsized	315	Total loss; wreck salvaged by 1943
California	2	2	Sunk	98	Salvaged in 1942; in service again early 1944 after repair and modernisation
West Virginia	2	6	Sunk	105	Salvaged in 1942; in service again early 1943 after repair and modernisation
Nevada	5	1	Grounded	50	Salvaged in 1942; in service again early 1943 after repair and modernisation
Maryland	2	–	Moderate damage	4	In service again February 1942
Pennsylvania	1	–	Moderate damage	15	In service again April 1942
Tennessee	2	–	Minor damage	–	In service again April 1942
Utah	2	2	Capsized	58	Total loss; wreck still *in situ*

Note

1 The following US battleships were absent from Pearl Harbor: *Arkansas*, *Texas*, *New York*, *New Mexico*, *Idaho* and *Mississippi*, which were all in the Atlantic (*Idaho* and *Mississippi* were at that time in Hvalfjord, Iceland, whilst *New York* was being overhauled at Norfolk). *Colorado* was undergoing modernisation at Bremerton.

An aerial view of the wreck of *Arizona*, seen from astern. The barbettes of the after turrets can be seen, only one of which is above water. *USN (Author's Collection)*

A monument was subsequently erected over the sunken *Arizona*. The cost of this was about half a million dollars, most of which was covered by donations; one concert given by the singer Elvis Presley brought in $160,000 for the project. The monument was dedicated on 30 May 1962, and since then millions of tourists from all over the world have visited it. *BfZ*

Appendix 3

The US Navy Experiments at Bikini Atoll[1]

World War II came to an end shortly after the atom bomb attacks on Hiroshima and Nagasaki, and the United States' military leaders then considered it necessary to carry out tests designed to establish the most effective method of deploying this new weapon and the limits of its effectiveness, and to investigate possible defensive measures in case an enemy were also to employ such weapons. A project of this type could only be carried out at a location where the environment would suffer the least damage, and the Pacific Ocean's vastness seemed the obvious choice. The uninhabited Bikini Atoll, the northernmost of the Marshall Islands, was chosen; the targets were warships of all types, from battleships to submarines and from aircraft carriers to landing craft. This series of tests was organised jointly by the Navy Department and the War Department: Vice-Admiral W H P Blandy, USN, was placed in command, with the command ship *Mount McKinley* as his headquarters. A total of 147 ships, 150 aircraft and about 42,000 men were placed under his command. Three tests were planned:

1 Test 'Abel' – the dropping of an atomic bomb to be detonated in the air at an undisclosed altitude at 09.00 local time, 1 July 1946

2 Test 'Baker' – the detonation of an atomic bomb under water at an undisclosed depth, at 08.34 local time on 25 July 1946

3 Test 'Charlie' – the detonation of an atomic bomb under water at a greater depth, on 1 March 1947. This test was not carried out, after the second experiment had shown its devastating effect.

The target area was the lagoon of Bikini Atoll, about 200 square miles in area, where the target ships were anchored across an area 1.33 nautical miles wide, in water averaging 30 fathoms (52m) deep. In test 'Abel' 77 vessels were used and in test 'Baker' 89; most of them carried measuring instruments, equipment and accessories, food, drinking and boiler water, fuel and much more, both on deck and inside the ships. Living animals were also accommodated on board. The US Navy, in short, was intent on achieving the maximum information from the tests. The main objective was to gather facts about the effect of shock and suction waves, and about radio-active contamination; the means available for this purpose included the results of the latest technology, such as unmanned, remote-controlled aircraft capable of flying through the 'mushroom' and transmitting back important information via radio. Boats, also unmanned, were also adapted to carry out tests on the water in the vicinity of the explosion.

In the first test the atomic bomb, whose TNT equivalent has not been disclosed, was dropped by a B-29 bomber and detonated above the surface of the water. Of the 77 vessels at anchor there, one destroyer and two transports sank immediately after the explosion, and one cruiser went down on the following day. The critical area was established as being a circle roughly 1300yds (1200m) in diameter: ships inside this circle either sank or suffered such severe damage that a protracted period in dock would have been needed to effect repairs; outside this circle the damage ranged from minor to moderate, and radio-active contamination was relatively low. The test showed that ships' crews had a good chance of surviving if they were below deck at the time of an atomic explosion.

The second test proved to be far more effective: in this experiment an atomic bomb of at least 20,000 tons TNT equivalent was set up and detonated precisely beneath a landing craft, which was completely destroyed by the explosion. Not only did more ships sink in test 'Baker', but the damage to the surviving vessels was also many times greater. Radiation also proved to be considerably more severe and of longer duration; even four days after the explosion it was extremely dangerous for personnel to spend even a short time on board the target ships in order to carry out the work necessary for taking measurements, showing that the problem of radioactive fallout was very serious.

Of all the vessels involved, the battleships proved to be the most capable of withstanding damage in these tests, their particularly rugged construction standing them in good stead. For them, the danger zone was a circle of about 1000yds (900m) radius, and only within 450 yds (400m) of the centre of the explosion did the danger prove fatal.

TEST 'ABEL', 1 JULY 1946

Name	Distance/position from centre of explosion	Damage
Nevada	550–650yds (500–600m)/135° starboard	Outer hull plating and stern considerably distorted; deck partially torn up and destroyed; fairly severe damage to superstructure; repairs possible
Arkansas	450–550yds (400–500m)/160° starboard	Approximately as *Nevada*, but rather more severe damage to superstructure and masts; some boilers and other fittings damaged, some fairly severely; repairs possible
Nagato	1100–1200yds (1000–1100m)/135° starboard	Insignificant damage to superstructure; differing degrees of shock damage to the heavy turrets; communications system partially disrupted; repairs possible
New York	1750–1850yds (1600–1700m)/130° starboard	Insignificant damage, mainly due to effects of heat, to upper deck and superstructure; repairs possible
Pennsylvania	1750–1850yds (1600–1700m)/65° starboard	Internal damage due to shock wave; other fairly slight damage due to heat and fire; slight distortion to superstructure; repairs possible
*Saratoga**	2600–2700yds (2400–2500m)/90° starboard	Slight heat and fire damage, wooden covering of flight deck burnt away; slight superstructure distortion

* *Saratoga*, an aircraft carrier, is included in this and the following summary, since the ship was laid down as a battlecruiser.

TEST 'BAKER', 25 JULY 1946

Name	Distance/position from centre of explosion	Damage
Nevada	1100yds (1000m)/115° starboard	Very minor damage to underwater hull; insignificant leakage; repairs possible
Arkansas	330–380yds (300–350m)/110° starboard	Thrown into the air by the explosion, capsized on falling back, hull shattered, outer plating largely torn open, starboard stern torn off; total loss
Nagato	1000yds (900m)/145° starboard	Very severe damage to underwater hull, especially to keel; fairly severe leakage; sank after 5 days; total loss
New York	1300yds (1200m)/150° starboard	Non-critical damage to stern and underwater hull; leaks altered trim slightly; repairs possible
Pennsylvania	1500yds (1400m)/50° starboard	A few small leaks, resulting in stern sinking deeper; repairs possible
Saratoga	450yds (400m)/70° starboard	Hull broken; underwater protective system badly damaged; outer plating partly torn away; funnel and superstructure detached by shock waves; 5° trim by stern; sank after $7^1/_2$ hours

Note

1 Terzibaschitsch has covered this in detail: 'Vor 31 Jahren: Atombombenversuche der US Navy bei Bikini', *Marine Rundschau*, 11/77, p635. Amongst other information, this includes a list of all the vessels which were involved.

25 July 1946, 08.25 hours: the second atomic bomb is detonated. It was set off under water, and its effect can be seen in this photograph. From left to right, the following ships can be made out: the battleship *New York* with the aircraft carrier *Saratoga* just behind, the heavy cruiser *Salt Lake City*, the Japanese battleship *Nagato* and finally the battleship *Nevada*. *USN (Author's Collection)*

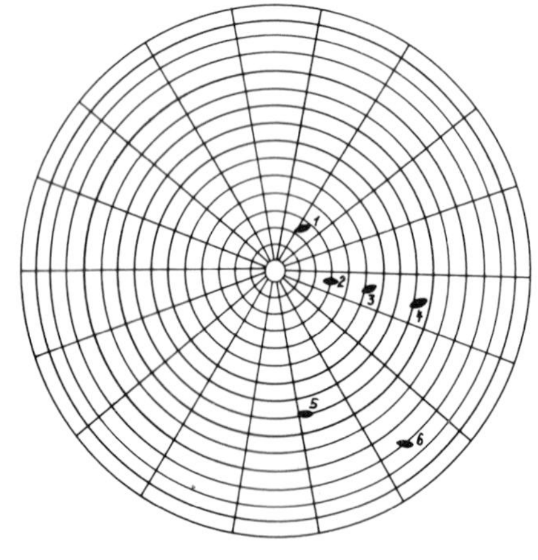

The positions of the battleships in relation to the centre of the atom bomb detonation 'Abel', on 1 July 1946: *Arkansas* (1), *Nevada* (2), *Nagato* (3), *New York* (4) and *Pennsylvania* (5). The drawing also includes the aircraft carrier *Saratoga* (6), which was laid down as a battlecruiser. *Author*

Arkansas withstood test 'Abel', although she was located no more than 550yds (500m) from the centre of the explosion: she did suffer fairly severe damage, but repairs would certainly have been possible. The ship is seen here after the first test. The markings on the hull were intended to be legible at a great distance, in order to ascertain how far she had settled in the water. *Author's Collection*

Nevada survived the first test tolerably well, and even the second only caused her relatively slight damage. Still quite able to float, she was used again as a target ship, but only for weapons with conventional charges. In all she proved to be extraordinarily rugged: she remained on the surface in spite of bombardment from heavy guns, the detonation of an underwater charge at very close range, and a near miss by a guided missile. It was a torpedo-bomber that finally sank the ship. The photo shows *Nevada* immediately before the start of Operation 'Crossroads'; markings have been painted on her orange and white hull, which were intended to register any degree of settling caused by flooding. *Author's Collection*

This photo of *Nevada* dates from 11 July 1946 and shows her after test 'Abel'. The devastation above decks is very apparent. *Author's Collection*

The positions of the battleships relative to the centre of atomic bomb detonation 'Baker', 25 July 1946: *Arkansas* (1), *Nevada* (2), *Nagato* (3), *New York* (4), *Pennsylvania* (5) and *Saratoga* (6). *Author*

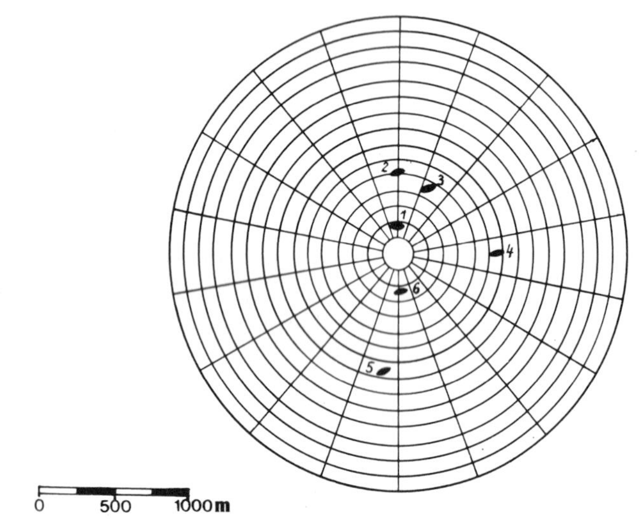

Pennsylvania survived both atom bomb tests without major damage. The cost of decontaminating, towing home and repairing the ship would have been far too high, however, and the ship was towed to Kwajalein – an island about 160 nautical miles further south – and beached there. At first she was used for scientific and technical experiments, and later as a target ship; as the latter, she was seriously damaged in 1948 and eventually totally destroyed. The photograph shows her at Kwajalein, still presumably in the hands of the scientists. The pyramid-shaped structures on the main turrets appear to be measuring devices. *Author's Collection*

Appendix 4

Capital shipbuilding in the Soviet Union 1938–1950

In the years immediately following the Civil War and the Revolution the building of capital ships in the Soviet Union was unthinkable; the effects of both meant that even the dreadnoughts which had been laid down before August 1914 and then abandoned could not be completed – with the exception of the *Borodino* class battlecruiser *Izmail*, which was the furthest advanced and for which the machinery was evidently ready for installation. *Izmail* was the only unfinished capital ship not to be scrapped; she was left in Leningrad to be completed later.

There were heated arguments in the Soviet Navy in the 1920s, in which the dreadnought advocates, who were demanding a total of eight battleships for the Baltic and Black Sea Fleets by 1930, were opposed by a body of mainly younger naval officers who wanted submarines, small vessels and naval aircraft. The battleship adherents were defeated, and in the longer term this meant that no more such ships would be built. The only concession to orthodoxy was a decision to repair and renovate the existing battleships (which were generally in very poor condition) and place them back in service. The completion of *Izmail* was abandoned in the early 1930s; the reasons for this decision have not been made known, but they probably reflected the industrial and economic problems with which the Soviet Union was faced at the time. Nevertheless, the Soviet Navy by no means wrote off the battleship as the principal type of warship; indeed, the opposite was true. Under the first Five Year Plan (1928–32) the shipyards still in existence were restored, and as part of the second Five Year Plan (1 January 1933–1 April 1937) efforts were made to modernise and expand these facilities and also construct new yards. Despite a number of setbacks, all of these projects succeeded, and the first vessels to be built were submarines and light surface craft, then destroyers and eventually cruisers. From the mid-1930s onwards it became clear that the third Five Year Plan (2 April 1937–1April 1942) would permit the construction of capital ships, although a number of problems remained which, for the foreseeable future, could only be solved with assistance from abroad.

The Soviet design offices had not been idle with regard to capital ships. In the early 1930s it was becoming more and more obvious that the great naval powers were rearming themselves with battleships, and the Soviet Union must have taken note. All the evidence shows that the Russians produced a whole series of design studies, and it seems that the most favoured projects were those based on the British *Nelson*s – at least, evidence for this can be found in the number of heavy guns, their calibre (40.6cm), their accommodation in triple turrets, and their disposition. However, it is fairly certain that other designs were drawn up and examined, but details of them have not been made known.

THE DECISION TO BUILD CAPITAL SHIPS

The resumption of battleship building by the leading powers evidently made little impression on the 'young school' of the Soviet Naval Officer corps, since more and more submarines, light surface craft and aircraft continued to be built. With the conclusion of the Anglo–German Naval Treaty, laying down the strength of the *Reichsmarine* as 35 per cent of British tonnage, and in practice cancelling the restrictions of the Treaty of Versailles, not only was the building of capital ships once more permitted, but the expansion of the entire fleet could now take place – to such an extent that the Soviet authorities must have been concerned, if not alarmed. For this reason Stalin put an end to the smouldering arguments and pronounced his decision against his 'young school': the Naval Construction Programme passed in 1937 was so extensive that it eclipsed any German naval rearmament that had taken place since 1935. Almost 400 units were included in the programme, including 14 cruisers, 12 flotilla leaders, 96 destroyers, 48 escorts and 198 submarines, plus a core of 8 battleships and 8 battlecruisers, although not a single aircraft carrier.

The original draft called for the designs to be completed by 1 January 1943, but eventually this was extended by three years, the new completion date being 1 January 1946. The first stage (21 January 1938) included four battleships and four battlecruisers, all of which were to be launched in 1939 and commissioned in 1941. In view of Soviet shipbuilding capacity at that time, this programme could not really have been completed in the time allowed; it was defeated – as were so many other Soviet intentions – by a total misjudgment of the feasibility of the project; even if foreign assistance had been obtained, this schedule could hardly have been met. The first overtures to a foreign concern were made in the autumn of 1935 when the Italian Ansaldo company was approached. The Soviets had two guardships for her Far East fleet built there, and an agreement was also signed which included technical assistance in the construction of destroyers and cruisers. Some time after this Ansaldo was given the contract for the design of a 42,000-ton battleship, which was drawn up by their *Ufficio Progetti Navali*.

This Ansaldo design ('UP41') dates from 14 July 1936, a time when the new battleship *Littorio*, destined for the Italian Navy, had been on the stocks for twenty months at the same shipyard; and one gets the impression when examining the 'UP41' design that it was influenced in major areas by *Littorio*. The similarity in hull shape makes this obvious, with its cut-down stern and short quarterdeck, on which a catapult is installed. The latter was pivoted not in the middle, as was usual, but at the rear end. Typical of the *Littorio* are the three triple turrets for the main armament, two forward and one aft on a high barbette, and the four triple turrets of the secondary battery, in pairs on each side close to Nos 2 and 3 turrets. Other features characteristic of Italian practice in warship building were the slim bridge tower, the two slim funnels with their raked caps, and the rangefinders – especially those arranged either side of the funnels on their slender, tubular pedestals. Platforms are grouped around these substructures in order to accommodate light AA weapons. The tall tripod mainmast by no means contradicts *Littorio*'s design, as she too was originally intended to be fitted with one. A peculiarity was the stowage area for two ship's aircraft (with folded wings) immediately behind No 3 turret; this was not a fully equipped hangar but just a 'parking space' enclosed on the sides and open-roofed.

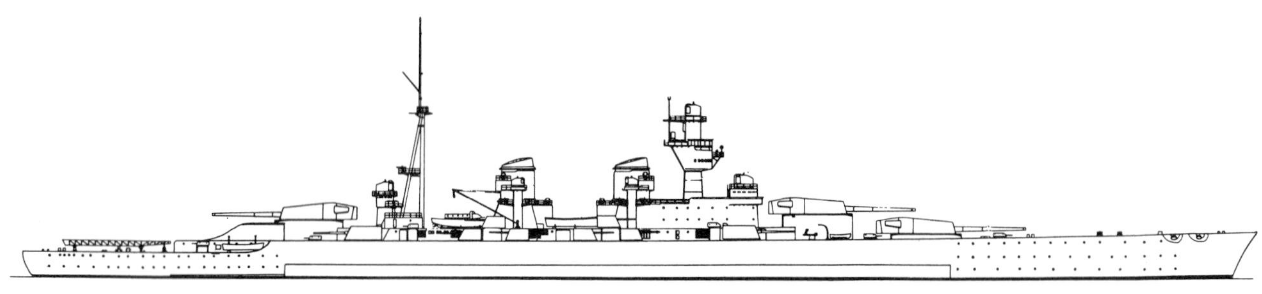

Side elevation of the Ansaldo design 'UP41'. *Author*

Two aspects of the ship's protection were also typically Italian: the external armour, which was inclined at 6° and had a thickness of 335mm (13.2in) tapering downwards to 145mm (5.71in) – *Littorio*'s was 350mm (13.78in) constant thickness at 15° inclination – and the Pugliese underwater system, which the Soviets probably had not encountered before and which might have been used later on their own new capital ships. At 120mm (4.72in) total, the horizontal armour was not as thick as that of *Littorio* which had a total thickness 148mm (5.83in) in the midship area. Bearing in mind the weight of the machinery (output almost 180,000shp) and the armament (a total of 117 barrels), and the relatively low standard displacement, there would not have been very much weight left for armouring the conning tower and the gun turrets.

DESIGN SPECIFICATIONS FOR 'UP41'

Displacement:	42,000 tons standard, 45,470 tons normal, 50,000 tons full load
Dimensions:	Length 236.00m (774ft 3in) pp, 245.00m (803ft 9in) wl, 248.95m (816ft 9in) oa; beam 35.50m (116ft 6in); draught 9.40m (30ft 9in)
Machinery:	4 sets turbines, 8 boilers, 177,538shp = 32kts
Armament:	9–40.6cm (16in)/50 (3 × 3), 12–18.0cm (7.1in)/57 (4 × 3), 24–10.0cm (3.9in) AA (12 × 2), 48–57mm AA (12 × 4), 24–13.2mm AA (12 × 2), 4 aircraft
Armour:	Fore and aft bulkheads 350mm–145mm (13.78in–5.71in), 6° inclined belt 335mm–145mm (13.9in–5.71in), upper deck 55mm (2.17in), main deck 65mm (2.56in) with 36mm (1.42in) slopes. Citadel armour apparently not provided. Pugliese underwater protection

Originally, the Russians had hoped to acquire the necessary heavy guns and armour plate from France, and then from Czechoslovakia. Negotiations with the French armaments industry – principally Schneider-Creusot in all probability – yielded nothing, but the Czech Škoda works were very interested in contracts of this type. However, they were not able to meet the Soviet requirements immediately as France had requisitioned the manufacturing equipment for heavy naval guns and all the associated documents when the young Czech state had been her protectorate immediately following the First World War. Even so, an arrangement was made in the summer of 1938, as part of which the Russians were to set up a design office at the Škoda works which would take over the development and construction of such guns. However, the political events of autumn 1938 and March 1939 – the Sudetenland crisis, the Munich agreement, and finally the occupation of the rest of Czechoslovakia – prevented co-operation before it had really begun.

The first approach to the USA was made in 1936–37, when Gibbs & Cox – a private company – were granted design contracts. It was only a few years ago that this firm published details of the Soviet projects which they developed at that time. This information made it clear that the series of projects began with hybrid designs, ie units with heavy guns and an air group. Three different designs were drawn up (see table), and in all three the flight deck was conceived as purely a landing deck, take-offs to be made via catapults. Flight operations would have proceeded as follows: the aircraft ordered to take off would be hoisted from the hangar by crane on to a carriage – which ran on rails installed on the upper deck – and taken aft. There the aircraft would have to be transferred once more, this time on to the catapult, from which it would be launched. On returning from its mission, the aircraft would land on the flight deck, and would immediately be taken back to the hangar via the lift.

'BATTLESHIP-CARRIER' DESIGNS BY GIBBS & COX

Design	Displacement		Length	Beam	Draught	Machinery		Speed	Armament	Aircraft
	Standard	Full load					Performance			
'A'	66,074 tons		1000ft 0in *304.80m*	126ft 0in *38.40m*	34ft 6in *10.50m*	Steam turbines	300,000shp	34.0kts	8–18in, 28–5in, 24–1.1in, 10 MG	36 wheeled, 4 floatplanes, 2 catapults
'B'	71,850 tons	74,000 tons	1005ft 0in *306.30m*	128ft 0in *39.00m*	34ft 6in *10.50m*	Steam turbines	300,000shp	31.9kts	12–16in, 28–5in, 32–1.1in, 12 MG	36 wheeled, 4 floatplanes, 2 catapults
'C'	44,200 tons	55,200 tons	845ft 0in *257.50m*	129ft 6in *39.50m*	33ft 6in *10.20m*	Steam turbines	200,000shp	31.9kts	10–16in, 20–5in numerous light guns	24 wheeled, 4 floatplanes, 2 catapults

Unfortunately, nothing is mentioned about protection; it would certainly be interesting to know how this was envisaged, as these very large vessels would have had to withstand engagements with battleships on occasions. Without discussing the alleged merits of such a 'hybrid' design, it is worth mentioning that there is evidence which shows that both Great Britain and the USA were quite clear about the paradox of these vessels – although this did not prevent them discussing and examining such projects again during the war. Thus it was hardly surprising that Gibbs & Cox simply tried to frighten their customers into abandoning their plans by preparing greatly exaggerated design drawings; whether the Russians realised the full extent of this is not known. In any event, such projects could never really have been carried out, as the US Government would certainly not have been prepared to give its shipbuilding industry the green light for the construction of a ship which far exceeded the qualitative limits for battleships at that time. This may well have been the reason why the Soviets lowered their requirements late in 1938. Gibbs & Cox then worked out a new design based on the hybrid 'Design B', this time for a conventional battleship.

Side elevation and plan of Gibbs & Cox's hybrid 'Design B'. *Marine Rundschau*

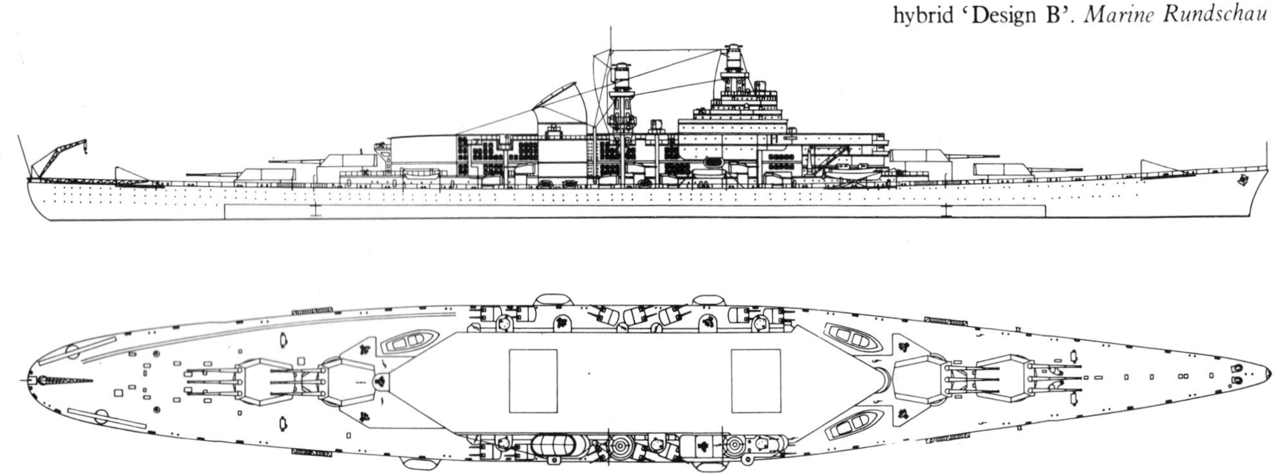

DESIGN SPECIFICATIONS FOR CONVENTIONAL BATTLESHIP BASED ON HYBRID DESIGN 'B'

Displacement:	45,000 tons standard, 53,680 tons full load
Dimensions:	Length 903ft 9in (275.50m); beam 113ft 6in (34.60m); draught 33ft 6in (10.20m)
Machinery:	Steam turbines, 200,000shp = 31kts
Armament:	10–16in (40.6cm), 20–5in (12.7cm), 16–1.1in (28mm), 10 MG, 4 aircraft, 2 catapults

The hybrid 'Design B', details of which have recently been made known, shows a ship with two 16in (40.6cm) triple turrets, one forward and one aft, a flight deck between them with the superstructure on the starboard side, and the secondary battery on either beam. The dimensions of the flight deck were 405ft 6in (123.60m) by 80ft 4in (24.50m) – not even as large as the flight deck of the smallest American escort carrier of World War II. For the aircraft, this would have been a perilously short landing strip, especially in view of the fact that no arrestor systems were included in the drawings. Every aircraft would have had to be taken down to the hangar immediately after it landed, as the landing deck was too small to provide parking space. Two centreline lifts connected the deck with the hangar; the height of the flight deck – measured from the level of the upper deck – was 44ft 4in (13.50m), which makes it probable that two hangar decks were provided, each slightly more than 20ft high and therefore adequate for aircraft of the period. Whether the combined floor area of both hangar decks would have been sufficient to accommodate all the aircraft planned is unknown. If this had been the case, then it must have been at the expense of extremely cramped conditions, which would have made maintenance and repairs more difficult. As already mentioned, the aircraft were all to be catapult-launched. The rails, extending from the flight deck area to the stern, were located on the port upper deck; the crane which would have been necessary to transfer the aircraft from the landing or hangar deck to the rails is not shown on the drawings – possibly it was just omitted. The exhaust fumes from the relatively low funnel would probably have obstructed flight operations to some extent. There are many other interesting aspects of this design, some of which were typically American: the arrangement of the two catapults with a stern crane; the two 'tower' masts (very similar to the *North Carolina* class design[1]); and the characteristic shape of the main and secondary turrets and their fire control systems. In addition to these, Gibbs & Cox supplied designs for a 62,000-ton battleship with 18in (45.7cm) guns in 1938, and a 45,000-ton ship with 16in (40.6cm) guns in 1939; details of these two have not been published.

Apart from their contacts with Gibbs & Cox, the Russians carried out direct negotiations with American government agencies, mainly concerned with the granting of export licences; they wanted 16in guns and mountings, 900 rounds of ammunition and armour plate, and in 1937 they wanted to order a battleship from a US yard. These negotiations became protracted; it seems that the Americans wanted to put off the Russians and await political developments in Europe. At that time it must have suited the USA to keep the building of capital ships, which had just been resumed by the great sea powers, within the qualitative limits laid down by the treaties – displacement 35,000 tons standard, raised to 45,000 tons in 1938, and maximum calibre 16in. It certainly would not have been wise for the USA to undermine the existing agreements by building a prototype for a foreign power which fully exploited or even exceeded those limits, as this would have been the signal for a new worldwide naval arms race. The American President and other high-ranking government representatives were therefore non-committal and did not grant final approval. Matters came to a head early in 1939 when Admiral Isakov, who was responsible for new warship construction in the Soviet Navy, visited the USA with the express purpose of securing a decision. As it happened, however, the problem was resolved in a different way: war broke out in Europe, and the Soviet Union's invasion of eastern Poland constituted the same crime as that perpetrated by the Germans – at least, to American eyes – and the US therefore ceased all work for Russia. From then on, no help could be expected from abroad – with one exception (although this was hardly likely to have any effect on Soviet battleship construction): as a result of the treaties concluded with German Reich in August 1939, which brought economic advantages to both nations, the Russians asked for assistance in the area of naval rearmament. Their requests in this respect included the plans of the *Bismarck* class, heavy guns and turrets, fire control systems, right up to complete warships. These demands were only partially met by the Germans, the promised supplies were deliberately delayed, and relatively little material actually reached Soviet hands. What was delivered was hardly enough to build capital ships from, and in any case the German attack of June 1941 put an abrupt end to all co-operation.

All these Soviet attempts to obtain technical help from abroad were apparently made only to speed up the acquisition of capital ships, which the Soviets had now resolved to build; the design and construction of such ships would still have been quite possible had help not been forthcoming. Even before 1930 A N Krylov had produced a design for a 33,000-ton capital ship whose dimensions were to be 225 × 35 × 9m (738ft 2in × 114ft 10in × 29ft 6in) and which was to achieve a speed of 30kts on 100,000shp. It is possible that elements of this design were included in the so-called 'Project 23', which referred to new battleships. The origins of 'Project 23' can be traced back to the year 1932.

THE SOVETSKIY SOYUZ CLASS

In the absence of foreign assistance, the Russians were forced to make their own technological strides, and in this respect they obviously worked very hard. Most of the problems were solved by the outbreak of war in September 1939, although there were still bottlenecks caused by many kinds of industrial, technical and economic shortcomings. Almost at the first attempt the Soviet Union seemed to be successful in developing heavy guns and heavy armour plate; the manufacture of these items evidently began as early as 1939–40, although only on a small scale to start with. By mid-1938 design work and building materials were so far advanced that the first ships could be laid down. The Russians were probably convinced that the armour plate and heavy guns needed would be available in time.

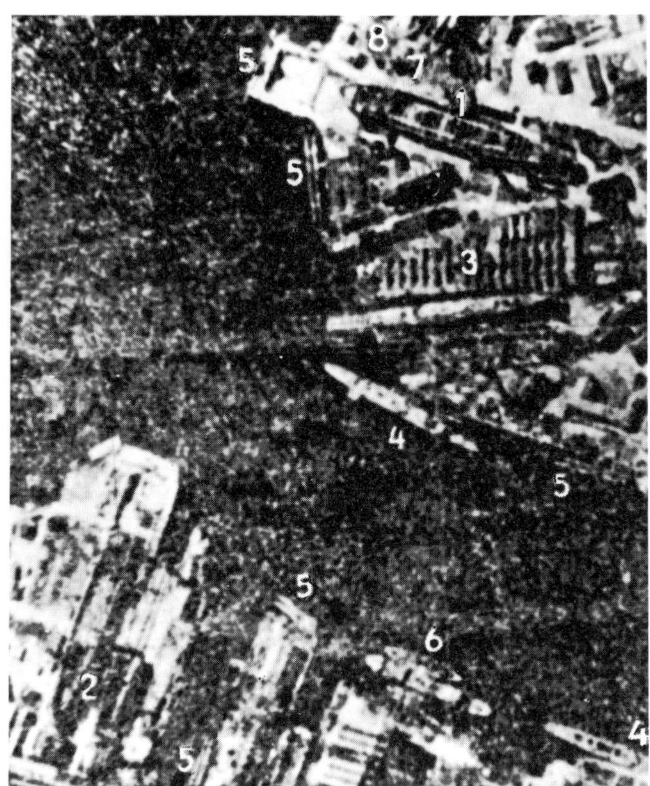

The first ship, *Sovetskiy Soyuz*, was laid down that summer at the Baltic Yard in Leningrad as No 299 – the actual date is often given as 28 August. A second, *Sovetskaya Ukraina*, followed, probably in the autumn of the same year (the date occasionally quoted in this case is 28 November), and at the latest in the first few months of 1939, as No 352, at the Marti (South) Yard at Nikolayev. *Sovetskaya Byelorossiya* was probably the third ship to be laid down, as No 101, at the newly built 402 Yard at what was then Molotovsk, a small town a few miles to the west of Archangelsk, which was renamed Severodvinsk in the mid-1950s. The fourth ship, *Sovetskaya Rossiya*, followed as No 102 around the early summer of 1940 at the same yard.

DESIGN SPECIFICATIONS FOR SOVETSKIY SOYUZ CLASS

Displacement:	44,190 tons standard
Dimensions:	Length 242.00m (793ft 11in); beam 36.30m (119ft 1in); draught 8.90m (29ft 2in)
Machinery:	150,000shp = 29kts
Armament:	9–40.6cm (16in), 12–15.2cm (6in), 12–10.0cm (3.9in), 20–7.6cm (3in), 2 aircraft

ACTUAL SPECIFICATIONS FOR SOVETSKIY SOYUZ CLASS

Displacement:	59,150 tons standard; 65,150 tons full load
Dimensions:	Length 261.00m (856ft 3in) wl, 271.00m (889ft 0in) oa; beam 38.90m (127ft 8in); draught 10.20m (33ft 6in); length-to-beam ratio about 7.17:1
Machinery:	3 or 4 shafts, 3 or 4 sets turbines, 231,000shp = 28.0kts; range 7200nm at 14.5kts
Armament:	9–40.6cm (16in)/50 (3 × 3), 12–15.2cm (6in)/50 (6 × 2), 8–10.0cm (3.9in)/50 (4 × 2), 32–37mm/56 (16 × 2), 8–12.7mm AA (2 × 4), 2 catapults, 4 aircraft
Armour:	Belt 375mm–435mm (14$^{3}/_{4}$in–17in), upper deck 25mm (1in), armour deck 150mm (6in) upper, 50mm (2in) lower, torpedo bulkhead 75mm (3in), main turrets 495mm (19$^{1}/_{2}$in) faces, secondary turrets 100mm (4in), conning tower 425mm (16$^{3}/_{4}$in); no citadel armour is given

◀ One of the most important centres of Soviet warship building was – and still is – Leningrad, with its two great yards and the numerous medium-sized and smaller yards. These photographs were taken early in July 1941 by German reconnaissance aircraft, a few days after the start of the German campaign in the east. Roughly in the middle of the picture is the mouth of the Neva, and the Baltic yard is close by, with the battleship *Sovetskiy Soyuz* on the stocks, her shadow showing up well. Directly opposite is the Marti Yard. The detail enlargement on the right shows both yards, in which a series of warships can be picked out. In the Baltic Yard (above the Neva in the picture) the ships are: the battleship *Sovetskiy Soyuz* (1) and the cruiser *Chkalov* (3), both on their slipways; the cruiser *Chapayev* (4) at the fitting-out stage; several submarines (5), three *Otlichny* class destroyer hulls (7); and probably a submarine (8). In the Marti Yard area (below the Neva) can be seen the battleship *Kronshtadt* on her slipway (2), thought to be an aircraft carrier at the time; the cruiser *Zheleznyakov* being fitted out (4), a few more submarines (5) and the hull of the naval icebreaker *Purga* (6). *Author's Collection*

The main characteristics of their new battleships were given by the Russians on 5 September 1938 under the terms of the 'Anglo-Soviet Qualitative Naval Agreement', and are given in the accompanying table. As far as the information on size and dimensions is concerned, that given at this time was not correct; the first ship had been laid down shortly beforehand, from which it could be assumed that its size and dimensions would not change. In reality these ships were substantially larger, following a directive from Stalin to this effect. True specifications and characteristics are given in the second table. The figures are taken from Soviet sources, and make it clear that the Russians in no way kept within the qualitative limits to which her accession to the London Fleet Treaty had bound her. This treaty laid down – as already mentioned elsewhere – the maximum standard displacement of battleships at 35,000 tons, which was raised to 45,000 tons in 1938. At virtually 60,000 tons the new Soviet vessels exceeded this upper limit by more than 14,000 tons. Thus the Soviet Union had overridden the treaties concerning armament restrictions just as unscrupulously as had the German Reich with its 'H' class ships begun in 1939 and Japan with her *Yamatos*, which exceeded these limits by around 7000 and 20,000 tons respectively, although in Japan's defence it must be said that she was not signatory to the 1936–37 treaty and had only promised unofficially not to build any battleships of 45,000 tons or over.

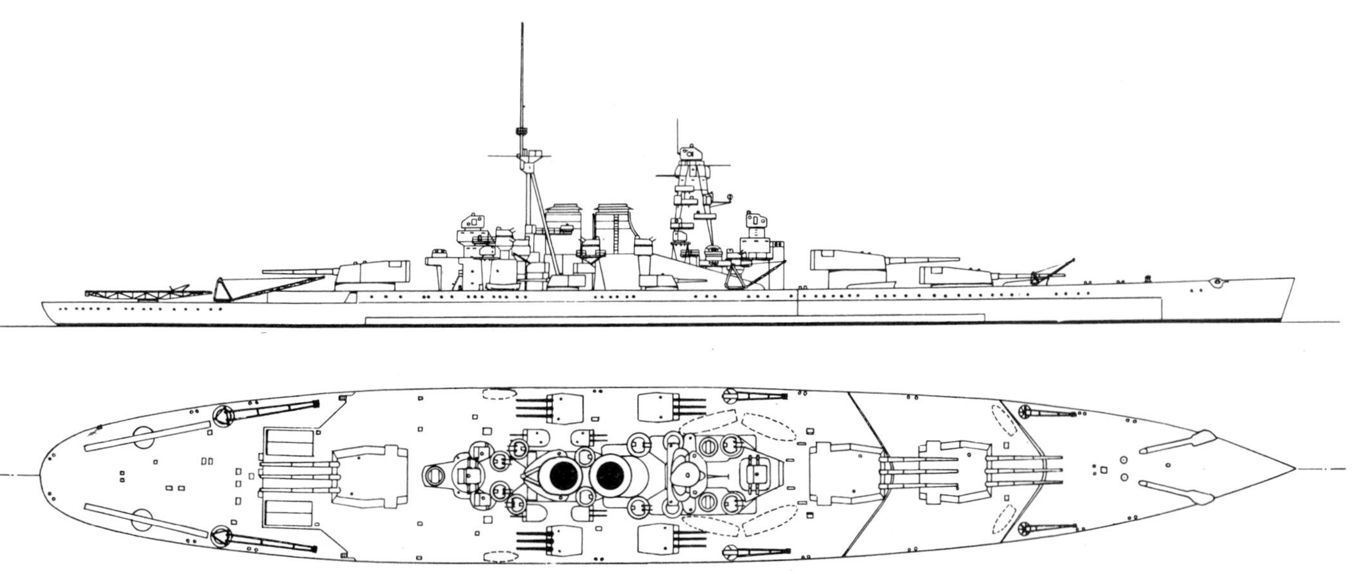

These two drawings were produced from a builder's (model) plan originating in the Soviet Union, and show one of the preliminary designs for 'Project 23', the later *Sovetskiy Soyuz* class. The drawings are unchanged from the original, although the fact that the forefunnel projects forward beneath the bridge superstructure has no plausible explanation. *Author*

The extent to which 'Project 23' was originally based on the 'UP41' design can be seen from their obvious similarity. If we examine the drawing of the *Sovetskiy Soyuz* class in what was probably one of its first design versions (the illustration comes from works drawings from the Soviet bloc), the similarity in hull shape and the almost identical accommodation for the ship's aircraft equipment is immediately apparent. The main armament layout, and even more so that of the medium artillery (in triple turrets) shows marked similarities, as does the sequence of the superstructure sections, and even the design of the superstructure itself. The ship's cranes fitted forward in 'Project 23' would certainly not only have been provided for normal small boats, but also for light torpedo-boats. This idea was by no means new, as older battleships had been fitted with installations for carrying such boats when they were modernised.

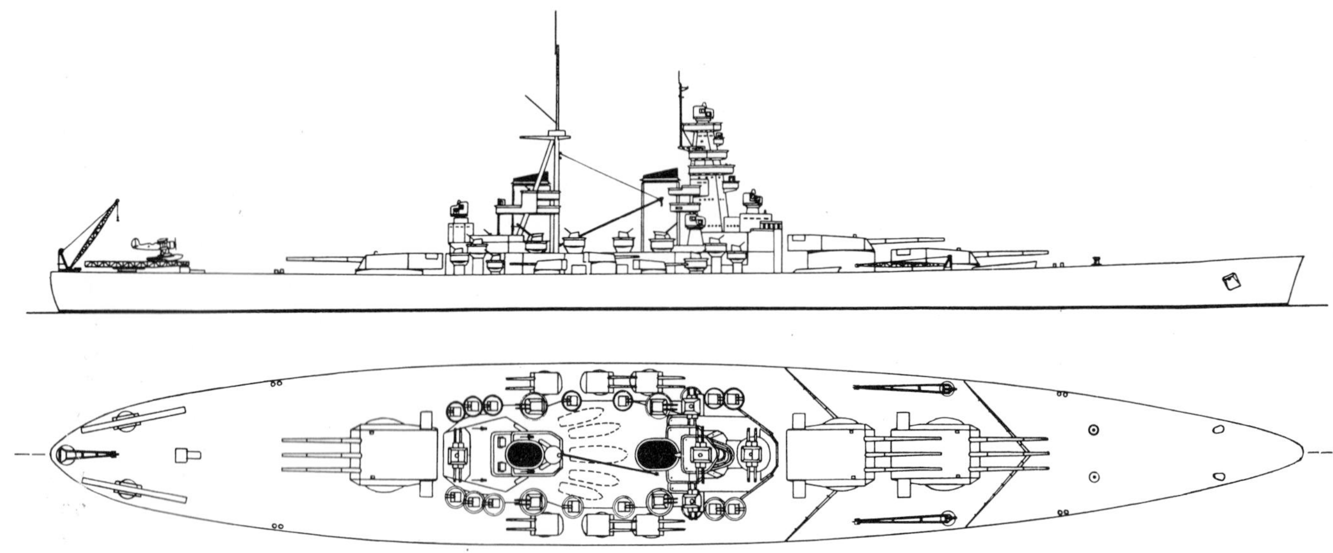

Side elevation and plan of the *Sovetskiy Soyuz* class in the probable final version. *Author*

In its final design form, the class showed both Italian and American influence. As far as US influence is concerned, a certain resemblance to both the *North Carolina* class and the *Iowa* class is inescapable, even though the latter postdated the Russian vessels. The bridge block is relatively small; it incorporates the conning tower, and a slender mast 'tower', slightly sloping on the front face, rises above it. Close behind is the forefunnel, and a somewhat greater distance away is the second funnel, of equal height. In front of this stands a massive tripod mainmast with a number of platforms in its middle and upper regions. There is a double-based rangefinder on each control position, on the foretop, and on both sides of the forefunnel; the last-mentioned appear to be the heavy AA gun directors, whilst the others control the main and secondary armament. The secondary turrets are closely grouped amidships, and in this respect they are reminiscent of the elevated middle turret of the British *Nelson* class. This concentration of lightly protected turrets in a confined space was rather dangerous – a single shell, even of medium calibre, would have been capable of wiping out half the secondary battery under certain circumstances. In front of and behind these turrets, all of them in elevated positions, were the AA mountings. These tub-shaped platforms appeared for the first time during the Second World War, mainly on US warships, and were designed to offer protection against splinters. It appears that the Russians recognised earlier than other naval powers that AA weapons and their mostly unprotected crews were especially vulnerable. This fact on the one hand and the relatively high number of light, rapid-firing AA weapons on the other, make it very clear that the Russians judged the threat from low-flying aircraft to be much greater than that from high-altitude bombers, for to counter the latter they had provided only eight barrels, and that was undoubtedly too few. It would certainly have meant that extra barrels would have had to be fitted subsequently. The stern was designed to accommodate ship's aircraft. Either one or two catapults were to be installed there (reports differ on this matter), plus a crane for hoisting the ship's aircraft back on board when they had landed on the water after a mission. The persistent use of cranes well forward – one each side of No 1 turret – makes it clear that the possibility of carrying light torpedo-boats was still considered, for the presence of such cranes is otherwise inexplicable. The regular small boats were stowed between the funnels, where the machinery for launching and hoisting them was also located. It must be considered doubtful whether in practice the Soviets could have managed to carry torpedo-boats: in this position they would be subject to unavoidable blast damage from the 40.6cm guns.

From the dimensions given, a length-to-beam ratio of 7.17:1 can be calculated. One cannot help but wonder whether the speed quoted, 28kts, is correct, especially if one compares this figure with the performance of ships most nearly comparable – the Japnese *Yamato* class. The latter had a full load displacement of 70,612 tons, a length-to-beam ratio of 6.90:1 and needed only 153,553shp to attain 27.46kts;

with about 5500 tons greater displacement and 77,447 less shp, the Japanese ships were only 0.54kts slower, and hence the *Sovetskiy Soyuz* class should really have been capable of a higher speed.

The question as to whether three- or four-shaft drive was to be fitted must remain open, as no reliable information exists on this point. In the text mentioned previously, a three-shaft system seems more likely, and the text also hints at turbo-electric machinery by occasionally mentioning the term 'turbo-aggregate', but this was certainly not correct. There is also little agreement on the manufacturer of the turbines: although at one time it seemed certain that the Stalin Turbine Works in Leningrad had received the contract for them, more recent sources indicate that the Charkov concern was involved. Whatever factory may have produced them, one thing is certain: the system must have been a purely Russian development. Evidently there were doubts initially about whether it would be possible to develop and build turbines of such high performance, and this might have been the reason why the Soviet Union ordered machinery for two battleships – one to be built at Leningrad and one at Nikolayev – from the Baden (Switzerland) based company of Brown, Boveri & Co in 1937. The order was for four turbines, each of 77,000shp, which thus might well have been intended for *Sovetskiy Soyuz* and *Sovetskaya Ukraina*. The turbines were never supplied. Reports say that they were purchased by Great Britain shortly after the Soviet invasion of eastern Poland, in order to prevent them being delivered to the Russians. This was by no means a sort of feeble revenge for their connivance with the Germans over Poland, but rather a measure of the anxiety felt about increased Soviet naval power, which could not have been less welcome to the British at this time. It is said that the turbines stood around at the manufacturer's premises for years, packed in crates; what eventually happened to them has never been satisfactorily explained.

This photo was taken by German reconnaissance before the German troops marched into Nikolayev, and shows the Marti (South) Yard with the battleship *Sovetskaya Ukraina* (1) on newly constructed stocks, whose slipway – as can be clearly seen – is still landlocked and would have had to be dredged away before the launch. Other ships visible include the cruiser *Ordzhonikidze* of the *Chapayev* class (2) on the dock's old pre-dreadnought slipway, on which the battleship *Imperator Aleksandr III* was built from 1911 to 1914, followed by the battleship *Imperator Nikolai I*, which was launched in 1916. Next to that is a covered double dock, and to the left are several slipways linked up to two 'S' class submarine hulls (3). In the narrow fitting-out bay are the destroyer *Ognevoi* (5) and three submarines. Other ships can be recognised by their distinctive shadows, namely the flotilla leader *Tashkent* and the ice-breaker *Mikoyan* (7); at right angles is the hull of another flotilla leader or destroyer (8). The *Chapayev* class cruiser *Kuibyshev*, launched early in 1941, can also be seen (9). With the exception of the vessels on the stocks, all the ships were brought to safety when Nikolayev was taken by the Germans. *Author's Collection*

It seems that the Russians had already begun to remove the strip of land blocking *Sovetskaya Ukraina*'s slipway by the time the Germans arrived, in order to launch the ship and tow her away; this is evident by comparing this photograph with the aerial photo taken before the yard was captured. The speed of the German advance, however, thwarted the plan at an early stage. On the right hand side of the illustration can be seen the cranes of the slipway occupied by the cruiser *Ordzhonikidze* at the same time. *Author's Collection*

On 19 October work stopped on the four ships which had been laid down, having been slowed down since mid-1940. The vessels were not, however, abandoned: completion was envisaged as soon as possible. What was the reason for this action? Until recently it appeared that work was halted because armour plate and the heavy guns could not be provided in time, but it now seems that other reasons caused the decision: the Soviet Union could not remain indifferent to German expansionism in Europe. In the early stages of the war the German machine had proved to be virtually unstoppable, and the Soviet Union realised that she was bound to become involved in the war herself sooner or later, for one reason or another. The only reaction to this realisation could be another round of rearmament, and this meant that the long term programmes had to be given up in favour of plans which could be carried out swiftly. With regard to the Navy, this meant that the building of smaller vessels was to be accelerated, and the large warships were to be postponed until such time as there was dockyard capacity available for them.

By this time the Russians had been able to achieve their first successes in the development of large calibre guns: around the beginning of 1940 the first 40.6cm (16in) gun was available, and in the following spring the first test firings were carried out, although the results were unsatisfactory. But by the summer of 1941 the problems were apparently overcome: it is certain that the only completed 40.6cm gun opened fire on the advancing German army units from the Leningrad area in August 1941, from a range of about 29 miles (46km). Three more 40.6cm guns are supposed to have been started, but it apparently did not prove possible to finish them[2].

It is not known whether work was ever resumed, but with the benefit of today's knowledge it seems most unlikely. Reconnaissance photos taken over Leningrad after the opening of the German attack on the Soviet Union show that only the armour deck needed to be sealed to make *Sovetskiy Soyuz* ready for launching; had work on her been restarted, she would have been able to leave her slipway around November. During the long months of the siege of Leningrad a large amount of material was removed from the hull and used for other armament purposes. When Leningrad was finally liberated from the German encirclement, the Western allies had another chance to see the hull of *Sovetskiy Soyuz*. One of the first was the American Naval Attaché in Moscow, Admiral Olsen, who had been invited to take part in a motor boat trip on the Neva on 10 June 1944. His comment on the state of the hull was 'about 20 per cent complete, and very rusty'. On 28 November 1945 the Russians allowed a member of the Attaché's staff to look over the Baltic Yard. *Sovetskiy Soyuz* was still on the stocks, next to the cruiser *Chkalov* (later renamed *Kosmomolec*), which had been laid down in 1939. At the time of this visit, no work was in progress on the two ships – at least, not that the visitors saw. Even on 29 June 1947, when the new American Naval Attaché, Admiral Maples, stopped off in Leningrad and climbed the dome of St Isaac's Cathedral, he could make out the hull of *Sovetskiy Soyuz* in the distance, apparently still in the same condition[3]. But in January 1949 the hull appeared to be no longer complete, and for the first time the impression was gained that scrapping had begun[4]. This was confirmed by another Attaché staff member after a stay in Leningrad from 6 to 9 May 1949[5], and again on 10 August 1949 during a short stay in Leningrad by American Attaché members, who could only make out a section of *Sovetskiy Soyuz* on the slipway[6]. The ship was obviously dismantled into sections on the slipway, and these were then 'launched' individually and broken up. The work evidently began in April 1948; by April 1949 it was finished.

Sovetskaya Ukraina was found in only a slightly damaged state because the Soviet demolition gangs had evidently not managed to carry out their work very well. The Germans considered launching the 75 per cent complete hull and finishing it; Soviet shipyard employees have reported that the ship was due to be launched in November 1942, according to the original schedule. The Germans would have had to overcome even greater problems than those facing the Russians, who would have had to transfer the ship to Sevastopol for fitting out owing to the relatively shallow water at Nikolayev. However, all the yards in the Black Sea area had been more or less destroyed, and it would have taken considerable efforts to complete the ship, as a suitable dock would have had to be repaired first. But what were they to do with a battleship which the Turkish government might not have allowed to leave the Black Sea for the duration of the war, under the terms of the Straits Convention of Montreux? These considerations may therefore have been more of academic character; they would certainly not have been seriously contemplated.

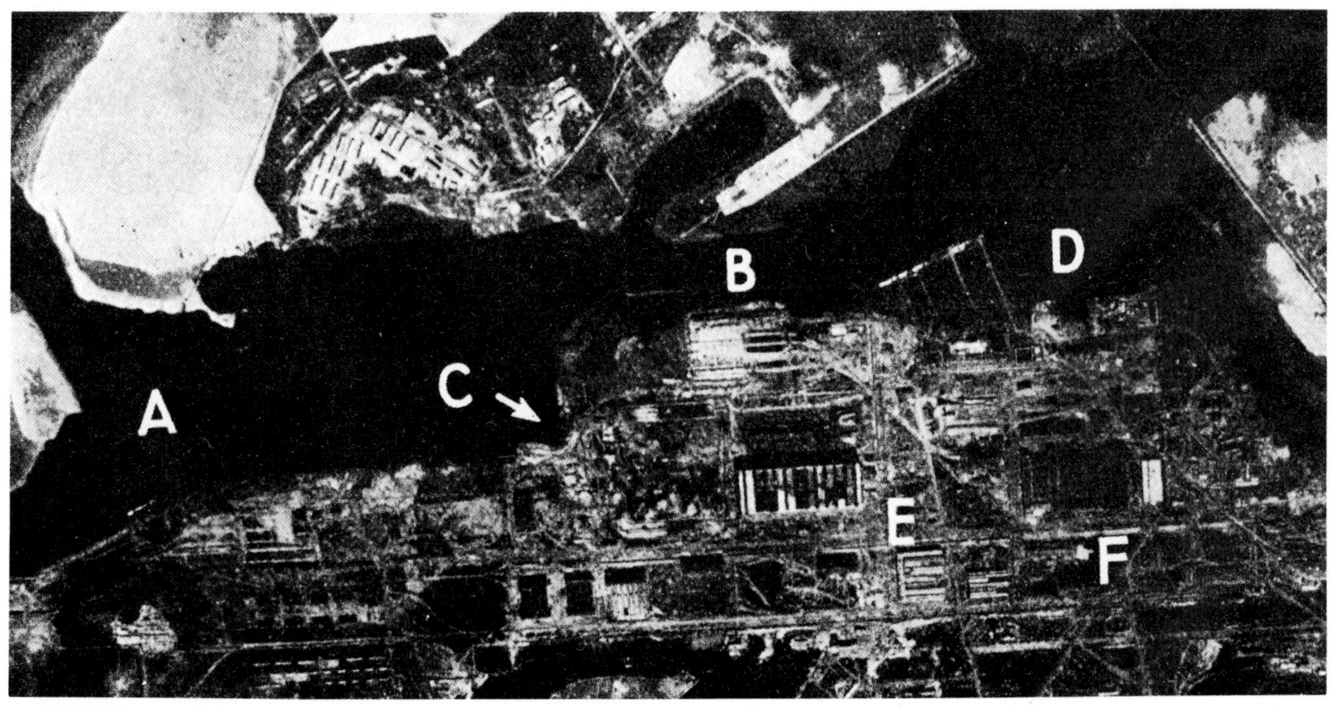

None of the great Soviet shipyards at Leningrad and Nikolayev can compare with the yard which was built in 1935 north of the Arctic Circle. This was the so-called 402 Yard at Molotovsk, (renamed Severodvinsk in the 1950s). It was literally dug out of the ground by a vast army of workers, and its special feature was the equipment which permitted work to be carried on despite the inclemency of the Arctic winter. Work on the yard advanced so swiftly that the construction – or, more accurately, assembly – of battleships could begin in 1939–40. Two large building docks had been built for these ships, both of them in a gigantic covered 'hangar'. This photo was taken by a German reconnaissance aircraft in July 1941, and shows the entire system from a great height: the harbour systems (A), slipways (B), fitting-out bays with entry locks under construction (C), quays (D), shipbuilding 'hangar' (E) and workshops (F). *Author's Collection*

An indication of the huge size of the 402 Yard complex is given by this photograph: the largest part of the yard is the 50,000m² 'hangar' which houses two construction docks able to take the largest warships and now used for building strategic nuclear-powered submarines. *USN (Author's Collection)*

A huge floating dock at the 402 Yard, Severodvinsk. *USN (Author's Collection)*

When the Russians recaptured Nikolayev in mid-March 1944, they found the battleship hull in a decrepit condition: partly cannibalised, and leaning 5–10° to one side because the Germans had blown up the wooden supports. There are more eye-witness accounts from this time. On 17 June 1944 the members of the Allied Minesweeping Command managed to see *Sovetskaya Ukraina*, and they were able to state that about 100ft (30m) of her stern and about 30ft (10m) of her bows were no longer complete[7]. A few weeks later a further visit showed that the wooden supports beneath half the ship's length had been destroyed, and now about 200ft (60m) forward and 100ft (30m) of stern were missing, in other words had been removed[8]. In the following years up to May 1946, all work seems to have ceased, and only from then on did work on breaking up the hull begin. This may have lasted until 1947–48.

These two photos, taken on 11 September 1942 from slightly different positions, show clearly how far the building of *Sovetskaya Ukraina* had progressed by that time. The angled frames projecting at the top indicate that the top deck had not yet been fitted. *BA/MA (Author's Collection)*

Another view of the hull of *Sovetskaya Ukraina*, showing the forward main turret shafts. The 'tubes' lying on the deck to port, most of them slightly tapered, are often said to belong to the Pugliese underwater defensive system, and are referred to as 'shock absorbing cylinders'. This opinion is probably incorrect, for at this advanced stage of construction it must be assumed that the underwater defence system was already installed. Possibly these tubes were pressure hulls for submarines; it was the Russians' intention to have the ship towed away after launch as the Germans advanced, and this would provide a convenient means of transport for other materials. *Author's Collection*

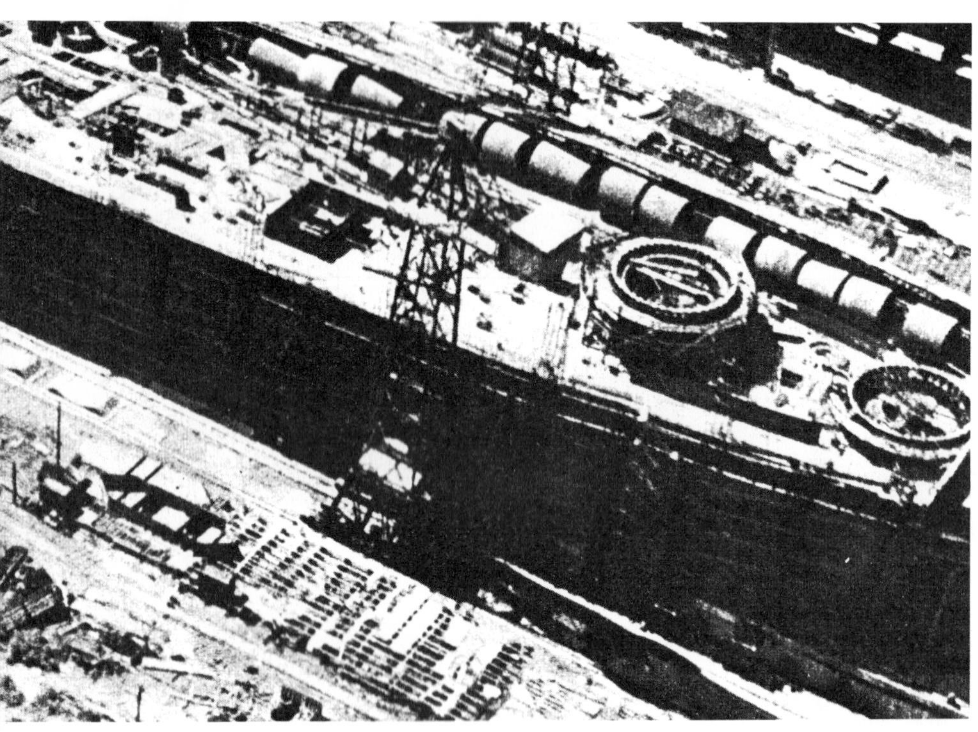

This photograph shows the bows of the battleship *Sovetskaya Ukraina*, which is clearly visible despite the large amount of scaffolding. Cross frames project out sideways at the top, and the longitudinal stringers have not yet been fitted. *BA/MA (Author's Collection)*

The ships begun at Molotovsk were not completed either. The rest of the world knew nothing of these vessels until 1944, evidently not even the Russians' British and American allies. It had been made known that the building of a large shipyard had begun in 1935 on the western arm of the northern estuary of the Dvina opposite the Yagri Islands, in the area of the former Nikolskiy monastery and an old cement factory. At the outbreak of war it covered $7^1/_2$ square miles (20km^2) of land, on which ten large 'hangars' and workshops, two covered building docks for destroyers and submarines and nine open slipways had been constructed. The most important installations of this yard were (and still are today) the two parallel building docks enclosed in a gigantic 'hangar' 1100ft (335m) long and 515ft (157m) wide, which was designed for the building of the largest warships. The plan drawn up at the time this yard was being built involved between 35,000 and 40,000 men working there; during the war, however, only about 11,000 were employed.

Hidden from unwelcome eyes and also well protected against the rigours of the long Arctic winter, two more battleships were laid down in 1939–40 in the building docks mentioned earlier, and their construction was easily kept secret under the exceptionally favourable conditions, although the yard was by no means complete at this time, especially in respect of the individual workshops. For this reason there was evidently still some dependence on material supplies from other yards, namely those in which two ships of this class were already being built. Hence the Baltic Yard at Leningrad was meant to be 'responsible' for *Sovetskaya Rossiya*, and the Marti Yard at Nikolayev for *Sovetskaya Byelorossiya*. It is doubtful whether *Sovetskaya Rossiya* was actually begun, since construction work on her was stopped even before the decree of 19 October 1940.

On 17 January 1944, the Russians allowed the American Naval Attaché in Moscow, Admiral Olsen, and his chief of staff, Commander K Tolley, to inspect the yard. The Americans were able to state that one of the two building docks was occupied by a battleship hull, which was advanced as far as the main deck. Both visitors gained the impression that work on this hull had ceased some time before. The vessel seen was obviously the third ship of the *Sovetskiy Soyuz* class, *Sovetskaya Byelorossiya*. The other great dock was empty, apart from a few sections of submarines, which were probably only being stored there temporarily; this dock might have been intended for *Sovetskaya Rossiya*, for which only the first floor sections (at most) had been assembled before work was halted.

This photograph was taken in July 1946 and shows the Baltic Yard at Leningrad. The hull of *Sovetskiy Soyuz* is on the stocks to the left, whilst in the foreground is the submarine *L21*. *BfZ*

This remarkable model of *Sovetskiy Soyuz* was completed by a Bulgarian shiplover after many hours of work. At a scale of 1/1250, the fastidious reproduction of many details is a considerable achievement. The stem appears to be slightly too curved; in reality, it was almost straight. *Todorov*

It is not known where *Sovetskaya Byelorossiya* was broken up: it may have been inside the construction dock, or possibly it was after she had been floated out. The only certain fact is that the dock was clear by 1948, as the *Sverdlov* class cruiser *Molotovsk* (renamed *Oktyabrskaya Revoluciya* in 1957) was begun there in that year. She was completed in 1952. Another *Sverdlov* class cruiser, probably *Murmansk*, was built in the neighbouring dock at the same time.

THE KRONSHTADT CLASS BATTLECRUISERS

The building of 'heavy cruisers' – a type of warship whose development began towards the end of the First World War – was taken up by all six great naval powers and a few minor ones by the mid-1930s. These ships' qualitative characteristics had been determined by the Washington Naval Treaty of 1922; a maximum standard displacement of 10,000 tons and a maximum gun calibre of 8in (20.3cm). Around 1936 the Soviet Union drew up a specification for a ship whose tasks would be as follows:

1 The defeat of enemy 'Washington cruisers' on the high seas
2 The support of her own light forces in operations on the high seas
3 The waging of a 'commerce war' along the main sea lanes

According to the ideas of Admiral Isakov, these *Istrebitel Vashingtonskich Krejsera* (lit: 'Washington cruiser-hunters') should have been around 22,000–23,000 tons standard displacement, armed with nine 25.4cm (10in) guns, and have a top speed of 33kts. They were to be weakly armoured, with a belt no thicker than 5.5in (140mm) maximum. The design was worked out in detail, but found no support when placed before the defence committee in June 1938, with Stalin as chairman. In spite of the ships' high speed, the committee was convinced that the design would be a failure, especially considering the German *Scharnhorst* class, which would have been the main opponents of such 'cruiser-hunters' at that time. A battlecruiser was demanded which would be clearly superior to the *Scharnhorst* class in terms of fighting qualities.

A corresponding design, 'ZKB-17', was presented on 11 July 1939, and was approved to the extent that the green light was given for building the ships even though design work was not yet complete. Only two ships could be built, however, as only two slipways of adequate size were available: *Kronshtadt*, to be built at the Marti Yard at Leningrad, was laid down on Slipway 4A in the autumn of 1939; and *Sevastopol* was laid down at the end of 1939 at the Marti (North) Yard at Nikolayev. The design was finalised early in 1940, and approved on 12 April that year. The accompanying table gives further details.

SPECIFICATIONS FOR KRONSHTADT CLASS

Displacement:	32,700 tons standard, 35,770 tons normal, 40,385 tons full load
Dimensions:	Length 238.00m (780ft 10in) wl, 248.00m (813ft 8in) oa; beam 29.20m (95ft 9in) wl, 31.40m (103ft 0in) max; draught 8.43m (27ft 8in); freeboard amidships 5.57m (18ft 3in); length-to-beam ratio 8.15:1
Machinery:	230,000shp = 32.0kts
Armament:	9–30.5cm (12in) (3 × 3), 8–15.2cm (6in) (4 × 2), 8–10.0cm (3.9in) AA (4 × 2), 24–37mm AA (6 × 4), 8–12.7mm AA (2 × 4), 1 catapult, 2 aircraft
Armour:	Belt 230mm (9in), deck 90mm (3½in), barbettes 330mm (13in), main turrets 330mm (13in) faces, conning tower 305mm (12in), deck 125mm (5in)

Just after the start of the German invasion of the Soviet Union, *Kronshtadt*'s hull was seen on the stocks at the Marti Yard at Leningrad, and was repeatedly photographed. German intelligence officers mistakenly believed that they were looking at an aircraft carrier under construction, although their estimation of the size of the hull was very accurate, the length being around 820ft (250m) and the beam 105ft (32m). Work on this ship ceased in the autumn of 1940 as was the case with the new battleships of the *Sovetskiy Soyuz* class, but by this time building had advanced as far as the armour deck. During the 2½-year siege of Leningrad, much material was also removed from this hull and used for other military purposes. After the liberation of Leningrad, officers of the Western allies had numerous opportunities to see the *Kronshtadt* hull, including Admiral Olsen on 10 June 1944 during the motor boat trip on the Neva which has already been mentioned. On this occasion he estimated that *Kronshtadt* was '5 per cent complete'. His successor, Admiral Maples, saw *Kronshtadt* on 29 June 1947, and stated that two-thirds of the hull was as good as complete, and that work on her had evidently been resumed to a limited extent, since one of the six cranes was working[9]. However, it later transpired that it was only preservation work that was being carried out, and only on certain fittings, in view of the coming winter. When the British Naval Attaché, Admiral L C Stevens, was on a visit to Leningrad from 6 to 9 May 1949, he was convinced that the *Kronshtadt* hull had not advanced past the stage reported by Admiral Maples two years earlier. But only a few weeks later members of the US Naval Attaché's staff finally learned the truth: *Kronshtadt*'s hull was still on the stocks, but it had been dismantled into several pieces; on this occasion the characteristic Pugliese underwater protective system was visible[10]. These sections were then launched one by one and on 7 October 1949 only two fairly small sections remained on the stocks, one roughly in the middle, one at the end of the slipway[11]. Shortly after this the slipway must have been completely cleared, because the keel of the *Sverdlov* class cruiser *Ordzhonikidze* was laid on it. This ship was launched on 20 September 1950[12]. The stern section of *Kronshtadt* was recognised in July 1950 as the caisson of Slipway 4A. Shortly before the cruiser *Ordzhonikidze* was launched, the section was released and anchored in a remote corner of the Neva not far from the Marti Yard.

This was the condition of the battlecruiser *Sevastopol* as she was found in the North Yard at Nikolayev. From this angle a section of the stern still appears to be missing; possibly the slipway was too small to accommodate the whole length of the hull, which meant that it would have had to be built in two parts. If this was true, then it would provide a plausible explanation for the existence of a single ship section which was used later on as a floating AA battery. In the background, in the 5000-ton floating dock belonging to the yard, is the Romanian freighter *Ardeal*, which was torpedoed by the Soviet submarine *A5*. The photo dates from 12 September 1942, one year after Nikolayev was captured. *BA/MA (Author's Collection)*

The second ship, *Sevastopol*, was found by the Germans on the stocks at the bulkhead stage when they entered Nikolayev in August 1941. Evidently they did not immediately realise what they had found, since otherwise there is no explanation why German propaganda suppressed news of this find when they reported other booty captured at Nikolayev, only mentioning one battleship. The reason obviously was that the ship was too little advanced to be recognisable as a capital ship. It was only later that she was recognised as a '35,000-ton battleship' by Kapt z S von Baumbach, who was the German Naval Attaché in Moscow from 1937 to 1941, and afterwards was Director of Naval Intelligence. Construction was not continued under the Germans, but parts were dismantled for use as raw materials for the armaments industry. The remains were then apparently made totally unusable by demolition crews when Nikolayev was cleared, leaving the Soviets absolutely nothing except a skeleton to break up. Scrapping is said to have been completed by June 1949.

When the Germans took Sevastopol, they found a destroyed, half-sunken ship's hull, which they thought to be the incomplete remains of a destroyer[13]. In fact it was a section of a capital ship, about 140 × 65ft (42 × 20m) in area and 26ft (8m) deep, which had been built before the German attack and after work was halted in October 1940 used for test purposes. In July 1941 this section was fitted out as a floating AA battery, three 130mm (5.1in), three 76mm (3in) and three 37mm AA and four machine guns being installed. From that time on it carried the designation 'PZB-3' (unofficially also *Ne Tron Menya*). At first it was used off Cherson, where it tore free from its anchorage in January 1942 and was driven southwards. It was salvaged and brought in to Sevastopol, where it was used as part of the airport's seaward defences from March 1942. On 27 June 1942 it was largely destroyed during the battles for Sevastopol, and was abandoned by its crew. The origin of this ship section remain unclear to this day, but there are two alternative theories:

1 The section was built by the Marti (South) Yard at Nikolayev from material being processed there for the battleship *Sovetskaya Byelorossiya*, which was being assembled at Molotovsk. This occurred after construction work on capital ships was halted in the autumn of 1940, and the intention was to exploit the knowledge gained from the other powers in the course of the war and carry out tests on the efficiency of underwater protective systems

2 It came from the battlecruiser *Sevastopol* and was possibly built elsewhere, as the slipway was perhaps too small to accommodate the entire hull. In this case this section would have been added on after the hull was launched – a thoroughly normal procedure even at that time. Explanations by Soviet historians tend to support this thesis.

The development of the 30.5cm (12in) guns intended for the *Kronshtadt*s could have been essentially completed by early 1940. Admiral Kuznecov – Navy Commissioner and therefore the highest-ranking officer at the time – himself bore witness to this in late 1940, and the Head of Naval Ordnance at Leningrad, Rear-Admiral Gren, evidently commended them as the 'best guns in the world'. The intended destiny of the eight twin turrets, which were ordered from Germany in 1940, remains a mystery. They comprised sixteen 38cm (15in) guns, and although Germany agreed to supply them, they were never delivered. These requests certainly had nothing to do with the *Kronshtadt* class battlecruisers.

THE STALINGRAD CLASS BATTLECRUISERS

The final chapter of Soviet capital shipbuilding was written only a few years after the end of the Second World War, and ended after the death of Stalin in 1953. During this period two battlecruisers were begun, although they were classed as *Tyazhelye Kreysera*, or heavy cruisers, in spite of their size and battle power: *Stalingrad*, laid down in 1949 on the same Marti (South) slipway at Nikolayev that *Sovetskaya Ukraina* had occupied up to 1947–48 (this yard was renamed the Nosenko Yard after the end of the war) and *Moskva*, which was begun in the second half of 1950 on the same slipway that *Sovetskiy Soyuz* had occupied until shortly beforehand.

Initial design work for this so-called 'Project 82' had been started in 1940, and the design was approved in March 1941. The German attack on the Soviet Union forced the Russians to abandon the project, or at least to postpone it, and it was only at a later stage of the war, when there was no longer any doubt that the Germans would be defeated, that the designs were reconsidered. By 1947 they had been brought up to more modern technical standards, reflecting the lessons learned during the war. The main features of this revised design are listed in the accompanying table.

DESIGN SPECIFICATIONS FOR 'PROJECT 82'

Displacement:	38,420 tons standard, 41,640 tons normal, 43,720 tons full load
Dimensions:	Length 240.00m (787ft 6in) wl, 250.50m (821ft 9in) oa; beam 29.40m (96ft 6in) wl; draught 8.88m (29ft); freeboard 5.67m (18ft 6in)

The two units were ordered under a ten-year naval programme passed in 1944, which is said to have included the construction of eight battleships. At this time the two great Western navies were still building capital ships, and the idea of halting work on them was still some time away. With these factors in mind, these new Soviet capital ships become more plausible.

Nothing is known about the drive system of this class, and very little about its armament. The latter was supposed to consist of nine 30.5cm (12in) guns in triple turrets, plus a corresponding AA battery – eight 10cm (3.9in) guns and twenty-eight 37mm AA guns in quadruple mounts. There can be no doubt that the 30.5cm guns were those which had been developed originally for the *Kronshtadt* class battlecruisers. US reports suggesting that these ships were to be equipped with 'Kennel' missiles which had been adapted for use against surface targets, cannot of course be proved. However, one question must be asked: could it be that here, in the last Soviet capital ships, are the roots of those sensational oft-repeated reports of the postwar period (which never quite died down) which persistently referred to Soviet rocket-equipped battleships? Were these reports, which have always been dismissed as fables, more than just rumours?

Is there anyone among the older generation of shiplovers who does not remember those 'artist's impressions' of Soviet battleships with heavy guns and rockets which were published so often in the Western world in the 1950s? These pictures even found their way into serious Fleet handbooks. This is one of them, showing a battleship whose main armament consisted of nine 16in and twenty medium guns. Also shown are two 'dome' turrets, from which missiles could be launched. The vast majority of experts considered these spectacular concoctions to be in the realms of fantasy, but present-day knowledge leads one to ask whether the sensational reports of the time might not have had a few grains of truth behind them. *Popular Science*

Work on both ships progressed very slowly. They should both have been laid down by the end of 1948, but there were serious problems. The slipway intended for *Moskva* at the Baltic Yard at Leningrad was still occupied by the hulk of *Sovetskiy Soyuz*, and when it had been cleared, time-consuming repairs needed to be carried out; hence *Moskva* was not laid down until the second half of 1950. Early in 1953 – the time of Stalin's death – the structure of the ship was 92 per cent complete, the machinery 20 per cent, the armament fittings and equipment 12 per cent and the navigation systems only 5 per cent. The anticipated date of completion, judging by her condition, must have been 1958–59. *Stalingrad* was about 60 per cent complete when she was launched.

Stalin's death in March 1953, and the change of leadership which followed, accelerated the reassessment of Soviet naval construction policy that began to emerge around the end of 1953. This involved a complete *volte-face*, away from the type of large warship typified by these two battlecruisers, and the abandonment of the previous building programmes in favour of others. As a result, *Moskva* was broken up on her slipway. *Stalingrad*, on the other hand, was probably almost complete, and was apparently used for tests with naval weapons systems. In 1956 she evidently grounded near Feodosiya (Eupatoriya?), yet was salvaged and then utilised as a target ship for guided missiles. Thus ended the final chapter of Soviet capital shipbuilding, in which not a single vessel was ever completed.

Notes

1 *See* Lott and Sumrall: *Ships Data 1: USS North Carolina (BB55)*, Leeward Publications (Pompton Lakes, USA, 1973).

2 Leningrad Naval Museum has evidently had on show for several years a shell which was manufactured for this gun. More details about Soviet naval guns of World War II can be found in Pierieczniew: 'Artyleraa Floty Baltyckiej w Operacjach Zaczepnych', *Voenno Istoriceskij* 1974, No 6, pp44–45. Information on the 40.6cm gun is given, together with details of the new 30.5cm (12in) gun for the *Kronshtadt* class battlecruisers.

3 NA Moscow Serial 175–47, 15 July 1947.

4 This comes from a report by Lt (jg) Levy, a member of the staff of the American Navy Attaché in Moscow (NA Moscow Serial 3-S-49, 7 February 1949).

5 Report by Lt (jg) Goloway (NA Moscow Serial 21-S-49, 3 June 1949).

6 Report from Admiral Leslie C Stevens USN and Lt (jg) Goloway (NA Moscow Serial 31-S-49, 28 August 1949).

7 Report from Cdr WS Lea RN, Lt Shirley RNVR and Lt (jg) Lexow USNR (NA Moscow Serial 96-44, 2 August 1944).

8 NA Moscow Serial 96-44, 2 August 1944.

9 NA Moscow Serial 175-47, 15 July 1947.

10 NA Moscow Serial 31-S-49, 23 August 1949.

11 Report by LT-Cdr C N Whited USN (NA Moscow Serial 43-S-49, 16 October 1949).

12 NA Moscow Serial 26-S-50, 31 October 1950.

13 Meister: *Der Seekrieg in den Osteuropäischen Gewässern 1941–45*, p360.

Sources

Greger: 'Sowjetischer Schlachtschiffbau', *Marine Rundschau* 1974, p461

Breyer: 'Sowjetischer Schlachtschiffbau' (a complementary comment on René Greger's article in *MR*, August 1974), *Marine Rundschau* 1975, p141

Erikson: 'Soviet Battleships – Part 2' *Warship International* 1974, p115

Lemachko and Erikson in readers' letters giving additional information on the subject of Soviet battleships, *Warship International* 1975, p159

Meister: *Soviet Warships of the Second World War* (London, 1977), p20

Huan and Rohwer: *La Marine Sovietique* (notes et études documentaires, 1978, No 4 479–4480)

Tables

The following summary lists all the capital ships which are dealt with or mentioned in this volume. The ships are presented under their respective classes, and the brief information following is intended to give the reader an idea of their fighting qualities. The data refers to the condition of the ships when they were first completed; modifications and equipment changes are not covered here – with some exceptions. Vessels which were never completed are indicated thus*; those lost are shown thus†.

Name	Built	Displacement (full load) (tons)	Speed (kts)	Armament		Armour	
				Main	Secondary	Belt	Horizontal
GREAT BRITAIN							
Lord Nelson	1905–08	17,863	18.0	4–12in (30.5cm), 10–9.2in (23.4cm)	–	12in (305mm)	4in ([illegible]02mm)
Agamemnon	1905–08	17,820	18.0	4–12in (30.5cm) 10–9.2in (23.4cm)	–	12in (305mm)	4in (102mm)
Dreadnought	1905–06	21,845	21.0	10–12in (30.5cm)	–	11in (279mm)	3in ([illegible]6mm)
Invincible†	1906–08		25.0	8–12in (30.5cm)	16–4in (10.2cm)	6in (152mm)	2½in (64mm)
Inflexible	1906–08	19,975–20,125	25.0	8–12in (30.5cm)	16–4in (10.2cm)	6in (152mm)	2½in (64mm)
Indomitable	1906–08		25.0	8–12in (30.5cm)	16–4in (10.2cm)	6in (152mm)	2½in (64mm)
Bellerophon	1906–09	22,102	20.7	10–12in (30.5cm)	16–4in (10.2cm)	10in (254mm)	3in (76mm)
Superb	1906–09	22,102	20.7	10–12in (30.5cm)	16–4in (10.2cm)	10in (254mm)	3in (76mm)
Temeraire	1907–09	22,102	20.7	10–12in (30.5cm)	16–4in (10.2cm)	10in (254mm)	3in (76mm)
Collingwood	1907–10	23,030	21.0	10–12in (30.5cm)	20–4in (10.2cm)	10in (254mm)	3in (76mm)
St Vincent	1907–09	23,030	21.0	10–12in (30.5cm)	20–4in (10.2cm)	10in (254mm)	3in (76mm)
Vanguard†	1908–10	23,030	21.0	10–12in (30.5cm)	20–4in (10.2cm)	10in (254mm)	3in (76mm)
Neptune	1909–11	22,720	21.0	10–12in (30.5cm)	16–4in (10.2cm)	10in (254mm)	3in (76mm)
Colossus	1909–11	23,050	21.0	10–12in (30.5cm)	16–4in (10.2cm)	11in (279mm)	3in (76mm)
Hercules	1909–11	23,050	21.0	10–12in (30.5cm)	16–4in (10.2cm)	11in (279mm)	3in (76mm)
Indefatigable†	1909–11	22,080	25.0	8–12in (30.5cm)	16–4in (10.2cm)	6in (152mm)	2in (51mm)
Australia	1909–11	22,080	25.0	8–12in (30.5cm)	16–4in (10.2cm)	6in (152mm)	2in (51mm)
New Zealand	1909–11	22,080	25.0	8–12in (30.5cm)	16–4in (10.2cm)	6in (152mm)	2in (51mm)
Orion	1909–12	25,870	21.0	10–13.5in (34.3cm)	16–4in (10.2cm)	12in (305mm)	4in (102mm)
Conqueror	1910–13	25,870	21.0	10–13.5in (34.3cm)	16–4in (10.2cm)	12in (305mm)	4in (102mm)
Monarch	1910–12	25,870	21.0	10–13.5in (34.3cm)	16–4in (10.2cm)	12in (305mm)	4in (102mm)
Thunderer	1910–12	25,870	21.0	10–13.5in (34.3cm)	16–4in (10.2cm)	12in (305mm)	4in (102mm)
Lion	1909–12	29,680	27.0	8–13.5in (34.3cm)	16–4in (10.2cm)	9in (229mm)	2½in (64mm)
Princess Royal	1909–12	29,680	27.0	8–13.5in (34.3cm)	16–4in (10.2cm)	9in (229mm)	2½in (64mm)
Queen Mary†	1911–13	29,680	27.0	8–13.5in (34.3cm)	16–4in (10.2cm)	9in (229mm)	2½in (64mm)
King George V	1911–12	25,700	21.7	10–13.5in (34.3cm)	16–4in (10.2cm)	12in (305mm)	4in (102mm)
Centurion	1911–13	25,700	21.7	10–13.5in (34.3cm)	16–4in (10.2cm)	12in (305mm)	4in (102mm)
Audacious†	1911–13	25,700	21.7	10–13.5in (34.3cm)	16–4in (10.2cm)	12in (305mm)	4in (102mm)
Ajax	1911–13	25,700	21.7	10–13.5in (34.3cm)	16–4in (10.2cm)	12in (305mm)	4in (102mm)
Iron Duke	1912–14	30,080	21.0	10–13.5in (34.3cm)	12–6in (15.2cm)	12in (305mm)	2½in (64mm)
Benbow	1912–14	30,080	21.0	10–13.5in (34.3cm)	12–6in (15.2cm)	12in (305mm)	2½in (64mm)
Emperor of India	1912–14	30,080	21.0	10–13.5in (34.3cm)	12–6in (15.2cm)	12in (305mm)	2½in (64mm)
Marlborough	1912–14	30,080	21.0	10–13.5in (34.3cm)	12–6in (15.2cm)	12in (305mm)	2½in (64mm)
Tiger	1912–14	35,160	29.0	8–13.5in (34.3cm)	12–6in (15.2cm)	9in (229mm)	2½in (64mm)
Agincourt	1911–14	30,250	22.4	14–12in (30.5cm)	20–6in (15.2cm)	9in (229mm)	1½in (38mm)
Erin	1911–14	25,250	21.0	10–13.5in (34.3cm)	16–6in (15.2cm)	12in (305mm)	3in (76m[illegible]
Canada	1911–15	28,600	22.7	10–14in (35.6cm)	16–6in (15.2cm)	9in (229mm)	4in (102[illegible])
Queen Elizabeth	1912–15	33,000	25.0	8–15in (38.1cm)	16–6in (15.2cm)	13in (330mm)	3in (76mm)
Valiant	1913–16	33,000	25.0	8–15in (38.1cm)	16–6in (15.2cm)	13in (330mm)	3in (76mm)
Barham†	1913–15	33,000	25.0	8–15in (38.1cm)	16–6in (15.2cm)	13in (330mm)	3in (76mm)
Malaya	1913–15	33,000	25.0	8–15in (38.1cm)	16–6in (15.2cm)	13in (330mm)	3in (76mm)
Warspite	1912–15	33,000	25.0	8–15in (38.1cm)	16–6in (15.2cm)	13in (330mm)	3in (76mm)

Name	Built	Displacement (full load) (tons)	Speed (kts)	Armament		Armour	
				Main	Secondary	Belt	Horizontal
Revenge	1913–16	31,200	23.0	8–15in (38.1cm)	14–6in (15.2cm)	13in (330mm)	4in (102mm)
Ramillies	1913–17	31,200	23.0	8–15in (38.1cm)	14–6in (15.2cm)	13in (330mm)	4in (102mm)
Resolution	1913–16	31,200	23.0	8–15in (38.1cm)	14–6in (15.2cm)	13in (330mm)	4in (102mm)
Royal Oak†	1914–16	31,200	23.0	8–15in (38.1cm)	14–6in (15.2cm)	13in (330mm)	4in (102mm)
Royal Sovereign	1914–16	31,200	23.0	8–15in (38.1cm)	14–6in (15.2cm)	13in (330mm)	4in (102mm)
Renown	1915–16	32,727	29.0	6–15in (38.1cm)	17–4in (10.2cm)	6in (152mm)	$3^{1}/_{2}$in (89mm)
Repulse†	1915–16	32,074	29.0	6–15in (38.1cm)	17–4in (10.2cm)	6in (152mm)	$3^{1}/_{2}$in (89mm)
Courageous†	1915–17	22,690	31.0	4–15in (38.1cm)	18–4in (10.2cm)	3in (76mm)	3in (76mm)
Glorious†	1915–17	22,690	31.0	4–15in (38.1cm)	18–4in (10.2cm)	3in (76mm)	3in (76mm)
Furious	1915–17	22,890	31.5	2–18in (45.7cm)	11–5.5in (14cm)	3in (76mm)	3in (76mm)
Hood	1916–20	44,700	31.0	8–15in (38.1cm)	12–5.5in (14cm)	12in (305mm)	3in (76mm)
Nelson	1922–27	38,000	23.0	9–16in (40.6cm)	12–6in (15.2cm)	14in (356mm)	$6^{1}/_{4}$in (159mm)
Rodney	1922–27	38,000	23.0	9–16in (40.6cm)	12–6in (15.2cm)	14in (356mm)	$6^{1}/_{4}$in (159mm)
King George V	1937–40		27.5	10–14in (35.6cm)	16–5.25in (13.3cm)	14in (356mm)	6in (152mm)
Prince of Wales†	1937–41		27.5	10–14in (35.6cm)	16–5.25in (13.3cm)	14in (356mm)	6in (152mm)
Duke of York	1937–41	44,460–45,360	27.5	10–14in (35.6cm)	16–5.25in (13.3cm)	14in (356mm)	6in (152mm)
Howe	1937–42		27.5	10–14in (35.6cm)	16–5.25in (13.3cm)	14in (356mm)	6in (152mm)
Anson	1937–42		27.5	10–14in (35.6cm)	16–5.25in (13.3cm)	14in (356mm)	6in (152mm)
Vanguard	1941–46	51,420	29.5	8–15in (38.1cm)	16–5.25in (13.3cm)	14in (356mm)	6in (152mm)
GERMANY							
Deutschland	1903–06	13,993	18.0	4–11in (28cm)	14–6.7in (17cm)	9.6in (240mm)	3.8in (97mm)
Hannover	1904–07	13,993	18.0	4–11in (28cm)	14–6.7in (17cm)	9.6in (240mm)	3.8in (97mm)
Pommern†	1904–07	13,993	18.0	4–11in (28cm)	14–6.7in (17cm)	9.6in (240mm)	3.8in (97mm)
Schlesien	1905–08	13,993	18.0	4–11in (28cm)	14–6.7in (17cm)	9.6in (240mm)	3.8in (97mm)
Schleswig-Holstein	1905–08	13,993	18.0	4–11in (28cm)	14–6.7in (17cm)	9.6in (240mm)	3.8in (97mm)
Nassau	1907–09	20,120	19.5	12–11in (28cm)	12–5.9in (15cm)	11.8in (300mm)	2.3in (58mm)
Westfalen	1907–09	20,120	19.5	12–11in (28cm)	12–5.9in (15cm)	11.8in (300mm)	2.3in (58mm)
Rheinland	1907–10	20,120	19.5	12–11in (28cm)	12–5.9in (15cm)	11.8in (300mm)	2.3in (58mm)
Posen	1907–10	20,120	19.5	12–11in (28cm)	12–5.9in (15cm)	11.8in (300mm)	2.3in (58mm)
Helgoland	1908–11	24,312	20.0	12–12in (30.5cm)	14–5.9in (15cm)	11.8in (300mm)	1.8in (45mm)
Ostfriesland	1908–11	24,312	20.0	12–12in (30.5cm)	14–5.9in (15cm)	11.8in (300mm)	1.8in (45mm)
Thüringen	1908–11	24,312	20.0	12–12in (30.5cm)	14–5.9in (15cm)	11.8in (300mm)	1.8in (45mm)
Oldenburg	1909–12	24,312	20.0	12–12in (30.5cm)	14–5.9in (15cm)	11.8in (300mm)	1.8in (45mm)
Blücher†	1907–09	17,500	24.5	12–8.3in (21cm)	8–5.9in (15cm)	7.1in (180mm)	2.8in (70mm)
Von der Tann	1908–10	21,802	24.8	8–11in (28cm)	10–5.9in (15cm)	9.8in (250mm)	2in (50mm)
Moltke	1908–11	24,999	25.5	10–11in (28cm)	12–5.9in (15cm)	10.6in (270mm)	2in (50mm)
Goeben	1909–12	24,999	25.5	10–11in (28cm)	12–5.9in (15cm)	10.6in (270mm)	2in (50mm)
Seydlitz	1911–13	25,146	26.5	10–11in (28cm)	12–5.9in (15cm)	11.8in (300mm)	3.1in (80mm)
Kaiser	1909–12	26,573	21.0	10–12in (30.5cm)	14–5.9in (15cm)	13.8in (350mm)	2in (50mm)
Kaiserin	1910–13	26,573	21.0	10–12in (30.5cm)	14–5.9in (15cm)	13.8in (350mm)	2in (50mm)
Friedrich der Grosse	1910–12	26,573	21.0	10–12in (30.5cm)	14–5.9in (15cm)	13.8in (350mm)	2in (50mm)
Prinzregent Luitpold	1910–13	26,573	21.0	10–12in (30.5cm)	14–5.9in (15cm)	13.8in (350mm)	2in (50mm)
König Albert	1910–13	26,573	21.0	10–12in (30.5cm)	14–5.9in (15cm)	13.8in (350mm)	2in (50mm)
König	1911–14	28,148	21.0	10–12in (30.5cm)	14–5.9in (15cm)	13.8in (350mm)	1.2in (30mm)
Grosser Kurfürst	1911–14	28,148	21.0	10–12in (30.5cm)	14–5.9in (15cm)	13.8in (350mm)	1.2in (30mm)
Markgraf	1911–14	28,148	21.0	10–12in (30.5cm)	14–5.9in (15cm)	13.8in (350mm)	1.2in (30mm)
Kronprinz Wilhelm	1912–14	28,148	21.0	10–12in (30.5cm)	14–5.9in (15cm)	13.8in (350mm)	1.2in (30mm)
Derfflinger	1912–14			8–12in (30.5cm)	14–5.9in (15cm)	11.8in (300mm)	3.1in (80mm)
Lützow†	1912–15	30,707–31,987	26.5–27.0	8–12in (30.5cm)	14–5.9in (15cm)	11.8in (300mm)	3.1in (80mm)
Hindenburg	1913–17			8–12in (30.5cm)	14–5.9in (15cm)	11.8in (300mm)	3.1in (80mm)

Name	Built	Displacement (full load) (tons)	Speed (kts)	Armament Main	Armament Secondary	Armour Belt	Armour Horizontal
Bayern	1913–16	31,961–31,987	22.0	8–15in (38cm)	16–5.9in (15cm)	13.8in (350mm)	4.7in (120mm)
Baden	1913–16		22.0	8–15in (38cm)	16–5.9in (15cm)	13.8in (350mm)	4.7in (120mm)
Sachsen	1914*		22.0	8–15in (38cm)	16–5.9in (15cm)	13.8in (350mm)	4.7in (120mm)
Württemberg	1915*		22.0	8–15in (38cm)	16–5.9in (15cm)	13.8in (350mm)	4.7in (120mm)
Mackensen	1915*	34,742	27.0	8–13.8in (35cm)	14–5.9in (15cm)	11.8in (300mm)	3.1in (80mm)
Graf Spee	1915*	34,742	27.0	8–13.8in (35cm)	14–5.9in (15cm)	11.8in (300mm)	3.1in (80mm)
'Ersatz Freya'	1915*	34,742	27.0	8–13.8in (35cm)	14–5.9in (15cm)	11.8in (300mm)	3.1in (80mm)
'A'	1915*	34,742	27.0	8–13.8in (35cm)	14–5.9in (15cm)	11.8in (300mm)	3.1in (80mm)
Lützow (ex-*Deutschland*)	1929–33	15,900–16,200	26.0	6–11in (28cm)	8–5.9in (15cm)	2.4–3.1in (50–80mm)	1.6–1.8in (40–45mm)
Admiral Scheer	1931–34		26.0	6–11in (28cm)	8–5.9in (15cm)		
Admiral Graf Spee	1932–36		26.0	6–11in (28cm)	8–5.9in (15cm)		
Scharnhorst	1935–39	38,900	32.0	9–11in (28cm)	12–5.9in (15cm)	13.8in (350mm)	4.1in (105mm)
Gneisenau	1935–38	38,900	32.0	9–11in (28cm)	12–5.9in (15cm)	13.8in (350mm)	4.1in (105mm)
Bismarck	1936–40	50,900	29.0	8–15in (38cm)	12–5.9in (15cm)	12.6in (320mm)	4.7in (120mm)
Tirpitz	1936–41	52,600	29.0	8–15in (38cm)	12–5.9in (15cm)	12.6in (320mm)	4.7in (120mm)
'H'	1939*	62,497	30.0	8–16in (40.6cm)	12–5.9in (15cm)	11.8in (300mm)	4.7in (120mm)
'J'	1939*	62,497	30.0	8–16in (40.6cm)	12–5.9in (15cm)	11.8in (300mm)	4.7in (120mm)

UNITED STATES OF AMERICA

Name	Built	Displacement (full load) (tons)	Speed (kts)	Armament Main	Armament Secondary	Armour Belt	Armour Horizontal
Connecticut (BB18)	1903–06	*c*18,000	18.0	4–12in (30.5cm), 8–8in (20.3cm)	12–7in (17.8cm)	11in (279mm)	1½in (38mm)
Louisiana (BB19)	1903–06	*c*18,000	18.0	4–12in (30.5cm), 8–8in (20.3cm)	12–7in (17.8cm)	11in (279mm)	1½in (38mm)
Vermont (BB20)	1904–07	*c*18,000	18.0	4–12in (30.5cm), 8–8in (20.3cm)	12–7in (17.8cm)	11in (279mm)	1½in (38mm)
Minnesota (BB22)	1903–07	*c*18,000	18.0	4–12in (30.5cm), 8–8in (20.3cm)	12–7in (17.8cm)	11in (279mm)	1½in (38mm)
New Hampshire (BB25)	1905–08	*c*18,000	18.0	4–12in (30.5cm), 8–8in (20.3cm)	12–7in (17.8cm)	11in (279mm)	1½in (38mm)
South Carolina (BB26)	1906–10	*c*18,000	18.8	8–12in (30.5cm)	–	12in (305mm)	1½in (38mm)
Michigan (BB27)	1906–10	*c*18,000	18.8	8–12in (30.5cm)	–	12in (305mm)	1½in (38mm)
Delaware (BB28)	1907–10	*c*22,500	21.0	10–12in (30.5cm)	14–5in (12.7cm)	11in (279mm)	3in (76mm)
North Dakota (BB29)	1907–10	*c*22,500	21.0	10–12in (30.5cm)	14–5in (12.7cm)	11in (279mm)	3in (76mm)
Florida (BB30)	1909–11	23,400	20.7	10–12in (30.5cm)	16–5in (12.7cm)	11in (279mm)	3in (76mm)
Utah (BB31)	1909–11	23,400	20.7	10–12in (30.5cm)	16–5in (12.7cm)	11in (279mm)	3in (76mm)
Wyoming (BB32)	1910–12	27,700	20.5	12–12in (30.5cm)	21–5in (12.7cm)	11in (279mm)	3in (76mm)
Arkansas (BB33)	1910–12	27,700	20.5	12–12in (30.5cm)	21–5in (12.7cm)	11in (279mm)	3in (76mm)
New York (BB34)	1911–14	28,400	21.0	10–14in (35.6cm)	21–5in (12.7cm)	12in (305mm)	3in (76mm)
Texas (BB35)	1911–14	28,400	21.0	10–14in (35.6cm)	21–5in (12.7cm)	12in (305mm)	3in (76mm)
Nevada (BB36)	1912–16	28,900	20.5	10–14in (35.6cm)	21–5in (12.7cm)	13½in (343mm)	3in (76mm)
Oklahoma (BB37)†	1912–16	28,900	20.5	10–14in (35.6cm)	21–5in (12.7cm)	13½in (343mm)	3in (76mm)
Pennsylvania (BB38)	1913–16	33,000	21.0	12–14in (35.6cm)	21–5in (12.7cm)	13½in (343mm)	3in (76mm)
Arizona (BB39)†	1914–16	33,000	21.0	12–14in (35.6cm)	21–5in (12.7cm)	13½in (343mm)	3in (76mm)
New Mexico (BB40)	1915–18	33,500	21.0	12–14in (35.6cm)	22–5in (12.7cm)	14in (356mm)	3½in (89mm)
Mississippi (BB41)	1915–17	33,500	21.0	12–14in (35.6cm)	22–5in (12.7cm)	14in (356mm)	3½in (89mm)
Idaho (BB42)	1915–17	33,500	21.0	12–14in (35.6cm)	22–5in (12.7cm)	14in (356mm)	3½in (89mm)
Tennessee (BB43)	1917–20	34,000	21.0	12–14in (35.6cm)	14–5in (12.7cm)	14in (356mm)	3½in (89mm)
California (BB44)	1916–21	34,000	21.0	12–14in (35.6cm)	14–5in (12.7cm)	14in (356mm)	3½in (89mm)

Name	Built	Displacement (full load) (tons)	Speed (kts)	Armament Main	Armament Secondary	Armour Belt	Armour Horizontal
Colorado (BB45)	1919–23	33,600	21.0	8–16in (40.6cm)	14–5in (12.7cm)	16in (406mm)	3½in (89mm)
Maryland (BB46)	1917–21	33,600	21.0	8–16in (40.6cm)	14–5in (12.7cm)	16in (406mm)	3½in (89mm)
Washington (BB47)	1919*	33,600	21.0	8–16in (40.6cm)	14–5in (12.7cm)	16in (406mm)	3½in (89mm)
West Virginia (BB48)	1920–23	33,600	21.0	8–16in (40.6cm)	14–5in (12.7cm)	16in (406mm)	3½in (89mm)
South Dakota (BB49)	1920*	c47,000	23.0	12–16in (40.6cm)	16–6in (15.2cm)	13½in (343mm)	3½in (89mm)
Indiana (BB50)	1920*	c47,000	23.0	12–16in (40.6cm)	16–6in (15.2cm)	13½in (343mm)	3½in (89mm)
Montana (BB51)	1920*	c47,000	23.0	12–16in (40.6cm)	16–6in (15.2cm)	13½in (343mm)	3½in (89mm)
North Carolina (BB52)	1920*	c47,000	23.0	12–16in (40.6cm)	16–6in (15.2cm)	13½in (343mm)	3½in (89mm)
Iowa (BB53)	1920*	c47,000	23.0	12–16in (40.6cm)	16–6in (15.2cm)	13½in (343mm)	3½in (89mm)
Massachusetts (BB54)	1921*	c47,000	23.0	12–16in (40.6cm)	16–6in (15.2cm)	13½in (343mm)	3½in (89mm)
Lexington (CC1)	1921*	c49,000	33.2	8–16in (40.6cm)	16–6in (15.2cm)	7in (178mm)	2¼in (57mm)
Constellation (CC2)	1920*	c49,000	33.2	8–16in (40.6cm)	16–6in (15.2cm)	7in (178mm)	2¼in (57mm)
Saratoga (CC3)	1920*	c49,000	33.2	8–16in (40.6cm)	16–6in (15.2cm)	7in (178mm)	2¼in (57mm)
Ranger (CC4)	1921*	c49,000	33.2	8–16in (40.6cm)	16–6in (15.2cm)	7in (178mm)	2¼in (57mm)
Constitution (CC5)	1920*	c49,000	33.2	8–16in (40.6cm)	16–6in (15.2cm)	7in (178mm)	2¼in (57mm)
United States (CC6)	1920*	c49,000	33.2	8–16in (40.6cm)	16–6in (15.2cm)	7in (178mm)	2¼in (57mm)
North Carolina (BB55)	1937–41	c46,000	28.0	9–16in (40.6cm)	20–5in (12.7cm)	12in (305mm)	3.6in (91mm)
Washington (BB56)	1938–41	c46,000	28.0	9–16in (40.6cm)	20–5in (12.7cm)	12in (305mm)	3.6in (91mm)
South Dakota (BB57)	1939–42	c45,000	27.8	9–16in (40.6cm)	20–5in (12.7cm)	12.2in (310mm)	5in (127mm)
Indiana (BB58)	1939–42	c45,000	27.8	9–16in (40.6cm)	20–5in (12.7cm)	12.2in (310mm)	5in (127mm)
Massachusetts (BB59)	1939–42	c45,000	27.8	9–16in (40.6cm)	20–5in (12.7cm)	12.2in (310mm)	5in (127mm)
Alabama (BB60)	1940–42	c45,000	27.8	9–16in (40.6cm)	20–5in (12.7cm)	12.2in (310mm)	5in (127mm)
Iowa (BB61)	1940–43	c57,000	33.0	9–16in (40.6cm)	20–5in (12.7cm)	12.1in (307mm)	4.8in (121mm)
New Jersey (BB62)	1940–43	c57,000	33.0	9–16in (40.6cm)	20–5in (12.7cm)	12.1in (307mm)	4.8in (121mm)
Missouri (BB63)	1941–44	c57,000	33.0	9–16in (40.6cm)	20–5in (12.7cm)	12.1in (307mm)	4.8in (121mm)
Wisconsin (BB64)	1941–44	c57,000	33.0	9–16in (40.6cm)	20–5in (12.7cm)	12.1in (307mm)	4.8in (121mm)
Illinois (BB65)	1944*	c57,000	33.0	9–16in (40.6cm)	20–5in (12.7cm)	12.1in (307mm)	4.8in (121mm)
Kentucky (BB66)	1942*	c57,000	33.0	9–16in (40.6cm)	20–5in (12.7cm)	12.1in (307mm)	4.8in (121mm)
Montana (BB67)	–	c71,000	28.0	12–16in (40.6cm)	20–5in (12.7cm)	16.1in (409mm)	5.8in (147mm)
Ohio (BB68)	–	c71,000	28.0	12–16in (40.6cm)	20–5in (12.7cm)	16.1in (409mm)	5.8in (147mm)
Maine (BB69)	–	c71,000	28.0	12–16in (40.6cm)	20–5in (12.7cm)	16.1in (409mm)	5.8in (147mm)
New Hampshire (BB70)	–	c71,000	28.0	12–16in (40.6cm)	20–5in (12.7cm)	16.1in (409mm)	5.8in (147mm)
Louisiana (BB71)	–	c71,000	28.0	12–16in (40.6cm)	20–5in (12.7cm)	16.1in (409mm)	5.8in (147mm)
Alaska (CB1)	1941–44	34,200	33.0	9–12in (30.5cm)	12–5in (12.7cm)	9in (229mm)	3in (76mm)
Guam (CB2)	1942–44	34,200	33.0	9–12in (30.5cm)	12–5in (12.7cm)	9in (229mm)	3in (76mm)
Hawaii (CB3)	1943*	34,200	33.0	9–12in (30.5cm)	12–5in (12.7cm)	9in (229mm)	3in (76mm)
Philippines (CB4)	–	34,200	33.0	9–12in (30.5cm)	12–5in (12.7cm)	9in (229mm)	3in (76mm)
Puerto Rico (CB5)	–	34,200	33.0	9–12in (30.5cm)	12–5in (12.7cm)	9in (229mm)	3in (76mm)
Samoa (CB6)	–	34,200	33.0	9–12in (30.5cm)	12–5in (12.7cm)	9in (229mm)	3in (76mm)

JAPAN

Name	Built	Displacement (full load) (tons)	Speed (kts)	Armament Main	Armament Secondary	Armour Belt	Armour Horizontal
Satsuma	1905–09	19,500	20.0	4–12in (30.5cm), 12–10in (25.4cm)	12–4.7in (12cm)	9in (229mm)	3in (76mm)
Aki	1905–11	19,500	20.0	4–12in (30.5cm), 12–10in (25.4cm)	8–6in (15.2cm)	9in (229mm)	3in (76mm)
Kawachi†	1909–12	23,000	21.0	12–12in (30.5cm)	10–6in (15.2cm), 8–4.7in (12cm)	12in (305mm)	2in (51mm)
Settsu	1909–12	23,000	21.0	12–12in (30.5cm)	10–6in (15.2cm), 8–4.7in (12cm)	12in (305mm)	2in (51mm)

Name	Built	Displacement (full load) (tons)	Speed (kts)	Armament Main	Armament Secondary	Armour Belt	Armour Horizontal
Kongo†	1911–13	27,500	27.5	8–14in (35.6cm)	16–6in (15.2cm)	8in (203mm)	2in (51mm)
Hiei†	1911–14	27,500	27.5	8–14in (35.6cm)	16–6in (15.2cm)	8in (203mm)	2in (51mm)
Haruna†	1912–15	27,500	27.5	8–14in (35.6cm)	16–6in (15.2cm)	8in (203mm)	2in (51mm)
Kirishima†	1912–15	27,500	27.5	8–14in (35.6cm)	16–6in (15.2cm)	8in (203mm)	2in (51mm)
Fuso†	1912–15	*c*31,000	23.0	12–14in (35.6cm)	16–6in (15.2cm)	12in (305mm)	2in (51mm)
Yamashiro†	1913–17	*c*31,000	23.0	12–14in (35.6cm)	16–6in (15.2cm)	12in (305mm)	2in (51mm)
Hyuga†	1915–18	*c*32,000	23.0	12–14in (35.6cm)	20–5.9in (15cm)	12in (305mm)	2in (51mm)
Ise†	1915–17	*c*32,000	23.0	12–14in (35.6cm)	20–5.9in (15cm)	12in (305mm)	2in (51mm)
Nagato	1917–20	*c*34,000	26.7	8–16in (40.6cm)	20–5.5in (14cm)	11.8in (300mm)	2.5in (63mm)
Mutsu†	1918–21	*c*34,000	26.7	8–16in (40.6cm)	20–5.5in (14cm)	11.8in (300mm)	2.5in (63mm)
Tosa	1920*	*c*44,200	27.5	10–16in (40.6cm)	20–5.5in (14cm)	11in (280mm)	6.4in (163mm)
Kaga	1920*	*c*44,200	27.5	10–16in (40.6cm)	20–5.5in (14cm)	11in (280mm)	6.4in (163mm)
Amagi	1920*	*c*47,000	30.0	10–16in (40.6cm)	16–5.5in (14cm)	10in (254mm)	6.4in (163mm)
Akagi	1920*	*c*47,000	30.0	10–16in (40.6cm)	16–5.5in (14cm)	10in (254mm)	6.4in (163mm)
Atago	1921*	*c*47,000	30.0	10–16in (40.6cm)	16–5.5in (14cm)	10in (254mm)	6.4in (163mm)
Takao	1921*	*c*47,000	30.0	10–16in (40.6cm)	16–5.5in (14cm)	10in (254mm)	6.4in (163mm)
Owari	–	*c*48,000	29.7	10–16in (40.6cm)	16–5.5in (14cm)	11.5in (293mm)	6.4in (163mm)
Kii	–	*c*48,000	29.7	10–16in (40.6cm)	16–5.5in (14cm)	11.5in (293mm)	6.4in (163mm)
No 11	–	*c*48,000	29.7	10–16in (40.6cm)	16–5.5in (14cm)	11.5in (293mm)	6.4in (163mm)
No 12	–	*c*48,000	29.7	10–16in (40.6cm)	16–5.5in (14cm)	11.5in (293mm)	6.4in (163mm)
No 13	–	*c*53,000	30.0	8–18in (45.7cm)	16–5.5in (14cm)	13in (330mm)	6.4in (163mm)
No 14	–	*c*53,000	30.0	8–18in (45.7cm)	16–5.5in (14cm)	13in (330mm)	6.4in (163mm)
No 15	–	*c*53,000	30.0	8–18in (45.7cm)	16–5.5in (14cm)	13in (330mm)	6.4in (163mm)
No 16	–	*c*53,000	30.0	8–18in (45.7cm)	16–5.5in (14cm)	13in (330mm)	6.4in (163mm)
Yamato†	1937–41	*c*73,000	27.0	9–18.1in (46cm)	12–6.1in (15.5cm)	16.1in (410mm)	9.1in (230mm)
Musashi†	1938–42	*c*73,000	27.0	9–18.1in (46cm)	12–6.1in (15.5cm)	16.1in (410mm)	9.1in (230mm)
Shinano†	1940*	*c*73,000	27.0	9–18.1in (46cm)	12–6.1in (15.5cm)	16.1in (410mm)	9.1in (230mm)
No 111	1940*	*c*73,000	27.0	9–18.1in (46cm)	12–6.1in (15.5cm)	16.1in (410mm)	9.1in (230mm)
No 797	–	*c*73,000	27.0	9–18.1in (46cm)	12–6.1in (15.5cm)	16.1in (410mm)	9.1in (230mm)
No 798	–	*c*78,000	?	6–20in (50.8cm)	?	?	?
No 799	–	*c*78,000	?	6–20in (50.8cm)	?	?	?
No 795	–	*c*35,000	33.0–34.0	6–14.2in (36cm)	16–3.9in (10cm)	7.5in (190mm)	4.9in (125mm)
No 796	–	*c*35,000		6–14.2in (36cm)	16–3.9in (10cm)	7.5in (190mm)	4.9in (125mm)
FRANCE							
Danton†	1908–11	19,450	19.2	4–12in (30.5cm), 12–9.4in (24cm)	16–3in (7.5cm)	10.6in (270mm)	1.9in (48mm)
Condorcet†	1909–11	19,450	19.2	4–12in (30.5cm), 12–9.4in (24cm)	16–3in (7.5cm)	10.6in (270mm)	1.9in (48mm)
Diderot	1907–11	19,450	19.2	4–12in (30.5cm), 12–9.4in (24cm)	16–3in (7.5cm)	10.6in (270mm)	1.9in (48mm)
Voltaire	1907–11	19,450	19.2	4–12in (30.5cm), 12–9.4in (24cm)	16–3in (7.5cm)	10.6in (270mm)	1.9in (48mm)
Mirabeau	1908–11	19,450	19.2	4–12in (30.5cm), 12–9.4in (24cm)	16–3in (7.5cm)	10.6in (270mm)	1.9in (48mm)
Vergniaud	1907–11	19,450	19.2	4–12in (30.5cm), 12–9.4in (24cm)	16–3in (7.5cm)	10.6in (270mm)	1.9in (48mm)
Courbet	1910–13	*c*26,000	20.0	12–12in (30.5cm)	22–5.4in (13.8cm)	10.6in (270mm)	1.6in (40mm)
Jean Bart	1910–13	*c*26,000	20.0	12–12in (30.5cm)	22–5.4in (13.8cm)	10.6in (270mm)	1.6in (40mm)
France†	1911–14	*c*26,000	20.0	12–12in (30.5cm)	22–5.4in (13.8cm)	10.6in (270mm)	1.6in (40mm)
Paris	1911–14	*c*26,000	20.0	12–12in (30.5cm)	22–5.4in (13.8cm)	10.6in (270mm)	1.6in (40mm)
Provence†	1912–15	*c*28,500	20.0	10–13.4in (34cm)	22–5.4in (13.8cm)	10.6in (270mm)	2.8in (70mm)
Bretagne†	1912–16	*c*28,500	20.0	10–13.4in (34cm)	22–5.4in (13.8cm)	10.6in (270mm)	2.8in (70mm)
Lorraine	1912–16	*c*28,500	20.0	10–13.4in (34cm)	22–5.4in (13.8cm)	10.6in (270mm)	2.8in (70mm)

Name	Built	Displacement (full load) (tons)	Speed (kts)	Armament Main	Armament Secondary	Armour Belt	Armour Horizontal
Normandie	1913*	c34,000	23.0	12–13.4in (34cm)	24–5.4in (13.8cm)	11.8in (300mm)	2.8in (70mm)
Languedoc	1913*	c34,000	23.0	12–13.4in (34cm)	24–5.4in (13.8cm)	11.8in (300mm)	2.8in (70mm)
Flandre	1913*	c34,000	23.0	12–13.4in (34cm)	24–5.4in (13.8cm)	11.8in (300mm)	2.8in (70mm)
Gascogne	1913*	c34,000	23.0	12–13.4in (34cm)	24–5.4in (13.8cm)	11.8in (300mm)	2.8in (70mm)
Béarn	1913*	c34,000	23.0	12–13.4in (34cm)	24–5.4in (13.8cm)	11.8in (300mm)	2.8in (70mm)
Lyon	–	c35,000	23.0	16–13.4in (34cm)	24–5.4in (13.8cm)	11.8in (300mm)	2.8in (70mm)
Lille	–	c35,000	23.0	16–13.4in (34cm)	24–5.4in (13.8cm)	11.8in (300mm)	2.8in (70mm)
Duquesne	–	c35,000	23.0	16–13.4in (34cm)	24–5.4in (13.8cm)	11.8in (300mm)	2.8in (70mm)
Tourville	–	c35,000	23.0	16–13.4in (34cm)	24–5.4in (13.8cm)	11.8in (300mm)	2.8in (70mm)
Dunkerque†	1932–37	35,500	29.5	8–13in (33cm)	16–5.1in (13cm)	9.5in (241mm)	5.1in (130mm)
Strasbourg†	1934–38	35,500	29.5	8–13in (33cm)	16–5.1in (13cm)	9.5in (241mm)	5.1in (130mm)
Richelieu	1935–40	c48,700	30.0	8–15in (38cm)	9–6in (15.2cm)	13.6in (345mm)	6.7in (170mm)
Jean Bart	1936–55	c48,700	30.0	8–15in (38cm)	9–6in (15.2cm)	13.6in (345mm)	6.7in (170mm)
Clemenceau	1939*	c48,000	30.0	8–15in (38cm)	12–6in (15.2cm)	13.6in (345mm)	6.7in (170mm)
Gascogne	1939*	c48,000	30.0	8–15in (38cm)	9–6in (15.2cm)	13.6in (345mm)	6.7in (170mm)

ITALY

Name	Built	Displacement (full load) (tons)	Speed (kts)	Armament Main	Armament Secondary	Armour Belt	Armour Horizontal
Vittorio Emanuele	1901–08	c14,000	21.0–22.0	2–12in (30.5cm), 12–8in (20.3cm)	16 to 24–3in (7.6cm)	9.8in (250mm)	2in (50mm)
Regina Elena	1901–07	c14,000		2–12in (30.5cm), 12–8in (20.3cm)		9.8in (250mm)	2in (50mm)
Napoli	1903–08	c14,000		2–12in (30.5cm), 12–8in (20.3cm)		9.8in (250mm)	2in (50mm)
Roma	1903–08	c14,000		2–12in (30.5cm), 12–8in (20.3cm)		9.8in (250mm)	2in (50mm)
Dante Alighieri	1909–13	21,800	23.0	12–12in (30.5cm)	20–4.7in (12cm)	9.8in (250mm)	1.2in (30mm)
Conte di Cavour†	1910–15	25,086	21.5	13–12in (30.5cm)	18–4.7in (12cm)	9.8in (250mm)	1.6in (40mm)
Giulio Cesare	1910–14	25,086	21.5	13–12in (30.5cm)	18–4.7in (12cm)	9.8in (250mm)	1.6in (40mm)
(After reconstruction)	1933–37	29,100	28.0	10–12in (30.5cm)	12–4.7in (12cm)	9.8in (250mm)	3.9in (100mm)
Leonardo da Vinci†	1910–15	25,086	21.5	13–12in (30.5cm)	18–4.7in (12cm)	9.8in (250mm)	1.6in (40mm)
Caio Dulio	1912–15	25,200	21.5	13–12in (30.5cm)	16–6in (15.2cm)	9.8in (250mm)	1.6in (40mm)
Andrea Doria	1912–16	25,200	21.5	13–12in (30.5cm)	16–6in (15.2cm)	9.8in (250mm)	1.6in (40mm)
(After reconstruction)	1937–40	29,400	27.0	10–12.6in (32cm)	12–5.3in (13.5cm)	9.8in (250mm)	3.1in (80mm)
Francesco Caracciolo	1914*	34,000	25.0–28.0	8–15in (38.1cm)	12–6in (15.2cm)	11.8in (300mm)	1.4in (35mm)
Cristoforo Colombo	1915*	34,000		8–15in (38.1cm)	12–6in (15.2cm)	11.8in (300mm)	1.4in (35mm)
Marcantonio Colonna	1915*	34,000		8–15in (38.1cm)	12–6in (15.2cm)	11.8in (300mm)	1.4in (35mm)
Francesco Morosini	1915*	34,000		8–15in (38.1cm)	12–6in (15.2cm)	11.8in (300mm)	1.4in (35mm)
Vittorio Veneto	1934–40	c46,000	30.0	9–15in (38.1cm)	12–6in (15.2cm)	13.8in (350mm)	6.4in (162mm)
Italia (ex-*Littorio*)	1934–40	c46,000	30.0	9–15in (38.1cm)	12–6in (15.2cm)	13.8in (350mm)	6.4in (162mm)
Impero	1938*	c46,000	30.0	9–15in (38.1cm)	12–6in (15.2cm)	13.8in (350mm)	6.4in (162mm)
Roma†	1938–42	c46,000	30.0	9–15in (38.1cm)	12–6in (15.2cm)	13.8in (350mm)	6.4in (162mm)

AUSTRIA-HUNGARY

Name	Built	Displacement (full load) (tons)	Speed (kts)	Armament Main	Armament Secondary	Armour Belt	Armour Horizontal
Radetzky	1907–10	15,851	20.5	4–12in (30.5cm), 8–9.4in (24cm)	20–3.9in (10cm)	9.1in (230mm)	2in (50mm)
Erzherzog Franz Ferdinand	1907–10	15,851	20.5	4–12in (30.5cm), 8–9.4in (24cm)	20–3.9in (10cm)	9.1in (230mm)	2in (50mm)
Zrinyi	1908–11	15,851	20.5	4–12in (30.5cm), 8–9.4in (24cm)	20–3.9in (10cm)	9.1in (230mm)	2in (50mm)
Viribus Unitis†	1910–12	c21,400	20.0	12–12in (30.5cm)	12–6in (15.2cm)	11in (280mm)	1.9in (48mm)
Tegetthoff	1910–13	c21,400	20.0	12–12in (30.5cm)	12–6in (15.2cm)	11in (280mm)	1.9in (48mm)
Prinz Eugen	1912–14	c21,400	20.0	12–12in (30.5cm)	12–6in (15.2cm)	11in (280mm)	1.9in (48mm)
Szent István†	1912–15	c21,400	20.0	12–12in (30.5cm)	12–6in (15.2cm)	11in (280mm)	1.9in (48mm)

Name	Built	Displacement (full load) (tons)	Speed (kts)	Armament Main	Armament Secondary	Armour Belt	Armour Horizontal
'Ersatz Monarch'	–	25,237	21.0	10–14in (35.5cm)	14–5.9in (15cm)	12.2in (310mm)	1.4in (36mm)
'Ersatz Wien'	–	25,237	21.0	10–14in (35.5cm)	14–5.9in (15cm)	12.2in (310mm)	1.4in (36mm)
'Ersatz Budapest'	–	25,237	21.0	10–14in (35.5cm)	14–5.9in (15cm)	12.2in (310mm)	1.4in (36mm)
'Ersatz Habsburg'	–	25,237	21.0	10–14in (35.5cm)	14–5.9in (15cm)	12.2in (310mm)	1.4in (36mm)
RUSSIA							
Andrey Pervozvannyiy	1903–10	18,306	18.0	4–12in (30.5cm), 14–8in (20.3cm)	12–4.7in (12cm)	8.5in (216mm)	2.2in (57mm)
Respublika (ex-*Imperator Pavel I*)	1904–10	18,306	18.0	4–12in (30.5cm), 14–8in (20.3cm)	12–4.7in (12cm)	8.5in (216mm)	2.2in (57mm)
Oktyabrskaya Revoluciya (ex-*Gangut*)	1909–15	25,850	23.0	12–12in (30.5cm)	16–4.7in (12cm)	8.9in (225mm)	1.5in (38mm)
Parizhskaya Kommuna (ex-*Sevastopol*)	1909–15	25,850	23.0	12–12in (30.5cm)	16–4.7in (12cm)	8.9in (225mm)	1.5in (38mm)
Marat (ex-*Petropavlovsk*)†	1909–15	25,850	23.0	12–12in (30.5cm)	16–4.7in (12cm)	8.9in (225mm)	1.5in (38mm)
Michail Frunze (ex-*Poltava*)	1909–15	25,850	23.0	12–12in (30.5cm)	16–4.7in (12cm)	8.9in (225mm)	1.5in (38mm)
Imperatrica Mariya†	1911–15	c24,000	21.0	12–12in (30.5cm)		10.4in (263mm)	1.5in (38mm)
Svobodnaya Rossiya (ex-*Ekaterina II*)†	1911–15	c24,000	21.0	12–12in (30.5cm)	18 to 20–5.1in (13cm)	10.4in (263mm)	1.5in (38mm)
General Alekseyev (ex-*Volya*, ex-*Imperator Aleksandr III*)	1911–17	c24,000	21.0	12–12in (30.5cm)		10.4in (263mm)	1.5in (38mm)
Borodino	1912*	32,500	26.6	12–14in (35.6cm)	24–5.1in (13cm)	9.3in (237mm)	3in (75mm)
Navarin	1912*	32,500	26.6	12–14in (35.6cm)	24–5.1in (13cm)	9.3in (237mm)	3in (75mm)
Kinburn	1912*	32,500	26.6	12–14in (35.6cm)	24–5.1in (13cm)	9.3in (237mm)	3in (75mm)
Izmail	1912*	32,500	26.6	12–14in (35.6cm)	24–5.1in (13cm)	9.3in (237mm)	3in (75mm)
Imperator Nikolai I	1914*	c31,000	23.0–24.0	12–12in (30.5cm)	20–5.1in (13cm)	10.6in (270mm)	2.5in (63mm)
Sovetskiy Soyuz	1938*	65,150	28.0	9–16in (40.6cm)	12–6in (15.2cm)	16.7in (425mm)	5.9in (150mm)
Sovetskaya Ukraina	1938*	65,150	28.0	9–16in (40.6cm)	12–6in (15.2cm)	16.7in (425mm)	5.9in (150mm)
Sovetskaya Byelorossiya	1940*	65,150	28.0	9–16in (40.6cm)	12–6in (15.2cm)	16.7in (425mm)	5.9in (150mm)
Sovetskaya Rossiya	1940*	65,150	28.0	9–16in (40.6cm)	12–6in (15.2cm)	16.7in (425mm)	5.9in (150mm)
Kronshtadt	1939*	40,385	32.0	9–12in (30.5cm)	8–6in (15.2cm)	9.1in (230mm)	3.5in (90mm)
Sevastopol	1939*	40,385	32.0	9–12in (30.5cm)	8–6in (15.2cm)	9.1in (230mm)	3.5in (90mm)
Stalingrad	1949*	43,720	?	9–12in (30.5cm)	8–6in (15.2cm)	?	?
Moskva	1950*	43,720	?	9–12in (30.5cm)	8–6in (15.2cm)	?	?
ARGENTINA							
Rivadavia	1910–14	c30,000	23.0	12–12in (30.5cm)	12–6in (15.2cm)	11in (279mm)	3in (76mm)
Moreno	1910–15	c30,000	23.0	12–12in (30.5cm)	12–6in (15.2cm)	11in (279mm)	3in (76mm)
BRAZIL							
Minas Gerais	1907–10	c21,500	21.0	12–12in (30.5cm)	22–4.7in (12cm)	9in (229mm)	2in (51mm)
São Paulo	1907–10	c21,500	21.0	12–12in (30.5cm)	22–4.7in (12cm)	9in (229mm)	2in (51mm)

Name	Built	Displacement (full load) (tons)	Speed (kts)	Armament Main	Armament Secondary	Armour Belt	Armour Horizontal
Rio de Janeiro	1911*	30,250	22.4	14–12in (30.5cm)	20–6in (15.2cm)	9in (229mm)	1½in (38mm)
Riachuelo	–	30,500	22.4	8–15in (38.1cm)	14–6in (15.2cm)	13.5in (343mm)	1.3in (32mm)
CHILE							
Almirante Latorre	1911–15	32,120	22.7	10–14in (35.6cm)	16–6in (15.2cm)	9in (229mm)	4in (102mm)
Almirante Cochrane	1913*	32,120	22.7	10–14in (35.6cm)	16–6in (15.2cm)	9in (229mm)	4in (102mm)
GREECE							
Salamis	1913*	c22,000	23.5	8–14in (35.6cm)	12–6in (15.2cm)	9.8in (250cm)	3in (75mm)
Vasilefs Konstantinos	–	c28,500	20.0	10–13.4in (34cm)	22–5.4in (13.8cm)	?	?
SPAIN							
España†	1909–13	15,840	19.5	8–12in (30.5cm)	20–4in (10.2cm)	9.1in (230mm)	1.5in (38mm)
España (ex-*Alfonso XIII*)†	1910–15	15,840	19.5	8–12in (30.5cm)	20–4in (10.2cm)	9.1in (230mm)	1.5in (38mm)
Jaime I	1912–21	15,840	19.5	8–12in (30.5cm)	20–4in (10.2cm)	9.1in (230mm)	1.5in (38mm)
THE NETHERLANDS							
1914 design	–	Of the designs ordered abroad, none was chosen					
1939 design	–	31,357	34.0	9–11in (28cm)	12–4.7in (12cm)	8.9in (225mm)	3.9in (100mm)
TURKEY							
Reshadieh	1911*	25,250	21.0	10–13.5in (34.3cm)	16–6in (15.2cm)	12in (305mm)	3in (76mm)
Reshad i Hamis	1911*	25,250	21.0	10–13.5in (34.3cm)	16–6in (15.2cm)	12in (305mm)	3in (76mm)
Fatikh		25,250	21.0	10–13.5in (34.3cm)	16–6in (15.2cm)	12in (305mm)	3in (76mm)
Sultan Osman I (ex-*Rio de Janeiro*)	1911*	30,250	22.4	14–12in (30.5cm)	20–6in (15.2cm)	9in (229mm)	1½in (38mm)
Yavuz (ex-*Goeben*)	1909–12	25,200	25.5	10–11in (28cm)	10–5.9in (15cm)	10.6in (270mm)	2in (50mm)